THE HISTORY OF THE GREEN BAY PACKERS

LOMBARDI'S DESTINY - PART ONE

FIRST EDITION

LARRY D. NAMES

EAGAN HILL PUBLISHERS
NESHKORO, WISCONSIN
USA

THE HISTORY

OF THE

GREEN BAY PACKERS

Lombardi's Destiny – Part One

ISBN-13: 978-0-910937-68-9

ISBN-10: 0-910937-68-0

Library of Congress Control Number: 2019915585

www.larrynames.com

Cover photo: Hall of Fame quarterback Bart Starr of the Green Bay Packers gets ready to fire downfield against the Los Angeles Rams at the Los Angeles Memorial Coliseum on December 16, 1962. The Packers went on to win the game 20-17. Bart Starr - Green Bay Packers – File Photos (AP Photo/NFL Photos) Copyright Associated Press.

Interior photographs courtesy of Jeff Everson Collection

To my long-time friends

Wayne and Linda Mausser

TABLE OF CONTENTS

Foreword

I met Larry Names in late December of 1990. I received a call from his spokesperson to set up a radio interview with me to promote his third installment of *The History of the Green Bay Packers.* I readily agreed. As we were doing the taping, I was impressed not only with Larry's knowledge but also his enthusiasm for the team and its history. The interview lasted 30 minutes but when it was done, we continued to talk, not only about the Packers but on other topics as well. From that time on, Larry and I have become good friends and have also worked on a few projects together.

In his latest book, *Lombardi's Destiny, Part 1,* Larry takes the reader on a very thorough journey through Lombardi's first four seasons in Green Bay. His extensive research into the man, a team in search of a coach, a city yearning for more championships and a return to glory, are clearly presented, step-by-step. From a winning team in his first season, to a near championship in his second and then two titles, Larry details not only Lombardi's football genius and his drive to win, but also the ability to teach his players how to win and be successful.

The National Football League's mindset in the late 1950s and early 1960s. Change was in the air and the owners were not interested. A new version of the American Football League was proposed and then launched in 1960. Larry chronicles the start-up of the new league and the NFL's reaction and its attempts to curtail it. But the AFL would survive and grow until a merger agreement was announced a few years later.

The book also looks at race relations and the gradual infusion of African-American players into the league. As you might expect from that time, there was resistance from some owners. As for Lombardi, he was very sensitive to the issue and took offense to any prejudice that his players might experience because he had gone through many similar experiences growing up as an Italian-American.

When Lombardi arrived as head coach in Green Bay to begin the 1959 season, he was a man desperate to show the football world that he belonged, that he was a winner. He had been passed up by his former team, the Giants, and the clock was ticking. Even though he wished to be in New York, "little" Green Bay gave him his opportunity and he would not waste it. The Giants tried to get him back, but that was not going to happen. He had more championships to win. You see, Green Bay was *Lombardi's Destiny.*

Larry, I can't wait for Part 2!

Wayne Mausser

Radio and TV Personality

§ § §

Introduction

Packer fans are everywhere. It wasn't always this way.

In the first two decades of pro football in the port city of Green Bay, Wisconsin, the local town team hardly ever played outside of their immediate neighborhood. They had no established nickname from season to season. They were just the Green Bay "This" or the Green Bay "That" in the local newspapers, which included tabloids in the other towns along the Fox River and within the counties adjacent to Brown County.

Then in 1919, a smooth-talking local hero joined the team. A meeting of potential players was announced by the one man who understood how important a good football team could be for a small city like Green Bay. His name was George Whitney Calhoun. The confab was held in the offices of the *Green Bay Press-Gazette*, and the boys who showed up elected the local hero to be their *captain*. He was Earl Louis "Curly" Lambeau, a true leader if there ever was one in this little duck pond at the mouth of the Fox. Lambeau accepted the post because he expected to be elected to it. After all, he had played at Notre Dame under the tutelage of the immortal Knute Rockne as the lead blocker for the immortal George Gipp. He'd also gone to the University of Wisconsin in Madison to play the year before, but when he failed to make the freshman team, he quit and went home to Green Bay. But nobody cared about that; Curly was still their guy, the big fish in their little pond.

On the following Saturday after meeting in the newspaper's offices, Lambeau married the girl of his dreams, and the two of them departed on their honeymoon, a train trip to Milwaukee, Chicago, and back into Wisconsin and north into the Upper Peninsula of Michigan. By the time of their return to Green Bay, his bride, Marguerite (nee Van Kessel), was glad to be home to set up housekeeping for them. Curly was glad to be home to announce the schedule of games he had arranged for the town's football team, a list that included an athletic club from Milwaukee and another from Chicago. He was going to lead the boys from Green Bay to bigger and better things, but to do that, "his" team needed uniforms.

Since he and several other members of the local aggregation worked for the same business, the Indian Packing Company, Curly asked his boss to cough up some money to buy the team some jerseys. He was given $500, which Curly used to purchase blue tops for his guys so they could look like a team and not a bunch of ragtag school boys that previous Green Bay town teams had looked like. He didn't buy gold pants for them because at that time every footballer just about everywhere in America wore leather pants and many of them wore leather helmets; hence, the nickname "leatherheads" and the title of a George Clooney movie in 2008.

George Whitney Calhoun christened the new town team as the Indians. It failed to stick for two reasons. The first was the racist attitude of the locals against the Oneida Nation, which was located just west of the city. It was the time, more than anything else. The second was a joke Calhoun made in the paper when he referred to the team as the Packers because so many of the players worked at the packing company. The footballers and the local fans got a giggle out of his little witticism, and they started calling themselves the Packers. When Curly convinced his boss to buy a franchise in the year-old professional league in 1921, he tried to get the nickname changed, but to no avail because a good joke has no end in the telling.

Over the next 30 years of their NFL existence, followers of the pro team from the little town in the Dairy State were clustered around Green Bay and the Fox River Valley. Then their numbers spread throughout Wisconsin, the Upper Peninsula of Michigan, and parts of Minnesota and Iowa, with a scattering in northern Illinois, during the 1950s. In 1959, a tough, hard-nosed Italian from Brooklyn came to town, and with sudden profusion, Packer Backers sprang up all across the United States. The man who caused this explosion was Vincent Thomas Lombardi.

The popularity of the Packers across the nation came as a result of the 1961 NFL title game being telecast on national TV.

The game was more or less promoted with a "David versus Goliath" theme. Meaning, of course, "Smallville against Gotham." This was verified by all the new fans the Packers picked up when Green Bay clobbered the New York Giants, 37-0.

The truth of this explosion in Packer fan numbers was confirmed by a friend of mine years ago. His name was Walt Craig. In a casual conversation during a Sunday brunch, Walt revealed his favorite team to be the Packers. When asked why the Packers since he was born and raised in New Jersey, he said he first saw the Packers on television in the 1961 title game in Green Bay against the Giants whom he hated because they were from New York City. When the Packers continued on their road to success throughout the 1960s, his love for them grew until he became a lifelong Packer fan.

Walt Craig is only one example of someone becoming a Packer fan from that title game. Over the years and through my travels promoting my Packer books, I've literally met hundreds of people who became Packer fans in the same way Walt did. They loved the team from little ol' Green Bay knocking off teams from all the big cities in America. Packer fan clubs are all over America. I've even heard of some being in England, Australia, Germany, and Mexico. I know because my Packer books sell in those countries. And it's because of them that I finally got around to writing this volume in Packer history.

Just a little spoiler alert here. In Chapter 19, I hope you enjoy the paragraphs about the game with the Lions in Green Bay. You can thank the most wonderful teacher any child could ever have for that piece of creative writing. Her name was Mrs. Sylva Martin. She never once raised her voice in class. She would only look at you—well, me—with a face so sad that you—yes, me—felt about two inches tall and she would say softly, "Oh, Larry, I'm so disappointed." Note that she didn't say she was disappointed in me, which truly eased my own guilt for causing her pain. Mrs. Martin was the first teacher who took the time to teach me how to write a story as opposed to making a report. I have always remembered her with love in my heart for the wonderful feeling she left on my soul.

This volume in *The History of the Green Bay Packers* series was 25 years in the making. Not that *Lombardi's Destiny* took that long to write in real hours, days, weeks, and months. No, it was because of all the books that have been written about the man who ranks among the greatest coaches of all time in the history of the National Football League. Of course, there are also all those books written about and by the players who gave their sweat, blood, and tears for Lombardi and all those countless millions of Packer fans who cheered them on, come win or loss. And then there are those few who were written about

Lombardi's teams.

My research started with *LOMBARDI* by Robert W. Wells, published by Wisconsin House in 1971. After that, it seemed a new book about Vince Lombardi came out every football season until the best of them all, the masterful biography, *VINCE*, by Dr. Michael O'Brien, was released in 1987. If you haven't read it, I urge you to get a copy from amazon.com. You won't be sorry.

So, you see, it was reading and re-reading all those other books that kept me from writing about Lombardi and his time with the Packers. Friends, fans, and even relatives, especially family members whether by blood or by marriage, kept nagging me to write about those incredible nine years when Lombardi stalked the sidelines at City Stadium, then at Lambeau Field after it was renamed shortly after the death of Earl Louis "Curly" Lambeau, the man who is credited by Packer officialdom for founding the team. All that time it never occurred to me that I wouldn't be writing about Vince any more than I had written about Curly Lambeau in three volumes and the first three men who succeeded Curly in just one book. As I had done in those earlier works, I will be writing about the history of the Green Bay Packers, the team, players, coaches, fans, and the front office from the president down to the volunteers who remove the snow from the stands before the next game after one of our frequently intense Wisconsin snowstorms. What a revelation! An epiphany, if you will!

Then I recalled something a close friend and member of our extended family said to me after he finished reading the fourth book in this series. His name is Marty Dylla, a giant of a man in heart, soul, and body. He said, "I can't wait to see how you handle the Lombardi years." I reveal these words of his because they typify the pressure I was getting from so many other people who had read the first four books in this collection as well as all five of my *Green Bay Packers Facts & Trivia* books.

Well, I had to accommodate them sooner or later. I chose later, sorry to say.

However, as my wife Peg has said to me so many times over the last 45 years, "If it's meant to be, it will happen."

So now is the time for this book. I started by again reading my copies of *VINCE* and *LOMBARDI*. As I wrote above, I searched the pages of other books by or about people from Lombardi's time in Green Bay. I read countless *Wikipedia* articles for tidbits of information on the many people associated with Packers history in one way or another. Some of them had a great deal to do with the Packers, but many of them never were a member of the team or a person within the organization. Then there was all the microfilm of all those newspapers and other print media that I had to read to make certain the details were correct. Sadly, I'm in need of a new prescription for eyeglasses now.

Anybody who knows even a smidgen about professional football history knows only one league has ever had the brains, the courage, and above all the finances to challenge the National Football League for a piece of the pro football pie and has succeeded in winning a war with the established circuit. It was the fourth incarnation to call itself the American Football League. None of the other circuits with that name came close to being successful, although the All-America Football Conference could claim some success because three of its franchises were absorbed by the NFL in 1950.

Because of the success of the latest AFL and the intertwining of its history with a certain individual in the NFL, I have included the story of how the AFL went from the drawing board to become an integral part of the NFL. Of course, that certain individual was none other than Vincent Thomas Lombardi. His involvement in all this has been overlooked by many other historians. Why? Beats me because I saw it as obvious while doing my research for this book and the one that will come in near future.

So, when you read about the AFL's history within these pages, be assured I added it here because it was more than pertinent to the central subject of this history, the Green Bay Packers, and to the one man who had the most to do with everything in the way of pro football during a decade that saw not only changes in all of sports but also in all of American history.

Finally, the really good part of researching a book like this is interviewing the people who lived this portion of the Packers history. It's a real joy to listen to those people. Through them, I felt like I was living those Lombardi years all over again. More than that, it was through them and all the other authors and scribes who wrote about Lombardi that I came to realize that Vincent Thomas Lombardi was destined to revive the legendary team that Curly Lambeau had coached for so long and to so much glory. Three men between their tenures tried and failed miserably. None since Lombardi to the time of this writing have come close to what either of those incredible men accomplished. Maybe one day, but not yet. Packer Backers can only hope and pray for a new deliverer.

When you finish reading this part of *The History of the Green Bay Packers,* I hope that you will also feel like you were living those years again and come to believe like I do that the Green Bay Packers were not just Lombardi's team but that they were *Lombardi's Destiny.*

§ § §

1
A New Era Begins

"Who the hell is Vince Lombardi?"

These famous words were spoken by John B. Torinus, Sr., a board member of the Green Bay Packers for over 30 years. He said them at a special meeting of the board of directors held January 28, 1959. He could have said them at the regular Packers executive committee meeting of December 15, 1958, the day after the Packers concluded their worst season in their 40-year history in the National Football League. He could have. He didn't because very few people outside of New York City had ever heard of Vincent T. Lombardi and nobody had yet put Lombardi's name in the hat to be the next coach of the Packers. But by the time Neil Armstrong set his foot on the moon, just about every sports fan in America would know something about Vince Lombardi.

But that's getting way ahead of things.

The major discussion at the December 15, 1958 meeting of the Packers executive committee concerned the fate of the team's head coach: the nice, likeable, gullible, too easy going, but very not-so-brilliant Ray "Scooter" McLean, the former Chicago Bears halfback who had been with the Packers as an assistant coach and head coach for a total of eight years. The committee members liked Scooter as a person, but as head coach of their team? Not so much. McLean's contract had only been for one year. They knew they weren't going to sign him for another year, but they were hesitant to make any such announcement to the public. So, they pinned their hopes on McLean being wise enough to "resign" his post.

Some of the Packers players tried to save Scooter's job. After being thrashed, 48-21, by the San Francisco 49ers the week before in the Golden Gate City, the boys sent a telegram to team President Dominic Olejniczak. Veteran tackle Dave Hanner stated, "The telegram was sent in hopes it would do some good at today's meeting." He meant the meeting on the 15th. Hanner added, "We were going to sign names, but we decided there were some players whose names shouldn't be on there or maybe they wouldn't even want to sign it. So, we made it from the players, meaning the majority, because I know that's how we feel."

Hanner also said the team's dismal showing was not the fault of Scooter and the other coaches. "Some of the players just let them down, that's all; some of the ones who were supposed to carry the load. A lot of us feel bad about Scooter."

Adding to Hanner's comments, backfield coach Ray Richards announced his retirement from pro football to go into business in California. Like any good assistant, he stuck up for his boss in his parting statement.

"Everything went against Scooter and his team this year. A host of injuries, pass interceptions, fumbles, everything."

These statements by Hanner and Richards failed to fool anyone; not the fans, not the players, and especially not the members of the executive committee.

The day after McLean resigned the rest of his staff decided to follow his example, even if reluctantly. Nick Skorich, Floyd "Breezy" Reid, and Jack Morton made it a clean sweep that suited just about everybody in Packerland.

At this time, the Packers organization was led by President Dominic Olejniczak, a former Green Bay city alderman and then the mayor for 10 years. A Green Bay native born August 18, 1908 he was raised on the east side of town. He became a Packer fan from day one of their official existence. In 1950 he was elected to the Packers board of directors. Two years later he was named to the executive committee, and six years after that he was elected to the post of executive vice-president. Four months after that he was elected team president.

A real take-charge kind of man Olejniczak ran the organization with enthusiastic leadership. Knowing success started at the top of any business, he threw himself into the job with the goal of returning the Packers to their glory days of the 1930s. Heartbroken over the 1958 season, Olejniczak wasted no time in searching for a new coach to replace McLean. He asked seven board members to act as a screening committee to find the right man to coach the Packers. They brought up a wish list of possible candidates that included Blanton Collier, head coach of the University of Kentucky Wildcats; Otto Graham, the former great quarterback of the Cleveland Browns; Forest Evashevski, head coach of the University of Iowa Hawkeyes; and the offensive coach of the New York Giants, Vince Lombardi.

Every Packer fan knew there was absolutely "no joy in Mudville—mighty Casey has struck out." Mighty Casey, in this case, was Scooter, the players, and the 13 members of the executive committee. All of them had disappointed the good people of Packerland that year. They had frustrated their fans for 11 straight seasons, in which the Packers had won a mere 37 games, lost 93, and tied two. The blame for such a string of disasters could only fall on one culprit: the one with 13 snarling, hissing, venomous serpent heads. The executive committee had not only mismanaged the business of professional football in little Green Bay, Wisconsin, but it had also fouled up the football side of the corporation.

The executive committee met regularly after lunch every Monday during the season to conduct business. Prior to their regular confab, these gentlemen came together with some invited guests, usually other board members, to question and second-guess McLean. They did this same thing with his two immediate predecessors, all three suffering the same indignity. These luncheons were more like torturous interrogations of the field boss than they were gatherings to break bread and enjoy the company of kindred spirits and the consumption of liquid spirits. "Poor Scooter," said John Torinus when recollecting those meetings. "He must have felt like the victim of a lynch mob after every single one of those losses."

History professor and author Dr. Michael O'Brien in his 1987 masterpiece *VINCE* summed up the situation with the Packers at that time in one very eloquent sentence. "Besides meddling with the coach, the committee was plagued by petty jealousies, archaic methods of administration through subcommittees, and reluctance to relinquish authority."

Renowned sports writer and editor Ollie Kuechle of the *Milwaukee Journal* took aim at the committee by calling it a "soviet," the communist term for a committee that runs things as a group rather unsuccessfully. He suggested to his readers that the Packers needed a general manager with some "real authority, a streamlined, compact executive committee, and a great coach with the security of a long-term contract."

Some dissatisfied fans vented their spleens on team officials as well as players. On the morning of December 9, 1958, a five-foot long effigy of Dominic Olejniczak was discovered hanging from a lamp post in front of the Packers' ticket office. Center Jim Ringo's daughter was harassed by classmates in school, calling her father and other Packers "bums" incessantly. Midway through the team's season, Ringo took his daughter out of a local school and sent her to live with family in Pennsylvania. Ringo's car was damaged when vandals spray-painted the roof in the middle of the night. More cowards hassled the future Hall-of-Famer at all hours of the day and night with crank calls. Sadly, he was not alone in receiving such abuse from those few Packer backers who felt it was their privilege to do something so ignominious to the team that far too many of them considered to be their own personal property. In newer times, these embarrassments to all sports fans everywhere would be the subjects of well-deserved legal action for behaving in such a disgraceful manner.

After all this hullaballoo from the fans and the media, several men on the executive committee thought they might be wise to discuss the suggestions Ollie Kuechle had made in his column as well as some ideas they'd picked up from other board members and stockholders. They came to the conclusion that real changes in how the corporation operated were absolutely in order. Executive committee member Jerry Atkinson put it succinctly. "We felt that no group, not even a group of successful businessmen, can run anything. Somebody has to be in charge." To paraphrase President Harry Truman, "The buck had to stop somewhere!"

Olejniczak had known weeks before this that several changes had to be made in how the corporation was managed and in how the team was coached. Of course, like the most excellent politician that he was, he kept everything on the "QT" as they used to say in that era. So, he formed a secret subcommittee to come up with some suggestions on what the executive committee should do to change the system for the better. He appointed Tony Canadeo, Richard Bourguignon, Leslie J. Kelly, Fred Trowbridge, and Jerry Atkinson to study the problems and come up with some answers on how to solve them.

On Tuesday, December 16, 1958, Olejniczak announced to the press that changes would be made, starting with the executive committee being reduced from 13 members to seven. The weekly meetings would become a monthly meeting in order to stem the lusty temptation for some committee members to intrude on the authority of the head coach. The most important change would be with the duties of the executive committee. Those austere gentlemen would confine themselves only to making organizational policy and to leaving administrative concerns to the team's general manager who had been the business manager in the past. Curly Lambeau had filled this position during his tenure as head coach. Former player and Packers Hall of Fame member Verne Lewellen held down the job at this time. Olejniczak added his own view on the subject of creating the post of general manager, saying succinctly that he wanted a man with a "dominant personality."

On this very same day, Art Daley printed a column in the *Green Bay Press-Gazette* that was a milk toast attempt at saving McLean's job. He made excuses for Scooter, saying the players took advantage of his soft-hearted nature. Then he blamed the players on the disciplinary committee for being too easy on their teammates when they broke training rules. Then he closed by stating the obvious about the team's play during the season. He cited the team's weaknesses, such as "spotty quarterbacking, inconsistency on defense, key injuries, among others." Injuries happen by accident, not by intention; thus, they are outside the coach's control. But the first two excuses aimed at the quarterbacks and the defense can be traced back to the coaches. A long-time high school coach at a private school in Oshkosh said of his players at the end of his 16th straight losing season, "They're still making the same mistakes they were making at the beginning of the year." This statement could be applied to Scooter and his staff. Poor blocking and poor tackling are the direct result of poor coaching.

With Olejniczak's announcement of the forthcoming changes in the operation of the Packer organization and Daley's apology for McLean's ineptitude as a head coach, the handwriting covered the walls of every drinking hole in Packerland. Scooter was about to be shown the door. The only question remaining on that topic was one word. When?

§ § §

2
The Hunt for a "Boss"

As rumors floated around the Packers offices about McLean's tenuous status, Jack Vainisi, the director of player personnel, thought he would throw in a suggestion of his own for who the team's next coach should be. He proffered the name of one Vincent Thomas Lombardi, the Italian genius behind the offense of the New York Giants, champions of the NFL's Eastern Conference two of the three previous years and NFL champ as recently as 1956.

Throwing Lombardi's hat in the ring was all well and good, but there was a definite "catch 22" involved here. In the business of professional sports, tampering with another team's personnel is strictly forbidden, whether it's players, coaches, or front office people. This made talking to Lombardi off limits until the Packers front office received official permission, whether in writing or verbally, from the New York Giants top brass. In this case, the man was co-owner and team secretary Wellington Mara, who also just happened to be a long-time friend of the topic at hand: Vincent T. Lombardi.

Knowing the rules and fearing someone in their organization might alert the media that the Packers were considering Lombardi for their next head coach—the media in this case being John B. Torinus, Sr., the secretary of the Packers, a local television commentator, and the managing editor of the *Green Bay Press-Gazette*—Olejniczak placed a long-distance telephone call himself to Mara shortly after McLean's resignation became official on December 17, 1958. Coming straight to the purpose of his call, the Packers president told Mara that Lombardi's name had come up as a possible candidate for Green Bay's now open head coaching job. The Giants official instantly became quite reticent with Olejniczak, who responded with another salvo, making it clear that all he wanted to do was talk to Lombardi about the position. The more Mara resisted Olejniczak's overtures, the more the

Packers president not only wanted to talk to Lombardi but actually began to think he just might have the right man for the Packers in the Giants assistant coach.

In his steadfast reluctance to permit the Packers to speak to Lombardi, Mara made an attempt to muddy the waters a bit by throwing out the name of the Giants defensive coach Tom Landry, the former University of Texas Longhorns fullback and defensive back and then an All-Pro DB for the Giants in the NFL. Mara pointed out that Landry had been an assistant coach with the Giants while still a player and then became a full-time assistant coach in 1956. According to Mara, Landry really understood the professional game because he had played it for seven years; one with the New York Yankees of the defunct All-America Football Conference and six with Mara's Gotham Goliaths. Olejniczak said something to the effect that all those platitudes about Landry were nice, but he still wanted to talk to Lombardi. Mara sighed and caved in, but with one caveat. "If Jim Lee (Howell, the Giants head coach) should retire, I'd like your permission to bring Vince back to New York." Without hesitation, Olejniczak and Fred Trowbridge, Sr., a member of the executive committee who was part of the conversation, both agreed to Mara's terms. This verbal agreement would come back to haunt Olejniczak in the not too distant future.

On December 22, a rally of sorts was conducted at Riverside Ballroom, where several speakers voiced their desire to see Curly Lambeau named the new general manager. Former Packer Pete Tinsley blamed the miserable showing by the Packers under McLean on "easy living." A crowd of nearly 200 fans showed up for the event that was meant to raise money to support an advertising campaign to bring Lambeau back into the fold. They collected a whole $28 that night and quickly learned their cause was little more than a whisper in a hurricane.

Two days later Lambeau denied having applied for the job. A week after that he reiterated that he had not applied for the position, but he said he would accept the post of general manager, *if* he was given enough authority to do the job. Gossip around town had it that, *if* Lambeau was hired to be the GM and given the power he wanted, *then* the first opportunity to fire the coach the executive committee would hire he would do so and name himself as head coach again. Little did Lambeau know the screening committee had absolutely no thoughts of hiring him to be anything with the Packers, not even ball boy. A few weeks later Lambeau changed his mind and submitted his application to Olejniczak. When Curly returned to Wisconsin in late January, the Packers president paid him the courtesy of an interview. This was a smoke screen by Olejniczak to divert public attention away from his true target, Lombardi, to be the boss on the field and in the office.

Expressing interest in both positions was former head coach Lisle "Liz" Blackbourn. Word around town about this possibility was that he had two chances of getting both jobs. Slim and none.

On January 3, 1959 after all the dust had settled on most of the college bowl games, Art Daley of the *Green Bay Press-Gazette* produced the first real public piece of gossip about the Packers of the New Year. The first portion of his piece concerned the 11 head coaches who would be returning to their jobs in the fall. He followed that with an essay on why many college coaches would want to be a head coach in the NFL and why most current NFL assistants would also want to be the boss of field of *any* NFL team. He topped that off with a one-sentence paragraph. "Thus, the Packer coaching job is a choice morsel."

Daley followed that with two succinct paragraphs that really summed up the situation in Green Bay.

"Who are the candidates for the Packer job? ...Just name anybody but the other 11 head coaches in the league and the long-time-established college coaches, and you have a candidate!

"This town is kicking every name from (Amos Alonzo) Stagg to (Forest) Evashevski to (Paul) Dietzel to (Bud) Wilkinson to (Vince) Lombardi to (Phil) Bengtson to (Milt) Bruhn to ("Fritz") Crisler to (Nick) Skorich to (Tom) Landry to (Blanton) Collier to (Earl "Red") Blaik to (Hamp) Pool to (Eddie) Erdelatz to (Jim) Trimble to Joe Blow."

Every man listed in Daley's article had served as a head coach in either college or professional football; every man except two: Tom Landry and Vince Lombardi. This was the first mention of either of them being in the running for the Packers head coaching job.

At that time, Packer fans wondered why Jim Trimble made Daley's list. Simple. Trimble had openly expressed his desire to take the head coaching reins for the Packers.

Jim Trimble played his college ball at Indiana University. With the start of World War II, he enlisted in the Navy. After the war, he became a line coach for the Wichita State University Shockers for two seasons before being named head coach in 1948. He led the Shockers to a 13-14-3 record over three campaigns, then moved on to become an assistant coach for the Philadelphia Eagles. Serving one year in that post, Trimble was promoted to head coach upon the resignation of Wayne Miller who had been appointed to the job the year before when Bo McMillin resigned due to being diagnosed with cancer. During his first three campaigns, the Eagles finished in second place in the East Division behind the Cleveland Browns. As a reward, Jim was given a three-year contract. Trimble's Eagles were expected give the Browns a run for the money in 1955, but not all went well in the City of Brotherly Love. Philly finished 4-7-1, and Trimble was fired. A few weeks later he was hired to coach the Hamilton Tiger-Cats of the Canadian Football League. Trimble directed his 1956 team into the Grey Cup Playoffs but did not reach the final game. His club placed first in the CFL East in 1957 and 1958, then into the Grey Cup final both years, but only winning the coveted trophy in 1957.

Trimble wanted to return to coaching in the U.S., but the only pro job available was in Green Bay. He might have gotten that post, if not for the fact that he wanted nothing to do with being the team's general manager and he did not want to be picked over by the entire Packers board of directors.

Getting down to the immediate business of seeking a new coach, Packers President Dominic Olejniczak, executive committee member Tony Canadeo, and head scout Jack Vainisi attended the NCAA annual meeting in Cincinnati. Their purpose for being there was to meet college coaches and get their opinions of the players the Packers were considering drafting in the remaining 26 rounds. Or so they said. Everyone knew their dual purpose was to see if any of the better coaches in the country had any interest in coming to Green Bay to coach the Packers. One *Associated Press* writer thought he would put a little spin on the rumor mill by reporting that the Packer officials were interested in Ben Schwartzwalder, head coach of the Syracuse University Orangemen, as their next field boss. Olejniczak said, "No comment!" to that notion, while Schwartzwalder unequivocally stated he had no interest in a head coaching job in the pro ranks.

A few days later Lou Brock, former Packers All-Pro center, spoke at a Fathers-Sons breakfast at a Catholic church in Fond du Lac. To put it politely, he had very little good to say about the Packers executive committee. Not mincing words, he called for every man on the committee to turn in his resignation immediately and have the board of directors elect a new committee and officers to revamp the whole Packer organization. Furthermore, he blamed the committee for the team's poor showing on the field for the last 11 years.

Brock's published remarks led Olejniczak to issue a statement to the press, explaining how the screening committee was going about its business of finding a new coach and general manager. However, he made no mention of any particular candidates for the two posts.

Two days later the American Legion Post No. 11 voted 23-9 to ask the Packers executive committee to resign immediately and an election be held to put new officers in place as soon as possible. They also recommended Dr. R.L. Cowles, a member of the Packers board of directors, be elected to replace Olejniczak.

Cowles replied that he was flattered, but he had no interest in ever becoming the president of the corporation.

Olejniczak responded very succinctly. "No comment."

The league meeting was held January 20-23 in Philadelphia. In attendance for the Packers were Olejniczak, sales promotion director Tom Miller, team attorney Fred N. Trowbridge, general manager Verne Lewellen, executive committee member Bernard Darling, and head scout Jack Vainisi. Olejniczak, Miller, and Trowbridge attended the business meetings, while Vainisi, Lewellen, and Darling manned the Packers table at the draft. Olejniczak had hopes of finding a new head coach and a general manager or a man who could handle both positions for the Packers.

At this same time, the early favorite for new head coach of the Packers was Forest Evashevski, whose University of Iowa Hawkeyes had just won the Big Ten title for the second time in three years and had gone to the Rose Bowl on New Year's Day, 1959, to face the Golden Bears of the University of California-Berkeley. After Iowa crushed Cal, 38-12, the Football Writers Association of America (FWAA) voted the Hawkeyes the winner of the Grantland Rice Trophy as the National Champion of college football. This was the first time Iowa had been so honored. This title whetted the appetites of Packer fans for Evashevski to be the next head coach in Green Bay. Evashevski's coaching resume was one factor behind the cry for his hiring, while the other was Packer fans hoped the Iowa mentor would be instrumental in signing QB Randy Duncan, the Packers' No. 1 draft pick for that year and Iowa's All-American signal-caller.

Evashevski played his college football at the University of Michigan in Ann Arbor as one of the many great quarterbacks under legendary coach Herbert Orin "Fritz" Crisler. Evashevski's nickname was Evy. He was a brilliant, hard-nosed leader on the field and in the classroom. Besides his intelligence, Evy owned a quick wit and playful character. In the Ohio State game of 1939, with 30 seconds to go and Michigan well ahead, Evy lit up a victory cigar on the sideline in full view of the Buckeye bench across the field. This was his way of pouring salt on their wounds and adding fuel to the annual feud game between the two schools that goes on to this day. In another game the next year, Crisler tried to inspire his team to beat Minnesota by asking them to play like lions on offense and like tigers on defense. Evy refused to play unless he could be a leopard. The players laughed at the joke, and Crisler said Evy could be a leopard. One day at practice, Crisler, who was a stickler for punctuality, arrived on the field a little late. "Fritz!" yelled Evashevski, boldly using the coach's nickname. "We start practice at 3:30. It's now 3:35. You're late. Take a lap around the field." Being the wise coach that he was, Crisler made no argument and proceeded to jog the circuit as ordered. His rules applied to his coaching staff and to him as well as to his players.

After graduating in 1941 Evashevski coached little Hamilton College in the little village of Clinton, New York, directing the Continentals (a nickname derived from the brave soldiers who served in the Continental Army during the Revolutionary War) to a 5-2 record in his only season there. He followed up that experience by serving as an assistant coach for spring football in 1942 at the University of Pittsburgh. That fall he enrolled at the Iowa Naval Pre-Flight School in Iowa City, Iowa, which was also the home of the University of Iowa Hawkeyes. Besides being a cadet in the school, he taught other students hand-to-hand combat and played for the Pre-Flight School Seahawks football team, which was coached by the notable former University of Minnesota Golden Gophers coach Bernie Bierman. Upon graduation from the Pre-Flight School, Evy joined the war in the Pacific with the Navy.

After the war, Evashevski returned to Ann Arbor, Michigan to enroll in the university's law school. Due to the housing shortage at the time, Evy and his wife Ruth failed to find any place to live there. When he heard about the plight of the Evashevski's, Clarence "Biggie" Munn, who had been Fritz Crisler's line coach at Michigan and who was now head coach of the Syracuse University Orangemen, offered Evy a position as an assistant coach on his team. Without a moment of hesitation, Evy took the job. When Munn was offered the head coaching spot with the Michigan State University Aggies (now Spartans) after the 1946 season, "Biggie" asked Evy to come along with him. Evy was glad to return to his native state and work as Munn's assistant for the next three years.

In 1950, opportunity struck for Evashevski again. The head coaching job of the Washington State University Cougars was offered to him, and he took it. After two seasons of winning ball in Pullman, Evy found himself in demand. Both Iowa and Indiana University offered him their head coaching posts. Unsure of which to accept, he asked Fritz Crisler for his take on it. Crisler urged him to take the Iowa job because it would be easier for him to get statewide support there than in Indiana where the Hoosiers had to compete with both the Purdue University Boilermakers and the University of Notre Dame Fighting Irish for a place in the media and fan spotlight. And there was the fact that Evashevski was already familiar with Iowa City, having spent several months there back in 1942 at the Pre-Flight School. So, with Crisler's recommendation to him and another to Iowa athletic director Paul Brechler, Evashevski took the position.

When the Packers came calling in January 1959, Evashevski had been at the helm in Iowa for eight seasons. He had compiled a record of 39-22-4 with two Big Ten Conference titles, two Rose Bowl victories, and one national crown. The Packers screening committee called Evashevski frequently to sound him out on the idea and to set up two meetings with him. The first was in early January at the NCAA Convention where a few members of the committee interviewed him. Later that month, they brought him to Green Bay, so he could see the stadium and be interviewed by the remaining committee members. All this was done without the knowledge of the local media and certainly not the fans, although speculation to what was going on with the committee was running rampant in every bar and barbershop in northeast Wisconsin.

After the Green Bay trip, Evashevski called Olejniczak and politely informed him he wasn't interested in taking the job. He preferred the life of a college coach over being a head coach in the pros and a general manager as well. Furthermore, he was making more money in Iowa City than the Packers were offering him. He wished them luck with their search for a new man.

Next on the Packers list of candidates was Blanton Collier, the mild-mannered head coach of the University of Kentucky Wildcats. The key part of the previous sentence is mild-mannered. Collier was born in Millersburg, Kentucky and raised in Paris, Kentucky. He attended college at nearby Georgetown College, graduated, and returned to Paris to teach and coach sports at the high school for 16 years. When World War II broke out, he joined the Navy at age 35 and was sent to Naval Station Great Lakes just north of Chicago, where he served as a survival swimming instructor. This was the big turning point in his life.

Naval Station Great Lakes was very similar in structure to the Pre-Flight School in Iowa City. Men who were stationed there to train the recruits had the same amenities as the other military training posts across the country, including a football team. The coach of the Great Lakes Bluejackets in 1944 was the famous Paul Brown, who would become very instrumental in the history of the Green Bay Packers.

Brown, a native of Norwalk, Ohio, moved with his family to Massillon when he was nine years old. Massillon was one of those Ohio cities that supported its own professional football team in the early decades of the 20th Century. Brown grew up watching the Massillon Tigers, one of the more fabled pro teams of the era. In 1920, he entered Massillon Washington High School at age 14 and 150 pounds, a weight that some considered to be too light for football. Not to be discouraged, he concentrated on being a pole vaulter on the track and field team. The football coach noticed how much grit Brown had as he practiced vaulting and asked him to join the pigskin squad. Massillon's quarterback that year and the next was Harry Stuhldreher, the same Harry Stuhldreher who would become famous first as one of the "Four Horsemen of Notre Dame" and then as a college head coach at Villanova University and the University of Wisconsin. Stuhldreher was no giant, not even in college where he tipped the scale at 151 pounds. Brown's high school coach Dave Stewart was a firm believer in Mark Twain's old adage, "It's not the size of the dog in the fight; it's the size of the fight in the dog." Stewart made Brown his starting quarterback in his junior and senior years. Brown led the Tigers to 15 wins in 18 games.

The next fall Brown enrolled at Ohio State University and

went out for the Buckeyes football team. He failed to make the squad. So, the next fall he enrolled at Miami University in Oxford, Ohio. Known as the "Cradle of Coaches because of the very large number of players and coaches who became famous elsewhere in their coaching careers, Miami was a really small college football powerhouse during the 1920s. The college was nicknamed the Reds at the time and then changed to the Redskins in 1928 until 1997 when the moniker was revamped again to its current RedHawks to be more politically correct for the times. Pro Football Hall of Fame coach Wilbur Charles "Weeb" Ewbank was one of the two starting quarterbacks when Brown arrived on campus. When Ewbank graduated, Brown became the starter in 1928 and over two seasons led the Miami eleven to a 14-3 record.

After graduating from Miami in 1929, Brown was forced to make a tough choice: either go to England and study history with the Rhodes Scholarship he'd been offered or take a job coaching football for a tiny prep school in Maryland. It's hard to imagine what football would be like in the United States today if Brown had gone to England and had been sucked into academia instead of the coaching profession. All fandom of football should be everlastingly grateful he accepted the position at Severn School, the prep school for the United States Naval Academy, because it was at Severn that he got his first real taste of victory as a coach. In his first year there, his Admirals posted a 7-0 record and won the Maryland state title. He already loved football but winning it all in his initial year as a head coach hooked him into the sport for life.

After one more season at Severn, Brown went home to Ohio. The head coaching job at Massillon Washington had become available, and he jumped at the chance to lead his alma mater to glory. The Tigers finished the 1931 season with a sad 2-6-2 record, calling for a new man to take the reins at Washington. Brown led them to an improved record of 5-4-1 in his first season back home. After that initial campaign, he directed the Tigers to an overall record of 75-4-1 over the next eight seasons, going 10-0-0 in 1935 and 1936 and earning national and Ohio state championship honors both years. His team finished 10-0-0 in 1938 and won the state title again. Their undefeated streak continued through the next two campaigns, earning Massillon Washington the state and national championships for both years.

Not often does a high school coach step up to the next level and succeed as well as he had in the lower rank. Brown was one of those rare exceptions.

In 1940, Ohio State's head coach Francis Schmidt resigned after losing to Michigan for the third consecutive year, a real no-no for coaches at both schools in this super tense rivalry. Brown applied for the open position and was hired, even though some of the university officials were skeptical about the 33-year-old coach making the transition to the college game.

In his first season in Columbus, Brown's Buckeyes won seven of their nine games. The only loss that year came at the hands of the Northwestern University Wildcats and its star tailback Otto Graham. Ohio State's ninth game was a 20-20 tie with Michigan, which many Buckeye fans considered a big step in the right direction. In his second year, Brown's squad lost only one game, a defeat by Wisconsin that was blamed on bad water that was drunk by several players, making them either too sick to play or too weak to perform up to their usual standards. The Buckeyes did beat Michigan at the end of year, which gave Ohio State its first national title. In 1943, with the war in full tilt, Brown suffered through his one and only losing season as a high school and college coach. The military draft depleted the talent pool so much that year that Brown was forced to play a lot of 17-year-olds, partly because Ohio State chose to affiliate itself with the Army Specialized Training Program, which forbade its trainees from playing in varsity sports. Schools such as Michigan and Purdue joined the Navy V-12 program, which allowed its trainees to play on varsity teams. This disparity put the Buckeyes at a distinct disadvantage that season, and they wound up 3-6 on the year.

Early in 1944, Brown was drafted by the Navy, commissioned as a lieutenant (the equivalent of a captain in the U.S. Army), and made the head coach of the Great Lakes Bluejackets football team at the Naval Station just north of Chicago. He was joined there by a former teammate at Miami, Weeb Ewbank, who became an assistant coach on the Naval Station team.

Each day at practice Brown observed an older man sitting in the bleachers and writing in a notebook. Curiosity got the better of him, so he approached the stranger and introduced himself. The man returned the courtesy, revealing he was a swimming instructor at the Recruit Training Center and his name was Blanton Collier. When asked what he was doing there, Collier replied that he coached high school sports back in his hometown of Paris, Kentucky and was hoping to pick up some pointers from watching Brown coach. Impressed and a bit flattered, Brown asked Collier to join him on the field and lend a hand coaching the team. Collier accepted without hesitation and became a volunteer assistant. Thus, began a lifelong friendship between the two men.

That first year at Great Lakes Brown coached the Bluejackets to a 9-2-1 record with a smattering of talented players. The only losses came to Ohio State and Notre Dame. On the roster that year were two very notable players: defensive end George Young and halfback Ara Parseghian. Young played his college ball with the University of Georgia Bulldogs, starting as a freshman and again as a sophomore before being called to duty in the Navy in 1943. Parseghian, who hailed from Akron, Ohio and grew up reading about Brown's coaching exploits at Massillon and Ohio State, suffered an ankle injury in pre-season practice and never played a down that year, but he did walk the sidelines with Brown, Ewbank, and Collier, learning from all three; knowledge that would serve him well in the years to come.

Why all this information about Paul Brown in a book about the Green Bay Packers? Keep reading and you'll find out how much he was connected to Packers history.

Sometimes great ideas and innovations come from people on the outside of an organization. In 1923, the eminent *Chicago Tribune* sports editor Arch Ward came up with the idea of having a city-wide amateur boxing tournament. This was the birth of Golden Gloves boxing. In the early years of "The Great Depression," he applied his imagination to both the National Football League and Major League Baseball. For the NFL, he suggested the champion of the league the previous season play a game in Chicago in August against a team of college all-stars that would be playing their first game in the NFL that fall. This was the birth of the College All-Star Game. At the same time, he tossed out the idea of an all-star game in the middle of the Major League Baseball season, pitting stars from the National League against the stars from the American League, also to be played in Chicago.

A decade later Ward suggested the NFL should expand after the cessation of hostilities in Europe and the Pacific. He even presented a list of possible cities to add to make it into a truly national league. The owners took exception to Ward's perceived meddling, especially George Preston Marshall, owner of the Washington Redskins. Ward countered by starting the All-America Football

Conference. He began by rounding up several very wealthy men as owners of teams in Buffalo, Chicago, Cleveland, Los Angeles, New York, and San Francisco. Later, he added Brooklyn and Miami.

The magnate for the Cleveland franchise was Arthur B. "Mickey" McBride, who started his fortune in the newspaper business and then in taxi cabs and finally in commercial real estate. McBride also had connections with various mobsters to whom he sold information to their bookmaking operations through his horse racing news wire.

McBride's first choice to coach his team was Notre Dame's coach Frank Leahy. The two men made a handshake deal that fell through when Notre Dame officials objected to losing their man on the sidelines. McBride then turned to *Cleveland Plain Dealer* sportswriter John Dietrich for his advice on whom to hire. Dietrich suggested Paul Brown. Not knowing Brown or much about him, McBride asked Ward to approach Brown about coaching his Cleveland team once the war was over. Like Don Corleone said in *The Godfather*, McBride made Brown an offer he couldn't refuse. As Brown said, he "couldn't turn down this deal in all fairness to my family."

Brown hired Collier to be his backfield coach with the new AAFC Cleveland team that the fans nicknamed the Browns after the coach in spite of his objections. Collier stayed with Brown through all four of Cleveland's four championship years in the AAFC and the first four years the franchise flourished in the NFL. After the 1953 season, Kentucky coach Bear Bryant resigned to take the head coaching job at Texas A&M University. Kentucky wasted little time hiring Collier away from the Browns. Over the next five years, his teams posted a total record of 27-21-2.

When Collier's name came up as a potential candidate for the Packers head coach's job—and possibly the general manager's post, too—the first thing the Green Bay executive committee did was call Paul Brown in Cleveland to hear what he had to say about Collier. Of course, they expected to hear all sorts of tributes and compliments about Collier. The gregarious Brown did not fail to disappoint them. He recommended Collier for the job, saying he was a good man, a good sport, and all their players liked him. When asked about his personality, Brown said he was easy-going. As far as Olejniczak was concerned, that killed any chances of the Packers hiring Blanton Collier. Olejniczak figured hiring Collier would be replacing one nice guy with another. The former mayor was fully familiar with the famous quote by former manager of MLB's Brooklyn Dodgers and New York Giants Leo "The Lip" Durorucher who said: "Nice guys finish last." Dominic wanted a tough guy to lead the Packers, not a wall flower.

The next man up for the search committee was Otto Graham, who up to that time in NFL history was inarguably the greatest quarterback ever to play the game of professional football. He remained top of the heap until Joe Montana replaced him nearly 40 years later.

Paul Brown had good things to say about Graham as well. He gave the Packers search committee a similar recommendation for Graham as he had given them for Collier. In his opinion, Graham possessed all the attributes of a real leader on the field and off. He could handle both the coaching job and the front office post of general manager.

Graham grew up in Waukegan, Illinois, the son of two music teachers. Because of his parents, he naturally took up music, learning to play the piano, the violin, the cornet, and the French horn. At the same time, he excelled in athletics, particularly basketball. In 1940, he earned a free ride to Northwestern on a hoops scholarship.

The Wildcats head football coach Lynn Osbert "Pappy" Waldorf saw Graham throw a football in an intramural game and invited him to come out to practice with the team. All the coaches were so impressed with his running and passing that Waldorf convinced him to join the squad. Football became Graham's primary sport in college, although he continued to play baseball and basketball. As a senior, he was named to both the All-American football and basketball teams, one of the very few ever to achieve such recognition.

Graham's collegiate career ended when the Navy called him to duty in February 1944. His first stop was the V-5 cadet pilot training program on the campus of Colgate University in New York. From there, he moved to the Navy Pre-Flight School in North Carolina, where he played football under coaches Glenn Killinger and Paul "Bear" Bryant. While he was at the Pre-Flight School, Paul Brown paid him a visit and offered him a contract for $7,500 to play for the new Cleveland team of the AAFC in 1946. To sweeten the pot, Brown gave him a stipend of $250 a month until the end of the war. Graham signed on without giving the offer a second thought.

To bide his time until the AAFC started play, Graham signed up to play basketball in the winter of 1945-46 for the Rochester Royals of the National Basketball League. His teammates included a few early professional basketball greats: Alfred Nicholas "Al" Cervi, Robert Edris "Bob" Davies, William "Red" Holzman, and Hollywood and television star performer Kevin Joseph Aloysius "Chuck" Connors, better known as The Rifleman. The Royals won the NBL title that season. Later that year, Graham led the Cleveland Browns to the AAFC title. This made him the only player to win championships in two major professional sports in the same year. Only one man has ever won two major professional sports titles during his career, and that would be Gene Conley who was a member of the 1957 Milwaukee Braves and the 1959, 1960, and 1961 Boston Celtics of the National Basketball Association.

Graham led the Browns to all four AAFC titles. He continued his winning ways throughout his career in the NFL. The Browns won their division all six years Graham played in the league, and they won three titles during that time: 1950, 1954, and 1955. To say Graham was a winner would be putting it mildly, which is why the Packers wanted him to be their head coach and general manager. The members of the search committee thought for sure he would bring his winning ways to Green Bay.

They were wrong.

Before he was even interviewed for the job, Graham let it be known that he wanted to coach in the college ranks because the pro game was too stressful. He said a few years later that he deplored the "win at all costs philosophy" that was necessary in the pros. Besides his attitude, Graham had applied for the head coaching job at the Coast Guard Academy in New London, Connecticut. He wanted to see how that turned out before considering any other post. Soon after he spoke with the Packers, Graham was hired by the Coast Guard Academy with the help of his friend George Steinbrenner, the future owner of the New York Yankees MLB team.

This left the name of Vince Lombardi as the only remaining option to be the next head coach and general manager of the Green Bay Packers as far as the executive committee was concerned. None of them worried that Lombardi might decline their offer, but that was only because none of them knew that Vince was looking elsewhere to become a head coach at a major institution in the college ranks or with another team in the National Football League.

§§§

3
Lombardi: BP (Before the Packers)

Vincent Thomas Lombardi was born in Brooklyn, New York, the first child of Enrico "Harry" Lombardi and his wife Matilda (nee Izzo). They named him after his paternal grandfather, which was the custom in many European countries through that time. His parents were second generation Italian-Americans. All four of his grandparents came to the United States in the late 19th Century. Both families—the Lombardi's and the Izzo's—were atypical of immigrants from southern Italy. Anthony Izzo and Harry Lombardi worked hard and saved their money as best as they could until they could move out of the slums of New York City to the newer, growing community of Sheepshead Bay just outside of Brooklyn. Here they prospered, and their children worked just as hard to give their children the same advantages of good homes, a solid education, and the so-called equal opportunity that all Americans needed to prosper.

"Vince loved sports," wrote Michael O'Brien in *VINCE*. He particularly enjoyed football; watching the New York Giants from the grandstands of the Polo Grounds and playing sandlot games, many of which he organized. "He had leadership even then," said his younger sister Madeline. "He was a perfectionist even in sandlot football. You played it right or you didn't play it at all."

Vince played basketball and baseball at Cathedral College of the Immaculate Conception, Preparatory School, where he had enrolled in order to become a Catholic priest. After three years there, he withdrew from Cathedral and came up with a new plan for his life. He would play football his senior year, work hard at the game, and hopefully earn a scholarship to college. His plan was aided by the offer of a scholarship to play football at St. Francis Prep, which was nine miles away in Brooklyn. Although this meant riding the subway 35 minutes each way to school, he saw it as just another obstacle to earn that scholarship to college he wanted so badly.

Lombardi received the football scholarship he desired with help from Dan Kern, his favorite teacher at St. Francis and a graduate of Fordham University. Kern wrote a letter to Jack Coffey, Fordham's athletic director, praising Vince's academic ability and his football prowess. That much was true, but to seal the deal, Kern added 15 pounds to Lombardi's actual 170 in order to make him a lot more appealing as a football player.

In 1933, Fordham ranked a very distant second in the nation among Catholic schools that played football. Of course, in those days as now, Notre Dame was first. This was about to change, thanks entirely to the new coaching staff. Former Fighting Irish halfback James "Sleepy Jim" Crowley, one of Grantland Rice's legendary "Four Horsemen of the Apocalypse "was the Rams' head coach, and his assistant was future College Football Hall of Fame member Frank Leahy. Other members of the coaching staff were Glenn Carberry, Earl Walsh, and Hugh Devore. This quartet of assistants had been with Crowley when he coached Michigan State University, then known as Michigan Agricultural College and nicknamed Moo U by students of in-state archrival University of Michigan.

Crowley was born in Illinois. When his father passed away, his mother took him and his older brother to live with her parents in Green Bay. Jim grew up there and attended East High School, the same school Earl L. "Curly" Lambeau called his alma mater. In 1919, Lambeau was Crowley's football coach at East. Still having ties to Notre Dame, Curly recommended Crowley to the legendary coach of the Fighting Irish Knute Rockne. Looking for a replacement for the immortal George Gipp, the Rock brought Crowley aboard.

After a standout career with the Fighting Irish as one of the fabled Four Horsemen of Notre Dame", Crowley played just three games in the NFL: two with the Packers and one with Providence. He served as an assistant coach at the University of Georgia. In 1929, he accepted the head coach's job at Michigan State, where he built up a winning team with an overall record of 22-8-3 in four seasons. In 1933, he took the same post at Fordham, taking his entire staff with him to "the Big Apple."

When Fordham coaches saw Lombardi on the practice field

for the first time, Crowley and Leahy instantly concluded he was too small to play fullback and not fast enough to be a halfback, so they opted to try him as a guard. Leahy lined up against Vince, and when Crowley said hike, the coach knocked the freshman on his backside. Vince bounced up and asked if he could try that again. Leahy okayed the idea, and this time the stout kid from Brooklyn put the coach on his butt. From that day forward, Lombardi played guard.

In that era of college football, freshmen were not permitted to play on the varsity, no matter how big or how good they were. So, Lombardi was relegated to the Fordham frosh. But due to an injury, he didn't play in any of their three games. As a sophomore, he made the varsity but did not start; too many upper classmen who were bigger and stronger. However, he did see a lot of action on both sides of the ball when the starters suffered any kind of injury, whether minor or major. In Lombardi's junior year, a new kid made the senior team with ease. Edmund Franco had been an outstanding guard as a freshman, and many people expected Vince to ride the bench again as his backup. Lombardi started the first three games before suffering an injury. This gave Franco his chance to start, and he did. Vince was his backup the rest of the season. The next year Leahy and Crowley decided to make a tackle out of Franco, so he could play alongside Lombardi. Their plan worked well. After the 1937 season, Ed Franco was proclaimed a consensus All-American.

Many writers in the second half of the 20th Century wrote that the "Seven Blocks of Granite" applied to Fordham's offensive line but not the defensive line. Before 1950, rules prevented teams on any level from platooning their players into offensive and defensive units. The seven men who played on the offensive line also played on the defensive side in the same positions with the center on offense being the exception. He would sometimes stand up in the middle of the line, or he would drop back a yard or two. It was believed this would give the defensive center a better opportunity to pursue a ball carrier on an end run or it would allow him to support a guard or tackle trying to stop a ball carrier from going through the line. Thus, a center on defense became a linebacker.

The 1936 "Blocks" were Leo Paquin (left end), Ed Franco (left tackle), Nat Pierce (left guard), Alex Wojciechowicz (center), Lombardi (right guard), Al Barbartsky (right tackle), and John Druze (right end).

In later years, Lombardi biographers would write that he was a three-year starter for Fordham. Not so. Somebody stated he was an All-American as well. Again, not so. His only real fame in college came from being a member of the "Seven Blocks of Granite" in the 1936 season. That moniker originated during the 1929 season when an unknown caption writer for the *Associated Press* penned the name on the Fordham linemen. After two seasons, it fell out of use. When Crowley and his cohorts from Notre Dame arrived in 1933, the name was revived by the school's publicist Tim Cohane, the same Tim Cohane who went on to become a famous sportswriter and editor for *Look* magazine. He kept the term alive for the first five seasons Crowley was the head coach.

The same biographers who boosted Lombardi's football skill would also grossly exaggerate his academic competence at Fordham. Some wrote that he was *magna cum laude* and that he made the Dean's list every semester he was there. Some said he graduated as a cum laude student. The truth about his academic standing is nowhere near those reports. Vince was a good student, a hard-working student, and his grades—at best—were decent. He passed all of his courses, but he only made the Dean's list once: his final semester.

Fans would argue that Lombardi had to be a genius because he was so brilliant as a football coach. Having talent to do something, such as painting or writing music or directing an orchestra to perform perfectly in synchronization, does not equal having a superb mental capacity to learn. The opposite of that is the person with a beautiful mind who can't function in society. Lombardi was truly the former as time would tell.

After graduating from Fordham in 1937, Lombardi struggled to find a career path that fit him. He attended Fordham Law School in the fall of 1938 and dropped out after completing just one semester because his grades weren't all that great. One job he took was for a finance company; he was a collector; he didn't like it and quit. He played some football for a semi-pro team and for a pro team in the American Football Association. A job with Du Pont Chemical Company in Wilmington, Delaware followed, but he didn't like being a chemist. He quit that position. Then in August 1939 came the break of his life.

Vince always wanted to be a teacher and a football coach on any level. The opportunity to be both came in a roundabout way.

Nat Pierce, the left guard at Fordham when Lombardi was the right guard, had secured a job as head football coach and teacher at St.

Cecilia High School in Englewood, New Jersey, only 10 miles by train from Times Square in Manhattan. Just before the start of school in the fall of 1939, Pierce quit his job at St. Cecilia to become the head coach of Fordham's freshman team. To replace him, St. Cecilia hired Andy Palau, Pierce's roommate and teammate at Fordham. Then Roger Mantell, head basketball coach, quit to take a post at another high school. His replacement then quit just before the school year began. Desperate for a head basketball coach and an assistant football coach, Palau turned to Jack Coffey, the athletic director at Fordham, for help. Coffey suggested three men, one being Lombardi. Knowing Vince as a teammate and a classmate at Fordham, Palau called him first and begged him to take the jobs of head basketball coach, assistant football coach, and teacher of physics, chemistry, Latin, and physical education. Lombardi accepted without hesitation.

Playing a game is one thing; coaching it is quite another. The world is full of Monday Morning Quarterbacks, but there is only one Knute Rockne, one Bear Bryant, one Darrell Royal, one Tom Landry, and one Vincent Thomas Lombardi. There are others who could be on this list, but you readers get the point. They are not *Knute Rocknes, Bear Bryants, Darrell Royals, Tom Landrys or Vince Lombardis.* These superstars of football coaching are each unique and one-of-a-kind in their own right. To pluralize them is insulting at the very least.

At St. Cecilia, Lombardi found out in a hurry the difference between coaching and being coached, between coaching and playing. As the head coach of the basketball team, he learned quickly and so did his players. After a slow start, the Saints finished with a record of 10-9. Five years later, they won the New Jersey state title. Over his eight years as the basketball mentor, Lombardi's teams posted a very outstanding record of 111-51 for a winning percentage of .681.

In 1942, Andy Palau left St. Cecilia to become backfield coach at Fordham. Lombardi was promoted to head football coach as well as head basketball coach. He stayed in both jobs for the next five years. His football Saints lost the very first game he was the top man on the sideline. They won six and tied two of their remaining eight games. Over the next two seasons and two games into the 1945 campaign, St. Cecilia didn't lose a single contest, running their unbeaten streak to 32 games. During that stretch, the Saints posted a 25-game winning streak. Lombardi's five-year record from 1942 through 1946 was a fabulous 39-7-5.

St. Cecilia High School had never been Lombardi's long-term goal. He enjoyed his time there, but he always had the welfare of his wife and family in mind. Vince arrived at the Catholic school a single man, then he married Marie Planitz, his sweetheart of six years, on August 31, 1940. The Lombardi's had their first child, son Vincent, Jr., in 1942. Vince sought jobs at other high schools and at colleges that would pay him better, but only one made him an acceptable deal. Hackensack (New Jersey) High School offered Lombardi twice the salary he was earning at St. Cecilia, topping that with some additional benefits that included tenure in three years. Because he and Marie wanted a bigger family, Vince could hardly say no. So, he made a verbal commitment to accept the Hackensack position. Lombardi would have signed the contract, if not for the pressure he received from everybody in his universe to back out of the arrangement with the public school and stay at St. Cecilia.

Lombardi stayed at the Englewood Catholic high school for two more years. Then he announced in January 1947 that he was leaving St. Cecilia to take the posts as assistant football coach and assistant athletic director at his alma mater.

Fordham's president Reverend Robert I. Gannon had always been very skeptical of the virtues of football in any academic setting. He had no love for the game and considered it to be out of control in almost every corner of the nation. When World War II broke out for the United States, Gannon suspended football at Fordham for the duration. Grudgingly, he allowed it to resume in 1946.

Ed Danowski, a Fordham alumnus, was given a three-year contract to be the new head coach. He captained the 1933 team and earned All-American honors as a triple-threat halfback. After college, he played six seasons for the New York Giants in the NFL. Then he turned to coaching at Haverstraw High School in New York until he enlisted in the Navy in 1942. Those who knew Danowski very well described him as quiet, shy, sincere, and exceptionally likeable. Note that nobody ever mentioned he was smart. His first team suffered through a disastrous season of being clobbered by every team they played, losing all seven of their games.

The next season would be better. Lombardi would be there.

Danowski had played halfback in the Rockne Box Formation when he was at Fordham and another version of the single-wing with the Giants. He wanted Vince as an assistant because Vince knew all the nuances of the now popular T-formation. Vince would teach the players and Danowski how to run the new offense. Although he was still teaching at St. Cecilia, Lombardi made the drive over the George Washington Bridge to Fordham to coach spring practice. It helped, but it didn't make a winner out of the 1947 Rams. They improved their record to a lowly 1-6-1.

The next season was filled with controversy. Many people close to the football team knew that Lombardi was the brains behind the team. The year before he had coached the freshman and won both of their games, defeating Rutgers, 12-0, and New York University, 33-0. Those players made the varsity in 1948, but they were still young and a little undersized. The Rams started the season well, winning two of their first five games. Then Boston College put the hurt on Fordham with a sound 33-7 whipping. But that wasn't the worst of it.

Notorious sports editor Joe Williams, who wrote a daily column for the *New York World-Telegram*, spilled the beans that Fordham was planning to fire Danowski at the end of the season and replace him with Lombardi. This news caught everybody—especially Vince and Danowski—by total surprise. Lombardi reacted with total embarrassment and mortification. He knew nothing about the plans of the school's three-man Athletic Council. Danowski was absolutely dumbfounded by the whole business, but he was so likeable that most people rallied around him with the hope that he would keep his job.

With all this distraction, the Rams lost their next two games to Holy Cross and Rutgers. Then the Friday before the last game of the season against NYU, Fordham star running back Langdon Viracola announced that "all the boys like Danowski and we're going win Saturday's game for him." The Rams made good with Viracola's prediction by sticking it to the Violets, 26-0. After the game in the locker room, Viracola triumphantly proclaimed to the press, "We did it for Danowski."

Langdon Viracola had issues. He had a terrible temper, and he hated Lombardi for conspiring with his father to keep him under control and out of trouble while he was at Fordham. After Lombardi moved on from Fordham, Viracola assaulted a police officer and was convicted of assault and battery. Being young, from a good family, and having a good attorney, the judge gave him a suspended sentence and put him on probation. Of course, Langdon broke his probation by getting into another fight. The next judge sent him to a reform school in New Jersey, and Fordham booted him out of school. Vince drove up to the reformatory once a month to visit Langdon. In time, he got Viracola released early and then reinstated at Fordham, where he eventually graduated.

The divide between Danowski and Lombardi was irreparable, in spite of the athletic committee stepping in and rehiring Vince for the 1949 season. Danowski didn't want him back, and Vince didn't want to stay at Fordham. In stepped Tim Cohane.

Cohane was now the sports editor for *Look* magazine. He had a little pull. Among his friends was Colonel Earl "Red" Blaik, head coach at the Military Academy, West Point, New York; better known as Army. They bumped into each other at the Biltmore Hotel in New York. It was well known that Blaik was looking to replace Sid Gillman, his offensive line coach, who had left to become the head coach at the University of Cincinnati. (This was the same Sid Gillman who went on to become a Pro Football Hall of Fame coach and a College Football Hall of Fame coach; the only man to do so to this date.) Cohane suggested Lombardi for the job Gillman had held. Blaik hesitated at first, then after a little more cajoling by his friend, he told Cohane to tell Vince to come up to West Point to see him. After three interviews with Blaik and other members of his staff, Blaik told Joe Cahill, the Academy's sports information director, to call Vince and offer him the job. Cahill called, identified himself, and before he could babble another word, Vince shouted, "I'll take it!"

Red Blaik was one of the top college coaches of his time and any other time. Born and raised in Dayton, Ohio, he earned his place at West Point in 1916 and graduated in 1920. The commandant at the Academy during his last year was General Douglas MacArthur, the grandson of a governor of Wisconsin (for only four days) and the son of a general. Blaik and MacArthur developed a close relationship that lasted until MacArthur's death in 1964. Blaik's coaching career began in 1924 as a part-time assistant coach at Miami University (Ohio). In 1926, he joined the staff at the University of Wisconsin. A year later he joined the coaching staff at West Point as a part-time assistant. His first full-time coaching job came in 1930 when he was promoted at the Military Academy. Dartmouth University hired him to be their head coach in 1934.

Attending Dartmouth at this time was John B. Torinus, Sr., the future secretary of the Green Bay Packers.

Blaik proved to be a gifted football coach. He believed the

game helped make men into leaders in all facets of life. At Dartmouth, he amassed a very impressive record, posting seven straight winning seasons for an overall mark of 45-15-4.

Then the Army came calling and he answered, becoming the head coach at West Point for the next 19 years. During his career at the Military Academy, his teams won 121 games, lost 33, and tied 10. Army won the national championship three years in a row: 1944, 1945, and 1946. The Cadets went unbeaten and untied three times and undefeated but tied three other times. They finished ranked in the Top 10 in the nation eight times and 13 times in the Top 20. Blaik didn't just turn out great officers for the Army and first team All-Americans for football fans, he also mentored several assistant coaches who became outstanding head coaches. Two of them won national titles in college football and two won pro titles.

By taking the Army position, Lombardi was not only free of his sticky situation at Fordham; he had a much better post at one of the top programs in the nation. As always, he threw himself completely into his new job, and he worked well with Blaik, the rest of the staff, and the players. During his five years at Army, the Black Knights posted a record of 30-13-2. Their mark would have been better, if not for the cribbing scandal that destroyed the 1951 season.

Cribbing is a form of academic cheating. In this case, upper classmen who took a test early in the morning would tell classmates who were taking the same exam later in the day what to look for in the test. This gave them a better opportunity to score higher. When all was discovered, 90 cadets were expelled from the Academy, 60 of them athletes, 37 of those from the football team just before the fall semester started in 1951. Blaik and his assistant coaches, especially Lombardi, were broken-hearted over this humiliating incident. They still went ahead with the season, playing with underclassmen and the best of the junior varsity. Their record was 2-7; Blaik's only losing season at West Point.

From that point on, Lombardi wanted a big-time college head coaching job more than ever. He applied whenever there was a post made available either by the retirement or dismissal of the present head coach. Nobody was interested in him because he had the reputation of being a hot-head; he could lose his temper at any moment, and this made most athletic directors shy away from him.

Then Lombardi got a break; one he wasn't sure he should take.

In 1924, the National Football League was still in its infancy, a mere five years old. The season started with a total of 18 teams. At the end, only 13 had played eight or more games. George Halas, the owner of the Chicago Bears, complained the league would never be considered to be a major sport until all the small-town teams withdrew and were replaced by teams from larger cities. In particular, he urged the other owners to look for someone from New York to buy a franchise in the league. Many agreed. They sent NFL commissioner Joe Carr to the Big Apple to find that man.

The first choice to own a franchise in New York was renowned boxing promoter Billy Gibson. In 1919, the New York Giants of Major League Baseball put together a team also named the New York Giants, but to distinguish the baseball team from the football team, they newspapers called them Brickley's New York Giants because their player-coach was fullback and kicker Charles Brickley, the famous All-American from Harvard. The team failed to play a single game because of New York's blue laws that prohibited professional sporting events on Sundays with the exception of baseball. The Giants were disbanded for the time being. Then after an exhibition game between the Canton Bulldogs and the Buffalo All-Americans played in the Polo Grounds in December 1920, drawing more than 20,000 spectators, Gibson started up the Giants again for the 1921 pro season. They played two games against league opponents and several exhibition contests against poorer teams. The next two years Gibson's Giants played as an independent and then he folded the team again. When Joe Carr came calling and asking him to take on yet another franchise in the now established NFL, Gibson politely turned him down. However, he did refer Carr to a friend of his, Tim Mara, an affable Irishman who had made his money as a bookmaker, a legal profession in those days in New York. Although he knew practically nothing about football, Mara knew people who did. His good friend Dr. Harry March knew a lot about professional football.

March had been born in 1875 in New Franklin, Ohio, and grew up in Canton, Ohio, the very heart of early professional football. He played football at Mount Union College in 1893 before becoming a newspaper reporter for the *Canton Repository*. His father was a friend of President William McKinley. When March moved to Washington, McKinley advised him to get into another line of work because, in his opinion, reporters were nothing more than "lounge lizards." March took his advice and studied medicine at the George Washington University Medical School. After graduation, he returned to Canton to start a practice. He joined the Army in World War I as a lieutenant in the Medical Corps. Post-war, he moved to New York City, where he met Tim Mara. March claimed to be the guiding force behind the formation of the National Football League. He told Mara that he had been around pro football most of his life and that he knew it was only a matter of time before the NFL became as big as the college game and Major League Baseball. Because he was so positive about the future of the pro game, March offered to be a minority owner of the Giants.

Mara made March the team's first secretary, then in 1928 made him the team's president until March became involved in a squabble with George Preston Marshall, the owner of the Boston Redskins, in 1934. This led to Mara firing March.

At this same time, Mara had two sons in college. Wellington and Jack were both at Fordham, of all places, in 1934. Wellington had a roommate, an Italian from Brooklyn named Vince Lombardi. Both brothers became close friends with Vince. They invited him to come to their home for dinner on many, many occasions. During these visits, the father advised Lombardi as if he were his own son, and Vince listened intently as if he were Mara's son.

In the late 1930s, Tim turned the team over to his sons. Jack, the older of the brothers, was named team president, and he ran the business end of things. Wellington was named team secretary, and he handled trades and personnel matters. They worked well together, and the Giants thrived.

The 1953 season was a real disaster for the Giants; they finished with a 3-9 record. The Maras assessed the situation and came to the conclusion that their head coach Steve Owen had been falling behind other coaches such as Cleveland's Paul Brown when it came to innovation and keeping up with the changes in the game. They let Owen go and tried to hire Red Blaik away from West Point. No luck there. Blaik wanted nothing to do with the pro game. The Maras then decided to promote from within by giving the head coach's job to Owen's assistant Jim Lee Howell, a huge surprise to everybody who knew anything about the Giants.

Howell had been an outstanding two-way end at the University of Arkansas in his college days. He came to the Giants in 1938 and played for eight seasons. In 1948, Owen made him assistant coach in charge of ends, a position he held until he made the leap to head coach. That was the extent of his coaching experience.

The Maras knew Howell would need two good assistants: one for offense and one for defense. They already had a solid man on defense.

Tom Landry played his college ball for the University of Texas as quarterback and fullback. At UT, he earned two degrees; one in business administration and the other in mechanical engineering. He possessed a brilliant intellect, which he used once he turned pro. In 1949, he signed with the New York Yankees of the AAFC and played defensive back. When the AAFC was melded into the NFL in 1950, the Giants picked him up and Owen made him a defensive back and quasi-assistant coach. With each passing season, he became more and more in charge of the defense until he became a full-time assistant in charge of the defense.

The Maras realized they needed someone to coach the offense for Howell. They thought they had their man in their present backfield coach, Allie Sherman, but when he was passed over for the head coaching job, he turned in his resignation and went to Canada to coach.

The Maras wanted someone who understood the nuances of the T-formation. That man was their friend Vince Lombardi. They offered him the job, but he appeared to be a bit reluctant to become an assistant coach in the pros. Wellington used his Irish persuasion to bring him on board with the Giants; that and a $5,000 raise over what he was making at West Point.

Lombardi had a little trouble learning the professional game. That little trouble was the passing game. In the pros, pass plays were much more intricate than they were in college offenses in that era. Realizing this, Vince turned to his players for tips, but more importantly than suggestions from them, he asked Bill Swiacki, the ends coach, for his help. Swiacki had been an outstanding end at Columbia. He was well aware of the subtle differences between the pro passing attack and airing the ball in the college game. Always a fast learner, Lombardi's game plan included more pass plays with each new game of the 1954 season. The Giants finished 7-5. A good start, according to head coach Howell.

Not quite so in Lombardi's mind. He felt he hadn't caught on with his players; many of them didn't like him or respect him. This made him very unhappy, and that led to depression over the holiday season. So, he decided to give up on the Giants and on his hopes of ever becoming a head coach in college.

Late in January 1955, Lombardi heard the news that Red Blaik had lost two assistant coaches. Vince's contract with the Giants had expired by this time, so he saw an opportunity to return to where he had been happiest. He called Blaik and asked to meet with him as soon as possible. They met for lunch that day, where Lombardi asked to be hired to fill his former position with the Academy. Blaik hired him on the spot with a handshake agreement that hadn't said a thing about how much Lombardi would be paid.

Out of courtesy and honor, Blaik phoned Wellington Mara to tell him that he had just rehired Lombardi. Mara's voice exploded into Blaik's ear. "You can't talk to him!" Blaik responded that he had already made a deal with Vince and that was that. That weekend the Giants general manager Ray Walsh begged Vince to stay and told him he'd be foolish to go back to West Point. Lombardi said his mind was made up. The next day Wellington Mara called him and made Vince an offer his wife couldn't refuse. If Lombardi would stay with the Giants, Mara would pay him $6,000 more than he had earned the year before. Marie Lombardi told Vince to go see Blaik on Monday and tell him she would be very unhappy to return to West Point. Lombardi did just that, and Blaik released him from their deal. Vince stayed in New York—for the time being.

Lombardi still wanted to become a head coach in the college ranks. His dream of coaching Fordham vanished when the school put an end to their football program after the 1954 season. He then reset his sights a lot higher. Having played for Frank Leahy, he wanted to coach for him as well. Before he could put that dream into motion, Leahy resigned from Notre Dame in January 1954, allegedly for health reasons. Later, he stated he left because he felt he was no longer wanted in South Bend.

Even though Leahy was gone, Lombardi continued to pursue his dream of coaching at Notre Dame. He wrote to Edward Walter "Moose" Krause, the athletic director for the Fighting Irish, expressing his interest in the head coach post, but Krause never responded one way or another. When the job became available again after the 1958 season, he wrote Krause to express his continued desire to coach at Notre Dame. Still no reply.

Prior to this misadventure with Notre Dame, Lombardi had become a desirable coaching commodity within the NFL. The Giants continued to improve under the triumvirate of Howell, Landry, and Lombardi, and in 1956, the Giants won the league title with a solid 47-7 whipping of the Chicago Bears at Yankee Stadium. The Giants finished second in their division in 1957, but they were still a strong contender.

The Philadelphia Eagles were a poor team during those two years. Their head coach was Hugh Devore, the same Hugh Devore who had been an assistant at Fordham when Lombardi was a player. Hughie, as he was known affectionately to those who knew him, was fired in early 1958 by Eagles general manager Vince McNally. After hearing great things about Lombardi, McNally consulted with the team's president Frank McNamee about offering the head coach's job to Lombardi. McNamee told McNally to call Lombardi directly because he thought the Maras would not grant the Eagles permission to talk to Vince. McNally and Lombardi met at a Philadelphia train station where McNally made Lombardi an offer of $22,500 a year for a contract that would only be for one or two years, depending on how the team did under Lombardi. Being the honorable man that he was, Lombardi said he would have to talk to the Maras first before giving him a definite answer.

Wellington Mara talked Vince into staying with Giants, citing a lot of reasons, especially the unsettled situation in Philadelphia where several minority stockholders kept meddling with the management of the organization. Vince considered everything Mara told him and eventually decided to remain with the Giants.

The 1958 NFL season was one of the most memorable in the history of the league to that time. Johnny Unitas led the Baltimore Colts to the Western Conference title, jumping out to 6-0 start and clinching the crown with two weeks remaining in the season. In the Eastern Conference, the Cleveland Browns also leaped ahead of the pack, winning their first five games before finally losing to the Giants in Week 6. The next week the Giants handed the Colts their first loss of the year, and the Browns went down to defeat to the Lions, to put the two teams into a first-place tie. The Giants suffered an upset in Week 8 at the hands of the lowly Steelers, while the Browns began a four-game winning streak. New York and Cleveland met in the final game of the regular season at Yankee Stadium. All the Browns had to do was win or tie the game to earn the conference crown. They did neither as the Giants forced a playoff game the following week again at Yankee Stadium. The Giants had won the regular season finale by a score of 13-10, as Frank Gifford completed a touchdown pass to Bob Schnelker to tie the game in the fourth quarter, and Pat Summerall booted a 49-yard field goal to win the game. New York's defense won the playoff game by completely dominating the Browns offense, proving it is possible to beat a team three times in a single season.

The 1958 season ended the following week also in New York at Yankee Stadium when the Giants took on the Colts in The Greatest Game Ever Played to that time. The National Broadcasting Corporation (NBC) telecast the game nationwide, and the viewing audience was given a thriller as the Giants and Colts played the first ever overtime game in NFL history. In sudden death, the Colts pulled off a victory, 23-17, when Alan "The Horse" Ameche barreled through the line for the winning score. Tom Landry reflected on the game sometime later. "It marked the time, the game, and the place where pro football really caught on, where the public attention was aroused and brought the game into the spotlight."

After this historic contest, two head coaching positions opened up for Lombardi. The first was at West Point. Red Blaik was retiring from coaching to take a job in the private sector. Lombardi seemed like the natural choice to succeed Blaik, but the athletic board had different ideas. Army's head coach had always been a former player and military officer. Lombardi was neither, so he was passed over in favor of Dale Hall, a former halfback at West Point who played alongside Doc Blanchard and Glenn Davis.

The news that he was no longer under consideration for the Army position reached Lombardi while he was having dinner at the home of the Giants team physician, Dr. Anthony Pisani. Although he was disappointed, Lombardi rallied instantly. He asked his host if he could use his phone to make a long-distance call. "Do you mind if I call Green Bay?"

With this call, Lombardi informed Olejniczak he would consider further discussion about the open coaching and general manager positions with the Packers.

§§§

4
The Packers Get Their Man

Most football coaches belong in some other coach's coaching tree, such as Sid Gillman's tree that you can find in a Wikipedia article about him. Not so with Vince Lombardi. Instead of him being a branch on the tree of Red Blaik or of Jim Lee Howell, Lombardi is the rare flower at the top of a tree that has Knute Rockne as the trunk.

Rockne coached Curly Lambeau in 1918. In 1919, Lambeau recommended Jim Crowley to Rockne to be a player for Notre Dame. Crowley was the head coach at Fordham when Lombardi played there. You can see where this is going. All the men who had some kind of influence on Lombardi's character, his personality, his knowledge of the game of football, and his business acumen are mentioned in the previous three chapters. They either made their mark on him directly, such as Frank Leahy his line coach at Fordham, or indirectly, such as Paul Brown who coached some of the men who worked with Vince before he became the head coach of the Packers. Even General Douglas MacArthur, Red Blaik's mentor, can be included on the tree of men who placed a mental or emotional impression on Lombardi at some point in his life. All of them came together in the rainbow of rainbows' aura around Lombardi the day he stepped into the offices of the Green Bay Packers.

The Packers search committee for a new head coach used Paul Brown as their model. Brown was the only man in the NFL who was head coach and general manager of his team. Lombardi only fit half that description; he had experience in business but none as a head coach in either the college or pro ranks. Even so, the search committee chose to interview him.

The first meeting between Lombardi and the Packers search

committee, held at the league meeting in Philadelphia in January, went very well, but the committee members still had their reservations about Vince. Yes, he had the strong personality that they wanted, and yes, he had some business experience, albeit not in pro football. So, they asked around about Lombardi within the NFL.

Bert Bell, the NFL Commissioner at the time, said Lombardi understood the business side of pro football, was an excellent coach, a student of the game, a real disciplinarian, and a gentleman, Bell added, "He's a great believer in desire and proper conduct. You'll like him."

On the field, the Packers and Chicago Bears were practically blood feud rivals. Away from the fans and the hoopla of game days, the two front offices were much like kissing cousins. Bears owner and head coach "Papa Bear" George Halas said, "I probably shouldn't be telling you this, but he'll be a good one. I shouldn't tell you because you're liable to kick the crap out of us!"

Red Blaik recommended Lombardi with great enthusiasm.

The final brick in the wall was placed by Paul Brown. He pushed hard for Lombardi because he felt Vince would be an excellent coach. Then he qualified all his praise with a last remark. "You'll never get him because he's married to the Maras. He's a New Yorker, and you just don't take New Yorkers out of New York."

With all those sterling recommendations for the Packers to hire Lombardi, the committee felt they should conduct one more interview with him. So, they flew him to Green Bay on the morning of January 26 without telling any of the local media about it. They took him to Prange's Department Store and spoke with him away from the prying eyes and donkey ears of anybody who might recognize any of the committee members.

Lombardi insisted he would only take the job of coaching the Packers, if he were also given the position of general manager. Some of the committee balked at this notion; others agreed to consider him for both; Olejniczak silently sided with Vince. They talked money next. The Packers offered him $36,000 a year for five years with a bonus package for finishing first, second, or third in the division. Lombardi knew how to haggle. He would take the deal, if they added the third-place money to the first-place money. They agreed. The meeting ended with Lombardi taking the deal and Olejniczak saying they still had to get approval from the board of directors.

During the several hours on the return flight to New York the next day, Lombardi repeatedly contemplated his meeting with the Packer selection committee members and Olejniczak. As soon as he was back in the Big Apple, he went to his church to pray and further consider his good fortune at being offered the Green Bay jobs. Then he met with his friend Wellington Mara to tell him about the Packers' proposition. Mara told him to take it. With Wellington's encouraging words in his pocket, Vince went home to break the news to his wife Marie. To say she was distraught over the prospect of leaving New York, the largest city in the NFL, for the long winters in Green Bay, the smallest town in any of the major professional sports in America, well, distraught seems less than apropos. Shocked might be better. Terrified would be best. That evening at a Fordham banquet she and Vince attended Marie pigeonholed Wellington Mara and begged him to enforce the Giants' contract with Vince, a deal that still had two years left on it. Mara told her the Green Bay job would be ideal for Vince and that she would be unhappy if Vince were unhappy. Although still broken up about leaving New York, Marie played the good wife and went along with Vince's decision to take the Green Bay positions.

On January 28 at a special meeting of the Packers board of directors held at the Hotel Northland the committee put the proposal they had made to Lombardi before Olejniczak asked the board to give the executive committee the authority to make the deal they had already made with Lombardi official. This was the moment John Torinus asked his now famous question. "Who the hell is Vince Lombardi?" After some brief discussion, the board voted 26-1 to do so. Then the executive committee voted unanimously to hire Lombardi to be both general manager and head coach.

Olejniczak called Vince to tell him the result of the meeting.

Lombardi couldn't have been happier.

Not so his wife Marie and their children. They were born and raised in the New York area. They knew no other place on the face of the planet. To them, West Point was practically in another country. Now Green Bay? Wisconsin? This was a whole different universe from their Big Apple. A dark cloud settled over all three of them.

But not over Vince.

When he spoke over the phone with Art Daley of the *Green Bay Press-Gazette*, Lombardi sounded downright effervescent. "Right now, I'm in the process of talking with seven or eight men as possible assistant coaches. I'll be in there (Green Bay) Monday to sign the contract and stay a few days. I'll have to get back here (New York) to close out some odds and ends. I expect to start in about the second week in February."

Now Coach Lombardi added that he was "anxious to review the game pictures (films). I know a few things about the club, and I know that there is a fine nucleus of veterans, but I'll get a better idea of the personnel from the pictures. It will help me know what we can do on offense and defense. I plan to use the T-formation with some flanking variations."

Lombardi the man said he had "enough football background generally and in particularly with the Giants to handle the general manager position. Of course, I'll have someone to take care of the details."

He continued by saying the politically correct thing to Daley and his readers. "I'm extremely happy to get this opportunity in Green Bay but I'm unhappy about leaving the Giants and their entire organization. The Maras are wonderful people and I'll miss them all."

Bob Daley, former Giants publicist, penned a piece about Vince in the team's press book.

"Howell may be considered as commanding officer, with Lombardi as his executive officer both on the practice field and on the bench during games.

"Basically, it is Lombardi who designs those intricate plays which result in long runs on Sunday afternoons. He not only plots and diagrams the movements of the offense, he teaches it in blackboard sessions and on the practice field, occasionally sharpening a particular play right up to game time."

Words such as these helped Olejniczak and the screening committee decide to make Vince the boss they wanted to lead the Packers back to their winning ways of Lambeau's first two and a half decades as head coach.

When asked about the rumor that the Packers were interested in trading for backup quarterback George Shaw of the Baltimore Colts, Lombardi replied quite diplomatically, "I know about Shaw, but I am going to give our boys a look before doing any trading." He added that he expected to "get an idea of their play—plus what I've seen myself from the pictures." Already, he was showing Daley and all of Packerland that he was now the Packers coach.

"I don't know much about the Packer personnel yet," he said

while discussing his new job. "But I'll put the best players on defense. That's the best way to build a team."

To show he meant business, Vince concluded his remarks to Art Daley, saying he was "making (a) complete break and I'm moving to Green Bay—lock, stock and barrel."

When Vince and his wife Marie flew into Green Bay Monday afternoon, the sky was clear, but the temperature was well below zero degrees. On the calendar, this was Groundhog Day. Lombardi smiled for the cameras, while Marie did all she could to keep her teeth from chattering. From her demeanor, she was not at all happy to be in Wisconsin.

While inside the airport terminal, a young man from a small radio station in the northern part of the state and carrying a tape recorder approached Lombardi. Someone in the entourage tried to brush him off, but Vince would have none of it.

"I promised this man an interview," said Lombardi. "So, he's going to get it."

Everybody that ever met Vincent T. Lombardi during his life knew he was truly a man of his word.

§§§

5
Lombardi Takes the Helm

Vince Lombardi, the general manager, wasted no time taking charge of the front office of the Green Bay Packers. He signed his initial contract on Groundhog Day, 1959. Then he held his first press conference immediately thereafter. It startled some, but it pleased most.

The next day Lombardi went to work. A photo of Lombardi in the *Milwaukee Journal* the next morning was captioned, "Coach Lombardi Takes Full Command of Packers." Makes one wonder if the writer of that line was truly aware of what lie ahead for the Packers or if he was just being wishful.

According to Michael O'Brien in his book, Vince "rented a house, hired two assistant coaches (Phil Bengtson and Red Cochran), reappointed the front office personnel, ordered remodeling of the South Washington Street offices, addressed the board of directors, met with the press and attended several meetings." He spoke to the board of directors over lunch at the Northland Hotel. According to John Torinus, Sr., the secretary of the corporation, Lombardi made himself perfectly clear to them. He started his speech by saying, "I want it understood that I'm in complete command. I expect full cooperation from you people, and you will get full cooperation from me in return. You have my confidence, and I want yours." Torinus, who had served in the Army during World War II with the rank of major, said he thought he was back in Europe and a new general had just taken command. He also remarked that Lombardi "scared Hell out of some of us."

Torinus was living proof of the six degrees of separation theory. He worked on the school newspaper in college. When Dartmouth hired Red Blaik to coach the football team, Torinus interviewed him before the team began spring practice in 1934. Of all the directors at that lunch, he was closest to Lombardi, even though he didn't know it at the time. He had completely forgotten about meeting Vince 25 years earlier.

At the press conference that followed, Lombardi repeated most of what he said to the board, adding, "I am responsible only to the executive board of six men through President Olejniczak."

Ole, as he was known among his friends, watched with pride, delighted to have a forceful, competent leader for the team and the organization.

"I've never been associated with a loser," Lombardi added, "and I don't expect to be now."

Dominic smiled ear-to-ear.

A month later at the stockholders annual meeting on March 2 Vince told them he would tolerate no meddling from anybody. "I have been hired to do a job without interference, and I don't expect to have any. If you don't like me ..., well, I don't believe that will happen. ... You will be proud of the team because I will be proud of the team." He paraphrased General MacArthur, saying, "There is no substitute for victory."

Lombardi spent much of his first few months with the Packers giving speeches, interviews, and press conferences all over Wisconsin and the Upper Peninsula of Michigan, which was nominally a part of Packerland. That in no way meant he was leaving all the business of the team to his office staff, and it certainly didn't mean he was letting his football staff sit around and collect dust while he was away. He gave specific orders to everybody who worked for him, and he expected them to be executed promptly and completely. Failure to carry out one's duties or an assignment resulted in a Lombardi rant. Nobody wanted one of those vocal explosions aimed at them, so everybody soon learned to get their work done Lombardi's way.

The first assistant Lombardi hired was his offensive backfield coach John Thurman "Red" Cochran, a native of Alabama and a true son of the South. Cochran had experience in the college ranks and in the pros. His collegiate playing career started out in 1942 with Wake Forest University. After playing one season, World War II got in the way, and he became a bomber pilot. After the war, he played one more year at Wake Forest before turning pro in 1947. He played four years for the Chicago Cardinals, then gave up playing due to a knee injury. In 1951, he joined the coaching staff at Wake Forest for the next five seasons. Then he took a job with the Detroit Lions and was their offensive backfield coach for three years before he was replaced by none other than Scooter McLean. Lombardi wasted no time in wooing Cochran into joining his staff in Green Bay to do the same job he'd done in the Motor City.

Immediately after hiring Cochran, Lombardi hired John Phillip Bengtson. A Minnesota native Bengtson played tackle at the University of Minnesota under fabled coach Bernie Bierman. He earned All-American honors in 1934. Bengtson went right from playing to coaching, starting as an assistant at the University of Missouri in 1935, then moving back to Minnesota as line coach through 1939. The following season he moved out West to take the same job at Stanford University in Palo Alto. He stayed in California for 12 years before jumping to the professional ranks with the San Francisco 49ers. That job lasted seven years until Bengtson was fired after the 1958 season along with his third head coach Frankie Albert. Lombardi had no trouble convincing Bengtson to come to Green Bay to coach the Packers defense.

Lombardi rounded out his staff with two relatively unknowns: Bill Austin and Norb Hecker.

William Lee Austin was born in California but grew up in Oregon. He played tackle for Oregon State College (now Oregon State University) in Corvallis. The Giants selected him in the 13th round of the 1949 Draft. He played seven years in New York, not including two years he served his country in the Korean War. After retiring from the Giants in 1957, he took his first coaching job with the Wichita State University Shockers. Lombardi convinced Austin to join his staff in Green Bay as the offensive line coach.

Born and raised in Ohio, Norbert Earl Hecker served his country briefly at the end of World War II. He came home and attended college at Baldwin-Wallace College where he played wide receiver and defensive back. Hecker won Small College All-American honors in 1950 and was drafted by the Los Angeles Rams in 1951. After three seasons in California, Hecker was traded to the Washington Redskins. Perturbed by the move, he signed to play the 1954 season with the Toronto Argonauts of the Canadian Football League. At the end of that campaign, the Toronto management chose to release all of its players from the United States. Hecker then signed with the Ottawa Rough Riders, but before playing a single down for Ottawa, he quit and returned to the U.S. to play for the Redskins. He played three seasons in Washington before being released in 1958, probably because he was one of the 12 players who formed the NFL Players Association. He returned briefly to the CFL with the Hamilton Tiger-Cats. On February 23, 1959, Hecker signed his first contract with Vince Lombardi and the Green Bay Packers as their secondary coach.

While lining up his coaching staff, Lombardi also faced the task of trying to sign draft picks, especially the Packers first round choice Randy Duncan, the All-American quarterback from the University of Iowa. Duncan was also the runner-up for the Heisman Trophy in 1958; he was that good. The problem was he knew he was that good, and he wanted to be paid accordingly. When Lombardi held the line on rookie salaries, Duncan basically told him to take his offer and put it where the sun doesn't shine. He then signed with the British Columbia Lions of the Canadian Football League. He played north of the border for two years before signing with the Dallas Texans of the American Football League. He played very little in the AFL and quit when the Texans traded for Len Dawson. That was the end of his football career.

The first four rounds of the draft were conducted on December 1, 1958 with the remaining 26 rounds being held January 21, 1959. Lombardi had no say in the Packers draft that year. Those duties were left almost entirely to Jack Vainisi, the team scout.

Gene Ronzani, the man who succeeded Curly Lambeau as head coach of the Packers, hired Vainisi in September of 1950 to be the team's scout. Jack had just graduated from Notre Dame that same spring. Ronzani had been friends with him and his family during his playing days with Chicago Bears. Jack went to Notre Dame to play football and lettered his freshman year as a tackle. He then entered the Army. While playing football in the military, he contracted a serious case of rheumatic fever that left him with an enlarged heart and prevented him from continuing the pursuit of his dream to play professional football. He remained with the Packers as team scout until Lombardi promoted him to business manager in March 1959.

With Randy Duncan balking at signing with the Packers, Lombardi concentrated on the rest of the draft. The number two pick, Alex Hawkins, a running back from the University of South Carolina, had already signed his contract the day before Scooter McLean turned in his resignation. Hawkins failed to measure up to Lombardi's standards, so the coach cut him from the team in training camp.

3rd Round pick Boyd Dowler didn't sign with the Packers until June 10. Dowler played just about everything for the University of Colorado. He stood 6'5" and weighed 220 pounds. His body size didn't impede his speed on the field. In his senior year on the Buffaloes track team, he ran the 100-yard dash in 9.9 seconds and was clocked at 14.2 seconds in 120-yard high hurdles. On the Buffaloes football roster, he was listed as a quarterback during his senior year, but as a junior, he played wide receiver, catching 25 passes for 376 yards. Dowler was also the team's punter with 33 kicks for an average of 43.3 yards. Lombardi said he planned to try Dowler as an end because of his speed and pass-catching ability.

The Packers traded away their 4th Round pick to the Cleveland Browns the previous season for defensive end Len Ford. Their next pick came in the 5th Round, and they took Andy Cvercko, a tackle from Northwestern University, where he played under the tutelage of Ara Parseghian. Cvercko was the second player to sign a deal with Green Bay. The Packers initial pick in the 5th Round had been traded away to the Washington Redskins the previous season for J. D. Kimmel, a defensive tackle.

After Cvercko, the Packers chose Willie Taylor, a center from Florida A&M (Agricultural & Mechanical) University; Bobby Jackson, halfback from the University of Alabama; Gary Raid, tackle from tiny Willamette College in Oregon; Buddy Mayfield, end from the University of South Carolina; Bob Laraba, quarterback from Texas Western University (now University of Texas-El Paso) who played two years in the American Football League before being killed in an automobile crash after the final game of the 1961 season with the San Diego Chargers; George Dixon, back from little Bridgeport College in Connecticut who was released by the Packers during the 1959 pre-season and then went on to play in Canada and earning a prominent place in the Canadian Football Hall of Fame; Sam Tuccio, a tackle from Mississippi Southern College; Bob Webb, back from tiny St. Ambrose College in Davenport, Iowa; Larry Hall, guard from Missouri Valley College in Marshall, Missouri; Jim Hurd, back from Albion College in Michigan; Ken Kerr, guard from Arizona State College (now University); Dick Teteak, guard from the University of Wisconsin; Dan Edgington, end from the University of Florida; Tom Secules, back from William & Mary College (now University) in

Virginia; Dick Nearents, tackle from Eastern Washington State College (now Eastern Washington University) in Cheney, Washington; William R. "Bill" Butler, safety from the University of Chattanooga (now University of Tennessee-Chattanooga); Charley Sample, back from the University of Arkansas; Dave Smith, back from the Ripon College in Ripon, Wisconsin; Charlie Anderson, back from Drake University in Des Moines, Iowa; Ben Lawyer, tackle from Lewis & Clark College in Portland, Oregon, and was a Modoc of the Klamath tribe of Native Americans; Joe Hergert, center from the University of Florida; Leroy Hardee, back from Florida A&M; Ken Higginbotham, end from Trinity University in San Antonio, Texas; Timothy Brown, back from Ball State College (now University) in Muncie, Indiana; Jerry Epps, guard from West Texas State University (now West Texas A&M University) in Canyon, Texas; Jack Flara, back from the University of Pittsburgh; and finally Dick Emmerich, tackle from West Chester State College (now University) in West Chester, Pennsylvania.

The annual meeting of stockholders of Green Bay Packers, Inc., was held March 2 in the Brown County Courthouse. Three men were expected to speak to the 150 attendees. First up was the new manager of the Green Bay Bluejays minor league baseball team Stan Wasiak. Knowing this was no more than an introduction of the hardball boss, Wasiak kept his words to a minimum, thanked the crowd, and then turned the podium over John Torinus, secretary-treasurer, who read a rosy financial report to the shareholders.

Although the Packers were lousy on the field in 1958, the fans still came out see them play, filling the bleacher seats every home game in Green Bay. The Packers turned a profit of $70,106.28. After taxes, the corporation cleared $37,302.61. This gave the Packers a war chest of $207,729.53, putting the organization on its soundest footing of all time.

The last speaker was the man of the hour, new head coach and general manager Vincent T. Lombardi.

"A good football team is my number one job," he said to start his speech, "and I am keeping that in mind at all times. I cannot make any predictions on the team because I don't know what kind of team I'll have. But I know this much. You will be proud of the team because I will be proud of the team.

"The Packers have many weak points, but they also have lots

of good points and it's around these good points that we will build our nucleus. We have finished grading every player in each of the 12 league games played last year and we discovered that some players who saw little action had high marks while some other players who we expected would get high marks had lower ratings.

"I am now holding a clinic with my coaches and we are discussing every phase, step by step, of our offense and the kinds of defenses we can use."

Lombardi closed his remarks by saying, "Hopes? I am very hopeful we'll win some games next fall—somehow and some way.

"I have been hired to do a job without interference and I don't expect to have any. If you don't like me—well, I don't believe that will happen."

The stockholders gave Lombardi a rousing cheer with the conclusion of his speech. He spoke with all the confidence of a leader facing a difficult but surmountable task.

Olejniczak smiled broadly as the shareholders continued the ovation. He knew for certain there would be no more effigies hung from trees in Packerland as long as Vince was holding the Packers' reins in one hand and the whip of leadership in the other.

After Hawkins and Cvercko, 22nd Rounder Charlie Anderson penned his contract with the Packers, along with Tom Newell, 15th Rounder drafted as a future in the previous year's draft. Both men attended Drake University in Des Moines. Neither Anderson nor Newell made the team in September.

General Manager Vince Lombardi had his hands full trying to sign all 30 draftees, while Coach Vince Lombardi studied game film from the previous years to see what kind of talent he had inherited from Scooter McLean and Lisle Blackbourn. Realizing the talent pool held some promise, he quickly surmised he needed more than he already had, if the Packers were to be at least a competitive team in the coming 1959 season. So, GM Lombardi decided to make a few trades to help Coach Lombardi build a better roster.

Coach Lombardi found weaknesses in the team's slow halfbacks, unaggressive defensive line, a confused defensive backfield, a weak offensive line, a lack of depth, and a riddle at quarterback. To make matters worse, offensive guard Hank Bullough retired from playing pro football to become an assistant coach at his alma mater Michigan State.

Now to solve the problems facing Coach Lombardi, General Manager Lombardi took to the telephone.

One hole was thought to be filled when Dick Teteak signed his deal with the Packers. A star at Wisconsin-Madison under Head Coach Milt Bruhn Teteak played center and linebacker for the Badgers. Standing 6'0" and weighing 215, he was bigger than his older brother Deral who had played five years for the Packers (1952-56) as a linebacker. An assistant coach for Bruhn, Deral recommended Dick to the Packers, who then took him in the 15th Round of the draft.

QB Bob Webb, known as "the Blond Bomber" in college because he broke 10 small school records for passing, signed in early March. The biggest of those records was his four-year total yards mark 5,114, which surpassed the total of 4,278 set from 1948 to 1951 by Bob Heinerdinger of Northern Illinois.

At the same time, Bob Skoronski, the big defensive tackle who had played for the Packers in 1956, returned from military duty in the Air Force. Lombardi greeted him with open arms. Skoronski had shown promise as a rookie.

Late in March, the Packers signed two potential defensive backs. Bobby Jackson played at Alabama as a quarterback as well as a safety. Bill Butler, a Wisconsin native from Berlin, played his college ball at Chattanooga. His coach, Andrew Cecil "Scrappy" Moore, rated him the best halfback in the school's history. Lombardi said both rookies would be given a chance on offense as well as defense.

Lombardi announced on April 1 that he and his coaching staff had finished reviewing game pictures to grade the Packers offense of 1958. Two days later Art Daley reported that versatile back Paul Hornung had been unhappy in how he had been used by McLean and his staff the previous season. Lombardi then told Hornung that he intended to play him at one position and only one position, and his place on the field was halfback on offense. "Let's face it," said Lombardi. "Hornung is the guy who can make us go. He's a key player, and much of our success will depend on him."

Daley also pointed out that the former Notre Dame standout was "stitched in threes." His third pro season would be 1959, and he would be playing his third different position for his third different head coach. Liz Blackbourn had used him primarily as a quarterback in his rookie year. Scooter McLean had him running at fullback. Now Lombardi intended to play him at halfback and possibly turn him into another Frank Gifford, the All-Pro halfback he had coached in New York.

On April 8, Lombardi announced the signing of a pair of defensive backs. Jim Morse had been the Packers' pick in the 13th Round of the 1957 Draft. A teammate of Hornung's at Notre Dame he opted to play in Canada for two years before taking a shot at the NFL. Also, penning his name to a Packer deal was Ken Wineberg, the Packers' 9th Round choice in the 1956 Draft. He passed on going pro until he had completed his education at Texas Christian University.

More roster news included the return of Jack Losch from duty in the Air Force. A halfback by trade Losch was the Packers top pick in the 1956 Draft. Defensive tackle Jerry Helluin, who had played for the Packers for four seasons, 1954-57, announced he was completely recovered from a shoulder separation he had suffered against the Eagles in a pre-season game and kept him out of the entire 1958 campaign. Adding further depth to the training camp roster was veteran tackle Volney Peters who had been drafted by the Chicago Cardinals in 1952. He also played for the Redskins and the Eagles. Philadelphia had released him the year before, making him available to Packers.

Lombardi received some good news and some bad news on April 10. The good news was the signing of veterans Bob Skoronski and Gary Knafelc. The bad news was the announcement of the retirement of Carlton Massey, the five-year veteran linebacker that the new coach was counting on as a key cog in his defense.

The Packers published the tentative roster for training camp, which was still three months away. It included four free agents, 28 rookies, and 39 veterans. Four were quarterbacks; veterans Bart Starr, Babe Parilli, and Joe Francis; and rookie Bob Webb. Hornung headed up a list of 10 halfbacks. Howie Ferguson, Jim Taylor, and Dave Smith filled out the fullback position. Veterans Billy Howton and Max McGee topped the list of seven pass catching ends. Bob Skoronski sat atop the list of tackles, while Jerry Kramer and Forrest Gregg led a group of six guards. Jim Ringo was the center, and Dan Currie was his backup, although his primary position was linebacker. The defensive line had five candidates for the two end spots, five for tackle, seven for linebacker, and 15 for the secondary.

In another transaction, Paul Brown traded defensive end Bill Quinlan and offensive back Lew Carpenter to Green Bay for wide receiver Billy Howton, the two-time All-Pro and at the time of the deal the second leading pass catcher in Packers history. Quinlan played his college ball at Michigan State and was taken by the Browns in the 3rd Round of the 1956 Draft. Carpenter was a two-sport star at the University of Arkansas, playing football and baseball. After playing minor league baseball in the summer of 1953, Carpenter accepted an offer from the Detroit Lions, who had chosen him in the 5th Round of the 1953 Draft. He helped the Lions win the NFL title that year. After 18 months in the U.S. Army, Carpenter was traded to the Browns who had picked his younger brother Preston, a tight end also from Arkansas, in the 1st Round of the 1956 Draft.

Shipping Howton out of Green Bay was a move that would have happened sooner or later. Although Billy had been an outstanding receiver in his first five campaigns with the Packers, his numbers had fallen off in the last two seasons. Furthermore, Howton had a reputation as a disciplinary problem. Then there was Howton's involvement in the newly formed Players Association. He was one of the founders, and in the Spring of 1959, he was the union's president. As such, he often spoke unfavorably about the league's owners and Commissioner Bert Bell. All of that failed to endear him to the Packers new coach and general manager. Lombardi revealed he had intended on making an example of Howton to the rest of the veterans on the Packers. So, the trade served more than its original purpose of improving the roster.

Right from the start of his regime as Green Bay's head coach, Lombardi wanted to make a deal with Baltimore for the services of backup quarterback George Shaw. Then Vince and his staff studied the films from the previous season and saw something they hadn't expected.

If any Packer fan had been asked who the best candidate was for starting signal-caller for the 1959, they would have replied that Parilli had the most experience or that Francis had the most potential.

Vito "Babe" Parilli was born in coal-mining, steel-making, and industrial Pennsylvania, one of the so-called hotbeds for college football recruiting in the 20th Century. Paul "Bear" Bryant, head coach for the Kentucky Wildcats, brought Parilli to Lexington to play his college ball. While there, he led Kentucky to two straight New Year's Day bowl victories. For personal achievement, he finished fourth and third in the Heisman Trophy voting for 1950 and 1951, respectively.

The Packers made Parilli the fourth overall pick in the 1952 Draft. He played two years in Green Bay before moving on to play two years for Ottawa Rough Riders in the Canadian Football League. Paul Brown coaxed him into returning to the NFL and play for him in Cleveland. One year there and he was traded back to the Packers.

Joseph Charles Naekauna Francis, Jr., was born and raised in Hawaii, and he was part Hawaiian, which allowed him to attend the Kamehameha Schools. Thus, Francis was the first Hawaiian to play for the Packers. In Oregon State's single-wing formation, Joe played tailback. The Packers took him in the 5th Round of the 1958 Draft as a quarterback, although he hadn't played that position very much in college. Francis started the last game of the 1958 season and performed fairly well for a third-string QB who hadn't seen much action that year.

After reviewing the game films of the previous year, Lombardi concluded that Bart Starr held the most promise to become an elite NFL quarterback. He did everything well, considering how weak the protection he received from the offensive line. The one factor that set him above the other candidates for the signal-calling job in 1959 was his potential to be a great field general. In Lombardi's mind, Starr knew the job; he only needed his teammates to recognize this quality in him.

Starr and linebacker Dan Currie submitted their signed deals on the same day in late April. Calling Michigan his alma mater, Currie developed quickly the year before at the linebacker position. Lombardi remarked that he might have to move Currie from the middle to the outside spot to replace the retired Carlton Massey.

A few days later Bobby Dillon and Nate Borden sent in their contracts signed and sealed. Dillon, who lived in Temple, Texas during the off-season, had been with the Packers since 1952 as one of their primary defensive backs. In that time, he had snared 51 passes thrown by the opposition. He also led the Packers in interceptions in each of those years. Borden came from Indiana, where he played end at a slight 220 pounds, which was fine for college but not the pros. So, he bulked up 20 pounds to make himself a tougher man to block.

The next two men to sign their pacts with Green Bay in the month of April were rookie Ken Higginbotham and veteran William Max McGee. Higginbotham decided to forego his senior year of eligibility at tiny Trinity College and take a shot at making the Packers. Tall and rangy, he was exceptionally fast and sure-handed. McGee had been with the Pack since 1954, being a 5th Round draft choice that year. He played in the shadow of Billy Howton his first four seasons, but in 1958 he led Green Bay in pass receptions with 37, one more than Howton, in yards receiving with 655 to Howton's 507, and in catches for TDs with seven to Howton's two.

The Packers board of directors met on April 29 for the dual purposes of electing a new executive committee and officially handing the reins for operating the team over to the general manager. Instead of reducing the committee to six members, the board voted to make it consist of seven. These were the president, vice-president, secretary, treasurer, and three members at large. Dominic Olejniczak continued to hold his post as president. Dick Bourguignon was vice-president. John Torinus remained as secretary, while Fred Trowbridge took over as treasurer. The three remaining at-large spots were voted to Jerry Atkinson, Tony Canadeo, and Les Kelly.

Having been the offensive coach for the Giants, Lombardi felt his first need was to shore up the offensive line. But while he was trying to make a deal for some linemen, he made a controversial trade with the Chicago Cardinals. Controversial? The trade was for Lamar McHan, a veteran quarterback. Green Bay would give the Cardinals a conditional draft choice the next year, if—and that's a major catch—if McHan can make the team in the fall. If he doesn't make the team, then he goes back to Chicago and the Packers retain their draft pick, whatever it might have been. As Lombardi put it, "We have nothing to lose. If McHan makes it, we will gain a veteran quarterback and if he doesn't make it, we will retain our draft selection. It amounts to a free look at a good quarterback prospect."

Clarence Lamar McHan was a super athlete. He earned 18 varsity letters in high school at Lake Village, Arkansas. Playing for the Arkansas Razorbacks in college, he earned All-American honors in 1953 and finished ninth in the Heisman Trophy balloting that same year. The Cardinals chose McHan with the second pick of the 1st Round in 1954. McHan played well for the Cardinals in his five seasons with them; so well, that by the end of his tenure in Chicago, he was very close to breaking all the passing records of the great Paul Christman. The Cards were glad to part with McHan because he was pretty much a prima donna on a bad team. Proof of that came in the middle of the 1956 season when he was fined and suspended for insubordination. Lombardi figured he could handle him.

When fullback Jim Taylor mailed in his contract, Art Daley of the *Press-Gazette* made a big deal about it. His article was headlined:

Taylor All-Time Fullback?

Daley compared Taylor's rookie stats of 1958 to those of six other Packer fullbacks: Fred Fritsch, Jack Cloud, Fred Cone, Bobby Jack Floyd, Bill Reichart, and Howie Ferguson. None of them came even close to Taylor's 247 yards on 52 carries for an average of 4.8 yards per. Fritsch did gain 223 yards, but he carried the ball 72 times for an average of 3.0 yards per. Daley tried to brush off his prediction about Taylor by stating, "Taylor ... isn't expected to set the Packers' all-time fullback records a-flaming just because of his rookie crashing average."

Still seeking linemen, Lombardi made another conditional trade to start off the month of June. His trading partner this time was the San Francisco 49ers. He obtained Lou Palatella, a guard with four years in the pros already. Assistant coach Phil Bengtson, who had been with the 49ers during those years, put his stamp of approval on Palatella as a player who performs with desire, a trait that Lombardi wanted in all his players.

On the same day that Boyd Dowler signed his first contract with the Packers, Bobby Dillon, the superstar defensive back for the Packers since 1952, announced his retirement from pro football. Lombardi called Dillon's decision "a very difficult blow" to his plans for the team that year. "He is the best in the league. A man like Dillon is irreplaceable at this time. It wasn't a question of finances at all because he had already signed his contract."

What was Lombardi to do? He picked up the phone and called his old friend in New York: Wellington Mara. Coming straight to the point, he asked Mara about the availability of any of his defensive backs. Mara answered with a question of his own. Who did Lombardi have in mind? After burping a laugh at Wellington's blunt response, Vince said, "Em Tunnell." Mara gasped at the mention of Tunnell. "Why would you want Em? He's 34 years old and probably soon to retire." Lombardi couldn't lie to Mara. He couldn't lie to anybody. Prevarication simply wasn't in his character. "Haven't you heard? I lost Bobby Dillon today. He's taking a regular job back in Texas." Mara interjected. "So, you need a leader for your secondary." Vince admitted he did. "What are you offering for Em?" They dickered a bit before settling on a price.

A few days after losing Dillon to retirement GM Lombardi purchased the contract of Emlen Tunnell from the New York Giants.

Tunnell joined the Giants in 1948, the first man of color to don a football uniform for the Goliaths of Gotham. He played collegiate ball at the University of Toledo in 1942 before joining the U.S. Coast Guard for World War II. Then he played at Iowa after the war in 1946 and 1947. Lombardi had seen Tunnell close up—on and off the field. He knew Tunnell to be an excellent leader on the field and a superb defender. Away from the gridiron, he knew him to be very likeable by just about everybody who knew him. He knew Tunnell worked as hard in the offseason to keep himself in condition as he did during the season. Lombardi expected Tunnell to lead by example and by deed, not by words. He had no doubt the nine-time All-Pro would do everything expected of him without Coach Lombardi saying a word to him.

More as a publicity stunt than real deal, Lombardi signed two local guys to join the Packers in training camp that summer. Neither Jerry Sprangers of Green Bay nor Bob Eiting of Kaukauna had any illusions about making the team as tackles on either side of the ball. Both had no college experience, but they did have size. Each man stood 6'5" and weighed 275 pounds. Sprangers graduated in 1953 from Premontre High in Green Bay, while Eiting was a 1952 graduate of Kaukauna High.

In the fourth week of June, Lombardi held a clinic for his six potential quarterbacks. This was his initial experience working with Parilli, Francis, Starr, Webb, McHan, and Boyd Dowler. Although Dowler was ticketed to be a pass-catching end for the Packers, Coach Lombardi thought it wouldn't hurt to see how he might fit in as a QB in his system. After the first day in the classroom, Lombardi said he was "impressed be the intelligence of the group." He singled out Starr as being "well built" for a quarterback, and he noted that Dowler was "quite a big boy." The signal-calling candidates worked with the entire coaching staff. They covered formations, terminology, the passing game, cadence, and some defenses they might see in games. The last item in the curriculum was Lombardi's "changeup system," meaning how the quarterback changes a play at the line of scrimmage. This was a very simple system that Lombardi had devised while he coached the offense for the Giants. The quarterback would call one play in the huddle, then line up to run it—unless he saw a defense that he didn't like. Then the QB would bark out an additional signal that told his team they would be running the same play but in a different direction or that he wanted to pass the ball instead of running it.

Lombardi felt the need for an assistant who could coach the offensive ends. He found one in mid-July in the form of Thomas Jesse Fears, the former All-Pro who played nine years for the Los Angeles Rams and set the single season record for pass receptions in 1950 with 86. On December 3, 1950 in Los Angeles, Fears caught 18 passes against the Packers to set the single game mark that would stand for 50 years.

Lombardi called Baltimore and asked about the availability of Charles Frederick "Fuzzy" Thurston, a guard who had played his college ball at little Valparaiso College (now University) in Valparaiso, Indiana. Thurston had been drafted by the Philadelphia Eagles in the 5th Round in 1956, but he failed to make the team. In 1958 he did make it on the Colts roster but only played in four games. For Thurston, GM Lombardi sent linebacker Marv Matuzak to Baltimore. Thurston, a native of Altoona, Wisconsin, couldn't have been happier.

The final deal between the Packers and Browns before the non-league games started was the acquisition of Bobby Freeman, a defensive back out of Auburn who was drafted by Cleveland in 1955. He spent two years in the military before joining the Browns in 1957. Lombardi gave up an undisclosed draft choice for him.

Satisfied that he now had some decent material to work with, Lombardi said again that his biggest problem was getting the defeatist attitude out of the men who had played in Green Bay the previous few seasons.

On Thursday July 23, the rookies reported to camp, along with some veterans eager to get going on the new season. None of them had any idea what they had signed up for.

§§§

6
New Coach, New Attitude

Veterans Max McGee and Howie Ferguson arrived at the Packers training camp at St. Norbert's College a few days early. They joined the rookies for the evening meal, then left camp to have one last night on the town before officially reporting to camp with the rest of the veterans. The next morning when they showed up at the dining hall Coach Lombardi was waiting for them. He ordered them to follow him to his office, where he proceeded to explain the rules to them.

"You start working today!" he shouted at them. "And you start keeping curfew today! As far as I'm concerned, when you ate a meal here yesterday, you became a part of this camp! Therefore, you abide by all my rules!"

"What the hell are you talking about?" Ferguson replied with nearly as much anger as Lombardi had displayed. "We don't have to report for two more days."

Lombardi exploded back at Ferguson. "Listen, mister. You get your ass out there on the field, or you get your ass out of here!"

The argument continued between coach and player, while McGee stood by quietly wondering if he should say anything or not. He chose the latter option. He and Ferguson got their equipment and joined the rookies and a few other veterans in the first practice.

Two days later Lombardi addressed the entire team.

"Gentlemen, we're going to have a football team. We are going to win some games. Do you know why? Because you are going to have confidence in me and my system. By being alert you are going to make fewer mistakes than your opponents. By working harder, you are going to out-execute, out-block, out-tackle every team that comes your way. I've never been a losing coach, and I don't intend to start here. There's nobody big enough to think he's got the team made or can do what he wants. Trains and planes are going in and coming out of Green Bay every day, and he'll be on one of them. I won't. I'm going to find 36 men who have the pride to make any sacrifice to win. There are such men. If they're not here, I'll get them. If you are not one, if you don't want to play, you might as well leave right now. I've been up here all year, and I've learned a lot. I know how the townspeople are and what they think of you men, and I know that in a small town you need definite rules and regulations. And anybody who breaks the rules will be taken care of in my own way. You may not be a tackle. You may not be a guard. You may not be a back. But you *will* be a professional."

From that moment forward, Lombardi had their attention.

After only two days of practicing and a 45-minute scrimmage by the rookies on camera day, Lombardi saw fit to start trimming his roster. He released six newcomers: ends Charles Anderson, Harry Hauffe, Chuck Brockmeyer; back LeRoy Hardee; and tackles Ken Kerr and Dick Nearents.

The first day of practice for the full squad was Monday July 27 at 10:00 a.m. That meant every player had to be on the practice field at 9:45, which was Lombardi's time. He demanded that every player show up at every practice, every meeting, every anything that was a team function 15 minutes before the appointed time. To arrive later would result in a money fine or running laps around the practice field.

Howie Ferguson helped Lombardi set another precedent for his Packers. Insubordination would not be tolerated by the boss. As a result of his shouting match with the coach the previous Friday morning, Ferguson was traded to the Pittsburgh Steelers for a draft choice first thing Tuesday morning. This basically handed the top spot for fullback on the depth chart to second-year player Jim Taylor. The move by Lombardi also taught a lesson to the rest of the team.

Wednesday morning Lombardi cut four more rookies from the team. Quarterback Bob Webb, tackle Bob Eiting, guard Larry Hall, and halfback Tom Newell were handed their pink slips.

Lombardi renamed Jim Ringo and Bill Forester as captains for the offense and defense, respectively. This would be their fourth year to hold down those spots.

Besides appointing field leaders, Lombardi set up a six-man players committee to confer with him on player problems. These were Dave Hanner, Bart Starr, Forrest Gregg, Emlen Tunnell, Bill Forester, and Jim Ringo.

Halfback Jim Morse, Hornung's teammate from Notre Dame, was the next player to be released. He was joined in the unemployed line by tackle Jerry Sprangers and linebacker Mel Schmidt.

Contract holdout Jesse Whittenton finally came to terms with Lombardi and joined the team August 3. Before coming to the Pack in 1958, Whittenton had played for the Bears and the Rams.

The next day Ken Russell, who had been traded to the Packers by the Detroit Lions for tackle Ollie Spencer at the start of training camp, quit the team. He had been very vocal about the workload in practice. The Packers were to receive a draft pick from Detroit for Russell.

Biggest surprise of the day was the return of Howie Ferguson to the Packers by the Steelers. Art Daley wrote that Ferguson had a chronic shoulder injury. The sportswriter hinted this was the reason for the fullback's return to Green Bay. At the same time, Daley wrote that he doubted Ferguson would play again in Green Bay, despite the fact that Lombardi said he would give him a chance. Daley proved to be correct in his prediction.

A week before the Packers were to play their first non-league contest against the Bears in Milwaukee, they played an intra-squad game at City Stadium. More than 11,000 turned to watch the offense score 28 points against the defense's seven, on a 56-yard punt return for a touchdown by Billy Butler, the Berlin, Wisconsin native. Lombardi was surprised that the offense played so well against his defense. As he said after the game, the defense is usually ahead of the offense at this stage of training camp.

On Monday morning, Lombardi put seven more players on waivers to reduce the camp roster to 47, not counting the four players in the College All-Stars camp in Chicago. Released were halfbacks Earl Miller, Des Koch, and Ken Wineberg; linemen Dick Grogg, Bill Yelverton, Jim Yeats, and Roger "Whip" Wypyszynski.

Prior to meeting the Bears in Milwaukee Saturday August 15 for their first non-league tussle, Lombardi had a few things to say. "I hate to think of that exhibition opener against the Bears. We'll be in a new system and the Bears know theirs. We'll probably look terrible. If they stand still, we might play them quite a game." The man had a sense of humor.

Two days before the game with the Bears Lombardi named his starting offensive lineup. Bart Starr at quarterback, Jim Taylor at fullback, Paul Hornung and Don McIlhenny at halfback, Jim Ringo at center, Fuzzy Thurston and Jerry Kramer at guard, Bob Skoronski and Forrest Gregg at tackle, and Max McGee and Gary Knafelc at end.

The headline in the *Press-Gazette* Monday afternoon read:

Packer-Bear Bow Makes Lombardi, Halas Smile

Both coaches were quite satisfied with the play of their teams. Although the Bears won the 10th Annual Midwest Shrine Game, 19-16, partially played in a downpour, Lombardi appeared to be ecstatic afterward. His boys had played fairly well against one of the better teams in the NFL. With the exception of two pass interceptions, one each by Bart Starr and Lamar McHan, a lost fumble, and a couple of 15-yard penalties when the Packers were in scoring position, the offense played nearly flawless football. Both coaches took the game seriously and used veteran players for most of the action. The two standouts in the game for the Packers were Starr and rookie Tim Brown. Starr completed seven of 13 pass attempts with a pair of TD tosses, and Brown gained 61 yards on just four carries. The post-game comment of the night was delivered by Halas. "They (the Packers) are a much better club already because they have Vince Lombardi for a coach."

On Monday, Lombardi further reduced the roster, giving walking papers to ends Ken Higginbotham and Buddy Mayfield, center Willie Taylor, linebacker Dick Teteak, and halfback Bob Laraba. He welcomed four players into camp at the same time. Boyd Dowler, Bobby Jackson, Andy Cvercko, and Gary Raid had all been with the College All-Stars up to this point. This left 47 players under Lombardi's tutelage with 12 of them being rookies.

The second non-league tilt for the Packers gave Lombardi his first win as a professional coach, albeit the game counted for nothing more than bragging rights. Final score for the game played in San Francisco's Kezar Stadium was Green Bay 24, San Francisco 17. The Packers dominated the 49ers for three quarters, taking a 10-3 lead into the last frame. Both teams scored two touchdowns in the fourth quarter, and the game ended with the 49ers having the ball on the one-foot line. R.C. Owens had just caught a 40-yard pass from Y.A. Tittle, landing inbounds just short of the goal line. The clock expired before the Frisco eleven could line up for one last play. Babe Parilli had an outstanding game, completing 10 of 11 passes for 130 yards but no TDs. Jim Taylor ran for 60 yards on 13 carries. Max McGee caught four passes for 52 yards. The highlight of the game was a 94-yard kickoff return by George Dixon, a rookie out of Bridgeport College in Connecticut. The Packers won the turnover battle, 4-0, by recovering two 49er fumbles and intercepting a pair of passes.

Besides the win over San Francisco, the big news for the Pack on Monday was the return of Bobby Dillon from a retirement that only lasted two months. He made it perfectly clear, though, that 1959 would be his final season. Dillon would enter the season as the Pack's all-time pass interceptor.

Six-year Packer Al Carmichael was released during the week. He had spent his entire Green Bay career as kickoff returner and punt returner. Carmichael held the record for longest kickoff return for a touchdown, a distance of 106 yards.

The Packers stayed on the West Coast to practice and prepare for their next non-league encounter, a Saturday night date with the Eagles in Portland, Oregon. Green Bay's offense couldn't be stopped in the 45-28 Packer victory. Lombardi gave Joe Francis the starting nod at quarterback. The Oregon State star played well, completing six out of eight passes for 167 yards, but no touchdowns. Hornung carried the ball six times for 45 yards and a touchdown. Boyd Dowler, seeing his first action with the Packers, caught two passes for 58 yards. The coach had nothing but praise for his offense, but he criticized the defense for its lack of tenacity and aggression; mostly because the Eagles gained 404 yards through the air.

Although Bobby Dillon was returning to the team, Lombardi felt the need for another experienced defensive back. So, he traded another undisclosed draft choice to the Cardinals for five-year veteran Dick Nolan. The coach was well acquainted with Nolan because he was drafted out of Maryland by the Giants and he spent four years with New York before being traded to Chicago.

At the same time, Lombardi released defensive back Billy Butler and tackle Gary Raid. Later in the week, rookie Bobby Jackson and veteran Al Romine, both defensive backs, and Jerry Helluin, a defensive tackle, were also released. Romine signed with the Ottawa Rough Riders of the Canadian league a few days later.

More good news for Lombardi and the Packers came in a phone call to the coach at the team's hotel in Bangor, Maine, where the

Pack would be squaring off with the New York Giants the next night. End Ron Kramer called Lombardi with word that he had been discharged by the Air Force and he was free to join the team as soon as the coach wanted him in camp.

Kramer had helped expose a scandal in the military when he refused to play football for the Bolling Air Force Base team. He had suffered a broken leg that required surgery before entering active duty and chose not to play to avoid reinjuring it and jeopardizing what was a promising pro career. The Packers made him their first draft choice in 1957, and he had played well as a rookie, catching 28 passes for 337 yards. Lombardi described Kramer as a natural to play tight end in his offensive scheme because he was "a murderous blocker and pass catcher."

The Giants had one of the best defenses in the NFL, showing it the week before meeting the Packers by handing the Detroit Lions a 31-0 whipping. Green Bay fared no better, losing 14-0 to New York. Lamar McHan started the game at quarterback and played most of the offensive downs. His passing numbers failed to impress with only five completions in 14 attempts for 65 yards. Green Bay's vaunted running attack failed to provide the punch it had displayed in the Packers' three previous non-league games, gaining 136 yards on 38 carries.

Lombardi reduced the roster by two to bring it down to 43 as prescribed by league rule. Halfback George Dixon was released, and newly acquired defensive back Dick Nolan was sold to the Giants. At the same time, Ron Kramer and linebacker Ray Nitschke were added to the player list; both recently discharged from military duty.

Howie Ferguson suffered a hamstring pull during practice on Labor Day as the Packers began preparing to meet the Washington Redskins in Winston-Salem, North Carolina. This injury, along with the shoulder separation he had been dealing with for some time, put him out of action for the season and ultimately led to his retirement from the Packers.

Paul Hornung was rapidly turning into the player Lombardi had thought he could be right from the start. Against the Redskins, the "Golden Boy of Notre Dame scored all of Green Bay's points in a 20-13 victory. He pounded his way into the end zone twice on 4-yard and 3-yard dives, booted a pair of field goals, and converted the point after touchdown on both of his scores from scrimmage. Bart Starr started the game at quarterback, but several miscues—two dropped passes, a penalty, and two lost fumbles, one by Starr himself—sent him to the bench early in the second quarter. Joe Francis came in and led the Packers to all 20 of their points. Jim Taylor led Green Bay's rushing attack with 72 yards on 11 carries. Hornung caught two of the Pack's meager five completions.

One of Lombardi's best moves came with a call from Paul Brown who felt a little responsible for Vince being in the spot he had chosen to be in with the Packers. The Cleveland general manager and head coach offered the Packers defensive tackle Henry Jordan, a 1957 5th Round draft pick from the University of Virginia, for Green Bay's 4th Round pick in the 1960 Draft. Jordan wasn't exactly thrilled about going to Green Bay until he heard Lombardi praise his play with the Browns and tell him the Packers really needed a man of his caliber.

The league mandated cut-down in each team's roster forced Lombardi to release three more players before the final non-league game. The toughest of those was the release of Babe Parilli, the most experienced quarterback on the team. Parilli wasn't out of work for long as the Ottawa Rough Riders signed him a few days later. Second to be released was Alex Hawkins, the Packers 2nd Round choice in the 1959 Draft. Hawkins was signed by the Colts soon after his departure from Green Bay. Third on cutting block was tackle Tom Saidock who was obtained from the Eagles. He went on to play three years in the forthcoming American Football League.

Offensive end Steve Meilinger suffered a broken arm against the Redskins and had to be placed on the injured reserve list.

The old saying goes something like this: "You can judge the true ability of a coach by how he handles the close games. Great ones win the close ones!"

Thus far in 1959 non-league games, Lombardi's Packers had played in three such close encounters. They lost to the Bears, 19-16; beat the 49ers, 24-17; and slipped by the Redskins, 20-13. This made Lombardi's record in "nip'n'tuckers" 2-1. The final tune-up game before the regular season would determine whether he was truly going to be a winner or just another frustrated coach marching up and down the sidelines screaming his displeasure at the referees and his erstwhile players.

Prior to the game with the Steelers, Lombardi had said Pittsburgh had the second-best defense in the NFL, sandwiched between those of New York and Cleveland. He couldn't have been more correct in his estimation of the defenders from Steel Town. They were good. So good that they held the Packers to just 13 points in their clash in the Twin Cities of Minnesota. But 13 was good enough for a win.

Once again Paul Hornung scored all of Green Bay's point. The most important of them coming with four seconds remaining in the game he booted a 44-yard field goal to break a 10-10 tie and put the final non-league contest in the win column for the Packers.

Lombardi admitted that he never expected his team to win four non-league games, but he was delighted they did. To those folks familiar with the old adage about coaches and close games, especially those who rooted for the Packers, the coming season held much more excitement than had been expected back on January 28 when John Torinus said, "Who the hell is Vince Lombardi?" Now he knew, and so did all of Packerdom.

Bring on the Bears!

§§§

7
Now the Real Challenge

Vince Lombardi joked way back in January when he first took the job as head coach of the Green Bay Packers that all he had to do to improve on his predecessor's record in 1958 was win two games in 1959. Everybody laughed with him at the time, but not many of those who heard him say thought he could do it, considering the team he was being handed.

How little they knew that Vince Lombardi was a steely-eyed football coach and innovator!

The league had voted the week before the final games of the non-league to raise the roster limit for the regular season from 35 players to 36. Lombardi still had 39 men aboard when the Packers faced off with Pittsburgh. He needed to pare three. Rookie fullback Dave Smith from Ripon College in Ripon, Wisconsin, rookie tackle Ed Buckingham, and linebacker Tom Braatz were placed on waivers.

The Packers and Bears had met 81 times in league clashes before their opener in 1959. Chicago was on a three-game winning streak over Green Bay, and the oddsmakers had the Monsters of the Midway six and a half point favorites to defeat the Packers. Nobody counted on the weather and field conditions factoring into the game. A heavy rain made the field sloppy and footing questionable. Then a roaring 25-mile wind out of the southwest changed the Packers' strategy from the very start. They won the coin toss, then chose which end of the field they wanted in the first quarter instead of receiving the first kickoff. Green Bay mistakes kept the Pack from scoring throughout the first three quarters. Meanwhile, the Bears, who weren't playing much better put up six points on a pair of field goals. With half the final stanza past, the Packers were forced to punt. The Bears roughed Max McGee, but he had gotten the kick away. Chicago return man Richie Petitbon fumbled, and center Jim Ringo recovered the ball on the Bears' 26. Green Bay took the ball instead of the penalty. Six plays later—Hornung for six, Taylor for five, Hornung for five, Taylor for two with a penalty for four, Hornung for a loss of one—Jim Taylor zipped around the left corner for the game's only touchdown, tying the score at six-apiece. Hornung split the uprights for the PAT to give Green Bay the lead. The Bears had two chances to retake the lead, but the Packers defense rose to the occasion on both possessions, the second one resulting in a safety when four Packers broke through the Chicago offensive line to trap quarterback Ed Brown in the end zone. Credit for the two-pointer was given to Dave Hanner. The game ended a few seconds later with the final score at 9-6 Green Bay.

So jubilant were the Green Bay players that they lifted their coach onto their shoulders and raced off the field in one of the iconic moments in Packers history. Lombardi knew his job was safe for at least one more year because his boys had struck down the mighty Monsters of the Midway.

The 1959 season was only one week old. It still had 11 weeks to go. This was the reality that Lombardi completely understood. "One game does not make a season. This is still a rebuilding year." He wasted no time starting preparations for his team's next opponent, the Detroit Lions, who had lost their opener to the Baltimore Colts, 21-9.

Results for rest of the league saw the New York Giants down Los Angeles, 23-21; Pittsburgh defeat Cleveland, 17-7; the Chicago Cardinals crush Washington, 49-21; and San Francisco get by Philadelphia, 24-14.

Rookie Andy Cvercko injured a leg and went on the injured reserve list on Monday. Later in the week, Lombardi resigned Billy Butler and released Timmy Brown who never really got a chance to show what he could after the first non-league game. Some writers have hinted this move was for racial reasons. Red Cochran, the backfield coach, was a Southerner, while Brown, LeRoy Hardee, and George Dixon, the latter two having already been released, were African-Americans. This left the Packers with an offensive backfield consisting of primarily white boys from the South. Joe Francis was the exception, hailing from Hawaii and being of Caucasian and Polynesian ancestry. Some might say Babe Parilli was from the South, too, because he starred at Kentucky. He may have played there, but he was born and raised in Pennsylvania. Makes one wonder because Brown and Dixon went on to have great professional careers in football; Brown in the

NFL and Dixon in the Canadian Football League.

The oddsmakers for the Detroit game called it even money. As the game played out, the final score was nothing close to even. In front of another sellout crowd, the Packers came away with a 28-10 victory. Lamar McHan once again quarterbacked the offense, this time playing a much better game than he had against the Bears. He threw 16 passes, completed 7 for 146 yards and four touchdowns, and one for an interception. He also fumbled once, which was recovered by the Lions, stifling a drive deep in Detroit territory. His scoring tosses went to Gary Knafelc for 12 yards and Don McIlhenny for four yards, both in the first quarter; and two to Max McGee in the fourth period for 41 and 36 yards, respectively.

Green Bay's win put Lombardi's boys on top of the Western Conference standings, tied with the 49ers who blasted the Rams, 34-0. The Bears upset the Colts, 26-21, to give both of them records of 1-1. Detroit and Los Angeles remained winless. The results in the Eastern Conference had Cleveland defeating Chicago, 34-7; Philly's Eagles throttling the Giants, 49-21; and Washington getting by the Steelers, 23-17. Thus, each team in the East had a record of 1-1.

The Packers came out of the Bears game nearly unscathed in the injury department. McHan suffered a leg cramp that hobbled him during the contest, but he recovered from it before the Detroit tilt. The Lions were not as kind to the Packers as Chicago had been. Jim Ringo and Nate Borden both came away with knee injuries. Borden's put him in the hospital and out of the lineup, while Ringo worked through his to start the next game. During the week, Jim Taylor was burned in a home accident. He spilled flaming grease on one foot and his right hand as he was trying to extinguish the fire. His burns kept Taylor from playing against San Francisco.

Bookies gave the Packers a four-point edge over the 49ers in their first meeting of 1959. To most fans in Packerland, it seemed a couple of centuries since the Pack had been favored to win a game.

Green Bay received the opening kickoff and returned it to their 20. Eight plays later Max McGee stretched out in the end zone to haul in a 30-yard pass from Lamar McHan. Hornung's PAT gave the home team a 7-0 lead with 11 minutes left in the first period. The 49ers managed a field goal on their first possession to bring the score to 7-3 Green Bay. Again, the Packers started their drive on their own 20. Frisco played tougher this time, making the Green Bay offense spend

13 plays to reach pay dirt with Hornung sweeping end for the final eight yards. His conversion put the Pack ahead, 14-3, with just five seconds gone in the second period. The 49ers stiffened more after that and went on the attack themselves scoring the next 17 points to take 20-14 lead into the final stanza. San Fran possessed the ball to begin the fourth, but Joe Perry fumbled a lateral on the Packers' 40 that was recovered by Dave Hanner. This turnover put the Green Bay offense into high gear again. In 10 plays, the Packers retook the lead on a 12-yard TD pass from McHan to Gary Knafelc and Hornung's third PAT. The two teams went back and forth until Frisco lined up for a field goal try from the Green Bay 37. Fortunately, the kick was wide and a tad short. The Packers then ran out the clock went into the locker room with a 21-20 victory.

Now 3-0 the Packers were the only undefeated team in the NFL and sat atop the Western Conference standings. Baltimore, by the virtue of their 31-24 win over Detroit, was tied with the 49ers for second place with 2-1 records. Los Angeles won their first game of the season, downing the Bears, 28-21, and moving into a fourth-place tie with Chicago at 1-2. Detroit was the only team without a win so far in 1959, and at 0-3 the Lions rested uncomfortably in the division cellar. Over in the Eastern Conference, New York beat Cleveland, 10-6; the Eagles downed the Steelers, 28-24; and Washington took down the Chicago Cardinals, 23-14. This placed the Giants, Redskins, and Eagles in a three-way tie for first at 2-1, and the Cards, Browns, and Steelers, all at 1-2, in a three-way tie for last place.

This was a great day for Green Bay, but it was a tragic Sunday for the NFL. Commissioner Bert Bell died from a heart attack while attending the Eagles-Steelers game at Franklin Field in Philadelphia. He was 65 years old and had been commissioner since January 1946.

The Los Angeles Rams came into Milwaukee County Stadium as three-point favorites to beat the Packers. Bettors who took the Pack may as well have flushed their money down the toilet. Green Bay made a reasonable showing in the first half, trailing 14-6, and the Pack continued to be competitive through half of the third quarter. Then they fell flat, and the Rams became supercharged by fullback Ollie Matson who burst through the line and raced 49 yards for six points with 6:52 left in the period. It was all Rams in the fourth stanza as LA romped to a 45-6 win.

The loss put the Packers in a three-way tie for first in the West with Baltimore, victors over the Bears, 21-7; and with San Francisco, easy 34-13 winners over the hapless last place Lions. The Rams moved into fourth place by themselves, and the Bears slipped into fifth. Back east, the Giants took sole possession of first at 3-1 with a 24-7 win over the Eagles, now 2-2 and tied for second with the Browns, Redskins, and Steelers. Pittsburgh defeated Washington, 27-6, and Cleveland got by the last place Cardinals, 17-7.

Going into football Sunday, the gamblers installed the Packers as 13-point underdogs to the Colts. Apparently, the betting crowd as well as the Colts saw something about the Packers from their games against the West Coast teams that Green Bay fans hadn't noticed up to now.

Still short of running backs, meaning Jim Taylor remained out due to his burns, Lombardi installed a new wrinkle into his offense. He put Boyd Dowler outside the tight end but not on the line, a yard into the backfield, making him a flanker in terms of that era, a wide-out in later jargon, a wide receiver in later football language. This formation confused the Baltimore defense initially, just long enough to allow the Packers a short-lived 7-0 lead in the second quarter. The Colts tallied their first TD six minutes later to tie the game and took the lead into the half with another six-pointer just before the gun. Not yet perturbed, the Packers came right back in the third stanza on a big bomb from McHan to McGee for 81 yards to tie the game. Then it all went south for the Packers. In less than six minutes of play, the Colts scored three touchdowns on two passes from Unitas, one set up by a pass interception, and one the result of a pick-six. Baltimore took a 35-14 lead into the final frame. The Pack scored a meaningless TD in the last minute of the game to make the final score, 38-21. McHan had his best and worst day passing. He completed 15 of 29, but he also threw four interceptions.

The loss dropped the Packers into third place by themselves at 3-2. Baltimore moved into a first-place tie with the 49ers (4-1) who slipped by the Bears, 20-17. Surprisingly, Detroit gained its first win by beating the 2-3 Rams, 17-7, and tying the Bears for the cellar at 1-4. The New York Giants (4-1) took a firm hold on first place in the East by downing the Steelers (2-3), 21-17. Cleveland and Philadelphia tied for second at 3-2 by respectively beating (2-3) Washington, 34-7, and Chicago's (1-4) Cardinals, 28-24.

For the second week in a row, Art Daley published a look at

the following week's standings, if the Packers won and other teams won. He had Green Bay at 4-1 the first week, and the Pack lost. For Week 6, he had them winning again and in a tie for first place with Frisco and Baltimore, providing they both lost their games, the 49ers to the Lions and the Colts. to the Browns. None of this was likely because both the Colts and the 49ers would be on their own turf, while the Packers were traveling to Yankee Stadium to face all-powerful Giants who were six-point favorites to beat Green Bay.

For most fans, this was not a good game. It lacked cohesive effort on both sides. The Packers made mistakes that resulted in easy scores for the Giants. A fumble at their own three set up a short run to pay dirt for the Giants. Then a pass interference call against Bobby Freeman gave New York another very short field to their second TD. The Packers could only mount a pair of decent drives, one resulting in a FG by Hornung and the other resulting in a field goal attempt that hit the right upright and bounced back into the field of play. New York added two field goals to their touchdowns to make the final score, 20-3.

Although this was their third straight loss, the Packers failed to lose their place in third because the Bears (2-4) beat the Rams (2-4), 26-21. San Francisco (5-1) set up shop in first place all alone by smacking the Lions (1-5) around, 33-6; while the Colts (4-2) took one on the chin from the Browns (4-2), 28-21, who remained in second in the East. The Eagles (4-2) defeated the Redskins (2-4), 30-23, to keep pace with Cleveland. Chicago's Cardinals (2-4) handed the Steelers (2-4) another loss, 45-24, to put them in a three-way tie for last in the division with Washington.

With the season only half over, Lombardi had reason to smile. His Packers had already won three times as many games as Scooter McLean's team had the year before. Coach and team continued to keep a positive attitude toward the second half, especially since Green Bay suffered no serious injuries in the New York game *and* their top backfield piece, Jim Taylor, was pronounced 100% fit to play after seeing limited fourth-quarter action against the Giants.

The Packers started the second half of the 1959 season the same way they started the first. Opponent: the Monsters of the Midway; only this time in the Windy City. Oddsmakers felt the Bears were still the better of the two teams, especially since they would be playing in Wrigley Field where they had a real home-field advantage.

The gamblers gave the Bears a seven-point edge.

For the first time in a month, the Packers entered a contest with all hands on deck. Fat lot of good it did them. The tone of the game was set early—very early. On the second play from scrimmage, Hornung fumbled and the Bears recovered the ball at the Green Bay 12-yard line. Two runs by Chicago and the Bears were up, 7-0, with 13:39 to play in the first quarter. Hornung fumbled again later in the period, and the Bears recovered it on the Green Bay 35. In just four plays, Chicago covered the short distance to the goal to increase their lead to 14-0. The Packers got back into the game in the second quarter on a Jim Taylor touchdown and a Hornung field goal to make the score 14-10 Bears. Chicago tacked on another seven in the last minute of the half to go into the locker room ahead, 21-10. Being down by 11 points concerned Lombardi just a little less than losing Lamar McHan to a pulled muscle with 21 seconds left in the half. Bart Starr replaced McHan in the second half and played well. The Bears scored their final TD on the opening drive of the third stanza. Then Starr went to work. He directed a drive down the field to the Chicago one, where Hornung lost another fumble to the Monsters of the Midway. On the very next possession, poor Paul let another slip from his hands, but this time Taylor recovered it for the Pack on the Bears' five. Kicking a three at this point in the game would leave Green Bay behind by 15 points, so Lombardi went for six only to turn the ball over on downs. Billy Butler returned a last-minute punt 61 yards for a TD to make the final score, 28-17.

Suffering their fourth loss in a row, the Packers remained in third place, now tied with the Bears (3-4). San Francisco (6-1) took a firmer hold on first place by beating the Rams (2-5), 24-14. Baltimore. (4-3) lost, 27-24, to Washington (3-4) to fall two games behind the 49ers. The Lions (1-5-1) and the Steelers (2-4-1) snoozed to the first tie of the year, 10-all. Over in the Eastern Conference, the Giants (6-1) dropped the Cardinals (2-5) into the cellar in a game of field goals, 9-3. Entering the day tied for second with Philadelphia (4-3), the Browns (5-2) spanked the Eagles, 28-7, to keep pace with New York.

The oddsmakers for the Packers tilt in Milwaukee against the Colts took one on the chin when they installed Baltimore to win by nine and a half points. At the half, with the Colts leading, 21-3, the gamblers felt very secure with their betting line. Then Lombardi had a little talk with his boys in the locker room. The Packers came out with a vengeance in the third quarter. Bart Starr replaced Lamar McHan as the starting quarterback. He hadn't played so well in the first half, but he made up for it in the second. Starr drove the offense 75 yards to pay dirt, with Taylor crashing into the end zone for the final two yards. After Henry Jordan recovered an Alan Ameche fumble on the Colts' 34, Starr and company wasted no time reaching the end zone again, this time on 15-yard pass to Taylor, bringing Green Bay back within four points at 21-17. Baltimore retaliated with an 80-yard drive that carried over into the fourth period to lift their lead to 28-17. Not yet ready to admit defeat, Starr drove his team 75 yards for another seven points with 2:12 left on the clock to bring the score to 28-24. Green Bay beat the spread but lost the game as the Colts made three first downs in the remaining time to hold on to their victory.

Five losses in a row would drag down almost every team, but not one being coached by Vince Lombardi. The Packers were now 3-5 on the year and residing in fourth place in the Western Conference. The second-place Colts (5-3) moved a game closer to the 49ers (6-2), tough-luck 14-3 losers to the Bears (4-4), who were now sole possessors of third place. Detroit (2-5-1) climbed out of the basement with a 23-17 beating of the now last place Rams (2-6). The Eastern Conference became much more of a race when New York (6-2) was upset, 14-9, by Pittsburgh (3-4-1) and Cleveland (6-2) took down Washington, 31-17, while Philadelphia (5-3) bumped off the Cardinals, 27-17. The losses by the Redskins (3-5) and Chicago (2-6) placed them in fifth and sixth, respectively.

The ever-optimistic Art Daley of the *Press-Gazette* hinted at the future once again in his Packers story for Tuesday, November 17, 1959. He wrote about the forthcoming home finale with the Redskins. "There's no place like home...And maybe the Packers can snap a losing streak and start a winning streak in friendly City Stadium." He added to that theme later in the article. "The Packers now have a 3-5 record ... the best they can do is sweep the last four and post 7-5, which could be good enough to tie for the title and force a playoff." He wasn't the first to voice this possibility. George Halas had spoken almost those exact words before his boys clipped the 49ers the past Sunday.

Once again, the old adage rang true for the Packers. There is no place like home, especially in sports. Lombardi's boys played a nearly flawless game on defense and their best game of the year so far on offense. Bart Starr was given the starting assignment at QB for the second week in a row, and he didn't let down a single fan in the stands at City Stadium or his coach on the sidelines. He had his best day as a pro against the Redskins, leading his team to a 21-0 win and breaking Green Bay's five-game losing streak. The signal-caller from Alabama completed 11 of 19 passes for 120 and two touchdowns, one each to Knafelc and McGee. Jim Taylor gained 81 on 15 carries to lead the ground game. Paul Hornung scored Green Bay's third touchdown on a five-yard run. The Golden Boy also picked up 78 yards on 16 runs. The shutout was the first for the Packers in 10 years.

Defeating Washington (3-6) kept the Packers (4-5) in fourth place in the West and dropped the Redskins into fifth in the East. At the same time, the Colts (6-3) gained a share of first place with the 49ers (6-3), crushing the California team, 45-14. The Bears (5-4) took their game, 24-14, from the Lions (2-6-1) to remain in third place and leaving Detroit in fifth place a half game in front of the Rams (2-7) who narrowly lost, 23-20, to the Eagles (6-3). Philadelphia's win put them in a tie for second in the East with Cleveland, narrow losers to the Steelers, 21-20. Pittsburgh (4-4-1) remained in contention with the first place Giants (7-2), 30-20 winners over last place Chicago (2-7).

Before their annual trip to the West Coast, the Packers had to face the Lions on Thanksgiving Day in Detroit's traditional Turkey Day game. The bookies picked the Lions to win by a narrow two points. The boys from Green Bay had other thoughts.

Lombardi played cat-and-mouse with the local press as well as the Detroit scribes. He refused to name his starting quarterback until the day of the game, which didn't give the Lions a chance to prepare for either Starr or McHan. The coach heaped loads of praise on both of his signal-callers to keep media guessing. When the Packers went on offense for the first time this Thanksgiving Day, the main man in the huddle was Starr.

Green Bay scored first on an 11-yard run by Hornung with 10:12 left in the first quarter. Less than two minutes later the Golden Boy from Notre Dame juked six yards for another TD. Hornung took a huge hit in the ribs, which hurt so much that he could hardly catch a breath. Fearing his star halfback might have a cracked rib, Lombardi removed him from the game and only let him back in the game to kick a field goal at the end of the period and to boot a PAT after Taylor's one-yard plunge for six with 6:51 gone in the second stanza. Detroit made a comeback, but it wasn't enough to take the lead away from a stalwart Green Bay defense. The Pack held on to win, 24-17, before a viewing audience of some 50 million fans around the country.

With the win in Detroit, the Packers (5-5) were still alive in the race for first place in the Western Conference. They waited anxiously for the remainder of the schedule to be played on Sunday.

On the Sabbath, Baltimore (7-3) defeated Los Angeles (2-8), 35-21, keeping the Colts in a first place in tie with San Francisco (7-3), winners, 21-20, over Cleveland (6-4). The Bears (6-4) remained a game ahead of the Pack by beating the Cardinals (2-8), 31-7. In the Eastern Conference, the Giants (8-2) smacked the Redskins (3-7) by a score of 45-14. The Steelers (5-4-1) put up a shutout, 31-0, over the Eagles (6-4).

Looking at the week ahead, the Packers did the math and realized there was no way they could win the division. The best record Green Bay could achieve would be 7-5. If the Colts and 49ers had both lost in Week 10, the Packers would still be in the race. Both won, and they would most likely settle the division crown on Saturday night in San Francisco when the Colts would come a-calling at Kezar Stadium in a nationally televised contest. The winner would take sole possession of first and clinch at least a tie for the title, while the loser would have to wait a week and hope the other team lost in Week 12.

When the Packers squared off with the Rams in Milwaukee in October, they were minus a few key cogs in their starting lineups. Jim Taylor sat out that game due to the burns he suffered in an accident at home. Nate Borden and Jim Temp sat out with injuries as well. To make matters worse, Lamar McHan was hobbled with a leg bruise that hampered his effectiveness. The Rams were also fresh off a win over the Bears, a victory that saved Coach Sid Gillman's job for one more week. Beating the Packers, the way the Rams did kept Gilman at the helm for the next two weeks. Then he lost six in a row and seemed ready to be fired at the end of the season. The oddsmakers felt Gilman's dismissal would fire up the LA boys, so they made them six-point favorites over Green Bay.

The Packers scored their highest point total for the regular season, cracked the West Coast jinx that had been plaguing them for the past three seasons, and assured themselves of what Art Daley called a miracle campaign at 6-6. In front of a crowd of 61,044 shocked fans in the LA Coliseum, the Packers came away with 38-20 victory over the star-studded LA team.

Led by Bart Starr who won his third straight game, the Packers pretty much had their way with LA. The Rams scored first in the initial period, but the Pack roared back with four touchdowns of their own, two each in the first and second quarters. After the Rams made a bid to get back into the game in the third stanza, Green Bay finished off the scoring with 10 points in the fourth frame. Starr completed 11 of 20 passes for 161 yards and a touchdown toss to Jim Taylor. Paul Hornung completed the two passes he attempted, both for TDs caught by Boyd Dowler. Taylor scored a second six-pointer on a six-yard burst to close the scoring in the first half. The final TD was put on the board by Don McIlhenny on a seven-yard scamper.

The win guaranteed Green Bay (6-5) at least a fourth-place finish in the conference. For the Rams (2-9), the loss guaranteed the cellar for them. Up in San Francisco the night before, the Colts (8-3) kicked the stuffing out of the 49ers, 34-14, to clinch at least a tie for first in the West. San Francisco (7-4) still had a prayer of tying the mighty Maryland team if Baltimore should fall to the Rams the last week of the season and the Packers should lie down and play dead for the 49ers. The Bears (7-4), victors over the Steelers (5-5-1), 27-21, had the same chance of tying for first. Although their chances of finishing first had vanished weeks earlier, the Lions (3-7-1) put the hurt on the Cardinals (2-9) to the tune of 45-21. In the East, the New York Giants (9-2) had the biggest win of the day, crushing Cleveland, 48-7, and putting the Browns (6-5) out of their misery for another year. The Eagles (7-4) tromped on the Redskins (3-8) by the score of 34-14 to stake a claim on second place in the division.

The last winning season for the Green Bay Packers was their title year of 1944 when they went 8-2. They broke that 14-year drought at Kezar Stadium in San Francisco when they came back from a 14-0 first-quarter deficit to crush the 49ers, 36-14. This was not a game for the ages. It was a game for the future.

Quarterback Bart Starr played his best game of his career up to then. He threw 25 passes, completed 20 for an amazing 80%, 249 yards, and two touchdowns. Halfback Paul Hornung ran for a trio of TDs and kicked four PATs for a total of 22 points to win the league scoring title with 96 points. The team gained a total of 479 yards, including 230 on the ground. Lew Carpenter ran for a season high 113 yards in just 16 carries for an average of 7.06 yards per carry. The defense shut down one of the league's best offenses for the final three periods.

The Packers played so well that they were left wishing this had not been their last game for 1959. Hank Gremminger summed the general feeling among his teammates when he said, "Why do we have to quit playing now? We're just rolling. Wait 'til next year."

The Packers win put them in a third-place tie with the 49ers as they finished 7-5 on the year. Baltimore (9-3) won the division by trouncing the Rams (2-10) again, 45-26. The Bears (8-4) finished in second place, closing their year with a six-game winning streak with a 25-14 trimming of the Lions (3-8-1) for fifth place. Back East, the Giants (9-3) closed out the campaign with a 24-10 victory over the Redskins (3-9) who finished a disappointing fifth. Cleveland (7-5) defeated the Eagles, 28-21, to finish in a tie with Philadelphia for second. Fourth-place Pittsburgh (6-5-1) put a 35-20 beat-down on the Cardinals (2-10) to keep Chicago all alone in the division cellar.

With the Colts and Giants winning their divisions, this set up a rematch of the game that turned America into a nation of pro football fans. The title game was close for three quarters with the Giants leading, 9-7. Then quarterback Johnny Unitas figured out the New York defense, and the Baltimore defense put the cuffs on the Giants' passer Charley Conerly, intercepting three of his throws in the final period. Baltimore tacked on 24 points in the fourth to win the NFL Championship again, 31-16.

When the Packers returned to Green Bay after their road trip to California, 7,500 screaming fans braved a rainy, sleeting day to greet their local heroes at Austin Straubel Airport. A stranger would have thought the Green Bay Packers had just won the NFL title and not a third-place finish. Lombardi addressed the fans, telling them the team played with determination all season long. He gave the players and his assistants all the credit for their successful season. A lesser man might have said, "You ain't seen nothin' yet!" But he didn't because Vincent Thomas Lombardi was not a lesser kind of guy.

§§§

8
Here We Go Again?

When the National Football League owners agreed to merge with the All-America Conference, they thought that would be the last time an upstart league would challenge their "monopoly" of pro football. Of course, they were wrong—as usual.

As the NFL teams began practicing for the forthcoming 1959 season, Commissioner Bert Bell testified before the U.S. Senate that a new pro league was in the works. He said he expected the new loop would start with six teams. He named the cities he thought would most likely make up the circuit: New York, Los Angeles, Denver, Houston, Dallas, and Minneapolis-St. Paul. Other cities that showed interest in having a team were Chicago, Louisville, Boston, Miami, Seattle, and San Francisco. Bell said a gross lie to the senators when he stated the NFL would support the new league wholeheartedly. Of course, he was trying to make his organization look good because the hearing the Senate was conducting concerned the exemption of big professional team sports from the anti-trust laws. The working name for the new loop was the Trans-America Conference.

The Green Bay Packers, Inc.., had faced extinction more than once in the past. Three different circuits, each one calling itself the American Football League, had sprung up and then faded away for one reason or another. The most recent challenge to the existence of a professional team in such a small city as Green Bay had been the All-America Football Conference. The first AFL lasted only one year, 1926, because it was started by a huckster who had the famous Red Grange under contract. His New York Yankees played teams much in the same manner that the Harlem Globetrotters play to this day; paid flunkies to give the crowds a good show. The next AFL rose up in 1936 and lasted two years. In 1940, the third AFL came to life and was the strongest of the three with some teams actually showing a profit.

When the Japanese bombed Pearl Harbor to draw the United States into World War II, the moguls of this third incarnation chose to suspend play until after the war was won. That never happened, mostly because the All-America Football Conference came to life and gave the NFL a real run for the professional football dollars.

Now in 1959 another American Football League was oozing its way from the drawing board to reality. Two Texas millionaire's, Bud Adams of Houston and H.L. Hunt of Dallas, decided they would get into the game. Hunt's 22-year-old son Lamar held the franchise for a team in Big D with the backing of his daddy's big bucks. Adams owned the Houston franchise. They had other millionaires from around the country interested in joining them in this new venture, and they had the "blessing" of the NFL owners, according to Bert Bell, the league commissioner. Truth be told, the NFL bosses were in panic mode at the thought of a new league challenging them again. Men like Hunt and Adams posed a real threat to their monopoly on the pro game. The Maras of New York, George Halas in Chicago, and the shareholders of the Green Bay Packers had been through four football wars in years past, and none of them wanted another conflict in this era of big television money, which could only get bigger with the passage of time.

Hunt and Adams knew this about the NFL, but unlike their predecessors who chose to butt heads with the established league, they opted to behave like gentlemen, like sound-minded men of business, instead of like mobsters.

"We think we have an advantage over the NFL," said young Lamar Hunt. "We can tell a boy (rookie) it's no sense in signing with Pittsburgh, for example. For $8,000 say, he can sign with Dallas and be sure of making the team." He further pointed out that each NFL team drafts 30 players a year. Of the 30, about four or five make the grade and land a spot on an NFL roster. "If he's a rookie, chances are 6-to-1 he won't make it." As for established players in the NFL, Hunt and Adams said they would not get into a bidding war for their services like the owners in the defunct AAFC had done a decade earlier.

In short, the new owners in this new professional football circuit had learned from the past. This attitude proved to be a great relief to the NFL owners.

On the Friday before the Packers were to play the Bears in the Shrine Charity Game in Milwaukee, Vince Lombardi and George Halas, Jr., Bears treasurer, spoke to reporters about the formation of the new pro loop, the American Football League. The Green Bay coach said, "I assume they (the AFL owners) will honor contracts the same as we will." When asked if the two leagues would arrange a playoff game for the world title, Lombardi displayed his talent for diplomacy. "That will be up to the football commissioner."

Halas remarked cautiously, "It could be a good thing and in the long run help football." He added, "Competition is always good, providing substantial people are behind it."

When asked about the possibility of a team in the AFL being placed in Minneapolis-St. Paul, Lombardi said he didn't believe it would be a bad thing for the Packers "because we don't draw from that area."

The big news of Week 5 of the 1959 NFL season came when Papa Bear George Halas issued a statement that said the NFL had been planning to expand the league for the past five years. "Our intent," said Halas, "was to expand when competition among our clubs began to equalize itself on an extremely high level. We now have reached that plateau.

"Conditions for expansion never will be more ideal," he continued. "Every team in the league is strong. There now is a sufficient backlog of experienced players available for the team in the new franchise city."

Halas introduced the prospective co-owners of the proposed Dallas franchise. They were oilman Clint Murchison, Jr., and attorney Bedford Wynne. Halas also introduced the man behind Houston interests in having a team in the NFL, Craig Cullinan, a broker in oil investments.

Murchison said he felt Dallas was ready for pro football after having had years of it on television. The Dallas Texans operated for one year in the NFL and folded after losing close to $200,000.

The fly in the ointment for the NFL getting teams in the two Texas cities was the newly formed American Football League, which planned to begin play in 1960 with teams in Dallas and Houston as the new circuit's center attraction. The owner of the AFL Houston franchise, Bud Adams, revealed he already had a stadium under lease for five years and that he planned to spend $150,000 to expand its seating to 40,000 for the 1960 season.

Halas let it be known that the NFL would put a team in the Twin Cities of Minnesota, if the franchise for Houston fell through for lack of a stadium.

In the third book in this series, the competition between the now defunct All-America Football Conference and National Football League was covered extensively, especially the dire threat that Green Bay faced the entire time; that menace being the loss of the Packers to one of several larger cities. Fortunately for Packer fans, their franchise was saved by the work of that legal genius Gerald R. Clifford who did everything possible to rally the stockholders and businesspeople for the cause. Of course, he had an "angel" in the enemy camp to help him where it counted the most. That man was George Halas, owner of the Chicago Bears. Papa Bear argued persistently in the value of retaining the Wisconsin franchise. To paraphrase his words, Green Bay represented the blue-collar working people, not just in Wisconsin, but all across America. He said all the other small-town teams had failed in the past because their owners were basically capitalists out to make a buck; whereas, the fans in the Dairy State only wanted their football team to survive, much like David in *The Bible* facing Goliath and the Philistines. Halas convinced enough of the other owners that the NFL needed tiny Green Bay more than Green Bay needed them. The Packers represented "the American way" as America's team.

So, a decade earlier, Halas helped save the Packers for the fans and the league by the merger of the NFL with the AAFC. Because of that history, the NFL owners voted to have Halas lead the expansion committee that dealt with adding more teams to the league. He wasted little time in trying to convince the owners of the Houston and Dallas franchises in the proposed American Football League to join the NFL in either 1960 or 1961 instead. Furthermore, the other teams of the fledgling circuit would join the NFL over the next few years until all eight were competitive members. AFL owners opposed this notion. He then said the NFL would put teams in both Houston and Dallas to compete with the two AFL franchises, providing the new Houston NFL team could find a suitable stadium. This only irked the seven confirmed AFL owners, a few of whom wanted to go to war by charging the NFL with trying to monopolize the pro game. Halas then added that his best suggestion "at this time is that the AFL go forward as an eight-team league."

Talk of expanding the NFL began to heat up when Charles Johnson, executive sports editor of the *Minneapolis Star and Tribune*, disclosed that 10 of the 12 NFL owners had agreed to accept a request by a financial group in the Twin Cities for membership in the older league. George Halas confirmed this report, saying the people in Minnesota initiated the contact, not anyone in the NFL. Johnson made it perfectly clear in his published article that this approach to the NFL had been made by people in Minneapolis-St. Paul and not by any person or persons within the NFL. Johnson also stated that one other city, presumably Dallas, would be acceptable to Halas and the other NFL owners as a member of their circuit.

Regardless of who instigated whatever, the fact that a second group of investors wanted the Twin Cities in the NFL raised the ire of the owners of the AFL. Contending for fans in New York and Los Angeles was one thing, thought the AFL moguls, because it was their opinion that both cities had enough people to support two franchises, one in each league. But to compete for fans in much smaller cities with smaller metropolitan areas—meaning Dallas and Minneapolis-St. Paul—was quite another. Both sides knew from the start such an arrangement would not work for one side. That one side was more than likely the AFL. That being the case, what should the AFL owners do in those two locales? For the time being, the AFL decided to go on as if the NFL didn't exist.

Weeks earlier the American Football League announced it would conduct its very first college draft a week before the National Football League planned to hold its annual draft. They did just that on Sunday November 22 in Minneapolis. Each of the eight franchises was allowed to make a "territorial bonus" choice; each franchise's territory having already been marked out on a map. After that, the teams drafted whoever from wherever.

Dallas made Don Meredith, two-time All-American star quarterback from Southern Methodist University, their bonus pick. Houston chose Billy Cannon, All-American halfback from Louisiana State. Buffalo drafted Richie Lucas, quarterback from Penn State (Pennsylvania State University). New York picked George Izo, quarterback from Notre Dame. Boston went for Gerhard Schwedes, halfback from Syracuse. Denver took Roger LeClerc, center from Trinity College (Connecticut). Los Angeles named Monty Stickles, end from Notre Dame. Minneapolis-St. Paul nabbed Dale Hackbart, quarterback from Wisconsin. Of these eight players, only three would sign and play for the AFL teams that drafted them. They were Lucas, Cannon, and Schwedes. The only one of the AFL 1st Round picks that the Packers drafted was Hackbart.

In the days that followed the AFL draft, press releases listed some of the players the new teams had chosen to fill out their rosters. NFL magnates looked at these lists with curiosity but not with much worry. Their thought was these were college boys, very few of whom would sign with the AFL before at least giving the senior league a try first.

The NFL held its draft Monday November 30 in Philadelphia. Green Bay's choice in the 1st Round was the fifth pick of the day Tom Moore, halfback from Vanderbilt. The Dallas Texans took Moore in the AFL's 3rd Round. In the 2nd Round with the 17th pick, the Packers selected Bob Jeter, halfback, Iowa; chosen in the AFL 2nd Round by the Los Angeles Chargers. Green Bay had no picks in the 3rd and 4th Rounds, having traded them away to the Cardinals for Lamar McHan and to Cleveland for Henry Jordan; but they had a pick in the 5th. This came from Detroit in the trade that sent tackle Ollie Spencer to the Motor City in exchange for Ken Russell who chose not to play for the Pack. With the 51st pick, the Packers took Dale Hackbart.

Moore wasn't Lombardi's first choice. He wanted LSU's Billy Cannon, but the Los Angeles Rams made him their first pick after winning a coin flip with the Chicago Cardinals for the privilege of choosing first in the draft. Next pick was George Izo, quarterback from Notre Dame, selected by the Cards. The Lions and Redskins had the third and fourth slots, then the Packers had their turn. Detroit chose John Robinson, halfback from LSU; and Washington's pick was Richie Lucas, quarterback from Penn State and the runner-up for the Heisman Trophy.

The NFL owners held a special meeting prior to the draft to discuss expansion, the AFL's draft, and the appointment of former governor of South Dakota Joe Foss. George Halas had said all along that the NFL wouldn't expand until 1961. When expansion would take place became a moot point after it was learned the Dallas Texans first choice in the AFL draft had already signed a personal services deal with Bedford Wynne and Clint Murchison, Jr, who claimed they had been promised a franchise in the NFL. The owners decided this threw a monkey wrench into their expansion plans. They knew the backers of a team in Minneapolis couldn't be ready to go until 1961, but they worried that since Don Meredith was drafted by the Texans he just might withdraw from his contract with Wynne and Murchison and play for the Texans who planned to take the field in 1960. This would be a major blow to the NFL, and an equally major coup for the AFL. The NFL owners decided they would wait until their annual meeting in January before making a final decision on expansion. George Halas then muddied the waters swirling around Meredith by selecting him in the 3rd Round. This was only the beginning of the troubles between the NFL and the AFL.

On the day of the draft, Billy Cannon let it be known that he planned to sign with the Rams, and the Cardinals announced they had already signed George Izo. The AFL owners cried foul, but they sat on their hands and nothing more than that for the time being. NFL moguls patted themselves on the back and puffed out their chests in typical contempt for the upstart league.

This paragraph appeared in an article written by Art Daley of the *Green Bay Press-Gazette*:

> **"National League clubs took 100 of the 286 players chosen in the American League draft, with the Redskins and the Lions each nabbing 12 ...The AFL took 132 of the 240 players chosen by the NFL. Denver's first choice, center Roger Leclerc of Trinity, wasn't even chosen in the NFL draft."**

Now does this make sense? If the NFL chose 100 players that were also chosen by the AFL, then how does the AFL choose 132 players picked by the NFL? So, how many players were selected by teams in *both* leagues? Is it 100 or 132? Can't be both!

The Packers took 17 players in the 1960 NFL Draft. After Dale Hackbart, their 6th Round choice was Mike Wright, tackle from Minnesota who was also picked by the Minneapolis-St. Paul AFL team. Then followed Kirk Phares, guard from South Carolina; Don Hitt, center from Oklahoma State; Frank Brocious, Minnesota tackle taken as a future for 1961; Ronald Ray, tackle from little Howard Payne College of Texas, the same school that produced Ken Gray, the guard-tackle that was drafted by the Packers in 1958 and traded to the Chicago Cardinals; Harry Ball, tackle from Boston College; Paul Winslow, halfback from North Carolina College (now North Carolina Central University); Jon Gilliam, center-linebacker from East Texas State; Carey Henley, halfback from Huron College in South Dakota; John Littlejohn, halfback from Kansas State; Joe Gomes, halfback from South Carolina; Royce Whittington, tackle from Southeastern

Louisiana; Rich Brooks, end from Purdue; and Gilmer Lewis, tackle from Oklahoma.

Dale Hackbart also played baseball at Wisconsin. The 6'3", 200-pound Badger also had his eye on a Major League Baseball deal. "If I play pro football, I'll probably play with the Packers," said Dale. "I've always been a Packer fan and watched them whenever I could."

Bob Jeter said, "I'm going to have a talk with Coach (Forest) Evashevski before I make up my mind. I'm going to play pro ball, but I haven't decided in which league yet."

Joe Foss, the newly hired AFL commissioner, said he doubted there would be a money war between the two leagues for established NFL players. "However," said the one-time flying ace who shot down 26 Japanese planes in World War II, "I can see that in some instances there will be heavy bidding for players."

The Packers won their first tussle with the AFL when they signed their 1st Round choice Tom Moore from Vanderbilt. The AFL Dallas Texans had also selected Moore, but the Packers wasted no time getting their man. Verne Lewellen traveled to Nashville right after the draft and got Moore's signature on a deal. "I plan to play pro football as long as I can," said Moore. "I like the idea of playing for Green Bay because it is building for the future..."

A few days after the NFL draft Lamar Hunt, owner of the Dallas Texans, issued a statement reiterating the AFL's plan to stay out of a bidding war for stars from the college ranks. "We want to build a solid team," he said. "The National Football League will have openings for only about 20 players from the new crop of college players. The American League will have 264 job openings." Hunt also divulged that 160 more college players had been picked by the AFL, bringing their total to 424 draftees.

On December 4, Art Daley wrote a few predictions in his column in the *Green Bay Press-Gazette.* "Here are a couple of good bets: (1) The American Football League won't operate in 1960, and (2) the National Football League will add two (new) clubs—Dallas and Minneapolis." He turned out to be wrong on the first wager and only half right on the second. Further along, he wrote that the AFL was "an overnight thing by comparison" with the defunct AAFC. He pointed out how the men who developed the former challenger to the NFL had spent two-to-three years planning their circuit, while the new AFL had only come to life less than six months earlier.

To support his analysis of the situation, Daley quoted Bobby Layne, the great quarterback of the Lions and then the Steelers. The Texas native said, "I don't think the AFL will get off the ground. We'll (the NFL) take a couple of new teams in our league this year, and I don't think they'll try to go with the rest. I know Bud Adams and Lamar Hunt (AFL organizers), and their daddies have got a lot of money, but they don't know anything about running a football team and are just beginning to realize the problems. Bud just saw a financial statement for one of the NFL clubs last week, and it worked him up a little."

Layne was considered a good source because during the off season he was a known drinking buddy of the two Texas millionaires. The reporters in the NFL cities, many of them also drinking buddies with Layne, cited Bobby on lots of subjects throughout his career. He was a good pal to them, and they reciprocated by not revealing how much and how often he drank, especially when he had a bad game here and there in his years in the pro game.

Besides signing Don Meredith to a personal services contract for five years, Clint Murchison also signed halfback Don Perkins to a similar deal. Like Halas did with Meredith by drafting him, the Colts did likewise with Perkins. Of course, both moves were only for the benefit of the NFL, if their clash with the AFL should wind up in court.

The Buffalo Bills signed the first head coach in the AFL. He was Garrard "Buster" Ramsey, the defensive coach for the Detroit Lions. This was a nice Christmas present for the fledgling league, but the bigger prize came in the signing of Ron Mix, the All-American offensive tackle from Southern California. Mix was the 1st Round pick of the Baltimore Colts and the Los Angeles Chargers. Mix was the first big name to put his signature to an AFL contract. Joining Mix with the Chargers was Garry Finneran, his teammate at USC and the other tackle. Their acceptance of deals with the Chargers opened the door for other quality draft picks to take a chance on the new circuit. If nothing else, Mix and Finneran gave the AFL its first taste of credibility.

Future Pro Football Hall of Fame quarterback Sammy Baugh was hired by the New York Titans to be their first coach. He told a press conference why he accepted the position in the AFL, saying he felt there was plenty of room for more pro teams in the country because college football was producing more good players than ever. When asked how long he thought it would take the AFL to reach parity with the NFL, he said three years, but that was only a guess. It could take longer, he added.

The NFL took another punch to the chin a few days later when Lamar Hunt of the Dallas Texans signed Jack Spikes, an All-Southwest Conference fullback and placekicker from Texas Christian University. Spikes had been drafted in the first round by the Pittsburgh Steelers and by the Denver Broncos of the AFL. Dallas acquired the rights to Spikes in a trade with Denver.

At the same time, Hunt announced he had signed Hank Stram to coach the Texans. Both Bud Wilkinson, the legendary head coach at Oklahoma University, and Tom Landry, the defensive coach of the New York Giants, turned down offers from Hunt prior to his hiring Stram. Hunt knew Stram from the season when Hunt had warmed the bench for the Southern Methodist University Mustangs and Stram was an assistant coach there. Previous to his time at SMU, Stram had been an assistant at his alma mater, Purdue University, and then the backfield coach under Terry Brennan at Notre Dame in 1957-58. He moved on to do the same job at the University of Miami (FL) in 1959. An irony here was Stram called the plays that led to the only score of the game when Notre Dame broke Oklahoma's historic 49-game winning streak under Wilkinson in 1957.

These signings by the Texans weren't the biggest news of the day in the growing fight between the two leagues. The huge story of the day was that a group of investors from Minneapolis had submitted their application *and* deposit check for $25,000 to the NFL office in Philadelphia for a franchise to start play in 1960. Heading up this group was Ole Haugsrud, the one-time owner of the long defunct Duluth Eskimos. Signing the application with him was Ernie Nevers who had played for the Eskimos and then the Chicago Cardinals.

H.P. Skoglund, part owner of the AFL franchise that intended to play in Minneapolis in 1960, said, "We intend to go right down the line with the American League no matter what happens." This was his denial that his group was planning to shift to the NFL.

Acting commissioner for the NFL Austin Gunsel confirmed receiving Haugsrud's check and application. He added the application would be considered *along with others* at the league meeting in January.

All this news and other rumors were beginning to make fans in

Wisconsin a little edgy, especially when it was announced that the AFL group in Minnesota had approached Packers defensive coach Phil Bengtson with an offer to be their head coach. When asked about the rumors, Bengtson said he was "pleased with the Packer set-up and I have no intention of leaving now." Bengtson admitted that he had talked with Haugsrud's group while he was in Minneapolis visiting his mother.

The following day another group in yet another city said it was in the market for an NFL franchise. Joseph Griesedieck, one of the owners of Falstaff Brewing in St. Louis, said he intended to make an application to the NFL for a franchise to play in the newly proposed stadium that was to be a part of a riverfront project in the Missouri city. Private interests reportedly had already raised $18 million of the $20 million needed to start the $80 million project that was to include a 55,000-seat venue for an NFL team.

Thus far, the NFL and the AFL had only been fighting a "cold" war of words mostly. Signing 1st Round draft picks by either league wasn't considered open warfare. Instead, the owners in the two loops thought of such things as mere maneuvering by the other side. Neither circuit had actually fired a "shot" by raiding the other for any players under contract. Of course, this would have been impossible for the NFL since the AFL had no experienced players under contract at this time. But everybody knew, even as the end of 1959 was close at hand, that it was only a matter of time and testosterone before one side or the other would break the gentlemen's agreement that the two had allegedly entered into back in the summer.

§§§

9

Coach of the Year! Now What?

Why did the *Associated Press* sportswriters even bother to vote for the NFL's Coach of the Year award? The only other coach to turn around a losing team in 1958 to a winner in 1959 was Philadelphia coach Buck Shaw. He did an admirable job with the Eagles, but he had begun rebuilding his team the year before when they finished with a record of 2-9-1, one win better than the team Lombardi inherited.

But the writers did vote, and 29 of them cast their ballots for the football genius from Brooklyn, Vince Lombardi. He won in a landslide. Jim Lee Howell of the Giants received four votes, while Weeb Ewbank and Red Hickey garnered two each.

After the final win of the season over the 49ers, the tributes for Lombardi, and for the season his team had delivered to their fans, began pouring in from all sides. He accepted them with the honest humility that made him man he was. Of course, he refused to take credit for the Packers rebirth as a power in the NFL. He paid tribute to his assistant coaches: on defense, Phil Bengtson and Norb Hecker, and on offense, Bill Austin and Red Cochran. "They are the finest staff in the National Football League. Any accolades at all belong to them and not me." Politicians often say such words, but Lombardi was not a political person. Far from it. He was a sincerely decent man, the kind that every man wished to be, that every parent prayed their son would be, and that every child wanted to idolize as their father.

Vince Lombardi accepted the honor of being voted Coach of the Year in the National Football League with all the grace and dignity that those who knew him believed he would. All Packerdom thanked their deity for bringing this man to coach their team. Yes, their team. For anyone who has never really visited Green Bay, it could be hard for them to understand how Packer fans feel about their team. It's *their team*, and thousands of them have a stock certificate to prove it. They actually believe it is their duty as fans to *protect* the players and coaches who live among them.

This love for their team was fueled by Lombardi whenever he spoke to a gathering of fans. He made them feel like they were a part of the Green Bay Packers story. When rumors started floating around the NFL that *their* coach might leave them for the Big Apple and the Gotham Giants, well, that's getting ahead of the historical facts.

Lombardi wasn't the only one to receive post-season honors. Boyd Dowler was named Rookie of the Year. Mentioned previously, Paul Hornung won the scoring title. Jim Ringo was named 1st Team All-Pro by both wire services. Hornung and Forrest Gregg made the *UPI*'s second offensive team. Bill Forester was on the *UPI*'s second defensive team. *UPI* Honorable Mentions went to Dave Hanner, Dan Currie, Tom Bettis, and Jerry Kramer.

Another honor was bestowed on Lombardi when Christian Brothers Academy in Lincroft, New Jersey named its new fieldhouse after him. The dedication of the building was attended by Lombardi and of his friends and supporters who had worked diligently to keep the name of the structure a secret from him right up to the actual time of the ceremony dedicating it in his honor. Heading up the list were Jack and Wellington Mara, owners of the New York Giants as well as player Alex Webster. Jerry Atkinson represented the Packers and made a speech praising Lombardi and conveying his appreciation to the Maras and their friends for giving up such a valuable coach to the Packers. Yogi Berra was there representing the New York Yankees. Also, in attendance were Alex Wojciechowicz and Johnny Druze, members of the famous Seven Blocks of Granite from Lombard's Fordham days.

Rumor mill: January 5, Art Daley reported that some Packer officials were privately talking about two things: raising ticket prices and expanding the seating at City Stadium. They felt there would be a bigger demand for season tickets now that the team was a winner again. This would mean they might need more seats. Their excuse for doing both was the threat posed by the AFL. Player salaries were bound to rise in the foreseeable future, and the executive committee wanted to be prepared for that inevitability.

The one rumor Daley didn't include in his column was the one making the rounds in New York. It started when Lombardi and his wife Marie went to the Big Apple before Christmas to visit their m-0====families and friends there. Of course, this included the Mara brothers, Jack and Wellington, owners of the New York Giants, who were very recognizable in public by football fans and definitely by members of the local media. When the gentlemen of the press heard Lombardi was in town, they immediately started tracking him down, only to find him in the company of the Maras. They added up the numbers one plus two and came out with four, meaning the Maras (2) and Vince (1) were talking about the Green Bay coach returning to New York to be the coach of the Giants (1). Maras, Lombardi, Giants? Their answer was definitely four! Had to be. Why else were the three men being so secretive about their meetings and so evasive with their responses when approached by members of the Fourth Estate? Daley knew better than to trust his fellow newsmen, especially those in New York.

Bad news hit the Packers when Lombardi learned that Bob Jeter, his second pick in the draft, had already signed a contract with the BC Lions in the Canadian Football League. To say Lombardi was disappointed in the loss of the man he planned to play the slot back position was a gross understatement. Lombardi said he would never pay a rookie more than a veteran playing the same position.

Lombardi's stance on rookie pay didn't seem to bother most of the Packers' draftees. First pick Tom Moore set the example by being the first to sign. Others inked to deals by the first week of February were Kirk Phares, Ron Ray, Paul Winslow, Jon Gilliam, John Littlejohn, Joe Gomes, Harry Ball, and Gilmer Lewis. Dale Hackbart withheld his signature on a compact because he still had baseball season to play at Wisconsin, which he hoped would result in an offer from a Major League club. Garney Henley, from little Huron College in South Dakota, also had eligibility remaining for the track season.

Besides Bob Jeter, the Packers also lost Richard Brooks and Mike Wright to Canada. Don Hitt, the center from Oklahoma State, chose to play with Houston in the AFL. Frank Brocious and Royce Whittington were both future choices for the 1961 season. Lombardi traded away four picks the previous summer and fall and acquired one that allowed him to draft Dale Hackbart for Green Bay. Losing three players to Canada, one to the AFL, four in trades, and two to the future, the Packers were left with 11 players from the draft, including the pair of spring athletes left to sign.

At a luncheon in Milwaukee the following week, Lombardi

talked about player salaries and season ticket sales. He mentioned how he was offered $125 a game to play for the Brooklyn Dodgers NFL team when he graduated from Fordham. He passed on the deal. "Many pros were paid at that rate then. But those days are gone forever. On our club, every man makes at least $7,000 a year. Other costs are up, too." He then revealed the Packers had to take in at least $65,000 a game after the visiting team received its share just to break even. Getting to the point, he spoke about player salaries being on the rise throughout the NFL, mostly because rookies would be receiving higher pay, thanks to competition from the AFL. These rising costs would make it necessary for more tickets to be sold in Milwaukee to help meet those increased expenditures.

"The name of the team is the Green Bay Packers," said Lombardi. "But the Packers are a state team. Playing a part of the home schedule in Milwaukee is in line with that thinking."

Lombardi didn't say it out loud, but he hinted at it. Plans were afoot to enlarge City Stadium to a seating capacity of 36,000 or more. The Packers expected those seats to be sold for every game played in Green Bay. If Milwaukee couldn't match that number, then possibly all home games in the future would be played in City Stadium.

Johnny Unitas, the fabulous quarterback of the Baltimore Colts, was in Milwaukee later that week on business. The local press interviewed him, and he said some very interesting things about the Packers.

Switch the Packers to the Eastern Conference, he said. "Then we wouldn't have to worry about them next season. Sure, we beat them twice last year, but the game here (Milwaukee) was touch and go. Vince Lombardi has meant the difference. Two years ago, the Packers couldn't do anything right. Now they are a proven power."

Over the winter whenever Vince Lombardi and either or both the Mara brothers were in the same city at the same time rumors began flying about the newly crowned Coach of the Year taking over the reins of the New York Giants. Of course, the usual denials would come from Lombardi, the Maras, and from Dominic Olejniczak of the Packers. But nobody in the media really believed these rather lukewarm disavowals. Not until February 24 when Jim Lee Howell, coach of the Giants, announced 1960 would be his final year coaching in New York. This led to more rumors that Lombardi would be taking over the Giants' job in 1961. For the time being, Lombardi would remain in Green Bay.

One thing was for certain as the calendar turned to March. The Packers were going to lose three plays to the expansion club, the Dallas Rangers. Which three, nobody knew just yet. However, there was certainty about three players rejoining the team for the coming pre-season. Ed Buckingham, Andy Cvercko, and Joe Falls signed new contracts for 1960. Buckingham was the last man to be cut before the regular began in 1959. Cvercko suffered an injury in the last exhibition game the summer before and went on the injured reserve list for the year. The Packers picked up Falls after he was released by the Giants, but he was a victim of numbers as the season approached.

Lombardi was one of the first general managers to announce which three players the new Dallas Rangers chose from the list of 11 players he submitted to them. The Texas team took halfback Don McIlhenny, defensive end Nate Borden, and Billy Butler who played backup safety, punt returner, and kickoff returner. Coach Lombardi expressed his regrets over losing each of the three, especially Butler because return men with his speed and agility were hard to come by and with the retirement of Bobby Dillon, the Green Bay coaches hoped Butler would fill the perennial all-star's spot on the field.

It had to happen sooner or later. It's called inflation. As the cost of living increases, so does the cost of leisure and entertainment. On March 24, 1960, the Packers announced ticket prices would be raised for the coming season. Seats between the two 30-yard lines would go up a dollar from $4.75 to $5.75. Other sideline seats would only be raised a quarter to $5.00. South end zone seats where fans would have the sun at their backs would be raised from $2.25 to $3.50, the largest boost of all. The north end grandstand would go up a quarter to $2.50. All other seating would remain the same.

Lombardi said he was hopeful that an additional 5,000 seats, probably in the north end zone, would be erected for coming season. These seats would be in the $3.50 and $2.50 category. When asked why the increase in prices and seating were necessary, he explained the need. "Increasing prices is an absolute necessity, if we are to compete with teams in our own league and against the American Football League. The increase in income from away games has been greater than the increase when playing at home. Therefore, we must be able to give visiting teams a sum more nearly equal to what we receive when we travel. We have reached the maximum in Green Bay unless we increase prices and add seats."

The general manager also pointed out this was the first price increase since 1946 when the cost of operating the team was 57 per cent less than it was in 1960.

Lombardi then revealed that ticket prices for games at County Stadium. in Milwaukee would also be going up. Lower and upper box seats would be increased from $4.75 to $5.75; mezzanine seats would be $5.75; the better sections in the lower grandstand would go up a quarter to $5.00; the better upper and lower grandstand seats would all be $4.00; all remaining upper and lower grandstand seats would be raised $1.25 to $3.50; and bleacher seats, meaning those that required spectators to see the game through binoculars, would be increased a quarter to $2.50.

At the same luncheon with the media, Lombardi listed three goals for the coming season. He wanted an improvement on field goal kicking, defense against passes, and an increase passing offense. "We may be asking Paul Hornung to do too much with his kicking." He pointed out that the Golden Boy made most of his long kicks but missed on some rather close ones. The coach reasoned that Hornung might have been gassed from having run several more plays to get in close to goal than when the team was halted closer to midfield. Then he mentioned the possibility of Ron Kramer as a possible placekicker. For passing defense, Lombardi said there was no chance of Bobby Dillon returning for one more season, so that hole needed filling. As for the passing attack, he felt sure that Bart Starr could lead the team to the 2,000 yards Lombardi felt was necessary to put a few more wins on their record for 1960. Finally, he said losing Nate Borden to Dallas might necessitate a move to defensive end by Henry Jordan, "if we can find a good tackle to take his place."

At an early April banquet, Lombardi rattled off a number of notable quotes.

Dallas – "The Cowboys will surprise somebody. I hope it won't be us."

The Draft – "Next year, with added competition, we'll be lucky to sign 10 of our 20 choices. As it is, only one per cent of the players selected after the fifth round make your club; 90 per cent of the first choices make it; 70 per cent of the second choices; and about 40 per cent of the third and fourth choices make it."

Green Bay – "It is not necessary to say 'those of you who are

Packer fans' in Green Bay as I do in other cities. Everybody's a Packer fan in Green Bay."

Future – "We believe we've got a team that wants to win and hates to lose. I was proud of our 1959 team. It was a team that played with great spirit, and it never quit."

Football – "Last year three and a half million people paid to see National Football League games. Attendance should go up again. Somebody called pro football 'a tornado of touchdown thrills,' and that's exactly what it is."

The following week the Green Bay city council threw a huge monkey wrench into the plan to increase seating at City Stadium. Like politicians all over the country when dealing with the private sector, they tried to play hardball with the Packers. Fred Leicht, the Packers' representative on the Stadium Commission said the Packers had presented two plans to the commission, but commission president, City Attorney Clarence Nier, denied the Packers had done this. That one offer was for the city to pay for the seating expansion, estimated to cost $100,000 and the Packers would repay the city $140,000 over the next 10 years.

In late April, Lombardi released the roster he planned to take into summer camp. The list included 33 veterans and 27 rookies. Two positions stood out: quarterback and fullback. The coach felt he had all the signal-callers he needed in Bart Starr, Lamar McHan, and Joe Francis. At fullback, he had Jim Taylor and a pair of rookies, Jim Hurd and Lee Nussbaum. Jim Ringo was the only vet at center with two rookies, Ken Iman and Jim Polen, trying to take his job away from him. For pass catching ends, six veterans and one rookie would be competing for five spots. One freshman was Joe Reese, and the returning corps consisted of Boyd Dowler, Gary Knafelc, Max McGee, Ron Kramer, Steve Meilinger, and A.D. Williams. At guard, Jerry Kramer, Fuzzy Thurston, and John Dittrich were still in the fold with rookies Jack Ashton, Mike Falls, and Kirk Phares fighting for a roster spot. Andy Cvercko was still considered to be a rookie because he had missed the entire previous campaign. Offensive tackles were a little thin on experience with Forrest Gregg and Bob Skoronski coming back. Challenging them were Harry Ball and Norm Masters.

The defense had lost two starters and one backup from the 1959 team. Lombardi needed to replace two secondary backs and a defensive end. Bobby Freeman, Hank Gremminger, John Symank,

Emlen Tunnell, and Jesse Whittenton were being counted on to anchor the pass defending group. Hoping to join them were Joe Gomes, Dale Hackbart, Garney Henley, John Littlejohn, and Willie Wood. Lombardi had three returning defensive ends in Jim Temp, Ken Beck, and Bill Quinlan, the first two having been used in 1959 as backups. Hoping to land a place with the Packers were rookies Ron Ray, Gilmer Lewis, and Jim Ward. For defensive tackles, Hawg Hanner and Henry Jordan, the two starters from the year before, were back for 1960 with Leo Bland, Ed Buckingham, Tony De Luca, Marv Rader, and Ed Wallace, all rookies, trying to win jobs. The most stable position on the team was linebacker. Tom Bettis, Dan Currie, Bill Forester, and Ray Nitschke, the four prime men at the position, would be fighting off challenges by a pair of rookies, Jon Gilliam and Joe Hergert.

All four of Lombardi's primary assistants would be with him in 1960, but his part-time aide, Tom Fears,, would not. Fears accepted the same post with the Rams because he wanted to stay in California more and because he had a natural affinity for the team, having played his entire career with LA.

Lombardi proudly announced the financial results for the Green Bay Packers, Inc., at the May meeting of the stockholders. For the first time in their history, the corporation's income surpassed the million-dollar mark, taking in a grand total of $1,006,914.18. The net profit was also a new record at $75,208.36. One key item sparked both new marks. The Packers share of the gate in the game played at Yankee Stadium against the New York Giants came to approximately $70,000. He warned the stockholders that no such check would be coming their way in 1960 because the Giants were being replaced on their schedule by the Pittsburgh Steelers. The best the Packers could expect from Art Rooney would be around $35,000.

The general manager wasn't through with the rainy part of his report. He looked several of the stockholders directly in the eyes and said, "And, gentlemen, this is a one-way street. These expenses always go up. They never level off or go down." He explained that player salaries would continue to rise with each succeeding season and all the other items on the negative side of the ledger would also increase with each passing year.

On a positive note, Lombardi reported season ticket sales had reached 22,227 for the four games that would be played at City

Stadium, well ahead of the previous year at this same time in the campaign. Also, season ticket sales were going well for the two games in Milwaukee with 4,032 renewals and 1,700 new requests for tickets to both games.

The coach concluded his remarks with more words of caution for the stockholders and the media. "We must have a better team in 1960, but that doesn't mean we'll win more games. We sneaked up on a few teams last year. Those teams will be waiting for us. But we won't have some of the problems that faced us in 1959. New coach, new offense, new terminology, new everything. Some of those problems will be gone, but don't forget we are still doing a rebuilding job."

Lombardi added another very important piece to the team he was remodeling in his own image. On July 11, he made another deal with Cleveland's Paul Brown. The Packers gave up offensive end A.D. Williams in exchange for defensive end Willie Davis. Brown took Davis in the 17th Round of the 1956 Draft. He made the team that fall, then went into the Army for a year. He came back to the Browns in 1958 and played for Cleveland that year and the next. Davis was a three-sport star at Booker T. Washington High School in Texarkana, Arkansas before attending Grambling College (University) where he captained the football team for two seasons and was named a Collier's NAIA All-America both years.

When training camp opened for the rookies on July 22, nearly all the veterans were already in their rooms at St. Norbert College. Joining the coaching staff for the pre-season was Bob Ghilotti from the University of Colorado. Ghilotti had been Boyd Dowler's coach there. His duties with the Packers would be the offensive ends.

Lombardi released eight rookies before the first weekend of practice was finished. Having 68 men in camp was a few too many.

A week into training camp Joe Francis suffered a broken leg that would sideline him for many weeks to come. Lombardi had been using Francis at both quarterback and halfback with the idea he could back up Hornung and also Starr and McHan.

Lombardi made another trade on the first day of August. This time his trading partner was the New York Giants. The Packers sent rookie linebacker Jon Gilliam to the Gothamites in exchange for Don Herndon, a halfback who was in Lombardi's last camp with New York.

For the first time in their history, Packer season ticket sales for the four games in Green Bay topped 30,000, reaching 30,009 on

August 1 and officially breaking the old record of 27,000. This left 2,141 seats up for sale. Because the demand was still out there, Lombardi decided to continue the season ticket sale through September 1, hoping they just might sell out the entire stadium. At the same time, season ticket sales in Milwaukee were marching right along with 10,327 being sold for the two games in the Cream City. Lombardi expressed his hope that the Milwaukee total would reach 15,000 to set a new record there.

Right after the annual intrasquad game Lombardi put several players on waivers and made one trade. He sent veteran guard John Dittrich to the Dallas Cowboys for a future draft choice. The *Press-Gazette* reported the deal was made with the Dallas Texans, but this couldn't have been correct. The Texans were in the AFL, and no accord had been reached between the two leagues that would have allowed such dealings between a team in one league with a team in the other league. This error was probably intentional by Art Daley for one very excellent reason. Such a mistake would stir up Packer fans and bring more attention to the team—and Daley and the newspaper—all of it being smart journalism.

Back at the second league meeting in March, the owners finally settled on a 1960 pre-season schedule for the NFL. The Packers would play the Steelers in New Orleans, the Giants in Jersey City, the Bears in Milwaukee, the Cardinals in Green Bay, the Cowboys in Minneapolis, and the Redskins in Winston-Salem, North Carolina. The Cowboys? Yes, the Cowboys. Dallas announced at this meeting their decision to change their nickname from the Rangers to the Cowboys.

The Packers opened their preseason schedule by defeating the Steelers, 20-13, on a hot, steamy night in The Big Easy. Big plays by both the offense and defense highlighted the game for Green Bay. A 79-yard field goal return by John Symank set up Paul Hornung's first field goal. Steve Meilinger pulled down a Bart Starr pass for 25 yards to set up the second three by Hornung. Jim Taylor burst through the line for 23 yards and a touchdown. Then Hank Gremminger killed the last hope for Pittsburgh by picking off a Bobby Layne pass and taking it back 47 yards to set up the final TD.

In their second preseason game, the Packers faced a tougher opponent in the New York Giants. Green Bay proved to be the better team in the game played on Monday night in Jersey City, New Jersey, coming away with a 16-7 victory. Paul Hornung booted three field goals, and Lamar McHan connected with Boyd Dowler for the lone Packer touchdown.

The 11th Annual Midwest Shrine Game was held in Milwaukee County Stadium before a crowd of 35,118, which was a superb showing of support for the Packers in a preseason game. Of course, having the Bears as invited guests didn't hurt any. The Packers put on an offensive show, slamming the Bears, 35-7. Green Bay scored four touchdowns: two by Jim Taylor and one each by Max McGee and Lew Carpenter. Paul Hornung put two field goals through the goal posts, and Willie Davis made a tackle for a safety. The loss broke Chicago's eight-game winning streak—six from the previous regular season and two in this preseason—while the Packers extended their victory skein to seven games—four from last year's regular schedule and three so far in the 1960 preseason.

The Packers made it four straight preseason wins on Labor Day by crushing the St. Louis Cardinals, 35-14, in front of a rousing crowd of 30,668 inside City Stadium. Lamar McHan, Ron Kramer, rookie Tom Moore, Paul Hornung, and former Cardinal Don Brown each scored a touchdown. Art Daley counted this 4th straight win in the preseason as the Packers 8th straight win going back to the 1959 regular season.

On Thursday of the following week, Lombardi announced the sellout of the Packers first three home games in Green Bay, which included the tickets allotted to the visiting teams. The game not a complete sellout yet was the contest against the Dallas Cowboys on November 13. The general manager added that he expected the Cowboys to return some of their allotted ducats for the game and these would go on sale in Green Bay as soon as they were returned.

The same day Lombardi received some more good news, this time on the player front. Dale Hackbart, the Packers' 5th Round draft choice, decided to give up pro baseball for the time being and report to the Packers. Lombardi was delighted because now he had the third quarterback, he'd desired all along. Hackbart had a lot to learn and only two weeks to learn how to play quarterback for Lombardi in his system.

Up next on the preseason schedule for the Packers was the annual game in Minneapolis. Their opponent would be the expansion Dallas Cowboys coached by Tom Landry, the former defensive coach for the New York Giants. Green bay came from behind to defeat the

Cowpokes, 28-23, with a 77-yard drive, culminated by a 12-yard pass from Bart Starr to Paul Hornung for the final score. Hornung also put up a touchdown in the second quarter on a 40-yard pass play from Starr. Ron Kramer and Max McGee scored the other two TDs.

Needing more beef in the offensive backfield, Lombardi traded a draft pick to the St. Louis Cardinals for fullback Larry Hickman, a one-year veteran who had played his college ball at Baylor University in Waco, Texas. At the same time, Lombardi traded Bobby Freeman to the Philadelphia Eagles for a draft choice.

In their final tune-up before the regular season, the Packers handed the Redskins a real shellacking, 41-7, in Winston-Salem, North Carolina. Lew Carpenter caught two touchdown passes, one each from Bart Starr and Lamar McHan. Max McGee and Steve Meilinger each scored on Starr passes, while Paul Hornung scampered eight yards for a TD, kicked five PATs, and booted two field goals.

Lombardi felt confident that his team was ready to play the regular season. Although the preseason had gone as well as any coach could expect, he knew Green Bay's 6-0 record meant nothing to the coming campaign. Art Daley, the Packers' primary cheerleader, might have tacked those half dozen wins onto the four straight victories the Pack finished the previous campaign with, but Lombardi knew this was nothing more than political propaganda of a sort. This was a new season ahead of the Packers, and every team in the league had the same mark of no wins and no losses. For Lombardi it was "Go, Pack, go!" again.

§§§

10
The Skirmishing Intensifies

Trivia question: What was the original nickname of the Dallas entry into the NFL?

A photo in the *Press-Gazette* called the potential new team the Rangers. The picture showed newly signed head coach Tom Landry between general manager Tex Schramm and co-owner Bedford Wynne.

On January 2, a short article stated the NFL would be voting on putting franchises in both Miami and Dallas when the owners held their annual meeting in Miami Beach on January 30. This was the first mention of Miami being considered for a franchise in the NFL. The Florida city had been named in several press releases the summer before, but these were always in articles about the AFL.

On the same day, the first legal battle between the two leagues was announced in the newspapers. All-American Billy Cannon had a change of heart about playing in the NFL with the Los Angeles Rams and had signed a contract with the Houston Oilers of the AFL. The Heisman Trophy winner had already signed a deal with Pete Rozelle, general manager of the Rams, nearly a month earlier. "The Rams have fulfilled their part of the bargain and expect him (Cannon) to respect his part of it. Neither Cannon nor Rozelle would say anything more about the deal because they were both assured the matter would wind up in court.

At the same time, the AFL pulled off another *coup d'état* when the Buffalo Bills snatched All-American quarterback Richie Lucas from the clutches of the Washington Redskins who had him their number one pick in the draft. Reports on the deal had Lucas signing a contract for $50,000 over three years. The clincher that convinced Lucas to do the deal was a "no release" clause that guaranteed he would remain with Buffalo for the term of the bargain.

The Los Angeles Chargers pulled off another victory over the NFL by signing Mississippi fullback Charlie Flowers. He was LA's 2nd Round choice, but he went undrafted by the NFL. However, the New York Giants' Wellington Mara signed Flowers soon after the NFL draft, but Flowers did so on the condition that the Giants keep his deal with them a secret until January 2, so he could remain eligible to play in the Sugar Bowl on New Year's Day. Mara agreed to do so. In the meantime, Flowers got a better offer from the Chargers and signed with them. The Giants attempted to enforce the contract, but their plea was rejected due to their "unclean hands" in making the deal.

The Boston Patriots also got into the act of signing players wanted by the NFL. Gerhard Schwedes, the Pats' top choice as well as the 4th Round choice of the Baltimore Colts, and Bob Yatees, the All-American center from Syracuse who was chosen by the Giants in the 7th Round, chose to play for Boston over New York.

More big news for the AFL came a few days later when Bud Adams of the Houston Oilers announced the signing of Lou Rymkus as the team's first head coach. Rymkus had a storied career as both a player and an assistant coach in both college and professional ranks that included a four-year stint as line coach for the Packers from 1954 thru 1957. During his time in Green Bay, he molded Jim Ringo and Forrest Gregg into the Hall of Fame linemen they became. In 1958, he left Green Bay to be the line coach for Sid Gillman and the Los Angeles Rams. When Gillman was fired at the end of the 1959 season, Rymkus was considered for the head coaching job of the Los Angeles Chargers by general manager Frank Leahy who had been Rymkus' coach at Notre Dame. The job was given to Gillman instead. Having played college ball for Leahy and his pro years after World War II for Paul Brown at Cleveland, he was part of the same coaching tree as Vince Lombardi. The Packers gave him some consideration to replace Lisle Blackbourn, but instead they chose Scooter McLean.

Then came the bad news for the AFL. Financial backers for the Minneapolis-St. Paul franchise backed out of their bid for a team in the Twin Cities. They cited the "hostility" on the part of the NFL advocates as the reason for their withdrawal. AFL founder Lamar Hunt called it sabotage by the NFL. The truth was the AFL backers appeared to be unable to build a team that fans in Minnesota would be willing to support. They had signed three players of little note, but they hadn't been able to sign a head coach who was willing to take a chance on the new circuit. With the AFL group calling it quits, the door to an NFL franchise was left wide open for Ole Haugsrud and his group.

AFL commissioner Joe Foss took up the gauntlet a few days later when he visited Washington. to chat with Senator Estes Kefauver about the bullying his league was getting from the NFL. The one-time candidate for vice-President on the Democratic ticket promised to launch an investigation into the NFL's tactics if any evidence of such misconduct was found. Foss followed up that move with a letter to all twelve NFL owners asking them to play fair. "We earnestly desire to be your good neighbor," he wrote, "working in parallel enterprise to promote professional football." This gave the NFL moguls a giggle. Well, some of them. The others saw the future. If the AFL proved to be successful, then either a serious war for players would break out, or the two circuits would merge into a much bigger league. Time would tell.

For now, the NFL had won the battle for the Twin Cities. The three groups that had been vying for the right to run a pro team in the Minneapolis-St. Paul area joined hands and combined their efforts to raise money to obtain that franchise. They announced their united front with the Minneapolis group putting up $600,000, the St. Paul contingent coming in with $300,000, and the Duluth organization led by Ole Haugsrud throwing in $100,000 to make their total bankroll a cool $1,000,000. All this and an application signed by Max Winter of Minneapolis and by Haugsrud they planned to put before the NFL owners at their annual meeting later in January in Miami Beach.

At the time, nobody knew publicly that the sole culprit in the fight for a team in Minnesota was none other than Papa Bear George Halas. As soon as the Lamar Hunt made his intentions known that he and Bud Adams were planning yet another professional loop known as the American Football League, Halas went to work with the goal of undermining their efforts. Since the NFL had once had a pro team in Texas, strangely enough named the Dallas Texans, Halas thought it would be good for his league to put Dallas on the NFL's map. He had the same idea when the AFL awarded a franchise to the Minneapolis group of backers. In his mind, extending the limits of the NFL into the upper Midwest and the Southwest would make the 40-year-old loop a truly *national* league. When he heard that Hunt intended to give his team the nickname of the failed NFL franchise of 1952, Halas felt this new incarnation was certain to fade into history as well.

With the Minnesota franchise already withdrawn from the AFL, the upstart league considered what to do with that eighth team. Three cities were under serious consideration. Atlanta entered the fray for the first time. Miami still wanted pro football. And then there was Oakland, across the bay from San Francisco. Hunt and Foss knew they had to act fast to pick one of them before the NFL stuck its big foot in the door.

As the owners and general managers for the NFL gathered in Miami Beach, Lombardi had a lot to say about the AFL. He initially appeared to be in favor of the new pro loop when Hunt first made the announcement back in the summer. That was before the NFL began losing draft choices to the new kids on the block. He took umbrage with Foss when he complained to Senator Kefauver about the NFL and its tactics in Dallas and Minnesota. Sure, the NFL had no interest in any expansion until the AFL sprouted from the fertile fields of Texas, but with Branch Rickey, the man who integrated baseball with the signing of Jackie Robinson in 1946, ballyhooing a whole new circuit for Major League Baseball that he wanted to name the Continental League, expansion fever struck all the major pro sports leagues.

The National Basketball Association started discussions about growing their league, especially since Abe Saperstein, founder and owner of the Harlem Globetrotters and other sports franchises, wanted to start and own an NBA team in California, preferably in Los Angeles. He even talked about starting up his own league and eventually did in 1961. To this critical time in sports history, the National Hockey League was the smallest pro organization with a mere six teams; four in the United States and two in Canada. The NHL owners were also considering expansion.

George Halas and a majority of owners in the NFL felt that expansion was the only way of maintaining their monopoly on pro football. They talked publicly about accepting the new league, but in no way did they want to share the growth of the game's popularity and give up a single dollar of the television revenue that was finally making all of them millionaires almost overnight.

When the NFL meeting did get underway a little earlier than originally announced, the owners listened to representatives from St. Louis, Dallas, and Minnesota stating their cases for admission into the NFL fraternity. The only real news of the day came in the form of a blockbuster telegram from Joe Foss to the NFL leaders.

"So long as inter-league relationships are kept on a two-way street, please advise all NFL teams I will require all existing valid NFL contracts be respected by all AFL teams. No tampering with players either under contract or option will be permitted. I will be pleased to resolve any existing conflicts in meeting with NFL commissioner on Jan. 26, 27, or 28."

The true purpose of this message was a pre-emptive strike at the NFL should the two leagues ever meet in a courtroom or in the halls of Congress in an anti-trust investigation. Halas and friends knew they had been "had" by the AFL. They didn't like it, but they still understood they were now on the defensive side of the game.

Art Daley reported all these goings-on back to the people of northeast Wisconsin by way of the *Press-Gazette*. He also mentioned he went to dinner the evening of the first day with one Charley Burton, a sports columnist for the *Dallas News*. Joining them were Bunker Hunt, brother of Lamar Hunt, and a couple of Texas attorneys who worked for Lamar and AFL commissioner Joe Foss. Bob Dedman, one of the lawyers, said he was eager to learn what "your league does on expansion. I have any number of lawyer friends who asked me to promise them a chance to work on the anti-trust case if the National League goes into Dallas. It's an open and shut case—a sure thing. The government couldn't rule any other way but for our league. We'll start proceedings right away if the NFL goes into Dallas."

Daley apparently defended the NFL by stating the AFL had gone into New York and Los Angeles, which were already established strongholds of the NFL. Bunker Hunt promptly countered with the AFL's argument. "My brother felt that those two cities were large enough to support two teams. We know we won't hurt the Giants or Rams if we go into their cities. We decided not to go into San Francisco because that city isn't large enough. But Lamar is trying to get a team into Oakland. That's actually larger than San Francisco." He then mentioned the Packers. "We took a look at Milwaukee, and I remember Lamar saying, 'We don't want to go into Green Bay's territory.' We had hoped to start a team in Minneapolis."

Dedman added his take on the Packers. "Green Bay is the most refreshing and wholesome happening in all American sports. We all in Texas hope they'll remain part of professional football forever."

Daley didn't offer any comment on Dedman's statement, but

the overall tone of his column implied he thought these gentlemen from Texas were what they call down that way "good ol' boys" and they had every right to have their own professional football league as long as it didn't have a negative impact on the Packers.

Finally, after a week of balloting and failing to elect a new commissioner in 22 tries, the NFL owners voted 8-1 with three abstentions for Pete Rozelle, general manager of the Los Angeles Rams, to be their new czar to replace the late Bert Bell. Frank McNamee, owner of the Philadelphia Eagles, said, "We won't have to wrestle with the problem of a commissioner for many years. He's young, intelligent, vigorous, and was well-thought of by Bert Bell." McNamee was right on all accounts.

At 33 years of age, Rozelle made all the right moves as soon as he took office. For one thing, he said he would keep the league office in Philadelphia before eventually moving it to New York. Then he mentioned the AFL. "I feel as (Bert) Bell did, that there is a place for two leagues. We'll cooperate with them. We ask only one thing (of the AFL)—honoring each other's contracts."

Now that they had a new commissioner, the owners turned their attention to expansion. This required a unanimous vote of the owners, according to league by-laws. Everybody knew that would never happen because George Preston Marshall, cantankerous owner of the Washington Redskins, absolutely opposed expanding the NFL. To counter Marshall's stiff-necked attitude, George Halas prompted Edward Anderson, president of the Detroit Lions, to propose an amendment to the league's by-laws that would require a vote of 10-2 to approve expansion. Halas got his way.

The next day the owners voted for expansion into Dallas for the 1960 season and into Minneapolis-St. Paul for the 1961 campaign. As an extra plum for Halas, they then voted to add two more teams within two or three years after the admission of the Minnesota team. Dallas was still nicknamed the Rangers at this time. They would have a 12-game schedule, playing each established team once; while the 12 teams already in the league would play their usual two games against each conference opponent but only play one team in the other conference plus Dallas to maintain the league's 12-game schedule. The next year the members of the Eastern Conference would vote to decide which of the two new teams would join them and the other would then become a member of the Western Conference.

George Halas said, "This is a big milestone in the history of the NFL. It has been planned and programmed for five years." Sad to say, there is nothing to back up this claim by Papa Bear. The fact is, nobody mentioned expansion in the NFL until Lamar Hunt and Bud Adams announced the formation of the American Football League *because they had applied to the NFL to join the established league and had been rejected outright.* If expansion had been in the works or even being talked about by NFL owners, why had they rejected two cities like Dallas and Houston? As he did often in his autobiography, *Halas on Halas*, old George stretched the truth.

In the meantime, the AFL had its issues to settle. Primary among them was the selection of a city to take the franchise that had been intended for Minneapolis-St. Paul. Hunt and the other owners had narrowed the candidates down to Atlanta and Oakland. Chatter outside the meeting in Dallas favored Oakland because a team there would be a natural rival for the Los Angeles Chargers. The other matter before the AFL owners was what to do about the NFL putting a team in Dallas in direct competition with Hunt's Texans. Foss and Hunt both called it "an act of war." They added they had attorneys looking into the possibility of court action. By the end of the next day, the AFL owners decided to go with Oakland as the eighth team in the league. All the new owners had to do was find a coach, a general manager, a home field, and 35 players to fill out each of their rosters. Nothing to it, right? It was about this time that the AFL owners dubbed themselves "The Foolish Club" because they knew they were about to take a big financial hit over the next few years.

After more than a month of rumors and new ideas floating around pro football circles, the NFL owners met in Los Angeles to hammer a few important issues. On the table were the stocking of the Dallas Rangers with players from the established teams, a nation-wide television contract, and the possibility of the Chicago Cardinals being relocated to St. Louis. The latter two items were considered by many as being tied together.

Although several ideas for stocking the new team were put forth and discussed heartily, the owners came up with a reasonable plan. Each team would submit a list of 11 players from their 1959 roster, and Dallas would be allowed to choose three from each team to give the Rangers a list of 36 veterans. As a bonus, Dallas would be permitted to carry a roster of 42 players throughout the season and would be given first chance to sign all players placed on waivers after the first three weeks of the season. If any players chosen by Dallas should refuse to play for the Rangers, those men would remain on the Texas team's reserve list. Packers president Dominic Olejniczak said, "I think we used foresight to go as far as we did. Many thought we were very generous. But if Dallas is to be a member of the NFL, we want it to be a strong member. Competition is what we want in the NFL."

The owners also wanted more television revenue that would be divided equally between the 13 teams in 1960 and the 14 teams in 1961. To increase viewership—and paydays for the owners—and to make the NFL appear to be more of a *national* league, the owners voted unanimously for the relocation of the Chicago Cardinals to St. Louis. Before the meeting, managing director of the franchise Walt Wolfner had denied every rumor that had the Cardinals moving to Missouri. He denied them emphatically and repeatedly right up until the announcement of the change was made at the conclusion of the league meeting.

The real story behind the Cardinals' move to the River City was much more intrigue than the newspapers reported. Wolfner made all those denials because he was playing for time and for cash. Shifting a franchise from one city to another doesn't come free. He wanted the other owners to pony up some dough to the Cardinals' expenses *and then some.* The only owner not to balk at this demand was Papa Bear George Halas. In order to get the rest of the owners to go along with him, Halas offered to assume the major share of the sum voted by the owners to compensate the Cardinals, meaning Wolfner's wife Violet Bidwill Wolfner, the widow of long-time owner Charles Bidwill, and the two adopted Bidwill sons, Charles, Jr., and William "Bill." Halas had everything to gain and little to lose by the Cardinals leaving the Windy City. What few Cardinal fans there were in Chicago would very likely shift their allegiance to the Bears, but more importantly to Halas, the Bears would have all their road games televised back to Chicago. For the rest of the league, the Cardinals move meant more television revenue for them as well because the Cardinals would be opening up a whole new market for the NFL, meaning the state of Missouri and all or part of the states that bordered it. Of course, as always, there was a hitch to the move. The Cardinals had to secure a contract for a stadium and a television deal for local broadcasts.

Speaking of television, Jay Michaels and Harry Wismer were

working on setting up a broadcasting deal with the Music Corporation of America) for the AFL. The New York Titans planned to play all of their home games on Friday nights, which would allow all of their Sunday road games to be broadcast in New York. Michaels and Wismer also came up with a plan to have a "Saturday Night Game of the Week" to be broadcast nationally. Regional networks would be set to cover areas that had no AFL team, and all teams would have their road games broadcast in their home areas. Sounded like a good plan. Now for it to work.

The new Oakland franchise in the AFL took a nickname that the owners hoped would appeal to Californians, especially those of Spanish descent. They called themselves the Oakland Señors. Of course, the moniker didn't stick, proving that racism was on the run in the Golden State.

On April 23, the AFL announced it signed a television pact with the American Broadcasting Corporation (ABC) for the 1960 season. Of course, the deal had "what if" clauses in it. The network said it had taken an option on 17 games and had until May 9 to sell the games to sponsors. If ABC sold 60 per cent of the air time, the contract would be closed. Otherwise, the AFL would be free to market the games to another network or to local stations. The league said the agreement could mean as much as $2,125,000 to the new loop, with each team getting $250,000 and the remainder going into the commissioner's office's coffers. This was a major step forward for the AFL, practically guaranteeing its survival through the first season.

The in early May, Harry Wismer, president of the New York Titans and chairman of the AFL's expansion committee, announced on May 3 that Atlanta and Chicago had been awarded franchises for the 1961 season. Eaton Chalkley, husband of movie actress Susan Hayward, said he had put down the $25,000 earnest money with the AFL for the Atlanta team. Wismer also said two different groups were vying for the Chicago franchise. One would be headed up by Tom King, Jr. and John Rigney, and the other would be led by Bill Veeck, Jr., the flamboyant owner of the Chicago White Sox. Rigney said he refused to put down the $25,000 to the AFL, and Veeck said his part in any Chicago AFL team would be as landlord, if the team wanted to use Comiskey Park as its home field. Putting a team in Atlanta had one major flaw. The two possible stadiums for the team were owned by the state of Georgia, which had a law prohibiting athletes of color from competing with whites on state property. Wismer said, if that law was repealed in the near future, then the Atlanta team would be ready to operate in 1961.

The following week a story appeared in the *Press-Gazette* that said two Canadian cities wanted to join the AFL. Businessmen in both Montreal and Toronto declared their intention to apply for franchises for the 1961 season. There were no comments from anybody in the AFL.

In the middle of June, a battle of words broke out between New York Titans owner Harry Wismer and Chicago Bears owner George Halas. Wismer defended his signing of Jack Sherer, a tackle from the University of Miami). Sherer was only a sophomore, but, as Wismer explained it, "The kid flunked out of school. He can't get into any other college. He wants to play football. I know the rule is that we aren't supposed to sign a boy until his class graduates, but this case is different. We have not induced the boy to leave school. We are trying to help him."

Halas fired back that the signing of undergraduates by AFL clubs could lead to wholesale raids of colleges.

"I know why Halas is mad," said Wismer. "He wanted the boy himself. Halas did the very same thing only a year ago. At the end of the 1958 college season, he signed Richie Petitbon, the best player Tulane had in 10 years, when he still had a year of eligibility at school. Halas has been getting away with this kind of stuff for years in Chicago."

Halas rebutted, "The two cases are entirely different. Petitbon's college class had already graduated. I tried to get him to finish his college career, but he was determined to play pro football and would have gone to the Canadian League. Signing Sherer sets a precedent for every college football player in the country to drop out of school if he thinks he can get a pro contract."

Halas lied.

Petitbon was born April 18, 1938. He first attended Loyola University (New Orleans) on a track scholarship, then transferred to Tulane after his freshman year. If he had started college in the fall of 1955 at the age of 17, his class would have graduated in 1959. This is not likely because he probably didn't graduate from high school until the spring of 1956 when he was 18. This would mean his class would not have graduated until 1960. Halas said Petitbon's class had already graduated, but he failed to mention that Petitbon did not graduate *at all.* This further proves that if Petitbon's class, supposedly of 1959, had graduated, then why didn't Petitbon graduate with his classmates?

A week later the AFL won the first pitched fight with the NFL when a Los Angeles judge ruled the contract between the Rams and Billy Cannon was null and void. Federal Judge William J. Lindberg said the Rams submitted three contracts to the NFL commissioner's office, but only the first of these, the one for the 1960 season, was signed by the acting commissioner Austin Gunsel. The other two were not signed; therefore, they were voided. Then he dismissed the 1960 contract, although signed by Gunsel, because he said it was part of an incomplete contract package. Finally, Judge Lindberg said Cannon was "unusually naïve for a college senior and anything but astute in business dealings."

At the same time in another court, the AFL filed an anti-trust suit against the NFL, asking for an award of $10,000,000. Lawyers for the two sides agreed that it would be a year before the case was heard and a judgment made.

Before the week was out, the AFL won the second pitched battle with the NFL; this time in Mississippi. Federal Judge Claude Clayton dismissed the lawsuit filed by the New York Giants that had attempted to prevent Charlie Flowers from playing the 1960 season for the Los Angeles Chargers. The judge ruled the contract signed by Flowers with the Giants a month before he accepted a deal with LA was not binding because Wellington Mara made an oral promise to the former Ole Miss star that he could void their pact before the first of January, if he changed his mind about playing for the Giants. This win put the AFL up 2-0 in court clashes.

On June 29 in New Orleans, Federal District Judge J. Skelly Wright ruled an agreement between former LSU star halfback Johnny Robinson and the Detroit Lions was not a binding contract because it was signed before Robinson's college eligibility had expired. Although the regular season had been completed by the signing date, Robinson still had one more game to play, the Sugar Bowl in January. After that game, Robinson signed another deal with the Dallas Texans. The court's decision freed Robinson to honor that pact. AFL 3, NFL zip in federal court rooms.

Although the AFL was riding a wave of good results in the courts, a piece of bad news hit the league on the first day of July. Frank

Leahy, the renowned football coach and general manager of the Los Angeles Chargers, had himself admitted to a hospital in Chicago because he had suffered a nervous breakdown. Never a man to deal with stress well, Leahy felt it was in his best interest and those of the LA club that he should resign from his post in the Chargers' front office. His brother Thomas Leahy said Frank's condition was caused by his worry over some oil stock he had sold to friends that hadn't turned out well. This may have been the truth, but the recent court case over Charlie Flowers' contract probably had something to do with his health as well. Leahy's resignation was a big blow to the AFL's growing prestige in professional sports circles.

When he took office in January, NFL Commissioner Pete Rozelle announced his intentions of moving the league's headquarters to New York City. The weekend after the 4th of July he made good on his promise. As he had stated in January, the NFL office should be located in Manhattan because New York was the media center of the country. The move, he felt, would result in more coverage for the NFL in particular and for professional football in general. With the passage of time, he would be proven absolutely correct.

The AFL began its pre-season games the last weekend of July by playing a pair of contests. Boston beat the Bills in Buffalo, and Dallas defeated Oakland at Kezar Stadium in San Francisco. The league moguls were overjoyed to be playing games, even if they were merely non-league affairs. The following week the Dallas Texans and the Houston Oilers met in Tulsa, Oklahoma, and Dallas came away with a win in front of a crowd of 8,000 enthusiastic fans. Out in California, the Los Angeles Chargers hosted the New York Titans and picked up a victory in front of a more impressive audience of 27,778 Angelinos. The AFL moguls were quite satisfied with the turnouts for these two games. The next game for the Chargers was on a Thursday night, and the crowd was much smaller. Only 11,491 people showed up to see Jack Kemp lead LA over the Houston Oilers.

The next week when the NFL preseason burst into full bloom with a slate of five games on the weekend, all of them being broadcast on local radio and a few of them on being broadcast on national TV, except in their home markets. Television and radio hurt the slate of three games played by the AFL at the same time. The NFL drew a total of 108,733 fans, while the fledgling AFL only attracted 26,796. Average attendance for the NFL came to 21,675 and only 8,932 for the

AFL contests. NFL cities like Green Bay boasted about the huge difference in the numbers, but not one of them mentioned how the coverage by television and radio of NFL games in the AFL markets just might have stunted the attendance figures for the AFL games. Of course, this was the preseason for the AFL. Only the regular season would tell the tale of the turn-styles.

§§§

11
Play Ball!

The Packers' regular season schedule for 1960 looked like this:

Sept. 25 – Bears at Green Bay
Oct. 2 – Lions at Green Bay
Oct. 9 – Colts at Green Bay
Oct. 16 – Open Date
Oct. 23 – 49ers at Milwaukee
Oct. 30 – Steelers at Pittsburgh
Nov. 6 – Colts at Baltimore
Nov. 13 – Cowboys at Green Bay
Nov. 20 – Rams at Milwaukee
Nov. 24 – Lions at Detroit
Dec. 4 – Bears at Chicago
Dec. 11 – 49ers at San Francisco
Dec. 18 – Rams at Los Angeles

Note October 16. Open Date. This was the first "bye" week for the Packers since the commissioner's office began making the entire league's schedules back in the days when Joe Carr was the NFL czar.

While the NFL teams were still playing the final two weeks of their preseason, the AFL kicked off its initial season on September 9, a Friday, with the Boston Patriots hosting the Denver Broncos. The Colorado eleven upset the New Englanders, 13-10. In other games that weekend, the Los Angeles Chargers nipped the Dallas Texans in La-La-Land, 21-20; the Houston Oilers spanked the Oakland Raiders, 37-22; and the New York Titans stuck it to the Buffalo Bills, 27-3, before a sparse crowd of 9,607 Big Apple fans. Attendance figures at the other three venues were better; not as much as the AFL owners had hoped for but still more than the NFL owners expected they would draw.

The next weekend the AFL card featured the Texans against the Raiders on Friday night. Dallas (1-1) came away with a 34-16 victory over Oakland (0-2). On Saturday night, Boston (1-1) edged New York (1-1), 28-24, on the final play of a thriller. Sunday had two games. Denver (2-0) defeated Buffalo (0-2), 27-21; and Houston (2-0) riddled the vaunted LA Chargers (1-1), 38-28. This put Houston in first place in the East and Denver in first in the West.

Finally, the NFL season was set to start on Friday night the 23rd of September with the Cardinals invading Los Angeles to play the Rams in the Coliseum. Five more games were set for Sunday with Detroit getting the bye the first week of the campaign.

For 1960, the NFL increased the roster size for each team from 36 to 38. This made room for six rookies on the Packer roster. They were Paul Winslow, Willie Wood, Tom Moore, Dick Pesonen, Ken Iman, and Andy Cvercko. Other newcomers were Larry Hickman, Ken Beck, and Willie Davis. Returning were Paul Hornung, Bart Starr, Lamar McHan, Joe Francis, John Symank, Jim Taylor, Lew Carpenter, Emlen Tunnell, Hank Gremminger, Jesse Whittenton, Jim Ringo, Dan Currie, Fred Thurston, Jerry Kramer, Tom Bettis, Ray Nitschke, Bill Forester, Henry Jordan, Forrest Gregg, Bob Skoronski, Norm Masters, Dave Hanner, Steve Meilinger, Jim Temp, Bill Quinlan, Gary Knafelc, Max McGee, Boyd Dowler, and Ron Kramer.

The Packers played hosts to the Bears who came into Green Bay as a one-point underdog. Both teams entered the fray with winning streaks carried over from the previous year. Green Bay won its last four games of 1959, while Chicago piled up seven straight victories to close the previous campaign. Based on what they had seen what their team had done the previous year and in the preseason of the current docket, Green Bay fans had good reason to be optimistic about their Packers against the Bears and the entire league.

A sellout crowd witnessed a tragedy for the Packers. After having one touchdown nullified by a penalty and a 22-yard field goal attempt by Paul Hornung was blocked, Jim Taylor got his team on the board with a one-yard plunge early in the second quarter. Then Green Bay upped their lead to 14-0 when Taylor ripped off 32 yards on a quick opener. Hornung followed with a two-yard bolt into the end zone. Then the roof fell in on the Packers in the fourth quarter. The

Bears scored two touchdowns in a minute and 55 seconds early in the final stanza to tie the game at 14-all. The first six came at the end of a long drive, while the second was on a short drive after Taylor fumbled on the Green Bay 31. Chicago mounted another drive late in the game that resulted in the winning field goal from 21 yards out.

After the game, George Halas declared the biggest play of the game came when he chose to go for it on fourth-and-one on the Bears own 30-yard line. Rick Casares made that last yard for a first down that kept the ball in Chicago hands and extended the possession into the Green Bay end zone to make the score 14-7. Halas said the big play was the turning point in the game.

Never one to make excuses, Lombardi said after the game, "The answer's not in the officiating or anything else like that. We just didn't play a good ball game. We made too many mistakes—that's it in a nutshell."

In the other games that first weekend, St. Louis ripped Los Angeles, 43-21, on Friday. Pittsburgh handed Dallas a loss, 35-28, on a rainy Saturday that limited attendance for the Cowboys' inaugural home opener. Baltimore showed why they were the reigning kings of the NFL when they crushed Washington, 20-0. Cleveland belted Philadelphia, 41-24; and New York slipped by San Francisco, 21-19.

In the AFL for their Week 3, New York (2-1) slipped past the Broncos (2-1), 28-24. Buffalo (1-2) upset Boston (1-2), 13-0. Dallas (2-1) shut down Los Angeles (1-2), 17-0. Oakland (1-2) upset Houston (2-1), 14-13, leaving the league without an unbeaten team.

On Monday, September 26, Judge Alexander Holtzoff ruled in Washington. that the lawsuit of the AFL against the NFL was only properly filed against the six teams in the Eastern Conference and the Baltimore Colts in the Western Conference. Commissioner Joe Foss of the AFL said the dismissal made no difference in their quest to prove the NFL was in violation of the antitrust laws and his league would continue to pursue the suit.

Embarrassed by the loss to Chicago, Lombardi and his staff put in a little overtime to prepare for the Detroit Lions, recipients of the season's first BYE week. The players took their cue from the men with the whistles and poured out more extra sweat than usual during the practices that week. All that special effort led to the Pack taming the Lions, 28-9.

Jim Taylor had a major day running the ball, carrying 26 times for 151 yards. He came up short of Billy Grimes' single game record of 167 set in 1950, and he tied Tony Canadeo 1949 record for rushing attempts in a game. Overall, the Packers rushed 52 times and gained 255 yards on the ground.

Detroit broke out to a 6-0 lead early in the second period before Green Bay put its first points on the board via a five-yard run by Tom Moore. The Lions regained the lead just before the half with their third and last field goal of the day. Taylor put the Pack ahead for good in the third stanza with a two-yard plunge. Paul Hornung scored twice in the final period, first on a 16-yard pass from Lamar McHan and then on an 11-yard run to seal the game for the Packers, now 1-1 on the young season.

In other NFL contests, Baltimore (2-0) became the only undefeated team in the Western Conference when the Colts broke Chicago's eight-game winning streak by trouncing the Bears (1-1), 42-7. San Francisco (1-1) slipped by Los Angeles (0-2) by the score of 13-9 to tie Chicago and Green Bay for second place. Dallas (0-2) came close to beating Philadelphia (1-1), losing by a mere two points, 27-25. Cleveland (2-0) downed Pittsburgh (1-1) by the tune of 28-20. New York (2-0) kept pace with Cleveland for first place in the East with a 35-14 smackdown on St. Louis (1-1)

Boston and Houston were recipients of byes for Week 4 in the AFL; but the rest of the league saw some decent action. Los Angeles tripped up Buffalo, 24-10. The Titans of New York held off Dallas, 37-35. The surprising Denver Broncos threw Oakland, 31-14. New York (3-1) moved into first place in the Eastern Division with their win, a half-game ahead of Houston (2-1). Boston (1-2) sat in third, and Buffalo (1-3) brought up the rear. Out West, Denver (3-1) elevated itself to first place. Dallas (2-2) dropped into a tie for second with Los Angeles (2-2), while Oakland (1-3) sank into the cellar.

Dale Hackbart became an official member of the Packers when he signed his contract the day after the win over the Lions. Hackbart had been practicing with the team for the last four weeks, first as an emergency quarterback and second as a defensive back. He joined the already outstanding secondary as his primary position.

The last time the Packers defeated a reigning NFL champion was in 1947 when they took it to the Bears, 29-26, winners of the 1946 title. Lombardi and company were hoping to repeat that performance against the Baltimore Colts at City Stadium on the third Sunday of the season. To add a little spice to the occasion, the league commissioner Pete Rozelle would be in attendance. Art Daley called the game the "acid test" for the Packers because the Colts appeared to be even better in 1960 than they had been in 1959. The oddsmakers made Baltimore six-point favorites over the Pack.

An old football axiom says something like this: "Offense is for pleasing your fans; defense is for winning games." That might not be the exact quote, but you get the point.

When the Colts roared into City Stadium on October 9, they had the most powerful offense in the NFL as shown by the whipping they gave the Bears the week before. By the time they left Green Bay that night, the Colts were no longer the mighty invincible scoring machine that the entire league had believed them to be. Not only that, they were no longer the only undefeated team in the Western Conference. The Colts returned to Baltimore with their tails bobbed by a Packer defense that swiped four of Johnny Unitas's passes and recovered two fumbles, while Green Bay's offense failed to turn the ball over even once. Baltimore amassed 435 yards of offense to the ' 245, but the Green Bay offense scored 35 points to the Colts' usually acceptable 21. Jim Taylor scored Green Bay's first three TDs on blasts of 12, three, and one yards. Tom Moore made a spectacular one-handed catch of a Lamar McHan pass for a 12-yard score that put the Packers ahead for good. Then McHan pulled a fast one with a QB sneak with 19 seconds to go in the game, racing past the demoralized defenders for 35 yards and the final six of the game.

Hank Gremminger had one of the finest games of his career. He held All-Pro Lenny Moore to just a pair of receptions, and he picked off two passes to set up a touchdown drives of 27 and 47 yards for the Green Bay offense. Emlen Tunnell and Jess Whittenton each grabbed an interception. Dan Currie recovered Baltimore's first fumble on the enemy 15, and the offense quickly converted it into a TD. The big play of the afternoon was made by Willie Davis near the midway point of the fourth quarter. Baltimore had the ball deep in their own territory when Davis busted into the Colts' backfield, forced Unitas to lose the ball, and then recovered it on the enemy four, setting up the Pack's fourth TD of the contest.

The win put the Packers into a four-way tie for first place in the Western Conference with Baltimore, Chicago winners over the Rams, 34-27, and San Francisco Lion tamers, 14-10, each having won twice and lost once. Detroit (0-2) sat in fifth, while Dallas beaten by Washington, 26-14 and Los Angeles were tied for last with three losses each.

New York (3-0) sat on top of the Eastern Conference after a narrow 19-17 defeat of Pittsburgh (1-2). Cleveland (2-0) now rested in second after having the week off. Philadelphia (2-1) owned third place for the moment by getting past St. Louis, 31-27. Washington (1-1) sat in fourth place, while the Steelers and Cards were tied for last.

The AFL races were in their fifth week, but neither division had yet to show a clear-cut leader. Houston (3-1) slipped by New York (3-2) for first place in the Eastern Division with a 27-21 win. The Patriots (2-2) occupied third, thanks to a 33-0 whipping they gave Los Angeles (2-3). The Buffalo Bills (1-3) had a bye and remained in the basement. Denver (3-1) had the other bye that week and held on to the top spot in the Western Division. Oakland (2-3) squeezed by Dallas (2-3) to create a three-way tie for second place.

Tragedy struck all of pro football that weekend when Howard Glenn, a guard for the New York Titans, was injured in the game with Houston. He left the game when the injury occurred and sat on the bench for the remainder of the contest. After showering, he took pills for the pain and drank a soft drink before being taken to a hospital after he became belligerent, hysterical, and going into a stupor while still in the locker room. Two hours later he died. An autopsy the next day revealed the cause of death to be a broken neck. As a result of the fracture, jagged pieces of bone eventually severed Glenn's spinal cord.

The AFL announced the league's average attendance had risen week-to-week for the first four weeks of the season. In Week 1, the average was 15,556; Week 2 average 16,506; Week 3 18,705; and Week 4 19,744. Dallas led the league in attendance with an average of 33,500 for three home games. No sellouts yet, but league officials had hopes for two the coming weekend when Dallas visited Houston and New York traveled to Buffalo.

On October 14, the AFL filed another lawsuit against the NFL, charging the older league with conspiracy to exclude the AFL and its eight teams from a share in the professional football business. The junior circuit asked the federal court to stop the NFL from granting new franchises in territories previously staked out by the AFL. This meant Atlanta, Miami, and New Orleans. On top of that request, the AFL asked the court to require the NFL to withdraw any franchises already granted, meaning the Dallas Cowboys and yet-to-be nicknamed Minnesota club. Of course, the suit had little merit, and the AFL owners knew it. Their true aim in suing the NFL was not to win a judgment, but to gain some parity with the older league in the eyes of the fans and the media, which was where they really expected to make some financial gain.

Owning a bye for the week was a two-edged sword for Green Bay. The week off gave Lombardi's boys a chance to heal up some of their bumps and bruises from playing three straight games against conference opponents, but it also meant they couldn't win a game and maintain a share of first place. Instead, the Packers slipped down a rung in the standings.

In games that were played in Week 4, the Bears (3-1) dropped the 49ers (2-2) into fourth place in the conference, 37-10, while keeping pace with the Colts (3-1), 31-17 winners over the Rams (0-4). The Lions (0-3) held on to their spot in fifth place, although losing to the Eagles by the score of 28-10. The Cowboys (0-4) took it on the chin from the Browns, 48-7, to remain in the cellar with the Rams.

Undefeated Cleveland (3-0) moved into first place in the Eastern Conference when the Giants (3-0-1) and Redskins (1-1-1) played to a 24-all tie. Philadelphia (3-1) continued to hold on to third place, and the Steelers (2-2) stepped up to fourth with a 27-14 win over the cellar-dwelling Cardinals (1-3).

The Houston Oilers (4-1) maintained a half-game lead in the AFL Eastern Division by downing the Dallas Texans (2-4), 20-10. New York (4-2) held on to second place with a 17-13 win over the cellar-dwelling Buffalo Bills (1-4). Boston (2-3) held on to third even though the Patriots lost, 27-14, to the Raiders (3-3). Denver (3-2) lost to Los Angeles (3-3), but the Broncos remained atop the Western Division. The Chargers and Oakland tied for second, and Dallas now occupied the basement.

After a week off for the players but not the coaches, the Pack returned to the practice field on Monday to begin preparing to meet the 49ers in Milwaukee. Lombardi had little to say about his team just before drills began. "They're all in good spirits." Then he blew a whistle to start them working again. All but John Symank were in good health. The defensive back suffered a severe leg bruise in the game against the Colts and had yet to heal.

The contest in Milwaukee would feature four of the NFL's

leading ground gainers. Jim Taylor and Paul Hornung for the Packers, and J.D. Smith and Hugh McElhenny for the 49ers. Green Bay had better averages than San Francisco by virtue of having played one less game. On paper, the 49ers appeared to have an edge over the Pack offensively because their quarterback was Y.A. Tittle, the eighth best passer in the league, whereas neither McHan nor Starr were even ranked. Fortunately, games are not played on paper.

Also confronting the Packers was the sad fact that they had lost nine straight regular season games in County Stadium.. This gave them more incentive to play well and hard come Sunday.

Fired up by a Lombardi pre-game speech, the Pack roared out of the dugout like the mounted Mongols of the Golden Horde racing across the Steppes to crush anybody foolish enough to stand in their way. In this case, the victims were invaders from the San Francisco Bay area of California. The game was half over before the 49ers came to the realization that they were totally outclassed by the boys from Green Bay.

Paul Hornung opened the scoring for the Packers with a one-yard leap into the end zone with 6:31 on the clock to complete Green Bay's 80-yard drive on its first drive of the day. Then Lamar McHan completed a 12-yard strike to Max McGee with 11 seconds left in the first quarter to put the Packers up 14-0. Rookie Tom Moore ran 12 yards to pay dirt early in the second stanza, and Hornung added three points to his count with a 47-yard field goal 5:31 before the half to give the Pack a 24-0 lead that held into the third quarter. Hornung booted his second field goal, this one for 32 yards, early in the second half to increase Green Bay's lead to 27-0. The 49ers finally erased their zero from the scoreboard late in the period to trail 27-7 going into the last period. The Packers countered with another touchdown by Hornung, a one-yard plunge, less than a minute into final frame. San Francisco scored once more on a short pass from Y.A. Tittle to R.C. Owens when the game was all but over. The last tally of the day was a three-yard run by Moore with a half minute on the clock to make the final score Green Bay 41, San Francisco 14.

The Packers' (3-1) win, combined with an upset of Detroit (1-3) over the Colts (3-2) and a tie between the Rams (0-4-1) and Bears (3-1-1), put Green Bay atop the Western Conference standings. In the Eastern Conference, idle New York (3-0-1) remained in first place. Philadelphia (4-1) nipped Cleveland (3-1) by a mere two points, 31-29, to move into second. The Steelers (2-2-1) held on to fourth by tying the Redskins (1-1-2), while St. Louis (2-3) started to show some life, narrowly squeezing by Dallas (0-5), 12-10.

In the junior circuit, Houston (5-1) increased its lead in the Eastern Division over New York (4-3) by handing the Titans a 42-29 loss. Buffalo (2-4) trounced Oakland (3-4) by a 38-9 count, moving the Bills into a tie for third with Boston (2-4), losers, 31-24, to Denver (4-2), leaders in the West. Los Angeles (3-3) and Dallas (2-4) both had the weekend off.

In the early days of football, eleven men were expected to play the entire game on both sides of the ball. As the years rolled by, substitutes became more and more important, especially as it became apparent that playing all 60 minutes of a game for 12 games a season was too taxing on the bodies of men who had been playing the game since childhood. Gradually, liberal substitution was allowed until the teams were no longer sending one, two, or more players at a time, but they were actually platooning with a first team offense and a first team defense. This eventually led to teams substituting running backs and receivers, depending on the game situation or just to let some of them catch their wind.

By 1960, the importance of bench players began reaching its peak. The next guy in had to be as good or nearly as good as the man he was replacing on the field. This was made very evident by remarks made by Lombardi after the game with the 49ers. Speaking about the Packers' backups, he said they were "better than last year." Then he rattled off a few names. "Meilinger, Carpenter, Masters, Ron Kramer, Wood," then added with a big grin, "and Moore." He could have put Cvercko, Temp, Beck, and Nitschke on that list as well. Each of them made solid contributions to the outcome of the game. Lombardi once again showed his touch for innovation by including several bench players on special teams. For example, the kickoff team included subs Hackbart, Winslow, Beck, Wood, Masters, Nitschke, Cvercko, Iman, and Pesonen.

The Packers faced the Steelers in Pittsburgh in Week 6. Bobby Layne led the Pitt offense, which was number one in the NFL going into the game. The oddsmakers favored Green Bay by a touchdown. For once the bookies nailed the spread on the head.

Green Bay wasn't the offensive machine that had ground out 14 touchdowns in its previous four games. The Pack controlled the ball all through the first quarter but couldn't cross the goal line once. Instead, Paul Hornung booted field goals of 35, 35, and 45 yards to put the Bays up 9-0. He added another three late in the second period, but the Steelers countered with a touchdown with just 13 seconds left in the half. After a scoreless third stanza, Pittsburgh took the lead with a TD with 12:07 remaining to be played. The home team held off the visitors until final five minutes of the contest. Bart Starr, who replaced Lamar McHan in the second half, engineered a 65-yard drive that culminated with Jim Taylor plunging over from a half-yard out with just 61 seconds left to play. The Packers' defense, which had been stout all day, held off a final push by Layne & Company to come away with Green Bay's fourth straight win, 19-13.

The victory gave the Pack a record of 4-1, strengthening their hold on first place in the Western Conference over 4-2 Baltimore, 45-7 winners over Dallas (0-6), and over the 3-2-1 Bears, victims of a resurgent San Francisco (3-3) club by a score of 25-7. Los Angeles (1-4-1) got into the win column by coming out on top in a 48-35 slugfest with Detroit (1-4). In the Eastern Conference, Cleveland (4-1) downed Washington (1-2-2) by a margin of 21 points, putting the Browns in a tie with the idle Eagles because St. Louis (3-3) slipped by New York, 20-13, moving the Giants (3-1-1) a half game behind the leaders. Pittsburgh's loss to Green Bay dropped the Steelers (2-3-1) into fifth place.

The AFL races tightened up when Buffalo (3-4) in the Eastern Division upset Houston (5-2) by the narrowest of margins, 25-24. Out West, Dallas (3-4) trimmed Denver (4-3) by a field goal, 17-14, to get back in contention. Los Angeles (4-3) tied for first place with their convincing 45-14 win over Boston (2-5), fourth place in the East. The Oakland Raiders (4-4) remained in the chase in the West, beating the New York Titans (4-4) by an extra point, 28-27.

"We're not any more wrought up over this game than we are for any other game," said Lombardi about the upcoming tiff with the Baltimore Colts. "This is our sixth game, and it happens that the Colts are our sixth opponent. This is like any other game. They're all tough. The only difference is the names. A week from today we'll be getting ready for Dallas. And they'll be tough."

This was the attitude Lombardi instilled in his team. No opponent could ever be taken for granted. As Pete Rozelle would say, "On any given Sunday…"

"We've got to beat the Packers, if we're going to win (another title)," said Baltimore coach Weeb Ewbank. "Nobody else is going to beat them for us."

The gamblers didn't pay much attention to all the rhetoric from the coaches. They installed the Colts as eight-point favorites to beat the Packers in Baltimore.

"Best game I've seen Packers play," said Lombardi after the tilt with the Colts.

Green Bay "played better than at home," said Ewbank.

The score might have indicated otherwise. Colts 38, Pack 24.

Baltimore jumped out to a 21-0 lead in the first half before the Packers offense finally found itself and put up a Jim Taylor four-yard touchdown just seconds before the two-minute warning signaled the closing of the second period. Paul Hornung scooted 10 yards for Green Bay's second TD with just 4:05 gone in the third stanza to bring the Pack to within seven points of the Colts who added a field goal to bring the score to 24-14. Hornung tacked on another six just 2:40 into the final quarter, and then he tied the game with a field goal five minutes later. That was the last of Green Bay's scoring. Baltimore mounted a drive on its next possession to retake the lead, 31-24. The Packers' next possession ended with an interception that set up the Colts' last touchdown.

The loss put Green Bay (4-2) a half-game behind Baltimore (5-2) in the Western Conference standings. Chicago (3-2-1) remained in third place with a bye. San Francisco (3-4) lost 24-0 to Detroit (2-4), while Los Angeles (2-4-1) pounded winless Dallas, 38-13. The Eastern Conference standings took a shuffle when Philadelphia (5-1) dominated Pittsburgh (2-4-1) to the tune of 34-7, and New York (4-1-1) stepped past Cleveland (4-2) for second place, 17-13. St. Louis (4-3) threw their hat in the race with a 44-7 whipping of last place Washington (1-3-2).

Now nine weeks into their inaugural campaign, the AFL was beginning to show some real competitive spirit. Houston (6-2) gave Denver (4-4) a 45-25 clipping to solidify its hold on first place in the Eastern Division. Los Angeles (5-3) took sole possession of the top spot in the Western Division with a 21-7 win over New York (4-5). Dallas (4-4) moved into second with Denver by downing Buffalo (3-5), 45-28. Oakland (4-5) dropped into last with a 34-28 loss to Boston (3-5).

In one of two off-field moves involving the two pro leagues, the Chicago Bears filed a $300,000 suit against the Los Angeles Chargers for inducing Ralph Anderson to break his contract with the Bears and play for the Chargers. George Halas said the suit was filed against the team rather than the player because he was convinced the Chargers' management had advised him to breach his deal with the NFL club. Papa Bear said, "There is no future for pro football unless responsible club officials adhere to ethical standards and honor contract obligations of all players and clubs." This was an amazing statement, considering the man who said it had committed many such violations of "ethical standards" over the past four decades.

The other piece of news was less provocative than the Bears' suit against the Chargers. NFL Commissioner Pete Rozelle issued an order to Harry Wismer to sell his stock in the Washington Redskins because he was the majority stockholder in the New York Titans of the AFL. Rozelle was perfectly within his authority to make such a declaration because to own stock in two pro teams, whether in the same league or in two, was a definite conflict of interest. Wismer had been vacillating about making the sale for some months, stating he had a buyer but not yet concluding the transaction. Rozelle stated he had waited long enough for Wismer to act and gave him a deadline to sell or the league would sell the stock for him. Wismer was hedging his bet on the success of the AFL franchise by holding on to his 25% interest in the Redskins. Rozelle merely called his bluff.

With their season half over now, the Packers stood as good a chance as any other team to win the division. They were only half a game behind the Colts, and that game was in the win column, not the loss column. Both Green Bay and Baltimore could win out, and if they did, they would be tied for first place, necessitating a playoff game for the right to play the Eastern Conference champ for the NFL title. That possibility haunted the hopes and dreams of Packer fans everywhere in the world.

The Dallas Cowboys sported seven former Packers on their roster when they came to town to play the Pack on November 13. Fred Cone, Billy Howton, Mike Falls, Don Mcllhenny, Tom Braatz, Nate Borden, and Billy Butler made up the list. Each hoped to play a prominent role in a potential upset of their former team, which was highly unlikely as the Packers were 21-point favorites to keep winless Dallas winless on the season. As things turned out, the oddsmakers were only being kind to the Cowboys.

In their first meeting of historic importance, Lombardi's boys easily handled Tom Landry's 'Boys, 41-7. Dallas proved to be totally overmatched from the very start.

The Cowboys received the opening kickoff, but they failed to do much and ended the possession with a punt. Green Bay's offense started their drive from their own 18 and drove the ball down the field to the Dallas 28, where Jim Taylor punched through the line and charged through the Cowboys' secondary for his first of three touchdowns. Dallas tried to return the favor, reaching the Packers 17 before Bill Quinlan forced a fumble that was recovered on the 25 by Henry Jordan. Starting his second straight game, Bart Starr engineered another scoring drive early in the second period, this time for 89 yards and ending with Taylor smashing through the line from the three for his second TD. Two minutes later Ray Nitschke snared a pass from Cowboys' quarterback Eddie LeBaron and returned it 43 yards for the third Green Bay touchdown. Just before the half ended, Jordan got a big mitt on a Dallas punt and Bill Forester returned it seven yards to the visitors' 25, setting up Paul Hornung for his first field goal of the day from the 21. With seconds left, Dan Currie intercepted another errant Dallas pass on the Cowboys' 47 and rumbled 34 yards to the 13 where Hornung booted another three to give the Packers a 27-0 lead at the midway point. Nitschke intercepted his second pass of the day on the Green Bay 35 and returned it to the Dallas 44. From there, Starr guided the offense to another Taylor touchdown from 20 yards out, to give the Packers an insurmountable lead, 34-0. Lamar McHan replaced Starr late in the period and engineered the last Green Bay scoring drive of the day with Hornung darting through the line from four yards out. Dallas scored a token touchdown with 7:03 left in the game to make the final margin. The Packers racked up 391 yards of offense to the Cowboys' 275, but the real difference in the game was the Green Bay defense that intercepted three passes, recovered two Dallas fumbles, and blocked one Dallas punt.

Green Bay's (5-2) victory only kept the Packers in pace with the Colts (6-2), 24-20 winners over the Bears (3-3-1). The Lions (3-4) moved into a tie for fourth with the idle 49ers (3-4) with a 12-10 win over the Rams (2-5-1). Dallas (0-8) remained on the bottom of the Western Conference pile. The Eastern Conference race was now down to a three-team finish with the Eagles (6-1) winners, 19-13, over the

Redskins (1-4-2), the Giants (5-1-1) victors, 27-24, over Pittsburgh (2-5-1), and the Browns (5-2) barely besting the 4-4 Cardinals, 28-27.

The AFL races tightened up with Los Angeles (6-3) beating Houston (6-3), Boston (4-5) defeating New York (4-6), Dallas (5-4) cruising by Denver (4-5), and Oakland (5-5) tripping up Buffalo (3-6).

Past incarnations of challengers to the NFL usually showed signs of failure in their first season. At least one team would be in deep financial difficulty by the halfway point of their inaugural season. Not so with the newest American Football League. Every franchise seemed to be on sound footing. Why? Simple answer. Television. The AFL's deal with the American Broadcasting Corporation, although not huge, provided some reliable cash flow, taking much of the burden off the owners to meet their regular payrolls. As long as the NFL didn't suck them into a bidding war for players, they felt certain their league would not only survive but would eventually thrive in the arena of professional football.

After the whipping the Pack put on Dallas, Art Daley pointed out the math for the rest of the season. Baltimore had four games left on their schedule, while Green Bay had five. Both teams had only two losses. Both teams could potentially win the rest of their regular games and tie for first place in the Western Conference. This would set up a playoff game between the two foes. In the words of Hall of Fame baseball pitcher and colorful analyst on CBS's Game of the Week Jay Hanna "Dizzy" Dean, the chances of a scenario like this happening were "slim and none." The Colts had to face the 49ers twice, the Lions, and the Rams. Ahead for the Packers were the Rams in Green Bay, the Lions on Thanksgiving Day in Detroit, the Bears in Chicago, and the 49ers and Rams in California. Neither the Colts nor the Packers had an easy road ahead of them and both teams knew it all too well.

The glamorous Rams from Los Angeles came to Wisconsin still smarting from a 12-10 loss to the Lions. Everybody knew what a dangerous opponent the Rams could be. In their last four games, LA had tied the Bears, tamed the Lions, lassoed the Cowboys, and lost by a mere two points to Detroit in the Motor City. In the parlance of the time, the Rams were getting it together and were ready to butt heads with anybody.

Oddsmakers installed the Packers as 13-point favorites to beat the Rams. Every bettor who took LA and the points cleaned up that Sunday. The gamblers failed to understand one key factor about the game of football. Turnovers. Fumbles and interceptions are totally unpredictable. History is full of upsets where the difference was one shocking miscue by the favored team. In this case, the Packers made five such misdemeanors; three lost fumbles and two stolen passes. The man in the hat, glasses, and overcoat stalking the home team's portion of the sideline lamented this as the reason for his team's defeat.

"We gave up the ball five times too many," said Lombardi.

Other than those mistakes, the Packers completely outplayed the visitors from La-La-Land. Green Bay trailed the Rams, 30-10, in the third quarter before playing a flawless eight minutes that produced three touchdowns and the lead, 31-30. Then just as victory appeared to be inevitable, Paul Hornung missed a 23-yard field goal. On the next possession, Hornung fumbled and the Rams recovered on their 40 with 3:44 left in the game. LA drove 58 yards to the Green Bay two where kicker Danny Villanueva booted a nine-yard field goal for the win, 33-31. Although Lombardi said his team committed five too many turnovers, the truth was it was the last giveaway that cost them the game.

Hornung scored 19 points on two TDs, four PATs, and one field goal. Tom Moore raced 60 yards around end for a touchdown, and Boyd Dowler caught an 18-yard pass from Hornung for a six. If not for the fumble and missed chip-shot field goal, the Golden Boy played one of his best games ever.

The loss put the Packers (5-3) a full game in back of the Colts (6-2). The Bears (4-3-1) thumped the Lions (3-5) by a 28-7 score to get back into contention. San Francisco (4-4) kept up their faint hopes of winning the Western Conference, defeating 0-9 Dallas, 26-14. With their win, the Rams (3-5-1) remained in sixth place. Philadelphia (7-1) still reigned over the Eastern Conference with a 17-10 defeat of the second place Giants (5-2-1). Pittsburgh (3-5-1) upset the Browns (5-3) by a 14-10 score, while St. Louis (5-4) handed Washington (1-5-2) a 26-14 loss. Dallas was eliminated from the Western Conference race two weeks earlier, while Pittsburgh and Washington fell out of the running this week.

Houston (7-3) was beginning to show dominance in the AFL with a 20-10 victory over Denver (4-6). Boston (5-5) kept pace with a 42-14 thrashing of Dallas (5-5). Buffalo (4-6) snared five interceptions and smacked Los Angeles (6-4), leaders in the Western Division, 32-3. With four weeks to play, all eight teams still had a mathematical chance of winning their division.

The Packers spent Thanksgiving in the Motor City as guests of the Detroit Lions. More often than not, the Lions were very rude hosts. On this Turkey Day, they didn't have to be unkind because the Packers played like a bunch of blithering idiots in front of a national television audience. Detroit came away with a 23-10 victory to the joy of 54,123 fans. As Art Daley put it, "Every club will get hit with at least one such catastrophe, but it was a shame that Green Bay's stinker came at this time." The loss dropped the Pack into third place a half game behind the Bears and two behind the Colts. Barring a total disaster by Baltimore in their last four games, Green Bay appeared to be out of the race for the Western Conference title. Their only consolation was the fact that they had 10 days to rest up for their next opponent, the Monsters of the Midway at Wrigley Field in Chicago.

Mathematically speaking, the Eagles (8-1) needed only one more win or one loss by both the Giants (5-3-1) and Browns (5-3-1) to clinch the Eastern Conference crown. Philadelphia handed New York its third loss, while St. Louis (5-4-1) held Cleveland to a tie. In a battle with cellar dweller Washington (1-6-2), Pittsburgh (4-5-1) came away with a win, 22-10.

Five teams remained in the Western Conference race. The Colts (6-3) fell to the 49ers (5-4) by a score of 30-22. Chicago (5-3-1) moved closer to Baltimore with a 17-7 defeat of Dallas (0-10) and stepped over the Packers (5-4), losers to Detroit (4-5). The Lions would need a miracle to overcome the four teams ahead of them, and Dallas would have to wait until next year before they could even think of challenging the existing powers of the West.

In the AFL, Houston (8-3) clinched at least a tie for first place in the Eastern Division with a 24-10 win over Boston (5-6) before a capacity crowd of 27,123 ardent Beantown fans. New York (5-6) sat in the same boat as Boston, but Buffalo (4-6-1) fell out of contention when the Bills played Denver (4-6-1) to the league's first ever tie, 38 all. Out west, Los Angeles (7-4) put the hurt on Oakland (5-6) by a 52-28 margin. This put the Raiders in a tie with idle Dallas (5-6). Both the Oilers and Chargers needed one more win to earn a spot in the AFL's first title game.

On a very sad note, tragedy struck Packerland that same weekend. Jack Vainisi, the man who practically built the Green Bay team of 1960 through the draft, died unexpectedly at his home that

Sunday afternoon. Players and team officials thought highly of Vainisi. The 33-year-old business manager and chief scout of the team collapsed in the bathroom of his home and was dead by the time a city rescue squad arrived. Physicians said his death was caused by a chronic rheumatic heart condition. His obituary appeared on the front page of the *Press-Gazette* of Monday November 28. Vainisi was inducted into the Green Bay Packers Hall of Fame in 1982.

With both the Bears and Colts ahead of them and the 49ers tied with them in the standings, the Packers' hopes of winning the Western Conference crown seemed dim at best. Green Bay needed two things to happen for them to find themselves atop the division at season's end. The Pack had to run the table on their own, while Baltimore dropped two out of three; the Monsters of the Midway lost twice, including once to Green Bay; and San Francisco dropped a pair. Was this a tall order? Only the tallest. But then again, the Packers had Vince Lombardi at their helm.

Going into Chicago, as history has shown, is never an easy task for the Packers, especially during the years that George Halas coached his own team. So far, the Bears were 2-1 over the Pack since Lombardi arrived in Green Bay. Everyone in Packerland hoped their Men of the Frozen Tundra would even the score this time around.

This game was the 85th regular season contest between the two teams. The Packers had won in Chicago only once in nearly two decades, beating the Bruins, 41-28, in 1952, 11 years after their previous victory in Wrigley Field, 16-14.

Players, coaches, fans, and sports media expected a brutal brawl by battling bruisers on both borders of the ball, and they weren't disappointed when neither eleven could gain an advantage in a scoreless first quarter. From that point forward, the Packers held sway over their hosts.

Paul Hornung kicked a 21-ard field goal to get the ball rolling at the 14:54 mark of the second period. Willie Davis blocked a punt and recovered it in the end zone for a six with 2:07 on the clock to give the Pack a 10-0 lead that they would not relinquish. The Bears managed a TD with 48 seconds left in the half, but Green Bay quickly retaliated with a 41-yard Hornung boot with one tick left in the half, increasing the lead to 13-6.

Hornung added a touchdown reception to his scoring early in the third frame on a pass from Bart Starr who played the best game of his career to date, completing 17 of 23 passes for 218 yards and a pair of scores and not throwing a single interception or losing a fumble. Jim Taylor put up a six of his own with 4:46 left in the stanza to give the Packers a 3-TD lead at 27-6. Chicago put up its final points of the game shortly afterward. From there, the game was all Green Bay with a 10-yard TD run by Hornung to start the final quarter and a 4-yard scoring pass from Starr to Max McGee at the 7:19 mark.

Taylor had a big day running the ball, gaining 140 yards on 24 carries. McGee hauled in six passes for 121 yards, and Boyd Dowler also caught six for 63 yards. The big stat of the day was the 23 points Hornung put on the board. This gave him 152 for the year, breaking the mark of 138 set by Don Hutson in 1942.

The 41-13 final was the biggest margin of victory by the Packers over the Bears to date. More importantly, the win over Chicago (5-4-1) put Green Bay (6-4) into a three-way tie for first place in the Western Conference with Baltimore (6-4) who lost, 20-15, to Detroit (5-5) and with the 49ers (6-4) who won, 23-7, over Los Angeles (3-6-1). Expansion team Dallas (0-10-1) finally made a positive move toward respectability by playing the Giants (5-3-2) to a 31-all tie.

Philadelphia (9-1) clinched the Eastern Conference title with a 20-6 win over St. Louis (5-5-1). Cleveland (6-3-1) won, 37-16, over Washington (1-7-2) in a valiant attempt to stay in the race with the Eagles that gained them the lead for second place.

The Dallas Texans (6-6) and the New York Titans (6-6) each kept their faint hopes alive to tie for first in their respective division of the AFL by winning crucial games. Dallas dumping Houston (8-4) by a 24-0 score, and New York nipping Denver (4-7-1) by a field goal, 30-27. Los Angeles (8-4) clinched a tie for first in the West, mauling Oakland (5-7) by a tally of 41-17. Buffalo (5-6-1) finally climbed out of the Eastern cellar by giving Boston (5-7) a 38-14 clubbing.

The Western Conference chase for the crown was now hotter than ever. Five of the division's seven entries still had a chance to rise to the top. The Packers still had their annual West Coast swing at San Francisco and Los Angeles. Baltimore would be playing the same two teams in California as well. The 49ers would face Green Bay and then the Colts. Chicago's first opponent was the Browns in Cleveland and then a visit to Detroit for their season finale. The Lions appeared to have the easiest schedule with home games against Dallas and Chicago. Of the five contenders, San Francisco appeared to have the best shot at winning the division because they had been playing excellent ball as of late and their last two games were at home. The Colts and the Packers found themselves in the same situation, as both needed wins on the road, a tough task to say the least.

The first fight in the frenzy to gain an upper hand in the standings was scheduled for Saturday at Kezar Stadium where the Pack would square off against San Francisco and its new shotgun offense. Both Lombardi and Red Hickey of the 49ers knew the key to the game would be their defenses. Which one could stop the other's vaunted offense? The Packers boasted one of the best running attacks in the league, while San Francisco's offense was led by quarterbacks Y.A. Tittle and young John Brodie. Lombardi prepared his team in secret at Stanford University, while Hickey worked his boys openly at their practice facility in San Francisco. The bookies placed the Packers as four-point favorites before it was announced that Paul Hornung and Forrest Gregg had injuries that might keep them from playing the game.

A 1973 song lyric (from the hit song, *It Never Rains in Southern California* by Albert Hammond) says, "It never rains in California, but, girl, don't they warn you, it pours, man, it pours."

On Saturday, December 10, 1960, the rain poured down on northern California, turning the gridiron of Kezar Stadium into a greasy quagmire. Noting the condition of the field, Lombardi and his defensive aide, Phil Bengtson, put their heads together and came up with a strategy to deal with the mud and the 49ers' offensive attack. "We gave them the middle and rushed hard to the outside," said the coach. This stratagem held San Francisco to a total of 81 yards and no points. Unable to get by the Packers on the ground, the Gold Rush Boys were forced to take to the air, throwing 25 passes, completing a mere nine, and having two intercepted—one by Hank Gremminger and the other by Jess Whittenton.

The sloppy field didn't affect the Packers offense as much as it did 49'ers. Lombardi knew that he had the best running tandem in the Western Conference in Jim Taylor and Paul Hornung, so he placed the burden of moving the ball squarely on their broad shoulders. The Golden Boy carried the ball 19 times for 86 yards; a good day's work. Taylor lugged the rock 27 carries for 161 yards. All 13 Packer points were put on the board by Hornung; six on a 28-yard dash to pay dirt, one on a PAT, and six more on a pair of field goals.

Taylor's day was record-setting. His 161 yards raised his total to 1,059 breaking Tony Canadeo's single-season mark of 1,052. As a cherry on the icing, his 27 carries upped his season total to 213. Both numbers broke Canadeo's records of 26 and 208, respectively. Green Bay's tough fullback was happy with the new standards he had set, but he took more joy out of the congratulatory hug and words he received from Canadeo who was present at the game.

"I'm glad you got it, Jim," said Canadeo in the locker room after the game. "It helped us win. Congratulations!"

Both men showed the true spirit of what it meant to be a Packer in that moment.

The 13-0 victory gave the Packers (7-4) sole possession of first place in the Western Conference. Trailing them in a three-way tie for second, one full game behind at 6-5, were Baltimore, losers to the Rams, 10-3; Detroit, 23-14 winners over Dallas (0-11-1); and San Francisco. To the delight of all Packerdom, the Bears (5-5-1) were eliminated from the race, 42-0, by Cleveland (7-3-1).

With first place in the Eastern Conference already locked up, the Eagles (9-2) lost, 27-21, to the Steelers (5-5-1). The Giants (6-3-2) put a lock on at least third place in the division, beating the Redskins (1-8-2) with defense, 17-3.

With a week remaining in the regular season, the two division titles were settled in the AFL. Houston (9-4) captured the Eastern crown with a 31-23 win over Buffalo ((5-7-1), and Los Angeles (9-4) clinched Western honors with a 41-33 victory over Denver (4-8-1). Dallas (7-6) guaranteed it would finish second in the West with a solid 34-0 whipping of Boston (5-8). New York (7-6) did likewise in the East by narrow 31-28 defeat of Oakland (5-8). LA and Houston would play for the AFL's initial championship on New Year's Day in Houston.

The Packers now held their fate in their own hands now. All they needed to win the division was a victory over or a tie with the Rams to claim the title.

If Green Bay were to lose to LA, the Pack would then be in a tie with the winner of the San Francisco-Baltimore game and possibly with Detroit as well, if the Lions should also win their game against the Bears. A tie of three teams would result in two weeks of playoffs to determine who would face Philadelphia in the championship game. Commissioner Pete Rozelle had already held a coin toss to determine who would get the bye in that scenario. It would be the winner of the 49ers-Colts game. Green Bay would travel to Detroit, and the winner of that game would get to play at home once more against either

Baltimore or San Francisco. The winner of that game would then play the Eagles on the second Sunday in January of 1961.

The next scenario would be a tie between Detroit and Green Bay, which could be caused by a tie between the 49ers and Colts, a loss by the Packers and a win by the Lions. Should Baltimore and San Francisco tie and Detroit win and the Pack lose, then the Lions would be tied for first with Green Bay and the playoff game would be held at City Stadium on the day after Christmas, a Monday but still a holiday for America.

Excitement was rampant in all four cities as the final weekend of the regular season approached. The Packers would be playing in Los Angeles on Saturday, December 17. Fans in Detroit, Baltimore, and San Francisco were all pulling for the Rams to repeat their performance of November 20 in when they came away with 33-31 victory over the Packers. Such an outcome would fire up the mood in Detroit when the Lions faced the Bears in the Eastern Time Zone and in Frisco when the 49ers squared off with Colts in the Pacific Time Zone. If Green Bay should lose, Sunday would be a real nail-biting day for Detroit, Baltimore, and San Francisco followers.

But if the Packers should defeat the Rams, then Sunday would be just another day in NFL history.

Thanks to television, the bonus money NFL players would receive for participating in the title game would amount to something close to $6,000. For some Packer players, this would be nearly a year's salary. For every Packer, the extra payday was real incentive for them to bust their tails in their preparations for the contest with the Rams. At Monday morning's team breakfast, the players requested practice that day instead of taking the day off as Lombardi had planned. The coach had absolutely no qualms about granting their wish. Big Dave Hanner remarked that the unscheduled practice was "good for everybody because I guess we've all been celebrating a little bit over the weekend." Art Daley punctuated Hanner's quote by writing: "That was an understatement."

The *Green Bay Press-Gazette* printed a special souvenir edition on Sunday, December 18, 1960 that consisted of four pages and no advertising whatsoever. Why? Because the Packers won the Western Division of the National Football League the day before by defeating the Los Angeles Rams, 35-21, and the special printing only cost five cents.

The headline read:

Packers Win Title; On to Philadelphia

The headline for the two-column game story read:

Beat Rams 35-21 On Aerial Bombs
Clinch First Western Crown Since '44:
Face Eagles in Dec. 26 Playoff

Art Daley did himself proud with the story he wrote that day of the game. He wrote with the heartfelt joy of a true Packer fan. "The Packers are Western Division champions." A temporary lapse of memory there. The Packers won the Western Conference, not division. But who really cared? The two words meant the same thing basically. He was excited that his team was headed to the title game in Philadelphia. So, who could fault him for his exuberance?

Green Bay won the game with big plays on offense, a timely defense that forced three pass interceptions and a fumble recovery, and a blocked punt and recovery for a touchdown by special teams.

Los Angeles scored on their first possession with a 40-yard pass play just three minutes and 32 seconds into the game. Green Bay balanced the board with 40 seconds left in the period when Bart Starr connected a on 57-yard bomb to Max McGee. At the 11:21 mark in the second quarter, the Packers took the lead for good on a 91-yard pass play from Starr to Boyd Dowler. After a 12-yard sack of Ram quarterback Bill Wade by Packer defensive end Bill Quinlan, LA was forced to punt from its own end zone. Little used Paul Winslow raced into the Ram backfield, blocked the kick, and then recovered it for a touchdown to give the invaders from Wisconsin a two-score lead. The quarter was capped off with a halfback pass from Paul Hornung to McGee for 42 yards and another six with 5:31 on the clock. Green Bay led, 28-7, at the half. After a scoreless third stanza, LA gave it the old college try in an attempt at a comeback. The Rams scored a TD just 48 seconds into the final frame. Then the Packers delivered the deathblow on their next possession. They drove down the field to the LA 35. On the next play, pass interference was called on the Rams at their own four-yard line. After two short gains by Jim Taylor, Hornung lunged into the end zone for the final Green Bay tally, giving Green Bay an insurmountable 35-14 lead with 5:31 left on the clock. LA scored quickly after that, but a short kickoff by the Rams was hauled in by Tom Moore and returned 16 yards to the Packer 35. Green Bay ran off the next four minutes before punting. With less than two minutes to go, LA threw in the towel replacing their regular QB with his backup to finish the game.

When the final gun sounded, the Packers hoisted their coach onto their shoulders and carried him off the field in triumph, a fete they hadn't done since the defeat of the Bears in Lombardi's first game as their new boss.

Back in Wisconsin, Packer fans throughout the state rushed outside their homes and places of business to honk their car horns in celebration of their team winning the Western Conference for the first time since 1944. People in rural areas even stepped out into the December cold with their shotguns and deer rifles to shoot them into the air to celebrate the victory. Men in drinking establishments shook hands with each other to share their jubilation over their boys taking the division crown. Women hugged each other as well and for the same reason. Strangers in town might have thought it was V-E Day or V-J Day all over again. Close. Very close. At least the displays of so much emotion was near to those two historic occasions. For Packer fans, that is.

The Packers, players and coaches and team officials alike, didn't have to watch the scoreboard or listen to the radio or watch the sports on television the next day. It made no difference to them who beat who on Sunday. Philadelphia had wrapped the Eastern title two weeks earlier, and now Green Bay had the Western. The outcomes on Sunday mattered only to the teams vying for second place in their respective divisions because the two clubs that won those spots would be playing one more game, which would be on January 7 in what was called the Playoff Bowl in Miami.

Detroit (7-5) and San Francisco (7-5) wound up sharing second place in the West as the Lions spanked the Bears, 36-0, and the 49ers downed the Colts, 34-10. The Lions earned a spot in the Miami game by virtue of having scored more points than the 49ers in their two encounters during the regular season. Baltimore (6-6) copped fourth, while Chicago (5-6-1) limped home in fifth. The loss to Green Bay kept the Rams (4-7-1) in sixth, and the expansion Cowboys (0-11-1) brought up the rear.

Oddly, the only team in the East without a tie in its record was the Eagles (10-2). Cleveland (8-3-1) finished second winning, 48-34, over New York (6-4-2), thus, garnering a shot at Detroit in the Playoff Bowl. The Giants claimed third place. Fourth place in the East went to St. Louis (6-5-1) who beat out Pittsburgh (5-6-1) with a Sunday victory over the Steelers, 38-7. Washington (1-9-2) lost to Philadelphia, 38-28, to wind up their dismal season in the cellar.

The AFL races had been settled a week earlier, but the league had one week to play out their inaugural season. Oakland (6-8), Dallas (8-6), Los Angeles (10-4), and Houston (10-4) won their last games, respectively, 48-10 over Denver (4-9-1), 24-7 over Buffalo (5-8-1), 50-43 over New York (7-7), and 37-21 over Boston (5-9).

The Packers set a new single season scoring record with 332 points, erasing the old mark of 300 set in 1942. They also tied the record for touchdowns scored in a single season, matching the number of 41 posted by the 1942 team. Lombardi's team shattered the record of 20 touchdowns scored on running plays set by the 1950 squad by crossing the goal line 31 times.

Paul Hornung raised his season scoring total to 176 points, far outdistancing Don Hutson's standard of 138 that had stood since 1942. Hornung's total came on 15 touchdowns, 15 field goals, and 41 extra points. His PAT total surpassed Hutson's 36 mark.

Jim Taylor finished the year with 1,101 yards gained on the ground on 230 carries, topping Tony Canadeo's records of 1,052 yards and 208 attempts set in 1949.

All things considered, the 1960 Packers must be hailed as the first great team of the post-World War II era. Not one ever to sit on his laurels, Coach Lombardi knew this was just the first of many titles he intended to win with the Green Bay Packers. Or just maybe, with the New York Giants. Only time would tell.

§§§

12

The "Cinderella Bowl"

"The Fearsome Foursome" was the title of an article published in the first edition of *Green Bay Packers Yearbook*. The author was the first professor emeritus of Packer history, trivia, and anecdotes, Lee Remmel. In the story, he wrote:

"Mountainous Ray Nitschke poked a huge index finger into the chest of his captive listener and declared with a vigor that brooked no disagreement, 'We've got the greatest football team in America right now. And you wanna know something else?' he asked, punctuating his rhetorical query with another jab of that meaty digit. 'We're going to win the championship next year, and I'll be in there all the way. They won't be able to keep me on the bench.'"

Nitschke's prediction was made for the 1961 season. With the Packers winning the Western Division title for 1960, it appeared he might be a little early with his prognostication.

Green Bay Press-Gazette writer Ralph Bernstein wrote a very interesting piece about the upcoming championship game. He called it the "Cinderella Bowl" because both the Eagles and the Packers had finished last in their respective divisions just two years earlier. That year Philadelphia won just one more game than Green Bay did. The Eagles were in the first year of rebuilding, while the Packers were just getting started.

In the years prior to World War II, the Eagles finished in third place once, 1934. Every other season they could rise no higher than fourth. They were no better in 1942, but in 1943, when they were mixed together with the Steelers and were known as the Steagles, they enjoyed their first winning season in their history. When they resumed their own identity in 1944, they started a streak of seven consecutive winning campaigns, including three division titles in a row, 1947-49, and back-to-back NFL Championships, shutting out the Chicago

Cardinals, 7-0, in 1948 and the Los Angeles Rams, 14-0, in 1949.

The 1950s started with a mediocre 6-6 record and a 4-8 mark. A new coach, Jim Trimble, took the reins in 1952 and reeled off three winning campaigns before suffering a 4-7-1 tally in 1955. Another coaching change, Hugh Devore, failed to improve the Eagles. They floundered in the division basement and could only rise to fifth place in 1957. A housecleaning was in order.

Enter Lawrence Timothy "Buck" Shaw.

Known more by his nickname than his given name, Buck Shaw was another memorable branch on the Knute Rockne coaching tree. Born in 1899 in Mitchellville, Iowa, a small town 10 miles east of Des Moines, Buck was one of five children. At age 10, his family moved to Stuart, Iowa just west of West Des Moines, where high school football had been abolished due to a fatality. The sport was not revived in Stuart until 1917. Shaw played only four football games at Stuart High School in his senior year. The following fall he enrolled at Creighton University in Omaha and went out for football. After only one game, the season was canceled due to the flu epidemic that was plaguing the country.

Fate seemed to be guiding Shaw's life. In the spring of 1919, he transferred to Notre Dame in order to participate on the track and field team. That was when he met Rockne who convinced him to try out for the football team in the fall. On the gridiron, Rockne molded Shaw into one of the greatest tackles and placekickers in Notre Dame history. Buck was a three-year starter, first at left tackle in 1919 and then at right tackle the following two seasons. He finished his playing career by being named an All-American by *Football World Magazine.*

Shaw. began his head coaching career at North Carolina State where he directed his team to 2-6-2 record. The South didn't appeal to him all that much, so he resigned and moved west to the University of Nevada. After four seasons there with little success, he joined the staff of former Notre Dame teammate Maurice "Clipper" Smith who had just taken the head coach's position at Santa Clara University in California. Shaw was the line coach under Smith.

Yet another branch on the Rockne coaching tree, Clipper Smith compiled a record of 108-76-12 over 22 seasons as a college head mentor with stops at Gonzaga University in Spokane, Washington; Santa Clara; Villanova University in Philadelphia; the University of San Francisco; and Lafayette University in Easton,

Pennsylvania. He also coached the Boston Yanks of the NFL in 1947-48. While at Gonzaga, he also coached the basketball team four all for years and the baseball team for one year.

When Smith resigned from Santa Clara to take the Villanova post, Shaw was named the head coach. He led the Broncos to seven consecutive winning seasons that included two Sugar Bowl victories over LSU and five top 20 finishes in the final *Associated Press* College Football Poll. World War II pre-empted football at Santa Clara after the 1942 campaign. After the war, Buck coached the Golden Bears of the University of California in Berkeley for one season before joining the pro ranks.

The organizers of the All-America Football Conference held off starting play in their new league until the war in Europe and the war with Japan came to an end. However, they did hire front office personnel and head coaches. The Morabito brothers, Victor and Tony, held the franchise for San Francisco. They hired Shaw. and his long-time assistant Al Ruffo to coach their 49ers. Shaw directed San Francisco to four consecutive second place finishes in the AAFC; three in the Western Division and one when the league was pared down to seven teams in its final season before merging with the NFL in 1950.

Shaw and his 49ers found the competition in the NFL to be a lot tougher than it had been in the AAFC. San Francisco suffered its first losing season in 1950, but it was the last under Shaw. He led the team to four more winning campaigns before leaving the club.

After a year off from coaching, Shaw became the second head coach of the Air Force Academy in 1956. He stayed only two seasons before accepting his next NFL job with the Philadelphia Eagles.

Buck knew he had a monster rebuilding task ahead of him. He started by trading two linemen and a first-round draft choice to the Los Angeles Rams for the rights to quarterback Norm Van Brocklin, a nine-year veteran who had announced his retirement from football in January that year. Rumors had it that "Stormin' Norman" had thrown in the towel due to a personality clash with Rams coach Sid Gillman. The truth was Van Brocklin didn't want to play another season in Gillman's offense. Shaw promised "The Dutchman" that he would have full control of the offense in Philadelphia. Van Brocklin had one question: "Where do I sign?"

Born in South Dakota, Van Brocklin grew up in California.

After three years of high school, he enlisted in the U.S. Navy at the age of 17. When the war ended, he enrolled at the University of Oregon at Eugene, Oregon and became the starting quarterback in 1947. The following year he led the Ducks to an undefeated season in the Pacific Coast Conference and an appearance in the Cotton Bowl against Southern Methodist University. Oregon lost, but Van Brocklin was named his team's most outstanding player for the game. The next year he left school to enter the 1949 pro football draft.

The Los Angeles Rams picked Van Brocklin in the 4th Round, 37th overall. LA already had a star quarterback in future Hall of Famer Bob Waterfield. Van Brocklin served as Waterfield's backup tin 1949, then new head coach Joe Stydahar platooned the two signal-callers the next year. Airing out the ball to receivers Tom Fears, and Elroy "Crazy Legs" Hirsch, the two passers finished first and second in the ratings of quarterbacks that year. The Rams scored 466 points for the regular season for an average of 38.8 per game, a record that still stands at the time of this writing. Van Brocklin and Waterfield failed to defeat the Cleveland Browns in the title game that year. The following season they led the Rams to their first and only NFL title in Los Angeles as of this writing.

When Waterfield retired after the 1952 campaign, the starting job fell to Van Brocklin alone. Over the next five years he posted a record of 30 wins, 18 losses, and three ties, not including a loss in the 1955 title game against Cleveland, the only year his Rams won the Western Conference title. After suffering through his worst season in the NFL in 1957, Van Brocklin decided he'd had enough of Sid Gilman's offense and "retired" to go into business in Oregon. Then along came Buck Shaw who talked him into playing just a few more years.

Buck Shaw had seen Van Brocklin play against his 49ers twice a year over five seasons. He recognized "The Dutchman" not just as a great passer, but also as a superb field general. To Shaw, Van Brocklin was a gridiron genius. He saw Norm as a true leader who could help him mold the Eagles into the same kind of scoring machine that the Rams had been. To Shaw, Norm Van Brocklin was the first and most important piece in his plan to restore the Philadelphia Eagles to the prominence they had achieved just a decade earlier.

Shaw inherited a team that had gone 4-8 for Hugh Devore, the man he replaced who was also a fellow Notre Dame alumnus. He retained just 17 of Devore's players for the 1958 season. The rest of the roster was filled with seven rookies and 11 veterans acquired by trades, free agent signings, or off the waiver wires. Shaw brought in Jerry Williams as his defensive backs coach, and he retained Charlie Gauer who had been with Eagles for several years coaching pass catchers. Despite having six Pro-Bowlers and three future Pro Football Hall of Famers, Philadelphia's record for Shaw's and Van Brocklin's first season together was a sad 2-9-1.

Just like the Packers in 1959, the Eagles showed remarkable improvement over their previous campaign, finishing with a record of 7-5 and landing in second place in their division. Again, Shaw did a lot of house-cleaning to his roster, adding 11 rookies and nine veterans by trades, free agency, or off waivers. He also added Nick Skorich to the coaching staff.

By the start of the 1960 season, the Philadelphia roster was made up 26 holdovers from 1959, five rookies, and eight pickups by trade, free agency, or off waivers. Counted among the first-year men were Tim Brown and Bobby Jackson, both drafted by the Packers in 1959 and then released; Brown after just one game and Jackson before the regular season began. The Eagles also picked up Bobby Freeman from the Packers that benefitted both teams.

The Eagles started off the 1960 season with a 41-24 loss to the Cleveland Browns. Then Shaw got his boys into high gear as they rattled off nine straight wins, six of them by eight points or less. After suffering an upset in Pittsburgh, the Eagles completed their division title season with a solid victory over the Redskins, 38-28, on the road. In seven of their 10 victories, the Eagles trailed heading into the fourth quarter, but still came out the victors.

Success for the Eagles in 1960 was often described as a team triumph. Philadelphia newspaper reporter Ralph Bernstein begged to differ. He wrote: "But if any one man ever hand-whipped a team to a championship, it was the fabulous Dutchman, Norm Van Brocklin." Bernstein supported his estimation of why the Eagles dominated their conference with a quote from quarterback Charley Conerly of the New York Giants. "Without Van the Eagles are nothing."

One of the great pro passers of his era, the 34-year old Van Brocklin made what he insisted was his last season as a player his greatest of his 12-year career. Bernstein declared: "Not only his passing, but his play direction an inspirational performance in the clutch lifted this team to heights beyond its visible capability." For the season, Van Brocklin completed 145 of 269 passes, good for 2,281 yards and 22 touchdowns.

After Van Brocklin, the Eagles had a host of heroes, but if the Philadelphia players had to pick out just one more, then the choice would most likely have gone to Chuck Bednarik, the team's old war horse and the last man to play on both sides of the ball for the full 60 minutes of a game. Bednarik had perhaps his greatest season since he broke in with the World Champion Eagles of 1949. Twice during the 1960 campaign the former Pennsylvania University All-American turned in two outstanding key performances; one against Cleveland and the other against the Giants. Art Donovan, the Hall of Fame defensive end for the Baltimore Colts, had one comment about the Eagles rugged center/linebacker: "He's nuts."

In Philadelphia's first game with the Giants, played in New York, Van Brocklin was blitzed unmercifully in the first half as Sam Huff, the Hall of Fame middle linebacker, and his teammates ran over rookie Eagles center Bill Lapham. Bednarik, who had been playing his usual linebacker spot on defense, took over the ball-snapping duties in the third quarter. On the first offensive play, Bednarik looked Huff in the eye and said, "Sam, the fun is over. The pros are in now." The Eagles rallied from a 10-0 deficit to win, 17-10.

Bernstein pointed out that any recap of the 1960 Philadelphia season had to contain special mentions for end Bobbie Walston who was second only to Paul Hornung in scoring with 97 points; for the sensational pass receiving of Van Brocklin's favorite target Tommy McDonald and for veteran Pete Retzlaff; for the punt and kickoff returns of Green Bay castoff Tim Brown; for the defensive secondary of Tom Brookshire, Jimmy Carr, and Don Burroughs, interceptors of 22 passes collectively; and for rookie running back Ted Dean who took over for starter Clarence Peaks after Peaks fractured an ankle.

In an article written by *Associated Press* reporter George Esper, Shaw summed up his feelings about facing the Packers in Franklin Field on Monday, December 26, which was a national holiday because Christmas fell on a Sunday that year.

"They've got a good, solid football team," said Shaw (of the Packers). "They've got good blocking offensive(ly) and good power running. They are one of the strongest, if not the strongest, running teams in the league."

Shaw said the Eagles' advantage would be "a little better passing attack. But I'm not discounting them on passing. If they get plenty of time to throw, they can hurt you as they did against the Rams. Bart Starr and Lamar McHan throw well and the line gives them plenty of protection. They've got good receivers in Boyd Dowler and Max McGee."

Shaw said that he hoped to stem the Packers running attack by using Chuck Bednarik at outside linebacker in addition to snapping the ball on offense. He indicated that he might call on Bednarik to play every down of the game because Bob Pelligrini, the regular outside linebacker, had suffered a severe knee injury in the Eagles' final game of the regular season and was thought to be facing surgery.

As for the preparation for the championship game, Lombardi said, "Our schedule is no different than for any other game. This is still another football game."

Lombardi had little to say about Philadelphia as he prepared the Packers for the title game. "They'll be ready for the Eagles. This is a new game, and they won't be under the pressure they were last week." And that was that until the game was over.

The oddsmakers had the Packers as 2½ point favorites in what many expected to be a high scoring contest. Chuck Bednarik said this gave the Eagles a little more incentive to play harder than usual. As he put it, being rated the underdog is "great. Makes you a little hungrier."

Philadelphia was seeking its fourth NFL title, while the Packers were hunting for their seventh.

Kickoff was set for noon Eastern Standard Time at Franklin Stadium. A sellout crowd of 67,325 would be in attendance, and millions of football fans across the country would be watching on TV as 190 televisions stations would be broadcasting the game.

The Eagles won the toss and elected to receive the ball. On the first play of the game, Norm Van Brocklin did something he rarely did all season. He threw an interception, a pass in the flat intended for halfback Billy Ray Barnes, that was picked off by Green Bay defensive end Bill Quinlan on the Philly 14. Jim Taylor and Paul Hornung gained nine yards on three carries. With fourth and a yard, Lombardi opted to go for the first down. Unfortunately, Taylor and Bart Starr mishandled the handoff and Taylor recovered the ball for no gain, turning the ball over to the Eagles on downs.

Van Brocklin led his team to a first down that dug the Eagles out of a hole, only to see fullback Ted Dean fumble on the Philly 23 and linebacker Bill Forester make the recovery. Hornung and Taylor moved the ball to the 12, but the drive stalled, ending with a 20-yard field goal by Hornung.

The next three possessions, two by the Eagles and one by the Packers, ended in punts. Green Bay started their next drive on their own 37. This one ended in 23-yard field goal by Hornung, giving the Pack a 6-0 lead.

The Packers defense held Philadelphia on its next drive, then the Eagles returned the favor. Finally, the Philly offense came to life. Van Brocklin completed two passes to wide receiver Tommy McDonald; one for 22 yards to the Green Bay 35 and the second for 35 yards and a touchdown. Walston's PAT gave the Eagles their first lead of the game, 7-6.

After another Max McGee punt, Van Brocklin kicked his boys into high gear again. He threw a 41-yard gain to wideout Pete Retzlaff to the Green Bay 33. After a gain of three, the Dutchman hit Dean for 22 yards to set up Walston's field goal from the 15, giving Philadelphia a 10-6 lead.

The Packers then went on the march again. Hornung ripped off 16 yards over left tackle, and Taylor picked up 13 on three carries. Both running backs followed up with eight-yard sprints, putting the ball on the Philadelphia 35. Bart Starr got into the act by completing passes to Taylor, Hornung, and Gary Knafelc that put the ball on the Philly seven. Then one of those rare quirks in the rules occurred. The Pack hurried to line up for a field goal try, causing the Eagles to jump offside. The rules of the day allowed the offense two choices: take the penalty or attempt a field goal without being rushed by the defense. With little time left in the half, Lombardi chose the latter. Good plan, but Hornung kicked the ball wide by a few feet.

The second half started pretty much the same way as the first half ended. Neither the Packers nor the Eagles could do anything on their first possession, and on their second, both mounted scoring threats, only to come away empty-handed. The Eagles halted Taylor from making a first down on a fourth down rushing attempt that left him a foot short of the Philadelphia 24. Then Green Bay defensive back John Symank snared a long pass in the end zone aimed for McDonald to thwart a solid drive by Van Brocklin and company.

Now the time arrived for Lombardi to reach into his bag of

tricks. After three failed passes, the Packers lined up to punt. McGee surveyed the Philadelphia defensive alignment and saw that the Eagles had overloaded the left side of the line. The Green Bay line had little trouble opening a hole on right side, and McGee rambled down the field for 35 yards to the Philly 46. On the next play, Starr hit Knafelc for a 17-yard gain. Tom Moore, now in the game for injured Paul Hornung, gained 11 yards the Eagles 23 on the first play of the fourth quarter. Taylor and Moore racked up 16 more yards on three carries to the seven where Starr hit McGee for the go-ahead touchdown and a 13-10 lead.

The Eagles then took their turn at scoring six. Dean took Hornung's kickoff on the three and raced up the sideline into Green Bay territory before Willie Wood and Ron Kramer forced him out of bounds on the 39. A holding penalty on the Pack was followed by a 12-uard gain by Dean. Linebacker Ray Nitschke sacked Van Brocklin for a seven-yard loss. The Dutchman then connected with Barnes on a screen pass that gained 13 yards to the Green Bay 14. Three more runs, the last by Dean, produced a touchdown to give the Eagles the lead again, 17-13.

After a Packers first down, Starr connected with McGee for 12 yards where Max took a hard hit and fumbled the ball at the Eagles 48. Bednarik recovered the loose ball. The Philly possession ended in another Van Brocklin punt. Green Bay's next drive stalled, and McGee punted the ball back to the Eagles. The Eagles couldn't move the ball again, and Van Brocklin punted to return man Lew Carpenter on the Packers 35 with 1:30 left in the game.

Starr then guided the Packers downfield in seven plays. He threw to Taylor for five yards and Moore for four. Taylor ran for eight more and a first down inside Philadelphia territory. Starr threw again, this time to Knafelc for 19 yards to the Eagles 30 with a mere 30 seconds left to play. A pass to Boyd Dowler in the corner of the end zone fell incomplete. Dowler complained righteously that he had been interfered with by defenders Jim Carr and Don Burroughs, but the refs didn't buy it. Starr then hit Knafelc again for eight yards to the 22. With time running out, Taylor caught Starr's final pass of the game and headed for pay dirt like a raging bull. When Taylor reached the Philly nine, the Eagles own beast Bednarik brought him down to save the game and the NFL Championship for the Eagles.

At the postgame press conference, Lombardi could only state

positives about his team. "I'm very proud of our ball club. I think they played a great football game. They stayed in there all the way."

Being the true man of sportsmanship that he was, Lombardi then congratulated Philadelphia coach Buck Shaw, saying he was "happy for Buck. Seeing he's going to retire, that's a nice note for him to go out on."

Lombardi made no excuses for the loss. "We were beaten, and that's all there is to it."

Back in Wisconsin, Packer fans were heartbroken, of course. Some people blamed a few local businesses who ran full page ads in the *Press-Gazette* that proclaimed the Packers as World Champions before the game was even played. They called those ads a jinx on the team. Most fans simply took it all in stride and said with confident pride in the hometown team, "Just wait until next year."

§§§

1959 Team Photo

1960 Team Photo

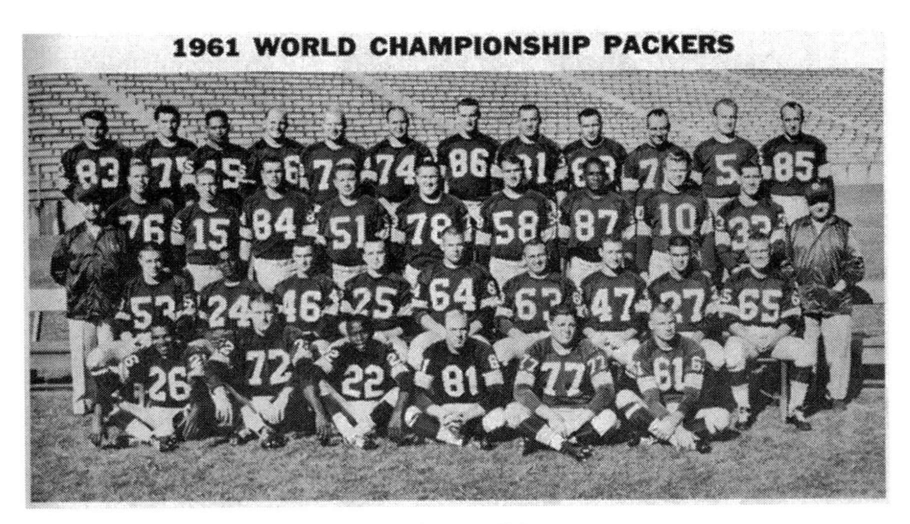

1961 Team Photo

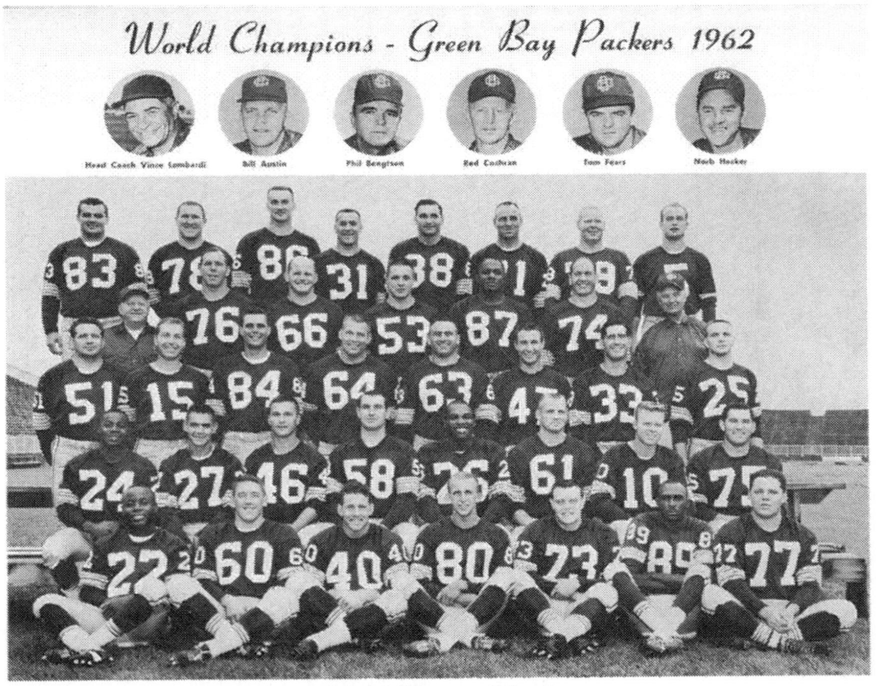

1962 Team Photo

Vince Lombardi and Bart Starr

Ray Nitschke

GREEN BAY PACKER
HALL OF FAME
BILL FORESTER
LINEBACKER #71

GREEN BAY PACKER
HALL OF FAME
FUZZY THURSTON
GUARD #63

GREEN BAY PACKER
HALL OF FAME
HOWIE FERGUSON
FULLBACK #84

GREEN BAY PACKER
HALL OF FAME
RON KRAMER
TIGHT END #88

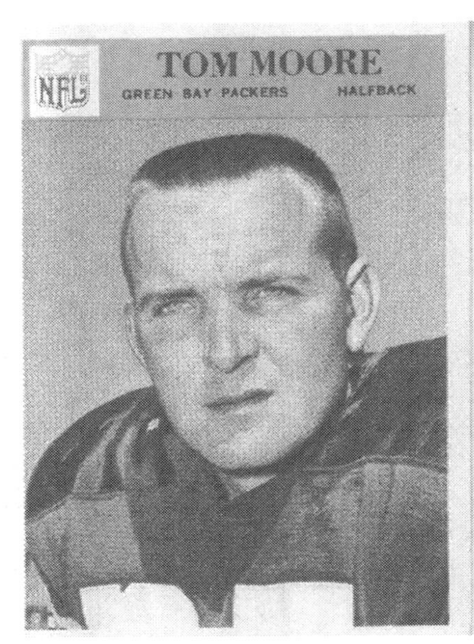
NFL
TOM MOORE
GREEN BAY PACKERS
HALFBACK

NFL
WILLIE WOOD
GREEN BAY PACKERS
HALFBACK

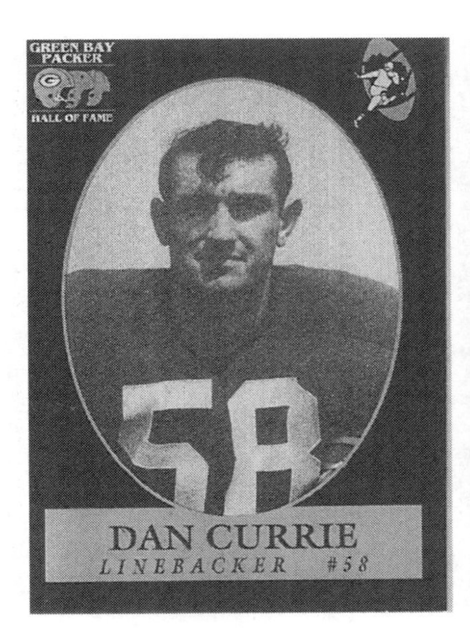
GREEN BAY
PACKER
HALL OF FAME
DAN CURRIE
LINEBACKER #58

GREEN BAY
PACKER
HALL OF FAME
ELIJAH PITTS
HALFBACK #22

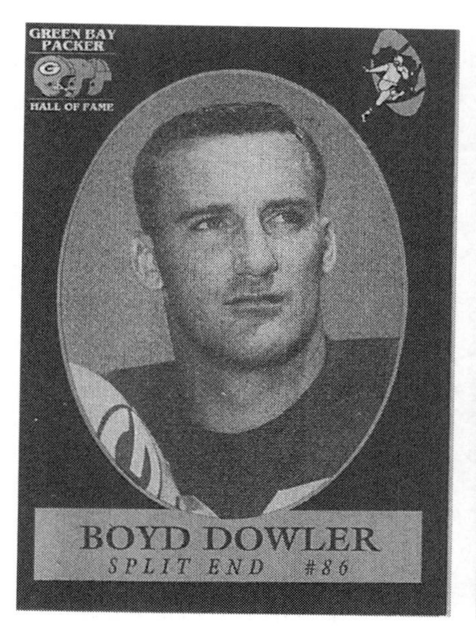
GREEN BAY
PACKER
HALL OF FAME
BOYD DOWLER
SPLIT END #86

GREEN BAY
PACKER
HALL OF FAME
JESS WHITTENTON
DEFENSIVE BACK #47

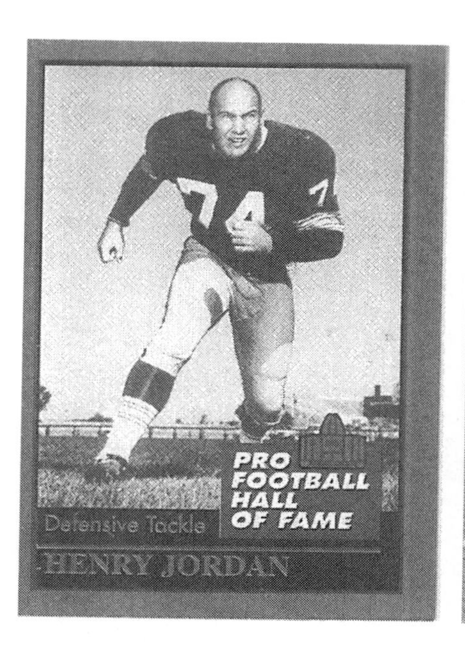
PRO
FOOTBALL
HALL
OF FAME
Defensive Tackle
HENRY JORDAN

SWELL
25
Anniversary
Jim Taylor
FULLBACK

SWELL
25
Anniversary
Jim Ringo
CENTER

SWELL
15
25
Anniversary
Bart Starr
QUARTERBACK

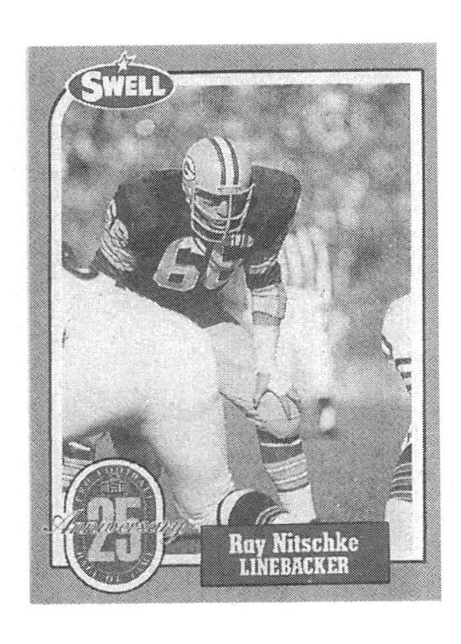
SWELL
25
Anniversary
Ray Nitschke
LINEBACKER

SWELL
25
Anniversary
Forrest Gregg
TACKLE, GUARD

SWELL
25
Willie Davis
DEFENSIVE END

NFL
WILLIE DAVIS
GREEN BAY PACKERS
END

NFL
HERB ADDERLY
GREEN BAY PACKERS
HALFBACK

SWELL
25
Herb Adderley
CORNERBACK

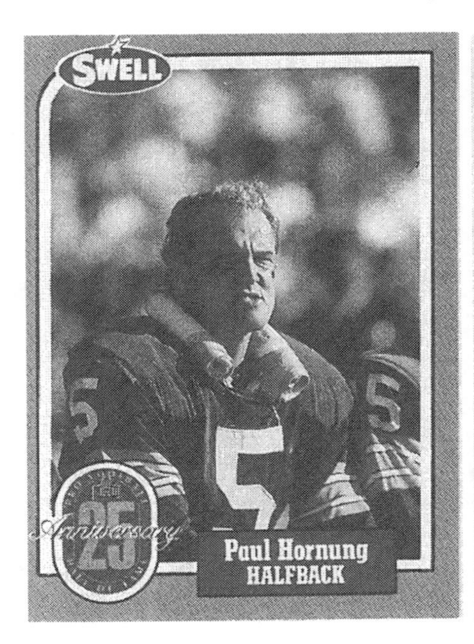
SWELL
25
Anniversary
Paul Hornung
HALFBACK

JERRY KRAMER
GUARD
GREEN BAY PACKERS

Dave Hanner

TACKLE-PACKERS

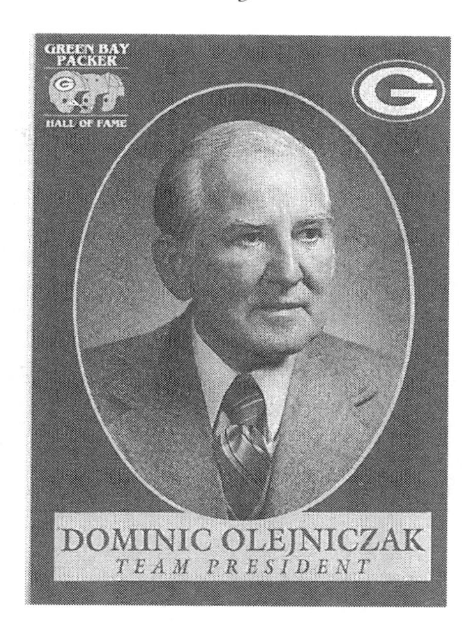
GREEN BAY PACKER
HALL OF FAME
DOMINIC OLEJNICZAK
TEAM PRESIDENT

SWELL
25
Anniversary
Vince Lombardi
COACH

A Tribute to Packer Fans Everywhere

The legend of the Green Bay Packers continues to be written in the pages of sports history and the entire sports world keeps on marveling at the prodigious "little town" with the great football team.

Many, many dedicated men are responsible to a great degree for the wonderful story that started unfolding back in 1919 with the founding of the Packers and is continuing today nearly 45 years later.

There have been Lambeau, Hutson, and Herber of the past, and there are Lombardi, Taylor, and Hornung of the present. These colorful figures and all of the other great Packers have done a tremendous job in putting the Packers in the national spotlight.

But it is the average fan of the Packers who has made the story a success. Their unwavering support when the Packers were suffering through the "lean" years was indication enough of the fans' great love for their team. Now they have a winner, and they truly deserve this reward.

"Salute to the Packers" congratulates Packer fans everywhere.

Eagles-Packers Championship Game 1960 - Franklin Field - Penn State University - *Courtesy Penn Today*

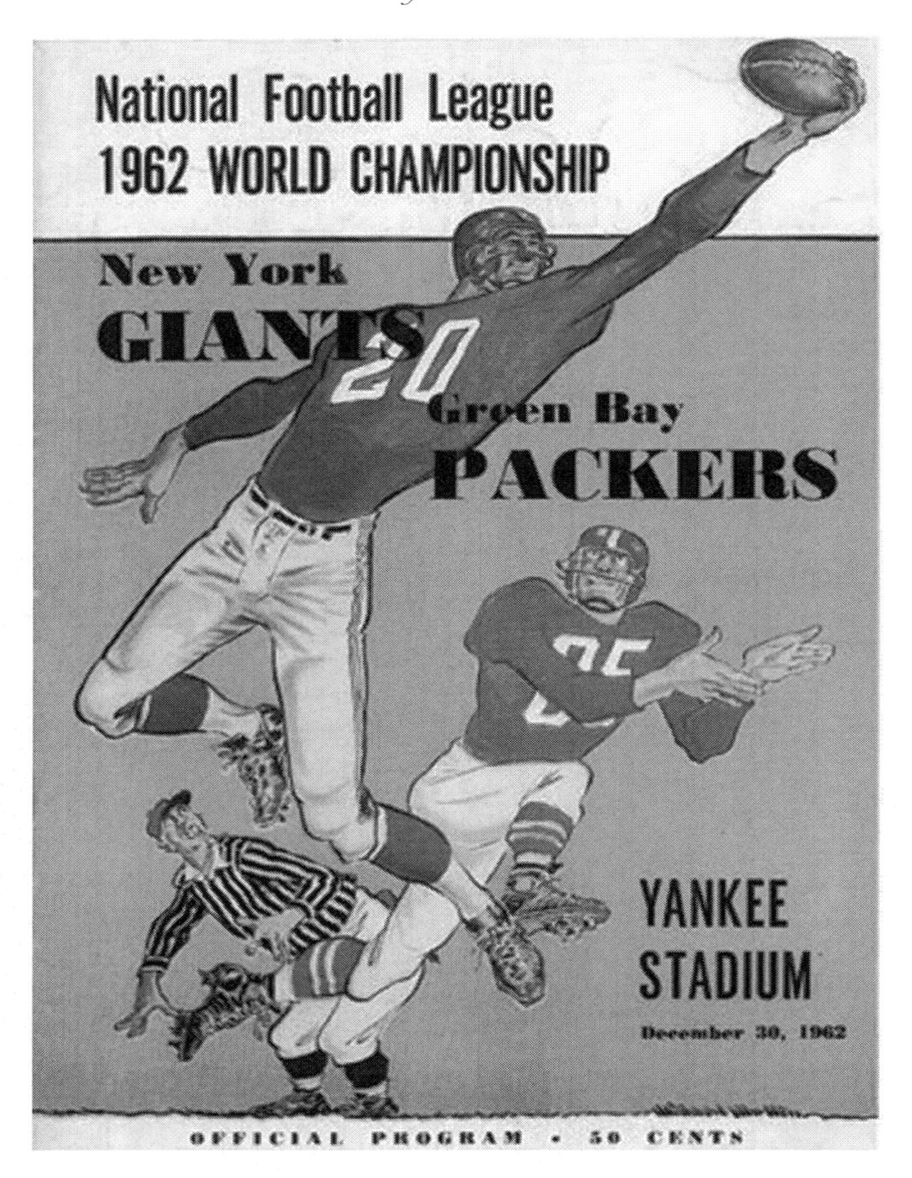
National Football League
1962 WORLD CHAMPIONSHIP
New York
GIANTS
Green Bay
PACKERS
YANKEE
STADIUM
December 30, 1962
OFFICIAL PROGRAM • 50 CENTS

Salute to the Packers
$1.00
COMMEMORATIVE ISSUE - 1962

GREEN BAY PACKERS
1962 YEARBOOK
One Dollar

13
The "Cold War" Resumes

Just as they had done the previous year, the AFL owners announced their plans to hold a "partial" draft of college players before the end of the collegiate regular season and the holiday bowl season. The loop's owners would conduct the draft of six rounds via a telephone conference call through the office of AFL Commissioner Joe Foss.

Because the draft would be conducted prior to the conclusion of the college season, Foss warned the owners not to sign any players who had not completed their college eligibility. He said he would personally void any AFL contract signed before the end of a player's college career.

The purpose of the early draft, said Foss, was to allow clubs to make their top selections and enable them to concentrate on scouting players of less well-known ability. The remainder of the league's draft would be conducted sometime in December.

Foss had learned well the art of shoveling out a horse stall when he was governor of South Dakota. "The purpose of the early draft was to allow the clubs to make their top selections and enable them to concentrate on scouting players of less well-known ability." He might have been trying to buffalo the public with this verbal road apple, but the NFL owners knew exactly why the AFL owners were holding this early "partial" draft. The upstart circuit's owners wanted to get the jump on the NFL in signing college players to post-dated contracts and to force the older league's owners to do the same thing with the hopes that one or several of them would make a mistake or two that would discredit the senior loop.

Men like George Halas who had been around the professional game for decades knew that fans wanted stars on their teams. Halas proved this when he made a deal with the immortal Red Grange, the great "Galloping Ghost" of the early 1920s. Papa Bear signed Grange to a contract to play for the Bears for a five games at the end of the NFL season and during a 19-game, 67-day barnstorming tour after that. Halas outsmarted himself with this sweetheart deal he made with Grange. He figured he had Grange locked up for the coming years. C.C. Pyle, Grange's manager, had other ideas. Halas signed Grange to play for the Bears in the National Football League. Their agreement said nothing about Grange playing for another team in another professional league nor did it have any wording giving Halas rights to Grange's services beyond the barnstorming tour. When Halas balked at giving Grange a bigger deal the next year, Pyle and Grange formed their own team, the New York Yankees, and then applied for membership in the NFL. They were denied entry into the league, so they started their own circuit, the first American Football League, which folded after one season. The Yankees were admitted to the NFL for the 1927 season, but the team folded after that campaign. Rights to Grange then reverted to the Bears.

This embarrassing episode in his career taught Halas a real lesson in the business of professional football, one he shared with his fellow owners every time a new challenger to the NFL came into existence.

Pete Rozelle hadn't been in the NFL commissioner's chair all that long, but he understood the power of his office. He also knew just how to use the media to his advantage. A few days after the AFL held its "secret" draft by telephone he put out a press release disguised as telegrams to about 50 leading senior players in college football. He urged them to wait for the NFL draft on December 27 before any of them committed themselves to any team in the United States or Canada. Very coyly, Rozelle stated the NFL's case in the telegrams.

"We were hopeful that the new league would co-operate with the colleges, but apparently they feel they need the six weeks edge for signing players. We will not change the date for our draft. We feel that the good seniors will wait to see which NFL clubs select them and will evaluate the offers. We are hopeful that we will not be hurt by our policy. It would be to your advantage to withhold any contractual commitments until you have a chance to consider the offer of the NFL team selecting you."

Clever man, Pete Rozelle. He started by calling the AFL "the new league," but then went on to refer to his circuit by its name, the

National Football League, not once but several times throughout the message. He followed that by making the AFL appear to be dishonest for failing to "co-operate with the colleges." Let's get real here. The colleges didn't care one iota what their players did after they had exhausted their college eligibility. There was no true co-operation between the colleges and the pros back then, even though both groups would have the general public think otherwise. Next, he called on the "good seniors" to wait for the NFL draft before making any deal to play for a pro team. The insinuation here is, if you wait, then you're a good senior; but if you don't wait, then you must be a bad senior. Finally, Rozelle played the pity card by saying, "We are hopeful we will not be hurt by our policy." Aw, poor NFL! The loop's owners were all raking in the bucks through the television contracts they had. Most of them could easily outbid any of the AFL teams for the services of new talent, but many of them chose not to pay "the come" as the expression went in those days.

Yes, Pete Rozelle was a clever man; a wise man, too, who could see into the future of pro football in the United States. For the time being, he was leading his league down the right path to success.

So, the NFL conducted its draft on December 27 as planned. The representatives of the now 14 clubs met at the Warwick Hotel in Philadelphia. First choice was awarded to the new team in the league, the Minnesota Vikings. The league would later hold an expansion draft for the Vikes. Besides this draft being the first for the Minnesota club, it was also the first for the Dallas Cowboys who had only been allowed an expansion draft the year before. Since the Cowboys had the worst record in the NFL in 1960, they were awarded the second position in the picking order.

Minnesota's first choice ever was Tommy Mason, a halfback from Tulane. The Cowboys had already traded its first draft choice ever the previous year to Washington for quarterback Eddie LeBaron. Dallas finally made their first pick ever with the 13th selection in the 1st Round, a choice acquired in a trade with the Cleveland Browns. The 'Boys did well, taking Bob Lilly, defensive tackle from Texas Christian University.

After the first two rounds of the draft were completed and had taken more than nine hours, Commissioner Pete Rozelle made the suggestion of a time limit for each pick. Each team could take five, 10 or 15 minutes to make their selection. The clubs finally agreed on middle option of 10 minutes. A second innovation was added after that when the group decided a two-minute warning, like in the games, would be given when necessary. Although this sped up the process, the draft did not finish until the next day.

Of the 14 players chosen in the 1st Round, only two were signed by the AFL. Among the remaining 12 were 11 men who were Pro Bowlers, and four of those All-Pros became members of the Professional Football Hall of Fame. They were Mike Ditka, James Earl "Jimmy" Johnson, Bob Lilly, and Herb Adderly.

The AFL had held its draft in two parts, conducting the first six rounds by telephone on November 21 and 22. The remaining 24 rounds were completed on December 5 and 6. Denver had the first choice and took Bob Gaiters, halfback, New Mexico State. Pickers 2-8 were the Boston Patriots, Buffalo Bills, Oakland Raiders, New York Titans, Dallas Texans, Los Angeles Chargers, and Houston Oilers. Their choices, in order of selection were Tommy Mason, halfback, Tulane; Ken Rice, tackle, Auburn; Joe Rutgens, tackle, Illinois; Tom Brown, guard, Minnesota; E.J. Holub, center and linebacker, Texas Tech; Earl Faison, defensive end, Indiana; Mike Ditka, end, Pittsburgh. Of these men, three—Ken Rice, E.J. Holub, and Earl Faison—put their signatures on AFL contracts and one—Tom Brown—signed with a Canadian Football League team.

With the NFL done with its draft, the signing war between the two leagues was about to get under full swing. The AFL picked a total of 240 collegians, while NFL chose 280.

With Minnesota coming into the league, the NFL decided to expand its regular season from 12 games to 14 games. Each club would play the clubs in its division twice for 12 contests and play two teams from the other division once to bring the schedule to 14 games.

The AFL owners felt expansion was out of the question this early in their circuit's history. Achieving profitability was their main priority for now, especially since Barron Hilton, owner of the Los Angeles Chargers, admitted to the press that his franchise had lost a whopping $900,000 in its initial campaign. Hoping to find a remedy for the red ink of the club's bottom line, Hilton planned to move the Chargers to San Diego for the coming season. A few weeks later Bud Adams, owner of the Huston Oilers, revealed he lost $710,000 in operating the AFL's first ever champion. The estimated losses for the entire AFL were said to amount to nearly $3,500,000. Of course, this led to rumors that junior loop would fold up before the start of the coming 1961 season.

The legal battles between the two leagues received a fresh start on December 30. Judge Dick Dixon, head of the 5th Civil Court of Appeals ruled that the Dallas Cowboys contract fight with the Dallas Texans' defensive star Jimmy Harris would have to go another round on March 3, 1961.

Harris, a former player for the NFL's Los Angeles Rams, was traded to the Cowboys back in July for Dallas's 5th Round selection in the recent NFL draft. Between the two dates, Harris signed a contract to play for the Texans. The Cowboys promptly charged into court to dispute the contract with the Texans. An injunction was issued against Harris, preventing him from playing football for any team. Harris filed an appeal against the injunction. While waiting for the appeal to be heard in court, Harris won the dispute over his contract with the Texans. He played the 1960 season with the Texans.

Everything seemed settled until Judge Dixon ruled the appeal had not been heard and the two parties had to come back to court to settle the matter.

Confused? So was just about everyone else involved in all this legal mumbo jumbo rigmarole. Except maybe the judge.

Another milestone in NFL history occurred the first week of the New Year. The players association held its first ever full-scale meeting. Financing a pension plan was the primary item on the agenda. Billy Howton, the union's leader, expressed hope that new sources of income for the fund would come out of the meeting with NFL Commissioner Pete Rozelle.

Player signings started plaguing the two leagues before the New Year was a week old. Houston (AFL) and Baltimore (NFL) squabbled over little Whittier College's Ken Gregory, the leading pass receiver in the nation for 1960. Dallas (AFL) and Detroit (NFL) each had a claim on Oklahoma fullback Ronnie Hartline. More disputes as these loomed over the horizon.

The AFL held its first meeting of the year in Houston during the second week of January. On the agenda were three very important items. The first and most significant was expansion. Commissioner Joe Foss stated the league had received deposits of $25,000 from each of three groups desiring entry into the AFL. Next item for discussion was the transfer of the Chargers to San Diego. Owner Barron Hilton felt his team would get better television ratings in San Diego and would draw better as well. The third point on the list to be considered was the shifting of the league office from Dallas to New York. Some of the owners felt it would help the league improve its relations with media. The argument for this move was based on the broadcast of the Senior Bowl by the National Broadcasting Company (NBC). AFL owners complained that the announcers showed favoritism for the NFL by mentioning the names of the senior circuit teams who had signed players in the game but refrained from mentioning which AFL clubs had signed players. In response to the anger with NBC, Foss revealed the fact that ratings for AFL games had doubled as the season progressed.

At the conclusion of the league confab, Houston owner Bud Adams announced that end Willard Dewveall of the Chicago Bears had jumped to the Oilers. This move by the Texas native made him the first NFL player to switch leagues without being released from a team's roster. Adams considered the signing to be a victory for the AFL. Chicago's owner George Halas said he "wasn't too surprised" Dewveall jumped to the junior circuit. He added that since the Bears had signed Mike Ditka, the All-American end from the University of Pittsburgh, Dewveall "would not be missed too much."

In an *Associated Press* story, Norman Miller cited a *United Press International* survey that stated the NFL was leading the AFL by a 2-1 margin in draftee signings through the 17th of January. Miller was right and wrong with the math. He forgot to take into account that the senior league had 14 teams while the junior loop only had eight. This discrepancy in numbers skews all of the *UPI*'s percentages.

Miller made a misleading hypothesis in the second paragraph of his story.

"Although the opportunities for making the grade appear to be better in the AFL, the leading college stars, by a ratio of more than 2-1, have indicated they would rather risk their pro playing chances in the tougher-to-make NFL."

Not exactly the whole truth. Many of the players who signed with NFL clubs were told by some general managers that they could always go play for the AFL club who owned rights to them, *if they failed to make the NFL team.* Keeping this in mind, a lot of the players who were released by the NFL team they signed with initially did turn around and signed either with an AFL team or a Canadian team.

The average NFL team retained five-to-seven of the players they drafted out of college. For the AFL teams, the numbers were close to the same: six-to-eight. This comparison showed the AFL was improving its talent pool and quality of competition. Was it proof the junior loop would be successful? No, but it did give the AFL owners hope that they were on the right track.

What initially appeared to be a minor sports story turned out to be rather intriguing for the future of the NFL.

Gene "Big Daddy" Lipscomb, huge tackle for the Baltimore Colts, signed a contract to play professional basketball for the minor league Baltimore Bullets of the Eastern Basketball League. Nobody seemed to care about this deal except one man, one very important and powerful gentleman named Pete Rozelle, commissioner of the National Football League, which had risen to new heights in the eyes of the sports public in just the last three years.

Rozelle said it would not be in the best interests of the NFL to allow one of its star players to compete in the EBL. Why? This particular league had players who had been involved with some rather very unsavory characters, mainly professional gamblers, while playing college hoops. So, Rozelle informed Lipscomb he had two choices: either walk away from the contract with the Bullets or be suspended from the NFL. Of course, Big Daddy chose the former.

Angry EBL president Harry Rudolph took exception to Rozelle's remarks about the players in his league and threatened to sue the NFL's top man for a million dollars for defaming his players and his league. Rudolph stated his position in the press. "People who live in glass houses shouldn't throw stones. Rozelle should put his own house in order before he goes around telling others what to do." The EBL president then pointed out that his league had sent 11 players up to the National Basketball Association over the last three years. He said this to show how the NBA, the "major league" of basketball felt it hadn't been "contaminated" by them.

A spokesperson for the Bullets said: "We know the fans are for us, and we hope he (Rozelle) is somehow aware of their feelings. Perhaps he will reconsider and correct what we believe to be a most regrettable injustice." Same person then added that the Colts had given Lipscomb permission to play for the Bullets.

Rudolph defended his position on these players who had been convicted of point-shaving when they were in college. "We have long felt that our allowing these boys to play in our league served as a good source of rehabilitation. They were young and immature when they made their mistakes, misled by selfish, corrupt people out for their own gains."

The EBL president was right when he spoke about people who live in glass houses. This story was just the beginning of a drawn-out investigation into gambling in the National Football League. For the moment, Rozelle had other matters that needed his attention far more than a few gambling rumors.

Rozelle announced the agenda for the winter league meeting to be held January 24 in New York. Primary point of contention was how to stock the first roster of the expansion Minnesota Vikings. Next, the owners would discuss whether to expand the season by two weeks by adding two games to the schedule. Finally, the league bosses had to decide which conference would get the Dallas Cowboys and which would get the Vikings. Unofficial sentiment favored Minnesota joining the Western Conference because of the proximity of the Twin Cities to Green Bay and Chicago, while the natural fit for Dallas was with the Eastern Conference.

Other matters included discussion of television broadcasting, proposals for a hall of fame, minor rules changes, reports on the pro bowl and playoff bowl, and the player pension plan, which to many was the most important issue of all.

On the first day of the NFL meeting, the owners split into two factions. One group wanted to limit to eight the number of players to be placed in the pool for the Vikings and their first ever coach Norm Van Brocklin. This bloc pointed out that the Vikings already had been permitted to participate in the draft—selecting 20 players—and had signed a pretty good quarterback in George Shaw.

The other group wanted to give the Vikings the same number of players from each of the 12 established teams that the Cowboys had been given the previous year. Commissioner Pete Rozelle supported this proposal even though he was not eligible to cast a ballot. After much discussion, the owners voted to make eight players available from each team except Dallas. Bert Rose, the general manager for the Vikings, called the decision "as equitable a solution as could be worked out."

During a break the first day of the conference, Pete Rozelle announced the total attendance for the 1960 was 3,128,296, marking the third straight season in which the aggregate season attendance exceeded the three-million mark. However, the total for 1960 was 12,113 less than the record set in 1959.

Rozelle failed to mention that the average attendance per game had dropped from 43,617 per game in 1959 to 40,106 in 1960. Of course, he had an excuse for the decline.

"Even though the league played six more games (because of the addition of a new franchise in Dallas), we had reached the point where, without stadium expansion, it was difficult to continue (raising) attendance figures each year." He blamed the decrease on the Los Angeles Rams because the Rams had "the lowest average ticket price in the league." Really, Pete? Cheaper seats were the reason the Rams attendance declined? The Los Angeles Chargers winning their division had nothing to do with the empty seats at Rams games? Of course, he would never admit that competition from the AFL was the actual reason for the drop off in LA.

The last news from the first day was the decrease in roster size from 38 players to 36 again. Why? Revenues may have gone up, but player salaries had increased even more. Again, competition from the AFL was the reason.

Good news for Barron Hilton, super-wealthy owner of the Los Angeles Chargers! The San Diego City Council agreed by a unanimous vote to fund the proposed improvements at city-owned Balboa Stadium. Their action assured the transfer of the Hilton's team from Los Angeles to San Diego in time for the 1961 season.

Having become the become the newest kid on the NFL block in 1961, the Minnesota Vikings were extended a privilege that was not given to the Dallas Cowboys the year before. The Vikes were allowed to participate in the NFL's draft of college players. A lot of owners thought this was unfair, especially the Dallas owner Clint Murchison. To put a little salve on his burning anger, the other owners voted to keep the Cowboys out of the league's program for stocking the new team. The move wasn't much of a consolation for Dallas, but it was better than nothing.

The legal scuffles resumed when halfback Ron Waller sued the Los Angeles Chargers for $25,300. Waller, a former star player for the Los Angeles Rams, claimed he was owed that amount under his 1960 contract with the Chargers. Under their agreement, Waller was to receive $12,000 for the 1960 season, then $15,000 for 1961 for a total of $27,000. He further stated he had only been paid $1,700 of the agreed amount. Waller had played four years for the Rams from 1955 through 1958. In 1959, he retired from the Rams to devote more time to his sports promotion business. Then the Chargers made him a lucrative offer to play for them the next year but did not play because of a knee injury suffered in an August pre-season game. Six weeks later, the Chargers released him instead of using him for promotion and publicity as his contract provided. Either Waller dropped the suit, lost the suit, or settled out of court because the outcome was never published in the newspapers.

More important news was the signing of John David Crow, the third leading rusher in the NFL in 1960. He ran for 1,071 yards on 183 carries for an average of 5.9 yards per carry, which was tops in the NFL. Jim Brown of the Cleveland Browns and Jim Taylor of the Green Bay Packers gained more yards but on many more attempts. All those numbers weren't nearly as important as the reported dollars on his new deal with the St. Louis Cardinals. Crow's 1961 contract would pay him $22,500. This pact made him one of the highest paid players in professional football. More importantly, the Cardinals were raising the ante for the services of the best players in the game. Above that, the NFL was signaling the AFL that if a bidding war was what the AFL wanted, then the NFL was locked and loaded for one.

On the last day of NFL's league meeting, Commissioner Pete Rozelle broke some startling news. "We are alarmed about the future of our league, if we do not change our television policy to conform to the times in which we live." He elaborated on that statement in depth.

The owners feared that under the present television program, whereby NFL games were televised on three different networks, some clubs might eventually wind up with no TV income.

"From the way costs of operating pro football teams have gone up, several teams could not survive without television income," Rozelle maintained. "Costs have more than doubled during the past decade."

Rozelle contended that a "package deal" or single-network program for the whole league would insure television income for all the cubs in the NFL. Commissioner and owners were in agreement on this proposal. The only catch was would the Department of Justice give its approval of such a plan.

The previous spring the DOJ told the NFL that such a

program would go against the anti-trust laws. That summer the AFL *did* make such a deal with the American Broadcasting Company and not one word was said publicly by anyone in the DOJ. Why was that? One reason. Money. The AFL owners were wealthier than the good old boys of the NFL.

All this prompted the NFL moguls to ask one question: "If they can, why can't we?"

Rozelle had more to say on the subject. "After innovating a television program all these years under Bert Bell, we suddenly have become copy-cats. We want to do what the NCAA and the National Basketball Association and the new league are doing. We want to put all clubs on the same network." Note that Pete referred to the AFL as the "new league," once again ignoring the AFL by name.

At that time, road games for nine NFL teams were televised by CBS, two by NBC, and one independently. Rozelle wanted all road games televised in each team's home area.

Rozelle stressed that television ratings for NFL games *as a whole* (author's italics) had remained high. However, the ratings for certain games had dropped drastically, particularly where several contests have been televised in the same area on a given Sunday. He pointed out that in Indianapolis, for example, four pro football games were shown on one Sunday last season (three NFL and one AFL). Such a dilution might result in the loss of sponsors, causing the TV networks to drop their options with some of the NFL clubs.

Note how Rozelle never mentioned the AFL by name. His saying that NFL games *as a whole* had remained high was a coverup for they were high but lower than last year in areas where AFL games were aired. He did say that it was his goal to get one network—and one network only—to televise all NFL road games outside each team's viewing area all across the country. Actually, he made it sound like it was going to be his life's work to achieve that goal.

The NFL winter meeting wound up with the owners voting to extend the regular season by two games to 14. Dallas and Minnesota would be swing teams, playing each of the other 12 teams once and each other twice. The rest of the teams would play each team in their division twice as usual and two teams from the other division once.

The final item on the agenda was roster limits. Thinking of their bottom lines first and the health of their players last, the owners voted to return to roster limits of 36 from 1960's 38. Vince Lombardi remarked that this was a problem. "We've got two more games and two less players." The implication was that every team would have players get hurt in a game and would need replacing in that game. What if a team suffered multiple injuries during a game and had to have someone play a position that he was unaccustomed to playing? The lack of those two extra players might cost a team a victory and in turn deny that team a division title. Lombardi made his argument for keeping rosters at 38, but he was voted down.

A week later the AFL fired the next shot in the pro football cold war. The year-old league filed an anti-trust suit against the NFL. Of course, the NFL denied the new circuit's claim. The AFL charged that its older rival engaged in an illegal restraint of trade to keep the AFL from getting a slice of the estimated $15,000,000 a year business that pro games generated. Stay tuned for how this one came out.

An article from the *Associated Press* announced that a young New Yorker named Bob Rappaport aimed to put an expansion team in Cincinnati for the 1962 AFL season and call it the Dukes. He said he already had an understanding with officials of Crosley Field, home of the Cincinnati Reds of Major League Baseball, to play games there. When asked why Cincinnati, he replied it was because Cincy was one of the few big cities without a pro football team. Finally, he said he already had a coach lined up; Pete Pihos, an assistant coach at Tulane for the present. Pihos had played for the Philadelphia Eagles for nine years (1947-1955) and was instrumental in the Eagles championship games in 1947 and 1948.

On Friday, February 10, Barron Hilton got his wish. He and the other owners voted unanimously to let Hilton move his Chargers from Los Angeles to San Diego of the coming 1961 season. This left LA with one professional football team, the Rams. San Diego was a city with a metropolitan area of 1,200,000 people.

Another would-be owner threw his hat in the ring for an AFL franchise. Robert Angus, manager of a meat packing firm, stated he had sent $25,000 in earnest money to the AFL office in Dallas. He talked with Commissioner Joe Foss about placing a team in Chicago that would play at either Soldier Field or Comiskey Park and that the team would be called the Bulls. Foss made him no promises except that the league would have an answer for Angus by early spring.

Does this sound a little hokey to you? The guy's name was Angus. He managed a meat packing plant. He wanted to call the team the Bulls. Angus? Meat packing? Bulls? Added up, this spelled cow pie. A practical joke by some *Associated Press* sportswriter with a very good sense of humor? More than likely.

Good news! Of a sort. The Dallas Cowboys and the Dallas Texans sat down together to work out their home playing schedules for the coming season. The two pro teams and Southern Methodist University played their home games in the Cotton Bowl. Why was SMU included in this negotiation? The Texans didn't want to play at home on weekends when the Mustangs used the stadium on Saturday. By the time all was concluded, all three parties were satisfied, setting a precedent for the other pro teams to follow.

Remember the lawsuit that the Eastern Basketball League filed against NFL Commissioner Pete Rozelle because Rozelle would not allow Baltimore Colts defensive tackle "Big Daddy" Lipscomb to play for the Baltimore Bullets of the EBL? Well, the EBL decided to drop the suit. EBL President Harry Rudolph said he just changed his mind about the suit. He changed his mind because he knew if the EBL lost the case, then the lawyer fees would bankrupt the league.

The original plan for the coming season had Minnesota and Dallas as swing teams, playing each team in the pre-expansion NFL once each and each other twice. That idea changed when the schedule was made. The Cowboys and Vikings would still play each other twice, but they would not play the remaining 12 teams once each. Instead, the planners placed Dallas in the Eastern Conference and Minnesota in the Western Conference and each of them would play their conference rivals twice. This new schedule made more sense than the original plan because it gave the two expansion clubs a better chance at winning their respective division, not that either really had much of a chance of doing that.

On April 20, a story hit the news wires that presented a good indication of how both leagues were operated when it came to signing draft choices.

Ken Rice, All-American lineman at Auburn University, stated he had been pressured into signing an undated contract with Buffalo of the AFL. He said the contract was later dated, without his approval or knowledge, with the day it was signed, December 1, 1960. Rice was also chosen by the St. Louis Cardinals in the first round of the NFL draft.

Both leagues would actually have agents of their teams in the stands waiting for the clock to expire on a prized player's collegiate eligibility. As soon as the field ticker showed nothing but zeroes for the time left in the game, these agents would rush onto the field with a contract in hand for a star player, quite often yelling out the player's name. In many cases, representatives from both teams that had made the same player a high pick would be screaming his name hoping to get his attention first. Smarter players would fend off the agents until they could meet under better circumstances. And then there were guys like Ken Rice.

At the annual meeting of the NFL owners, Pete Rozelle and Bill MacPhail, vice-president in charge of sports for the Columbia Broadcasting System (CBS) announced that they had made a deal to televise all 98 regular season league contests on CBS for the next two seasons. The two-year pact called for a total of $9,300,000 to be paid to the league. Each club would receive $332,000 per year. The network would feed the road games back to their affiliates in each team's viewing area. Affiliates outside all NFL viewing areas could more or less choose which games they wanted to telecast.

The NFL won a big victory over the AFL when Detroit won a contract fight with the Dallas Texans for the services of two rookies. Dick Mills and Ronnie Hartline, picks 3 and 4 for the Lions, had both signed deals with the two pro clubs. Instead of waging an expensive court battle over the players, Dallas threw in the towel and let Detroit have them.

More precipitous to the overall tug-of-war between the two pro leagues, Joe Foss, AFL commissioner, declared: "There will be no court fight this year between any of our clubs and the NFL. We also have quit giving no-cut contracts to new players. As far as I know there are only two contracts of this type for 1961. We got burned plenty last year."

Wow! An honest and straightforward statement. Something rarely heard in the pro football cold war. And practically never when the speaker was Pete Rozelle, the spin-king of the NFL during these early years of the conflict.

On June 8, Rozelle announced the NFL title game would be played Sunday afternoon, December 31. The only thing that could possibly affect a change to the following Sunday, January 7, would be a three-way tie for first in one division or both divisions. He added that the payout for players in the championship game should be much more than it was in 1960, primarily because of the new television deal with the National Broadcasting Company. Revenue for radio and TV rights to the game were being increased from $200,000 to $615,000 with $315,000 of that going to the players.

A week later the AFL reported a small boost in publicity for their league. ABC announced it would be televising taped highlights of AFL games played the previous weekend right after airing a college game of the week on Saturday. The purpose of this was to advertise the games that would be televised live on Sunday with the hope of boosting ratings.

All the joy the NFL owners had for their television deal with CBS was kicked out the window on July 20. The query made by the U.S. Justice Department about the validity of the contract was made in federal court in Philadelphia. Judge Allen K. Grim declared the pact null and void because it violated the antitrust laws. Judge Grim failed to mention the contract the AFL had with ABC. Neither did he remark on the exclusive contracts with networks held by the National Basketball Association (NBA) and the National Collegiate Athletic Association (NCAA). Both the AFL and NBA were in doubt as to what the ruling would mean to them.

Pete Rozelle said, "The NFL entered into the contract in order to ensure the continuation of its policy of televising all road games of a league team to its home area. Changing television economic factors (back to where they were) make it impossible for us to arrange for a continuation of this plan in the future without a single network arrangement. It will mean that many of our teams will be without the necessary television income to operate successfully and preserve the balance of competition in the NFL."

Rozelle also pointed out what Judge Grim failed to mention, the contracts held by the AFL, NBA, and NCAA. The commissioner said he was consulting league attorneys concerning future action by the NFL.

In his decision, the judge said: "By this agreement the member clubs have eliminated competition among themselves in the sale of television rights to their games. Clearly, this restricts the individual clubs from determining from which areas the telecasts of their games may be made since the defendants have by their contract given to CBS the power to determine which games shall be telecast and where."

One has to ask how this contract violated the antitrust laws. All 14 teams agreed to the deal, so who was being monopolized? The AFL? That league had their own deal with ABC that was shared by all eight of their clubs. Something seems fishy here. Either this judge was very erroneous in his judgement or somebody had it in for the NFL.

Let us not forget that the justice department was headed up by a rich lawyer from Massachusetts and his boss was also from the Bay State. History tells us that President Kennedy owed a lot of political favors for his narrow victory the previous fall in the presidential election. Add that to the facts that Boston had a team in the AFL and that much bitterness remained over George Preston Marshall taking his Redskins to Washington 25 years earlier. Some might say the old cliché, "Where there's smoke..."

And there were all those millionaires who started the AFL. Who's to say any one of them or just a few of them didn't spread a little of their political influence in the justice department? To paraphrase the fictional television character, not the real historical boss of Atlantic City, the immortal Enoch "Nucky" Thompson, portrayed by the award-winning actor Steve Buscemi, "Money talks wherever it goes."

The NFL's lawyers initial reply to Judge Grim's decision was they were studying a possible appeal. Their bosses, the owners of the 14 NFL teams, could only shudder and ask, "And what's that gonna cost us?" The boys over in the AFL giggled over the NFL's troubles, but they kept their snickering to themselves.

Lawyers for the NFL did file an appeal, and a hearing was held July 27. Again, the same judge ruled the NFL could not have a contract with CBS. Judge Grim based his decision on a 1953 decision of his. The league then appealed to the judge to hold a full hearing on December 31 on whether his earlier decision should be modified. Like judges on almost every level, he didn't want his decision to be appealed, so he said no dice to the NFL. This left the league no other option except to appeal to a higher court. Until then, CBS could broadcast the NFL games as planned in their deal.

In mid-August, the NFL let be known that the senior league had only signed 133 of the 280 players it had drafted. What happened to the rest? A majority signed with AFL teams, while a few dozen went north of the border to the CFL or were juniors with another year of college eligibility left.

A few days later the NFL put out a propaganda piece through the *UPI* wire service. The article was boastful about season ticket sales so far and how the league expected to break the previous record for ticket sales. Again, the NFL's publicity department counted on the ignorance of the average pro football fan. Yes, the chances were the NFL would break its 1959 record for attendance, but the writer failed to mention that the NFL would have two more teams than in 1959 and that the Packers would have an additional 6,300 seats for games in Green Bay's City Stadium. The seven Vikings games would add more than 210,000 occupied seats to the previous record. He also failed to mention that the new schedule of 14 games per team with each one gaining one more home game would add another 280,000 people in the stands. Of course, the NFL would set a new attendance record, but not because the league was that much more popular. It was simply that much bigger.

NFL Commissioner Pete Rozelle reported some good news to the press at the Chicago-Green Bay pre-season game in Milwaukee in late August. New York Congressman Emanuel Celler introduced a bill that would essentially nullify Judge Grim's decision to cancel the contract between the NFL and CBS. "Representative Celler has introduced a bill we want to get through. It's a simple, limited purpose bill which would clear up the confusion about single network deals. It would permit all clubs to negotiate for a single contract." Rozelle also said he expected the bill to clear the House shortly after the hearing by the sub-committee and that the Senate would pass the bill by the end of September. He made no mention of what President Kennedy might do when the bill reached his desk.

Because of the point-shaving scandals and the interference of professional gamblers in college basketball, Pete Rozelle took steps to prevent such misdeeds in the NFL. He started by hiring 100 former Federal Bureau of Investigation agents who would operate a system of watching what the gamblers were doing and keeping an eye on the players and coaches in the league. Rozelle made the rounds of all the teams to speak with the players about this new division of surveillance with the game. He warned that violators would be dealt with severely, although he hoped no one would break the loop's rules on gambling. Much to his chagrin, his warning would not go heeded by everyone in the league.

Autumn was coming soon, so it was time for both leagues to turn their attention to the 1961 season. The NFL was still pinning its hopes on a resolution of their television contract with CBS in the halls of Congress, while the AFL would be trying to put more fans in their stadiums every weekend.

Just before the start of the regular season for the NFL, the

House of Representatives judiciary committee approved a bill to permit professional football, baseball, basketball, and hockey to enter into package television agreements. The bill contained a provision that would prohibit the televising of professional football games on Friday nights and Saturday afternoons between the second Friday in September and the second Saturday in December.

The following week Representative John William Byrnes, a Republican from the 8th District in Wisconsin and a native of Green Bay, appeared before the rules committee of the House to urge that it permit the bill approved by judiciary committee be brought before the House for debate. In an article published in the *Congressional Record,* he described the need for the legislation from the point of view of the Green Bay Packers.

"The reason for this is that the television networks, if the member clubs negotiated separately, would look to their own economic interests and negotiate contracts only with those teams which operate in areas of intense viewer concentration. The teams which represent the largest metropolitan areas could obtain lucrative contracts, while the other teams would have difficulty in obtaining any kind of contract at all.

"Thus, the televising of games would be largely under the control of the networks. Many fans would be deprived of watching their home teams play its out-of-town games. Since television revenue is important in the economic structure of football, some teams would become richer and some poorer, but, in the long run, if the teams are not balanced, both financially and competitively, they would all suffer since evenly-matched contests are the essence of a successfully operated league.

"The Green Bay Packers, one of the first professional football teams in the nation, have been able to compete successfully against teams representing much larger cities because of the wise policies of the National Football League which strive for balanced teams.

"The team is owned by a non-profit corporation which has had its struggles, through lean years, to field a representative club. In recent years, however, the club has strengthened its financial position through increasingly successful teams. Green Bay, in 1960, was the Western Division champion.

"With costs mounting, however, Green Bay, like other clubs, is increasingly dependent upon television revenues.

"Negotiating singly, it has never been able to sell its television rights at the level of the clubs which represent the large cities. When its present contract expires, and if it is forced to approach the networks on its own, it will be competing against clubs who offer vastly greater TV markets, and it could wind up without any television contract or with one at a greatly reduced figure. The difference the size of the TV market makes can be judged by the fact that Green Bay's present contract, as champions, is $120,000 for radio-TV rights, while the Washington Redskins, who finished last in the Eastern Division last year, have a $250,000 contract. Under a contract negotiated by all of the clubs, and subsequently ruled out by the court, Green Bay and all other clubs would have received $325,000 in 1962 for television."

The committee agreed to an amendment aimed at making sure professional football telecasts do not compete with college football broadcasts.

The House wasted no time approving the bill, and the next week the Senate approved it by a voice vote.

President John Fitzgerald Kennedy penned his name to the act on Saturday, September 30, 1961; an historic day in the histories of both the telecasting industry and the professional sports industry. The new law practically guaranteed big money every year in perpetuity to the NFL, the AFL, and all three TV networks in existence at the time.

It could be argued that it was an historic day for major college football. The only benefit college football received was protection of the televising of their own games. Although the law didn't specify either league by name, the NFL and AFL were the villains here as they were the only professional football organizations that broadcast their games on national networks. This was a practice that the two leagues already had in use.

This was the dawn of a new era in professional sports. But in Green Bay, Wisconsin it was more than that. To every single fan in Packerland, it meant financial security and life for their team in green and gold for as long as the NFL existed. That TV dough meant one more thing to Packer fans. Their team would never have to worry about the NFL moving them to another, bigger city. With a man around like Vincent T. Lombardi running the business of the Green Bay Packers, Inc., they wouldn't dare.

§§§

14
"Staying in Green Bay"

The *Associated Press* reported the second biggest story coming out of Philadelphia on December 26, 1960.

"Green Bay Coach Vince Lombardi is hopping mad over persistent reports that he plans to leave the Packers and succeed Jim Lee Howell as head mentor of the New York Giants.

"'I'll be going back to Green Bay,' Lombardi snapped Monday after the Packers had lost 17-13 to the Philadelphia Eagles in the National Football League Championship .

"Lombardi, a former offense coach with the Giants, has three years to run on a five-year Packer contract.

"Giant co-owner Wellington Mara, in Philadelphia for the playoff, also denied another rumor. He said, 'Contrary to report, Vince never made any commitment to return to the Giants if and when Jim Lee Howell retired.'

"'Another thing. Vince has a five-year contract at Green Bay,' Mara said, 'and we wouldn't interfere with it.'"

All that was for public consumption. As previously written here, Wellington Mara agreed to let the Packers interview Lombardi for the job of head coach *provided* the Giants could get him back when Jim Lee Howell retired, which they expected to happen after the 1959 season. When Mara reminded Lombardi of that deal, Lombardi told Mara to give him one more year in Green Bay and if Howell planned to hang it up at that time, then he, Lombardi, would resign from the Packers and take the head coach's job for the Giants.

Season completely over now, Lombardi initiated step one. He flew back to Green Bay and turned in his resignation. Step two, the Packers were supposed to announce Lombardi's resignation. The third step never happened.

Just one problem with this plan. Packers top man Dominic

Olejniczak nixed the deal by reminding Lombardi he still had three years left on his contract and he wasn't going anywhere. Mara then reminded Olejniczak about their verbal agreement made during their initial telephone conversation concerning the Packers interviewing Lombardi for the Packers post as head coach. Ole reminded Mara that their agreement was for one year, not two. If the Giants wanted Lombardi back after the 1959 season, then they should have spoken up then. He then reminded Mara that Lombardi had asked them to wait another year and then he would come back to them. Mara was fit to be hogtied for just a few reasons. The first was they felt Olejniczak backing out of the deal, and the second was not getting Lombardi to coach the Giants. To make matters worse, his second choice to replace Howell was now the head coach of the Dallas Cowboys.

The one person who was more upset than the Mara brothers was Lombardi's wife Marie. She had been looking forward to moving back to New York and everything it stood for: Macy's, Gimbels, Park Avenue, Broadway, the theatres, and all those people who spoke like she did. Three more years in Green Bay, Wisconsin? She would gladly have traded twice that many in Hell, if at the end she could return to the Big Apple.

Packer fans were delighted that Lombardi was staying—at least for the coming season. They knew better than to look ahead too far, especially after those ads in the *Press-Gazette* that had jinxed their boys from winning the NFL crown in 1960.

Lombardi, being a straight-shooter and a pragmatist, put all the rumors aside and went back to work. The New Year was only a few days away, and he had to take part in the NFL's college draft. The general manager and his scouting brain trust looked to bolster three different positions: one on offense and two on defense.

The Packers first pick was the 12th of the 1st Round, and with it they decided to fill their top need: an offensive halfback with speed to run outside. They chose Herb Adderly from Michigan State.

Lombardi was always a coach who understood that football games are won in the trenches. In the 2nd Round, the Packers selected Ron Kostelnik, a 255-pound defender from Cincinnati who could player either tackle or end. Kostelnik was the 26th overall pick.

Green Bay then opted to fill their final need: a solid defensive back. Although he still had a year of eligibility remaining at Tulane, the Packers chose Phil Nugent in the 3rd Round with the 40th overall pick.

From there, Lombardi and staff chose players that would only have an outside chance of making the 1961 roster. In draft order, they selected Paul Dudley, back, Arkansas; Joe LeSage, guard, Tulane; Jack Novak, guard, Miami (Florida); Lee Folkins, tight end, Washington; Lewis Johnson, Back, Florida A&M; Fred Cox, halfback, Pittsburgh; Vester Flanagan, tackle, Humboldt State (California); Roger Hagberg, fullback, Minnesota; Buck McLeod, tackle, Baylor; Val Keckin, back, Mississippi Southern; John Denvir, tackle, Colorado; Elijah Pitts, Halfback, Philander Smith College; Nelson Toburen, linebacker, Wichita State; Ray Lardani, tackle, Miami (Florida); Clarence Mason, end, Bowling Green; Jim Brewington, tackle, North Carolina Central; Arthur Sims, back, Texas A&M; Leland Bondhus, tackle, South Dakota State; and Ray Ratkowski, back, Notre Dame.

Because the Packers had won the Western Conference title, Lombardi was given the privilege—and a paid vacation and a bonus check from the league—of coaching his division's all-stars in the Pro Bowl set to be played January 15 at the Coliseum in Los Angeles. As general manager for the Packers, he set up a temporary office for himself to conduct the team's business during his two-week stay in California. From there, he made the first big announcement of the year for the fans back in Green Bay.

Art Daley reported the good news on January 9 with a huge headline that spanned the top of the sports page in the *Press-Gazette*.

Pack Signs First Three Draft Picks; Win for NFL

Why was this such big news? Not losing a single one of your top three picks to the AFL was reason one. Signing them all in a short time after the NFL draft was the second reason. Lombardi considered this to be a major victory in the cold war with the AFL. Herb Adderly had been drafted by the New York Titans in the AFL's 2nd Round; Ron Kostelnik by the Buffalo Bills in the 14th Round; and Phil Nugent by the Denver Broncos in the 9th Round. This announcement was the first official business of the year conducted by Lombardi. With it, he also labeled Ron Kostelnik "The Mad Russian" because the 6'4" – 255 lb. defensive end rushed passers like a hungry beast while he was playing for the University of Cincinnati Bearcats.

Lombardi was not too keen about coaching the West team in the Pro Bowl in Los Angeles. He felt it took up too much of his time and wasn't fair to coaches who were also general managers. As the GM for the Packers, he had to prepare for the league meeting later in the month.

While still in California, Lombardi announced the signings of Mississippi Southern quarterback Valdemar Christian (Val) Keckin and Washington end Lloyd LeRoy (Lee) Folkins. The Packers needed a new third string passer, and Lombardi hoped Keckin would fill that need. As for Folkins, Lombardi felt the 6'5" end would beef up some and fill the backup tight end spot behind Ron Kramer.

The next day Lombardi let it be known that Roger Hagberg, Green Bay's 10th Pick in the recent draft, had signed to play with the Winnipeg Blue Bombers of the Canadian Football League. Hagberg, a fullback, saw that he would be competing with Jim Taylor for a spot on the Packers roster and realized he would have a better chance of making the Canadian team.

When the time came for the new Minnesota Vikings to pick players from the 12 teams that had made up the NFL in 1959, each club presented the Vikes with a list of eight players from which they could choose three. The whole list that Lombardi gave Minnesota was never revealed; only the names of the trio snatched up by the Vikings. Green Bay lost defensive tackle Ken Beck, offensive back Paul Winslow, and defensive back Dick Pesonen. All three played only on special teams for the Packers.

At the same time, Lombardi announced the hiring of Richard J. "Dick" Voris to replace Jack Vainisi as the team's chief talent scout. Voris had been a very successful high school and junior college coach in California during the early 1950s. Then he was an assistant coach with the Los Angeles Rams in 1954, defensive line coach under Red Blaik at Army from 1955-57, and head coach of the Virginia Cavaliers from 1958-60. After going 1-29 and suffering through a 26-game losing streak, a record for major colleges at the time, he resigned his post and looked elsewhere for work in football. Lombardi knew Voris by his work at Army and concluded he could help the Packers.

Although Lombardi signed a few free agents and a middle of the list draft pick, the Packers lost another draft choice. This time it was 7th Rounder Lewis Johnson, a halfback from Florida A&M. He chose to sign with the Houston Oilers. Johnson was the second pick to sign elsewhere; the first being Roger Hagberg, the fullback from Minnesota who penned a deal with a CFL team.

The Packers set a new home attendance record in 1960. For the first time in the club's history, Green Bay broke the 200,000 mark with a total of 204,423 delirious fans attending games. Four sellouts in Green Bay accounted for 128,744 of the total. The two Milwaukee games made up the other 75,679. Green Bay averaged 32,186 fans in City Stadium, while Milwaukee averaged 37,839-plus per contest at County Stadium.. These numbers again raised the cry for more seating in City Stadium.

General Manager Vince Lombardi said the capacity would be raised in Milwaukee to 45,000 from the current 43,000. When asked about increasing seating at City Stadium, he answered, "More seats here will depend on how much money we made." How much the club profited in 1960 would be known within short time.

Asked whether the extra game would be played in Milwaukee or in Green Bay, Lombardi said, "We'll decide that later." He also pointed out that the verdict on additional seating at City Stadium would also include the surveys on possible ticket sales.

After nearly a month of skimpy news releases that mentioned little more than some minor signings of draft choices and free agents, Lombardi finally gave fans something they had been waiting to hear since the subject was first breached in January. The Packers would be building 6,200 additional seats at City Stadium. Yes, the Packer Football Corporation. would be paying for the increase in seating, not the taxpayers, thus boosting capacity to 38,613 seats.

Why the increase? One reason was 1961 was an odd year, and in odd years, the Western Conference champion would have the NFL title game at their stadium. Nobody in the front office was counting their chickens just yet, but after seeing how the Packers finished the 1960 campaign, chances seemed very good that the Pack just might repeat. So, why not be prepared for that possibility?

On March 14, the Beaver Dam (Wis.) Knights of Columbus held a banquet to honor Vince Lombard. He addressed the assembly of 300 with his usual voice of confidence, assurance, and authority.

"We should have a better team in 1961. We've been together for two years and we know each other very well. We have three great running backs in (Tom) Moore, (Jim) Taylor, and (Paul) Hornung. We have an improving quarterback (Bart Starr) who won it for us last year and who should have gained the confidence necessary to return us to the top. We will have a young team to play a young man's game. The team will have great desire, and while we are extremely proud of the 1960 club, we can't forget that the season was marred by the loss in the championship game, and thus, we will not rest as a Packer team or organization until we return to another championship game."

Of course, the audience rose almost in unison, clapping and cheering their approval.

"It's a tough job to repeat as a champion because each opponent prepares just a little harder for you. Everybody wants to beat the champion. The other teams will be especially ready for us.

"Also, management is reluctant to make changes. There is a tendency to stay with the players that won the championship, even if he isn't as good as he was. And it's the very human thing to do. However, there is no room for that type of emotion. Football is a hard-headed, cold business. No matter what a player did last year, he must go if he can't do it this year.

"Then there is a tendency to get fat-headed by the players and coaches. The ego becomes the dominant factor, and you are no longer willing to pay the price.

"The singleness of purpose must be greater than ever when you are trying to repeat; a complete dedication to winning. Our staff and players will have a complete devotion to winning again this year.

"This is a state team, and you people in Beaver Dam, in Fond du Lac, Appleton, Milwaukee, and every other city in Wisconsin are all a part of it ... just as the fans in Green Bay."

On March 25, Lombardi made a major trade, sending Lamar McHan to the Baltimore Colts for an undisclosed draft choice. A story had been circulating among Packer fans that McHan was on his way out since the flight home from Philadelphia after the title game. Allegedly, McHan had referred to Lombardi as a "Nigger Dago" and the coach had overheard him. The likelihood of this tale being true is very remote at best. Passenger airplanes in those days were extremely noisy because of the roaring engines and poor sound-proofing in the fuselage, whether prop planes or jets. The only way Lombardi could have heard McHan say anything would be if he was sitting or standing very close to him. Being the big dog on the plane, Lombardi would have been sitting up front, while McHan would have been several rows behind him.

There was also this finer point to consider when searching for the veracity of this rumor. Lombardi was so sensitive to racial slurs aimed at him or anyone in his family that he wouldn't have waited three months to act on it. He would have found a way to get rid of the bigot as soon as possible.

If the story was true, then to his credit Lombardi took the high road when he traded McHan to Baltimore. He said in the papers that the time had come to develop a young quarterback to back up the designated field general Bart Starr. He noted that "the most successful teams are those with only one number one quarterback. Starr showed us a lot of stature and confidence last season, and we feel he can do the job for us."

On April 11, the NFL announced the schedule for the coming regular season. It was the exact nightmare that Lombardi feared. The Packers would be playing their first four games of the campaign in Green Bay. In Lombardi's mind, this meant the Pack would be on the "road" for the rest of the year. Yes, three games would be played in Milwaukee, but the Packers still had to travel there to play. No other teams had to play a schedule anywhere near that of the Pack.

Lombardi made his displeasure over this schedule known to anybody who would listen, especially Commissioner Pete Rozelle. He wanted to make a couple of changes to the game calendar. Good for the Packers, Rozelle agreed. The first game of the season would be played in Milwaukee against the Lions, and the game the Sunday before Thanksgiving would be played in Green Bay against the Rams. Lombardi also wanted to switch the two games with the Colts, but that was more than Rozelle would allow.

Packer fans in the Green Bay and Milwaukee viewing areas received some excellent news from the NFL annual meeting in San Francisco. The Pack's $75,000 a year television contract with CBS was cancelled, and a new league-wide deal was consummated with the same network. Green Bay would now receive $332,000 a year for the next two years. The additional $257,000 to the Packers budget would allow the club to pay all their players higher salaries, which would certainly make all of them happy. More importantly, the extra cash would give Lombardi more money to offer their top draft choices. In a nutshell, the Packers could better compete with the AFL teams who had drafted the same players.

Because the Packers had come so very close to becoming a footnote in the history of professional sports, publication of the club's financial results each year was almost like an orphanage full of kids waiting to see if they would get any presents for Christmas or would their stockings be stuffed lumps of coal. Instead of lonely children, the persons waiting anxiously for the big meeting where they would learn whether it would be coal or candy this year were the fans and the corporation's stockholders.

General Manager Vince Lombardi announced the numbers at the annual stockholders' meeting of the Green Bay Packers, Inc., at the WBAY (local television station) Auditorium May 8. The club had a net profit of $115,128.25. This was not a record but close. What was a record was the total operating income of $1,177,733. Income from football games totaled $1,026,506 for another record. Home receipts came to $512,192 for yet another highwater mark.

This record year showed the fans that their team had finally reached the financial stability everybody had been working toward for decades. To the people who had purchased stock in the club for only one reason—to keep their team alive and in Green Bay—their faith in the officers of the corporation was confirmed. Their Green Bay Packers, were no longer on life-support; they were alive and well on their way into an infinite future.

Lombardi announced the practice schedule for training camp. A four-day school for quarterbacks would be held at the Packers office, starting June 12. The class would consist of six signal-callers: veterans Bart Starr and Joe Francis, and rookies Danny Bridges from Southwest Louisiana, Roger Johnson from Whitewater (Wis.) State, Val Keckin from Mississippi Southern, and Phil Nugent from Tulane. Rookies would report July 16 with veterans reporting two days later. The Green Bay roster would consist of 36 vets and 21 draftees and free agents for a total of 57 players, three men below the league mandated 60. August 11 was the date for the first pre-season game, a tussle at the Cotton Bowl in Dallas with the Cowboys.

In the second week of July, Lombardi released the terms of the new deal with the Milwaukee County Park Commission (MCPC) for the lease of Milwaukee County Stadium by the Packers. The contract's terms called for the Packers to pay 10% of the gross revenue after taxes for each league game. If this 10% failed to amount to $10,000 or more, then the MCPC's share would increase to 15%. The money was not the important part of the deal. Lombardi, having worked in the banking business for a short time early in his adult life, negotiated a three-year pact for the first time in the history of the club's use of facilities in

Milwaukee. He wisely understood that going back to the bargaining table year-after-year was a waste of time and money on his part as general manager of the Packers. So, he pursued a pact that would run through the end of 1963 and got it.

The Packers opened training camp on July 17 with 17 rookies and six veterans reporting. Before the practice was 15 minutes old, Royce Whittington, 319-pound rookie from Southwest Louisiana became Lombardi's first casualty. After taking three laps around the field, the 19th Round pick was advised to leave camp by Lombardi, who had expected the recruit to report at 265.

Lombardi's problem of evaluating the rookies was reduced a little more on the second day of practice. Halfback Randy Sims from Texas A&M and tackle Buck McLeod from Baylor left camp on their own accord. Both men took one look at the veterans who reported that night and quickly concluded they had only two chances of making the team: slim and none. Another victim of the Turk was free agent guard Sterling Parnel from Howard University.

More than once Lombardi said that placekicking and playing a regular position on offense was too much to ask of Paul Hornung. So, the coach invited Italian immigrant and soccer player Aldo Santaga to camp for a tryout as the Packers placekicker. Santaga played soccer for the Croatian Eagles in the Wisconsin State Soccer League. He was invited back for a second look the next day, but he failed to make the team.

A financial crisis struck the Packers during the first week of training camp. The big television money that was expected to come from CBS was suddenly canceled by a federal judge in Philadelphia. This was money the Packers had practically already spent on the future of the franchise and more especially on the expansion and upgrading of City Stadium.

On the good news side, Lombardi reported that every season ducat had been sold for the coming campaign. All that remained were tickets that were held for visiting teams. The general manager expected all of those would be snapped up by game time at every home game in Green Bay.

The Packers played their annual intra-squad game Saturday August 5. Nothing unusual about the game except for one little detail. For the first time, the Green Bay helmets sported the famous Packers "G" on each side of the head gear. Everybody loved the new emblem.

Better news hit the wires on August 7. The Packers executive committee presented Lombardi with a new five-year contract that was pre-dated to February 1, 1961. Lombardi received more money; the Packers and their fans were given security that Vince would be with them at least through the 1965 season.

The reality of it all was Lombardi had wanted to leave Green Bay and return to New York to be the head coach of the Giants. He even turned in his resignation. Olejniczak said he wouldn't let Vince out of the five-year deal he had signed in 1959. Vince argued that contracts could be broken. Dominick countered with an offer to give him a new deal. Lombardi agreed to stay in Green Bay, and Ole and the executive committee came up with a new pact. Everybody came out winners. Well, almost everybody. The Giants were left with their second choice for their head coach. Allie Sherman was a good coach, but he was no Vince Lombardi.

Because of the Packers' sudden turnaround from worst to first in just two seasons. Coach Vince Lombardi began his new role of football's innovative genius. College coaching staffs began attending his practice sessions with the team to observe his coaching techniques and hopefully get an opportunity to question him about some of his football philosophy.

On the roster front, Lombardi made a couple of trades. He picked up veteran quarterback John Roach from Cleveland for the proverbial undisclosed draft choice. Then he traded tight end Steve Meilinger to the Cowboy for an undisclosed draft choice.

The Packers opened their 1961 pre-season schedule with a trip to the Cotton Bowl to face the Dallas Cowboys. Always the competitor, Lombardi directed the game to win, and win the Pack did, 30-7, before a light crowd of 30,000. Bart Starr connected 14 times on 24 pass attempts for 188 yards. Jim Taylor racked up 112 yards in 13 rushes.

The only bad news for the Packers came at halftime when the team returned to the locker room to discover they had been robbed. Wallets and clothing were strewn all over the dressing room. Once Lombardi got his team quieted down, an inventory of the situation was taken, revealing that 15 of the 42 players had been victimized by thieves who entered the room through a window in the ceiling. About $400 in cash, watches, rings, and other personal items were stolen. Em Tunnell lost a medal he had been carrying for 16 years, plus his championship ring won as a Giant. Boyd Dowler lost his East-West Shrine Game watch. Those who hadn't lost anything had given their wallets and personal items to Dad Braisher, the team's property chief, for safekeeping. Braisher locked up those things in a team trunk that went untouched by the burglars.

Before the next exhibition game, Lombardi released Pineapple Joe Francis from the roster. In his short career, he had played sparingly in the regular season when he was healthy, which wasn't often. He missed the entire 1960 season with a broken leg suffered in training camp. The Montreal Alouettes of the CFL signed him shortly after his release from Green Bay.

The Packers flew down to St. Louis to face the Cardinals in the annual Cardinal Glennon Memorial Charity Game in front of the largest crowd ever, 31,056, to see a pro football game in St. Louis. As expected, Green Bay rolled over the Redbirds, 31-10, scoring three TDs and a field goal on the Packers' first four possessions.

Whenever the Packers played the rival Bears, whether in the regular season or the pre-season, no love was lost between the players or the fans. This was more than evident in the third game of the 1961 exhibition season when the two squads squared off in the 12th Annual Midwest Shrine Game in Milwaukee County Stadium. A record crowd of 42,560 delirious paid patrons turned out to root home the Packers, snapping the old mark of 40,199 set in 1955 when the Packers faced the Colts. After trailing 14-7 at the half, Green Bay roared back in the second 30 minutes to come away winners, 24-14. The size of the crowd pleased Lombardi more than the victory because it seemed more like a home game than a road game as most previous contests in Milwaukee had in the past.

The Packers aimed for a third straight attendance record when they readied for their battle with the New York Giants in the Bishop's Charities Game at City Stadium on Monday night September 4. Green Bay figured in the largest crowd ever to see a pro football game in St. Louis when 31,056 fans turned out to watch the Pack play the Cards in Busch Stadium. Then there was the game between the Packers and Bears in Milwaukee that was another record attendance for a pro game in Wisconsin. The Packers were expecting another record crowd for their game against the Giants.

On the television front, CBS announced that eight Packer games would be televised via WBAY-TV in Green Bay, including the three Milwaukee contests and five of the seven on the road. Only the two West Coast battles at the end of the regular season would not be viewed in Green Bay. The four home games in Green Bay would be televised on WISN-TV in Milwaukee. WISC Channel 3 in Madison, WKBT Channel 8 in La Crosse, and WSAU Channel 7 in Wausau would be carrying all 14 regular season Packer games, adding to the Packers' claim as Wisconsin's team.

The headline in the *Press-Gazette* for Green Bay's fourth pre-season game read: "Pack Tips Giants on Hornung Field Goal, 20-17." Of course, that wasn't the whole story of the game. The score went back and forth during the course of the game. Giants led 7-0 in the first quarter. Packers led 10-7 at the half. Giants led 14-10 in the third period before the Bays regained the lead, 17-14. The final score was a field goal of 13 yards with 4:08 to go in the game. New York made one final push to recover the lead, but an interception by Willie Wood canceled that threat, sending 33,452 delirious Packer fans home happy.

The following week Lombardi pared the roster by trading guard Andy Cvercko to the Dallas Cowboys for a draft choice to be determined. Then he waived fullback Larry Hickman. Defensive tackle John Miller was also released. These moves meant rookie running backs Herb Adderly and Elijah Pitts would be making the opening day roster. Lombardi made another deal that week; this one with the Giants, sending New York a draft choice for 6'8", 285-pound tackle Ben Davidson who played at the University of Washington.

The Packers finished up the pre-season with a solid win over the Washington Redskins in Columbus, Georgia. Their 31-24 victory gave them their second straight undefeated exhibition season, and it extended their pre-season winning streak to 13. Of course, Lombardi downplayed these numbers because the games were nothing more than practice in front of paying audiences. In his mind, these contests were teaching chances for him to show his team how to win during the regular season. And learn they did.

§§§

15
Time to Get Down and Dirty

The American Football League opened its 1961 season on Saturday September 9, a full week ahead of the NFL. Rosters for the new year would be limited to 33 players compared to the 35 from the previous campaign. Like the NFL, this was a cost-cutting move for the AFL. In another budget-reduction act, the AFL owners urged their coaches and general managers to keep less expensive rookies over veterans who were near the ends of their playing careers. The result was 96 new faces on the eight teams opening the season. Of those, 50 were rookies. The remaining 156 were veterans.

Houston started the 1961 AFL campaign with a record setting thrashing of Oakland, 55-0. The Chargers, now in San Diego, mashed Dallas, 26-10. New York nosed out Boston, 21-20; and Denver clipped Buffalo, 22-10.

Meanwhile, the Packers set their sights on the Detroit Lions as Lombardi pared down the roster to 36 players. Veteran Jim Temp decided to hang up his cleats because he reinjured the same shoulder that had plagued him the year before. Then rookie quarterback Val Keckin was waived. Lombardi retained the services of six rookies on the team: linebacker Nelson Toburen, defensive tackle Ron Kostelnik, defensive end Ben Davidson, end Lee Folkins, and halfbacks Elijah Pitts and Herb Adderly. Returning veterans were secondary men Jess Whittenton, Hank Gremminger, John Symank, Em Tunnell, Willie Wood, and Dale Hackbart; linebackers Bill Forester, Dan Currie, and Ray Nitschke; defensive linemen Bill Quinlan, Dave Hanner, Henry Jordan, and Willie Davis; offensive linemen Jim Ringo, Forrest Gregg, Bob Skoronski Jerry Kramer, Fred Thurston, Norm Masters, and Ken Iman; quarterbacks Bart Starr and John Roach; running backs Paul Hornung, Jim Taylor, and Tom Moore; and ends Max McGee, Boyd Dowler, Gary Knafelc, Ron Kramer, and Lew Carpenter. LB Bill

Quinlan was not on the opening day roster due to an injury.

Lombardi surprised everybody by announcing Willie Wood as the starter at safety, replacing Em Tunnell. Wood was in his second year with the Pack, while Tunnell was entering his third in Green Bay and 14th in the NFL. As Art Daley put it, this was the start of one era and the end of another.

All weeklong Lombardi had been telling reporters that he expected a real defensive battle with the Lions and a record crowd in their opener at County Stadium in Milwaukee. Both teams sported talented defenses, so a low-scoring affair was also expected. The coach proved correct on all three accounts.

A record 44,307 showed up for the game against the Lions, setting a new attendance mark for a professional football game played in Wisconsin. The Packers took the opening kickoff and roared down the field in eight snappy plays covering 69 yards and ending in a Jim Taylor touchdown on a one-yard plunge. The drive took all of 3:23 off the clock. Packer fans were sure their guys were off and running to a win in the pursuit to repeat as champs. A TD plunge by Detroit's Nick Pietrosante tied the game at seven-all just under 10 minutes later. Then a 13-yard scoring toss from Earl Morrall to Pietrosante with 1:40 left in the half put the Lions ahead for good, 14-7. The Packers retaliated slightly with a Paul Hornung field goal from 14 yards out with 12 seconds left in the half. Neither team put any points on the scoreboard in the third period. Then Hornung closed the gap to 14-13 just two minutes into the final period with a 26-yard boot. Five minutes later kicker Jim Martin extended Detroit's lead to 17-13. The Packers made it into scoring territory twice in the second half. The first time they reached the Detroit two before turning the ball over on downs. Their final threat was thwarted by Dick "Night Train" Lane when he intercepted a pass in the red zone with 1:06 left in the game. The Lions ran out the clock and came away with a 17-13 upset of the Pack.

Bart Starr had a tough day passing, completing 14 of 26 tosses for 173 yards with two intercepted. Jim Taylor gained 85 yards on 15 carries, while the rest of the backs could only muster 47 yards on 13 rushes. Max McGee had a big day receiving, hauling in seven throws from Starr for 127 yards.

Lombardi summed up his thoughts on the outcome of the game in one short sentence. "It was those two goal line things." He was referring to the two possessions where his guys fought their way into the red zone and came away empty-handed. Two field goals would have won the game. "You don't get down there that often. If you don't score, you don't win."

Folks in Packerland could only say, "Things will be different next week."

The Packers weren't the only team upset in the league's first week of action. As Gomer Pyle would have put it, "Surprise! Surprise! Surprise!" The Dallas Cowboys won their first NFL game in 13 tries by downing the Steelers, 27-24. But the bigger stunner was pulled off by the infant Minnesota Vikings when they manhandled the Chicago Bears, 37-13. In the fourth upset of the day, the St. Louis Cardinals handed the New York Giants a loss in their opener, 21-10. The NFL Champion Philadelphia Eagles slipped by the Cleveland Browns, 27-20. Baltimore's Colts sheared the Los Angeles Rams, 27-24, while the San Francisco 49ers gave the Washington Redskins a beatdown by the score of 35-3.

In the AFL, the Chargers (2-0) kept the Raiders (0-2) scoreless on the year by handing them a 44-0 crushing. The Patriots (1-1) gave the Broncos (1-1) a thumping, 45-17. Buffalo (1-1) made it by the 1-1 New York Titans, 41-31. Houston (1-0) and Dallas (0-1) had the weekend off.

Two days after the loss to Detroit Packer defensive tackle Dave "Hawg" Hanner came down with appendicitis that required an emergency operation. The doctor told him he would be out of action for three weeks. Lombardi wasted no time inserting rookie tackles Ron Kostelnik and Ben Davidson in Hanner's spot.

Green Bay's next opponent was San Francisco at City Stadium with its new seating of 38,650. Since joining the NFL from the defunct AAFC, the 49ers had beaten the Packers 13 out of 20 regular season meetings. The Pack won the first game, then lost seven in a row before winning a pair in 1955. San Francisco took the next six, but then Lombardi became head coach. He had directed the Packers to four straight wins over the 49ers and had them aiming for number five.

A record crowd of 38,669 fans turned out at City Stadium to watch the Packers face off against San Francisco's vaunted shotgun offense led by quarterback John Brodie.

Paul Hornung had a big day, scoring 18 points in total. He started the day with a one-yard dive into end zone for his one TD. The 49ers tied the game on their only entrance into the red zone. New return man Willie Wood scored the Pack's second touchdown with a 39-yard punt return in the second quarter. Hornung booted his first three of the day with 3:34 left in the half to give the Packers a 17-7 lead. San Francisco countered with a field goal of their own with 40 seconds left in the period. Hornung put up his second three, a 43-yarder, with five seconds remaining in the half, putting Green Bay ahead, 20-10.

The Packers defense played superb football in the second half, holding the 49ers scoreless and never allowing them to reach the red zone. Hornung added his third field goal in the third quarter, and Max McGee caught a 21-yard TD pass from Bart Starr in the final stanza to close out the day's scoring. The final tally was Packers 30, 49ers 10.

Around the NFL, the Cowboys (2-0) continued their first winning streak by stopping the Vikings' (1-1) first victory skein at one, 21-17. The Eagles (2-0) remained tied for first in the East with a 14-7 win over the Redskins (0-2). Cleveland (1-1) downed St. Louis (1-1) by a 20-17 margin. New York (1-1) got on the winning track with a 17-14 victory over Pittsburgh (0-2).

Detroit (2-0) played Baltimore (1-1) just like they played the Packers the week before. The Lions' strong defense held the Colts to a touchdown, two field goals, and a safety to slip by them, 16-15. The Bears (1-1) and Rams (0-2) played on Saturday in Los Angeles with Chicago coming away with 21-17 win.

Over in the AFL, Boston (2-1) handed Buffalo (1-2) a 23-21 loss to remain in a tie for first in the East with the Titans (2-1), who dumped Denver (1-2) by a tally of 35-28. San Diego (3-0) remained the only unbeaten team in the league with a 34-24 win over Houston (1-1). The Texans (1-1) added to Oakland's (0-3) woes by handing the Raiders a 42-35 defeat.

Feeling he had too many defensive backs, Lombardi traded Dale Hackbart to the Washington Redskins two days after the game with San Francisco. In return for Hackbart, the Packers received an undisclosed draft choice in the 1962 NFL Draft. Tom Bettis came off the injured list to replace Hackbart on the roster.

Whenever a team changes their head coach, everything starts all over in that team's history book. New coach, new history. That last statement is what they say when two archrivals meet in a game as in, "You can throw out the history books whenever the Green Bay Packers face off with the Chicago Bears."

In Week 3 of the NFL season, that's exactly what fans were

saying everywhere because that's what the sports media were telling them over and over and over right up to and even for days after the game between the Bears and Packers at City Stadium in Green Bay.

This game between the Packers and Bears would be their 85th regular season meeting in the 41 years both teams were in the NFL. Of course, the Pack was favored in this one based on their records of the previous two years when Green Bay finished ahead of Chicago in the Western Conference standings. However, the two teams had split their four contests in those two seasons, which were the only two where Lombardi and Halas roamed opposing sidelines.

In 1959, the Bears were the favored 11 in the first game in City Stadium. The Packers won. In the second game in Wrigley Field, the Packers were favored. Yes, Chicago won. In 1960, the Packers were favored in game one in Green Bay. The Bears won. In game two in Chicago, the Bears were favored. The Packers won. As opposing head coaches, Halas and Lombardi had the exact same records. Each was 1-1 on the other's field and 2-2 overall. Would any of this change in 1961?

Art Daley began his story on the game with the perfect lead-in. "The Packers shut out the Bears!" He followed up with a more potent graph. "That hasn't been written for 26 years, but it's the real word today on the heels of the Packers' historic 24 to 0 victory over the Bears before 38,669 fans in City Stadium Sunday afternoon."

If that didn't make you want to read the rest of his game story and all the other game-related articles in that *Press-Gazette* Monday edition, then you couldn't call yourself a real Packer Backer in those days.

Just by the final score, you knew the Pack's defense forced the outcome. Green Bay twice took the ball away from the Bears on fourth down plays deep in Packer territory in the first half. This led to the first Packers' shutout of the Monsters of the Midway since 1935. Was this an omen of what was to come in the rest of the season?

Here's how the Pack pulled it off:

Defensive back John Symank snared a pass from Chicago's Ed Brown late in the first period and ran it back 41 yards. Three plays later Bart Starr slung a pass to Boyd Dowler for 18 yards and a GB touchdown, putting the Bays up, 7-0. Paul Hornung booted a three in the second quarter to make the halftime score, 10-0. Midway in the third period, Willie Wood made a gutsy return through the Chicago punt team for 22 yards to the Bear 42. Three plays later Jim Taylor crashed over from the three to make it 17-0. On the second play of the fourth quarter, Dan Currie intercepted a Bill Wade pass on the Bears 46. A half dozen plays later Bart Starr connected with Ron Kramer for 17 yards and the final score of the game.

Jim Taylor bull-dozed his way for 130 yards on 19 carries with one going for 59 yards. Paul Hornung picked up 59 yards on nine attempts. Starr completed 13 of 22 passes for 111 yards. The Packers intercepted four Chicago passes; two by Dan Currie and one each by Hank Gremminger and John Symank.

As in nearly every game between the two archrivals, no mercy was shown on either side of the ball. Both teams took no prisoners. Yet when the game was concluded, Lombardi and Halas met in the center of the field and shook hands like the two friends that they were.

This was only Week 3 in the NFL campaign of 1961, and no clear-cut leader could be found in either division. The two previously undefeated "D" teams, Dallas and Detroit, and Philadelphia were handed their first losses of the year; Dallas (2-1) to Cleveland (2-1) by 25-7 and Detroit (2-1) to San Francisco (2-1) by a whopping 49-0; and Philadelphia (2-1) to St. Louis (2-1) by a narrow 30-27. Green Bay (2-1) and Baltimore (2-1) joined the top of the Western standings with their wins, 24-0 over Chicago (1-2) and 34-23 over Minnesota (1-2). New York (2-1) joined the top of the East with a close win, 24-21, over Washington (0-3). Los Angeles (1-2) got into the win column, downing Pittsburgh (0-3) by a 24-14 margin.

San Diego (4-0) remained undefeated and on top of the AFL West with a 19-11 victory over Buffalo (1-3), holder of last place in the East. Dallas (2-1) slipped into second in the West with a close 26-21 win over Houston (1-2) now third in the East. New York (3-1) broke the tie for first in the East by clipping Boston (2-2) in a high-scoring affair, 37-30. And finally, Oakland (1-3) won its first game of the season with a 33-19 win over Denver (1-3).

Coming up for the Packers in Week 4 of the season was a visit from the Baltimore Colts at City Stadium. In the four games between the two teams since Lombardi took the reins in Green Bay, the Pack had won only one contest. Former Packer and now backup QB for the Colts, Lamar McHan, led the charge for the men in green and gold. Bart Starr had yet to defeat Johnny Unitas and his Baltimore club. One of the two teams would come out of the game in first place in the

Western Division, possibly tied for the top spot with the Lions and/or the 49ers, both of them at home that Sunday against the Bears and Rams, respectively.

Until this week, the Packers had relied almost totally on their defense to win games, giving up 27 points in all with 17 of those being scored by the Lions in Green Bay's only loss. That trend on defense continued against Baltimore, but the slightly sluggish offense got their game together and slashed the Colts, 45-7, in front of another sellout crowd of 38,699 delirious fans.

Paul Hornung put the Pack on the board first with a 54-yard gallop to pay dirt just 2:04 into the game. Baltimore mounted their only scoring drive late in the same period and finally crossed the Green Bay goal line 15 seconds into the second stanza. From there on, it was all Packers. Hornung scored from the one, He booted a field goal later in the quarter to give the Pack a 17-7 lead at halftime. At the 2:48 mark of the third, Hornung took in a pass from Bart Starr from eight yards out, then with 2:06 remaining in the period, Hornung put up his fourth touchdown of the day, giving his team a comfortable 31-7 lead over the Colts. Willie Wood returned a punt for 72 yards for the Pack's fifth touchdown with 1:15 expired in the final quarter. Jim Taylor capped off the day's scoring with a three-yard burst to pay dirt with 10:58 to go in the game.

The four touchdowns scored by Hornung tied Don Hutson's record set back on October 7, 1945 at State Fair Park in Milwaukee against the Detroit Lions. He also set a new record for points scored by a Packer with 33, surpassing Hutson's mark of 31 set that same day 16 years earlier. Hutson put 29 points on the board in the second quarter that day, a mark that may never be equaled or surpassed.

Hornung also gained 111 yards on the ground and 28 through the air for a game high total of 139. Taylor ran for 82 yards and caught two passes for another 24 to give him a total of 106 yards on the day. In the passing column, Starr completed 13 of 25 attempts for 157 yards and the one touchdown to Hornung.

Baltimore's offense was almost as potent as the Pack's attack, but the Colts committed eight turnovers; two lost fumbles and a half dozen passes intercepted. Jess Whittenton picked off a pair, while Hank Gremminger, Willie Wood, John Symank, and Dave Hanner took in one each. Symank and Dan Currie each recovered a fumble.

The Packers' (3-1) huge day over the Colts (2-2) kept them in a tie for first in the West with the 49ers (3-1) who had a big day of their own, a 35-0 spanking for the Rams (1-3). Chicago (2-2) clipped Detroit (2-2) by 14 points, 31-17, to bring the Lions back down to earth, while the Vikings (1-3) joined the Rams in the cellar by taking a 28-0 beating from Dallas (3-1). New York (3-1), Philadelphia (3-1), and Cleveland (3-1) kept pace with the Cowboys in the East. The Giants shutout St. Louis (2-2) by the score of 24-0. The Eagles got by Pittsburgh (0-4) narrowly, 21-16. The Browns stuck it to Washington (0-4) by a 31-7 margin.

In the AFL, Oakland (1-3) and New York (3-1) had their bye week. San Diego (5-0) continued to cruise along with a 38-27 victory over Boston (2-3). Dallas (3-1) kept pace in the West with a 19-12 defeat of Denver (1-4). Most surprising was the 22-12 loss by Houston (1-3) to Buffalo (2-3).

Week 5 for the Packers promised to be an historic event. Why? Because the Pack was off to Cleveland to face the Browns for the first time in five years. In three previous encounters, Cleveland had come out victorious. The Packers were looking to change that trend.

The game promised to be a real slugfest as Coach Paul Brown of Cleveland faced off with Vince Lombardi for the first time ever. Brown was already a legendary figure in the annals of pro football, Lombardi was just beginning to make his mark on the game. Looking back, this contest appeared to be a clash of titans.

Both teams were riding a three-game winning streak and were tied for first place in their respective divisions.

Brown had a phenomenal career to date as a professional football coach. His record in the AAFC was 47-4-3 over four seasons and four straight AAFC titles. When the AAFC and the NFL merged in 1950, his teams won five consecutive Eastern Conference titles and two NFL titles in 1954 and 1955. After suffering his first losing season in 1956, he bounced back in 1957 with the division crown and then tied for first in 1958 before losing to the New York Giants in a playoff game. To date, his record in the NFL was 99-34-3 in regular season games and 4-5 in post-season play to give him an overall mark of 103-39-3 in the NFL and a total record of 155-43-6 for his career in pro football.

Lombardi's record to date as a head coach in the NFL was a mere 18-11 with one division title to his credit. Hardly comparable to Brown's mark.

Marsh Samuel, publicity director for the Browns, announced the expected attendance for the game would be in the neighborhood of 70,000. Advanced sales had already reached 45,000 by the middle of the week. By game day, the crowd was predicted to reach 82,000, a new record for Cleveland.

Former Cleveland players, and now Packers, Willie Davis, Henry Jordan, Bill Quinlan, and Lew Carpenter all looked forward to facing their old team over the line of scrimmage.

Attendance for the game failed to meet expectations. Only 75,642 fans showed up to see the Packers pick up right where they left off the week before against Baltimore.

On their first possession of the ball, Jim Taylor made both teams and all the fans aware that he intended to make his mark on the game. He wasn't just competing against the Cleveland Browns; he was also putting himself up against the arguably greatest ball carrier of all time, at least in the 20th Century, the one and only Jim Brown.

Taylor opened his day by carrying twice for 17 yards, catching a pass from Bart Starr for six yards, then adding three more yards to the Browns' 46. Three plays later he hit off left guard, picked up a sharp block by Paul Hornung on Del Shofner on the 10 and then lugged the ball and a Cleveland defender into the end zone with him for a run of 26 yards and his first touchdown of the day.

Cleveland ended the following possession by punting. The Packers started their attack again on their own 33. Taylor picked up 16 yards on two runs and a pass reception. With first-and-10 on Green Bay's 49, Starr hooked up with Boyd Dowler for 25 yards and another first down on the Cleveland 26. Taylor took the ball the rest of the way to the end zone from there, scoring his second touchdown of the game and putting the Packers ahead, 14-0.

Cleveland managed to get on the board on their next time on offense. Their drive ended with Lou Groza kicking a 17-yard field goal.

Taylor then led off the next scoring drive with a two-yard loss. Them Starr connected with Ron Kramer who fought his way down the field for 35 yards before lateraling to Dowler for an additional 12 yards, reaching Cleveland's 35. After a pair of short gains, Starr found Max McGee for 13 yards to the Cleveland 19. Taylor zipped 16 yards to the three to set up Hornung's rush for the score, giving Green Bay a 21-3 halftime lead.

Starting their first drive of the second half on their own 20, the

Packers mounted another long scoring possession. Taylor and Hornung gained 12 yards between them before Starr passed twice to Ron Kramer for 23 yards. Then Taylor rumbled 45 yards to the end zone for his third TD of the day to build the lead to 28-3.

After the Browns countered with their first touchdown, the Pack failed to score, giving a breath of life to Cleveland. They appeared to be headed for pay dirt when Jess Whittenton intercepted a pass that was deflected by John Symank and returned it 35 yards. Starr passed to McGee for 12 yards. Hornung rushed for 19 yards to the Cleveland four where Taylor followed Jerry Kramer into the end zone for his fourth TD of the game to build the lead to 35-10.

The Browns still fought back to score another TD making the game a little tighter at 35-17.

After an exchange of fumbles, the Packers found high gear again. Starr was sacked for a six-yard loss, but not to be deterred, he connected with McGee on the Browns' 20 where McGee juked a pass defender and then raced into the end zone. The Packers now led by a healthy margin of 42-17.

The Packers scored once more when backup quarterback John Roach recovered his own fumble at the one and slipped into the end zone to bring final score to 49-17.

Statistically, Taylor, McGee, and Starr had a great day. Besides his four touchdowns to tie the record held by Hornung and Don Hutson, Taylor carved out 158 yards on the day, 47 more yards than Jim Brown and Bob Mitchell combined for Cleveland. McGee hauled in five passes for 120 yards, and Starr completed 13 of 15 passes for 272 yards.

Green Bay's masterful victory over the Browns kept the Pack (4-1) in step with San Francisco (4-1), winners, 38-24, over the Vikes (1-4), for first place in the West. The Bears (3-2) and the Lions (3-2) held on to third place with wins over Baltimore (2-3) and Los Angeles (1-4), respectively, 24-10 and 14-13.

Back East, Philadelphia (4-1) and New York (4-1) remained on top with wins over St. Louis (2-3) and Dallas (3-2), respectively, 20-7 and 31-10. Washington (0-5) booted Pittsburgh (1-4) out of the cellar, losing 20-0 to the Steelers.

The AFL standings began to take real shape in its Week 6. San Diego (6-0) remained the only pro team without a loss by handing New York (3-2) a 25-10 loss. Buffalo (3-3) moved into second in the East with a 27-24 win over Dallas (3-2), now a distant second in the West. Denver (2-4) stepped out of the basement in the West with a 27-24 win over Oakland (1-4). Houston (1-3-1) continued to reside at the bottom of the Eastern Division, being held to a 31-all tie by Boston (2-2-1).

With the Packers on a four-game winning streak, bad news found its way into the locker room on Tuesday morning, October 17. Uncle Sam pointed his bony index finger at Paul Hornung and Ray Nitschke and said, "Report for duty on October 30, Mr. Hornung, with the 896th Engineer Corps at Fort Riley, Kansas. And you, Mr. Nitschke, report to 32nd National Guard Division of Wisconsin at Fort Lewis, Washington by November 2. You're in the Army now, men. Not behind the line of scrimmage, waiting to plow up the dirt with your cleats."

Vince Lombardi never took any opponent lightly. He believed in and understood Pete Rozelle's famous quote quite seriously. "On any given Sunday ..." Lombardi prepared for every game as if the title was on the line. Minnesota might have been an expansion team, but that made no difference to him. The Vikings were all pros, and Norm Van Brocklin, their coach, although a rookie at the helm, was no fool on the sidelines. Finally, Lombardi told his team to remember how the Vikings handled the Bears in their first league game ever. To him, that kid Fran Tarkenton was hell on wheels and the key to defending Minnesota was stopping the scrambler from Georgia. Containment, containment, containment! The Bears hadn't been ready to do this. Lombardi's Packers would be.

Van Brocklin's game plan was to stop Jim Taylor and Paul Hornung. That would have been a gargantuan task if both men had been playing on healthy wheels. Both men had taken a beating the week before in Cleveland, and neither was totally healed from all those bumps and bruises at the hands of the Browns.

Playing before a record crowd of 42,007, the game started with the Vikings winning the coin toss and receiving the ball. After holding the ball for almost four minutes and three first downs, they were forced to punt. The Packers set up on their own 21, and Bart Starr went for the goal on the very first play. He found Boyd Dowler racing down the sideline all alone and dropped the ball into the speedy receiver's arms at the Minnesota 40. Dowler then scampered straight to the end zone untouched for the first touchdown of the day. Paul Hornung booted his first field goal of the day later in the period, and the Packers went into the second stanza, leading, 10-0.

Minnesota made its only scoring drive early in the second on the legs of Fran Tarkenton who plunged into end zone from the one. The Packers countered the Vikings with Hornung's second field goal, an 18-yarder, to bring the halftime score to Packers 13, Vikings 7.

The Packers received the second half kickoff and marched down the field to the Minnesota six. Bart Starr provided the big action with completions of 11 yards to Tom Moore and 13 and 22 yards to Max McGee. The attack bogged down in the red zone, and Green Bay had to settle for another Hornung field goal, this from 13 yards out, giving the Bays a 16-7 lead.

An interception by Ray Nitschke ended the Vikes' next threat. Each team then punted on their next possession before Tom Moore ended the third quarter with a 14-yard gallop. On the first play of the final stanza, Moore connected with Ron Kramer for a 20-yard gain. Moore followed that with another sprint of 18 yards to the Minnesota 14. The attack stalled at this point, bringing Hornung into the game to boot his final field goal of the day, this one from 16 yards out.

Willie Wood intercepted Tarkenton's first pass of the fourth to demoralize the Vikes. After an incomplete pass by Starr, Moore took the handoff and raced 69 yards before being pushed across the sideline on the Minnesota 13. Ron Kramer gained nine yards on an end around before Jim Taylor waltzed in from the three, raising the lead to 26-7. Not much later, Dan Currie intercepted another Vikings pass and returned it 21 yards for the last touchdown of the day to make the final score, 33-7.

Hornung tied his own record of four field goals in one game that he set the year before against Pittsburgh. The Vikings did a fairly good job of holding back Jim Taylor who only gained 46 yards on 16 carries, but there was no stopping Tom Moore who ran for 159 yards on 16 carries. Bart Starr had a so-so day, completing just nine passes of the 19 he threw, but he still managed rack up 206 yards.

Lombardi said after the game that the Packers could have played better, but he gave credit to a spirited Minnesota team, saying they were better than Dallas was the year before. The victory was far from perfect, but a win is still a win in the standings.

The win was the fifth straight for Green Bay (5-1). Minnesota (1-5) suffered its fifth straight loss. Good news for the Packers! The Bears (4-2) shut down the 49ers (4-2) to grab a share of second place in the West, dominating San Francisco, 31-0. Baltimore (3-3) got back on the winning track with a 17-14 victory over Detroit (3-3).

In the East, New York (5-1) and Philadelphia (5-1) remained tied for first with wins over Los Angeles (1-5) and Dallas (3-3) by the scores of 24-14 and 43-7, respectively. Cleveland (4-2) stayed in the race by giving Pittsburgh (1-5) another narrow loss, 30-28. St. Louis (3-3) continued to be a dark horse with their 24-0 shutout of winless Washington (0-6).

The Chargers (7-0) continued to be the only undefeated team in either league, whipping Oakland (1-5) big, 41-10. Denver (3-4) took down New York (3-3), still leading the East, 27-10. Boston (3-3-1), in second in the East, gave a 52-21 beating to Buffalo (3-4). Houston (2-3-1), still in last in the East, began showing signs of life with a 38-7 tromping of in-state rival Dallas (3-3).

First Paul Hornung and Ray Nitschke got called to active duty in the military, then Boyd Dowler received word to report to report to Fort Lewis, Washington on November 3. Lombardi sent requests to the Army to defer the reporting dates for all three, but he held out little hope that they would be approved. Hornung was still nursing a pinched nerve in his neck. He went to the Army induction center in Milwaukee to have a physical to determine whether he should still report for duty at Fort Riley, Kansas. While waiting for the results of that examination, Hornung received another order to report for a physical; this one at the U.S. Navy Hospital in Great Lakes, Illinois on Monday, October 30.

Packer fans got into the act on behalf of the team's players who had been called to active duty. They requested Senator Alexander Wiley (R-Wis.) to help them gain deferments for Hornung, Nitschke, and Dowler to report after the conclusion of the NFL season. Wiley complied to their wishes, and when he did, two congressmen from Wisconsin spoke against deferments for entertainers such as pro football players. Representatives Alvin E. O'Konski and Melvin Laird voiced their opinions that deferments for these people would be absolutely unfair to other men being called up who weren't entertainers.

Bill Forester of the Packers spoke up for his teammates. "If the Colts can get Lamar McHan deferred until the end of the season because of seasonal occupation, there's no reason why we can't get our three deferred for the same reason."

When the NFL decided to split into two divisions in 1933 and schedule each team to play the other teams in its division twice in a home-and-away series every season, the intention of doing so was to increase the level of competition in the league. The owners figured it would be more difficult for one team to dominate its division because it would have to play a majority of its games within the division. In 1935, they added the college player draft to balance the level of competition even further. It didn't take long for the coaches to figure out they had to change their strategies every time they played a team for the second time in a season, especially if their games were only two or three weeks apart. Defeating a divisional opponent twice in one campaign gradually became more difficult as the years went on. Very seldom did two teams square off on back-to-back Sundays. But when they did, it was usually a nightmare for the coach trying to win two in a row.

This was the dilemma facing Vince Lombardi in Week 7 of the 1961 schedule. His Packers handed the Vikings what seemed like an easy beating, 33-7, but the truth was Minnesota had played a fairly tough game. With a break or two here and there during the course of the game, the outcome could have been different or at the very least the final score would have been much closer. Lombardi knew his next opponent wasn't just the Vikings in Milwaukee; it was complacency by his players. They had won five straight and sat all alone on top of their division. Game 7 appeared to be another certain victory for the boys in green and gold. The Vikings had other thoughts.

A spirited crowd of 44,112 turned out at Milwaukee County Stadium to see the rematch between the Packers and expansion club Minnesota. The game got off on a sour note for Green Bay as Jerry Kramer suffered a severe ankle injury on the opening kickoff. Green Bay's defense forced the Vikes to punt on their first possession. Then Bart Starr directed his team 67 yards to pay dirt on a one-yard plunge by Paul Hornung to give the Packers an early lead of 7-0. Minnesota was stymied again on its next drive. Starr engineered a second scoring drive, this one for 70 yards, culminated with a 10-yard toss to Max McGee by Hornung, putting Green Bay ahead at the end of the first period, 14-0.

Both teams had trouble getting into the end zone in the second quarter. Bart Starr, who was having a great day, connected with Jim Taylor for eight yards and a TD with 2:35 left on the clock. The

Vikings finally got on the scoreboard with 1:24 to go in the half. Green Bay led, 21-7.

The second half was mostly a defensive contest as neither of the teams could do much damage to the other. Minnesota managed a field goal in the final minute of the third stanza to close the gap to 21-10, but that was all the offense the visitors could muster the rest of the way. The Packers did manage to score an insurance six with 4:33 remaining in the game as Bart Starr hooked up with Max McGee for a 22-yard scoring pass to put the game away, 28-10.

Bart Starr put up the best performance of the day, completing 18 of 24 passes for 311 yards, two touchdowns, and no interceptions. Max McGee hauled in six passes for 102 yards and a touchdown. Boyd Dowler caught five throws for 121 yards. Paul Hornung gained 70 yards on 12 carries, while Jim Taylor managed just 54 yards on 16 attempts.

Green Bay (6-1) kept its hold on first place in the West just one game ahead of Chicago (5-2), winners over Baltimore (3-4) by the narrowest of margins, 21-20. Detroit (4-3) moved into a tie for third with a 28-10 victory over Los Angeles (1-6). In the upset of the week, San Francisco (4-3) took on one the chin, 20-10, from the lowly Pittsburgh Steelers (2-5). Minnesota (1-6) remained in the West's cellar with the Rams.

Philadelphia (6-1) maintained its hold on first place in the East with a close 27-24 win over Washington (0-7). New York (5-2) fell into a tie for second by losing, 17-16, to Dallas (4-3), now in fourth all alone. Cleveland (5-2) regained a share of second place by trimming St. Louis (3-4) on the road, 21-10.

The race for the Western Division title was all but over in the AFL's Week 8. Still undefeated, San Diego (8-0) put the big hurt on Denver (3-5), shutting out the Broncos, 37-0. New York (4-3) held on to the Eastern Division lead, winning 14-6 over poor Oakland (1-6). Boston (4-3-1) held on to second place in the East with a narrow 18-17 win over Dallas (3-4). Houston (3-3-1) continued its comeback with a 28-16 victory over Buffalo (3-5).

Good news, bad news for the AFL as the new league reached its halfway point for the 1961 season. On the positive side, league attendance was up 7.4 percent over the previous year for the same time period. Leading the way was undefeated San Diego with an average of 27,352 for three home games. Chargers management expected to top

30,000 for each of its four remaining home games. The bad news was the squabbling of the three Oakland partners on where the Raiders should play their home games in 1962. Two wanted to play in Oakland, while the senior partner wanted to continue using Kezar Stadium and Candlestick Park in San Francisco. Time would tell if and when this would play out.

Green Bay finished the first half of the season with a six-game winning streak. The second half loomed ominously for the Pack. In their first seven games, two were on the road. two at County Stadium in Milwaukee, and three at home. The next seven were nearly the opposite; five on the road, one in Milwaukee, and one at City Stadium. Oddsmakers projected a tougher than tough schedule over the final two months. Six of the seven were against Western Conference opponents, and the seventh was against the always brutal New York Giants. The bookies conceded wins against Los Angeles because the Rams were the dregs of the division. The other four contests had the Packers in Baltimore, Chicago, Detroit, and San Francisco; none of them exactly soft-touch venues for any visitor.

Lombardi cautioned Packer fans about his team's chances as the second half approached. "Everybody's in it. We won six straight. Somebody could go out and win seven in a row." He recognized the truth of the matter. There were no guarantees, looking ahead.

His immediate problems were preparing for the Colts with his roster shrunken by injuries and military call-ups. Missing in action were Paul Hornung, Ray Nitschke, and Jerry Kramer.

Hornung was down in Illinois getting a physical at Great Lakes Naval Training Base to see if his pinched nerve would be a hindrance to his Army duties. The report on his condition wouldn't be known for as much as 10 days. In the meantime, he would have to stay at the hospital for three or four days. If all this were to transpire as predicted, he might have a chance of playing in Baltimore.

Nitschke left the team at least for the duration of the current season. He was due to report for active duty with the 32nd Division at Fort Lewis, Washington by the coming Friday, November 3.

Kramer suffered a badly stretched ligament in his ankle on the opening kickoff in Sunday's game against Minnesota. He was in a cast in the hospital, recuperating from the injury. Lombardi said Kramer was expected to miss three or four games.

Boyd Dowler had received a reprieve from reporting to Fort

Lewis with Nitschke because his orders didn't arrive at the same time as Nitschke's. Dowler would be available for the Colts and possibly for the game after that.

Ron Kramer sprained an ankle in the Minnesota game, but he was already feeling better by Tuesday morning. He was expected to be good to go on Sunday against the Colts.

Two days later the Packers were informed that Hornung would be available for the next two games. The next day word came that the Army declared him fit for duty and that he would have to report to Fort Riley, Kansas on November 14.

At the same time, Lombardi and staff were trying to figure out how to fill the holes left by the departure of Nitschke and the injury to Jerry Kramer. The first was a no-brainer. Veteran Tom Bettis was moved into the starting linebacker position Nitschke had been playing. When Kramer went down against the Vikings, Ken Iman and Norm Masters filled in for him. During the week, Lombardi toyed with the idea of moving Forrest Gregg into Kramer's guard position and using big Ben Davidson at Gregg's usual position of right tackle. The experiment with Big Ben didn't work out, and Lombardi decided to go with Masters in Kramer's spot.

Baltimore was having a mediocre season so far. The Colts had narrow wins over Los Angeles, Minnesota, and Detroit by a total of 10 points. Of their four losses, the only one that was a blowout came at the hands of the Packers in Green Bay. They lost both games to the Bears; the second defeat by a single point. Baltimore's record could have been 5-2 or just as easily an embarrassing 0-7.

Lombardi told his players not to judge the Colts by their record. Baltimore still had the horses to beat anybody in the league. The Colts were not to be taken lightly.

Game day saw a capacity crowd filling the stands at Baltimore Memorial Stadium; the 10th consecutive sellout for the Colts. The fiery Baltimore fans put a charge into the home team right from the start. Lenny Lyles took Paul Hornung's opening kickoff on the two and returned it 64 yards to the Pack's 34. Six plays later Joe Perry burst into the end zone with the first touchdown of the day. The Packers came right back with a 70-yard seven play drive of their own to tie the game at seven on a 21-yard scramble by Bart Starr.

The Colts fumbled the ball away on their next possession, and the Packers were forced to punt on theirs. Starting on their own 40,

Baltimore drove 60 yards on 13 plays to score their second TD on a six-yard toss from Johnny Unitas to one-time Green Bay draft pick Alex Hawkins. Unaccustomed to being behind, the Packers roared right back, moving the ball 75 yards in seven plays. Hornung bulled into the end zone from 17 yards out to tie the score again, 14-14. This was the final show of offense for the Packers. From this point on, the Colts dominated on both sides of the ball, scoring 31 unanswered points before Jess Whittenton picked off an errant pass from Lamar McHan and raced 41 yards to the end zone to make the final tally a blistering victory for the Colts, 45-21.

Although the winning streak ended there, Green Bay's lead in the division was still intact. The Packers (6-2) remained a game ahead of the Bears (5-3), 16-14 losers to the Eagles (7-1). Detroit (4-3-1) and San Francisco (4-3-1) played a 20-20 "sister-kisser" to pick up a half game on the Packers and Bears. The Colts (4-4) got back in the race with their win over the Pack. Los Angeles (2-7) climbed out of the cellar by defeating Minnesota (1-7) handily, 31-17. The Giants (6-2) stayed tight with Philadelphia by humiliating the Redskins (0-8) by a whopping 53-0. Cleveland (5-3) dropped into third place in the East by losing, 17-13, to Pittsburgh ((3-5). St. Louis (4-4) moved into a tie for fourth by winning, 31-17, over Dallas (4-4).

On the ledger side of things, the NFL set a new one-day record for attendance. Pittsburgh-Cleveland led the way with 62,723 paid fans. Chicago-Philadelphia came in a close second with 60,471. The Packers-Colts did their part with 57,641. Detroit-San Francisco played before 56,878 disappointed patrons. Washington-New York had 56,077 show up at Yankee Stadium. Minnesota-Los Angeles could only muster 38,594 even though the AFL Chargers had moved to San Diego. St. Louis-Dallas brought up the rear with 20,500. The grand total for the day was 353,084, beating the old mark of 326,594, which was set earlier in the year.

Over in the AFL, three games on the same day drew 61,982 with more than half that number, 33,391, in San Diego to see the Chargers play New York. Houston at Denver only attracted 11,564 die-hard fans. Oakland-Buffalo wasn't much better with 17,027.

The Chargers (9-0) won again, 48-13, over New York (4-4). San Diego's victory clinched at least a tie for first place in the West. Dallas (4-5) lost, 28-21, to Boston (5-3-1). Houston (4-3-1) kept pace with the Patriots by crushing the Broncos (3-6) in Denver, 55-14.

Oakland (2-6) won its second game of the year, 31-22, over Buffalo (3-6). Although the Chargers had a stranglehold on first place in the West, the Eastern Division was still a wide-open race. The last place Bills still had a mathematical chance of taking first, but it was highly unlikely they could climb over all three teams ahead of them. After starting the season 0-3, the Oilers had won four and tied one, making them the hottest team in the East. Still, they had six weeks to play, and anything could happen.

For the Packers, Week 9 was "Hell Week" for them; meaning a trip to Chicago to fight with the Monsters of the Midway at Wrigley Field. Lombardi kept up his usual stiff upper lip and positive attitude in the public eye, but the reality of it was he felt he was going into the game with one arm tied behind his back. Meaning? The Pack's roster was already two players short with Ray Nitschke wearing Army khakis and Jerry Kramer still in the hospital and now probably done for the season due to surgery on his ankle. Those two out of the lineup was bad enough. Now Lombardi was worried about losing the services of Ron Kramer due to an ankle in injury suffered against the Colts. A devout Catholic who attended mass daily the coach now had one more prayer to add to his devotions.

The coach's prayers were answered. Word came late Friday that the Army had given Private Ray Nitschke a weekend pass like any other soldier. What they didn't say was his pass had no restrictions on it limiting how far he go within the contiguous 48 states like nearly every other serviceman's liberty pass did. Nitschke boarded a plane for Chicago on Saturday morning and was due back at Fort Lewis by midnight Sunday. The fact that the 32nd Division, Nitschke's unit, was based in Janesville, Wisconsin allegedly had nothing to do with him being allowed to travel anywhere within the mainland United States. Some of those guys in the 32nd were actually Bear fans, and they didn't care if Nitschke made it to the game or not. Sure, they didn't care. Not much, they didn't!

Certainly, Lombardi thanked his Maker for having a hand in getting Nitschke to Chicago for the game. It was more than likely he asked the Almighty for another bit of help as well. Just maybe he prayed for a win over the Bears that Sunday afternoon. Most likely, he did.

After the game was over, Lombardi told the press that the Pack won a half and the Bears won a half and the difference in the game was a toe. He didn't mention the outcome of the contest because everyone in the room already knew that.

Green Bay's biggest headache all day was Chicago's tight end Mike Ditka who caught nine passes for 190 yards and three TDs. He set a new Bears record for yards gained receiving in a game with 190.

After an exchange of punts following the opening kickoff, the Bears took possession when Dave Whitsell intercepted a Bart Starr pass aimed at Max McGee. With first down on the Pack's 47, Ditka slipped past John Symank and snared Billy Wade's aerial on the 10 and charged into the end zone to put Chicago ahead, 7-0.

The Bays stormed back, going 80 yards in nine plays to tie the score. On the ninth play, Starr drifted to his right and rifled the ball to Ron Kramer who took it away from defender Harlon Hill and raced into the end zone.

Chicago reached Green Bay's 26 before their drive stalled. This set up a field attempt by Roger LeClerc from 33 yards out. The kick sailed wide to the left.

That happy turn of events set the Packers off on yet another 80-yard charge to paydirt, in 13 plays this time. The drive ended with an eight-yard Starr pass to Ron Kramer in the left flat for the TD, making the score 14-7 Packers.

A holding penalty on the Bears and timely tackling by Dan Currie and Bill Quinlan, and a sack by Willie Davis put the ball just one-foot away from being a safety forced Chicago to punt. Ed Brown could only pooch the kick to the Bears' 35 yard-line. Lew Carpenter hauled it in and returned the ball to the Chicago eight, thanks mostly to a solid block by John Symank. From there, Hornung took Starr's handoff and found the hole off right tackle to burst into the end zone for the Pack's third touchdown of the day, making the score 21-7.

An exchange of punts followed before Wade hit Ditka on the Chicago 34 where he fumbled on a solid hit by Willie Wood who made the recovery for Green Bay. On the very next play, Starr rolled to his right and zipped the ball to Hornung for the last score of the half, putting the Packers up, 28-7.

The Bears received the second-half kickoff, made one first down, and then were forced to punt. Green Bay moved the ball to the Chicago 44 before being forced to punt or kick a field goal. Lombardi chose the second option. Hornung came through with a 51-yarder that barely made it over the crossbar, giving the Packers a 31-7 lead that appeared to be insurmountable.

These were the Monsters of the Midway the Packers were playing. On the ensuing kickoff, the Bears rose up on their hind legs and mounted a ferocious comeback. While totally stifling Green Bay's offense, Chicago scored three unanswered touchdowns, the last with just 2:53 left in the game. The Packers then ran out the clock, keeping the ball for 10 plays to preserve a 31-28 victory, defeating the Bears twice in one season for the first time since 1935.

Hornung had the big day for Green Bay, rushing for 94 yards a TD on 22 carries and catching one pass for 34 yards and a touchdown. Ron Kramer caught just two passes for 61 yards, but both put sixes on the board.

The win increased Green Bay's (7-2) lead in the West to a game and a half over Detroit (5-3-1), a big winner, 45-14, over St. Louis (4-5) and two games over Chicago (5-4). San Francisco (4-4-1) continued to slip in the standings, losing, 17-7, to rising Los Angeles (3-6). Baltimore (4-5) continued its slide, losing, 28-20, to Minnesota (2-7). New York (7-2) moved into a tie for first in the East with a 38-21 win over Philadelphia (7-2). Cleveland (6-3) remained in the running for the Eastern title with a 17-6 victory over lowly Washington (0-9). Dallas (4-5) began to lose hope for a winning season when Pittsburgh (4-5) handed them a loss, 37-7.

San Diego (10-0) clinched the AFL's Western Division title with a 19-14 victory over Denver (3-7). Houston (5-3-1) continued its winning streak with a 27-15 win over Boston (5-4-1). New York (5-4) kept pace with a 23-12 defeat of Oakland (2-7). Buffalo (4-6) stayed in the Eastern Division race with a 30-20 come-from-behind win over Dallas (3-6), losers for the fourth straight week.

The AFL did have some other good news that week. Joe Foss reported overall attendance was up 11 percent over the league's first season. "What has happened this season is something we didn't quite expect—the development of a nucleus of at least three, maybe four, solid franchises." He admitted that the junior circuit still had problems with four clubs, those being Dallas, New York, Oakland, and Denver. However, he was cheered by the news that the city of Oakland had voted to construct a 25,000-seat stadium. This news was positive because the Raiders were currently playing their home games in old Kezar Stadium in San Francisco. He stated that Buffalo, Houston, and San Diego looked solid for the year and the future. Boston was close to joining that group. Buffalo was the real surprise with a 20 percent increase over the previous year, considering the Bills record at home for the two campaigns was 4-14, including exhibition games. Houston was up 25 percent, while San Diego was ahead of the prior season in Los Angeles by 80%. Foss wrapped up his comments by saying there was no doubt that the AFL would be around to play in 1962.

Next up for the Packers at City Stadium were the resurgent Los Angeles Rams, winners of their last two games. Lombardi felt the Pack could win the Western Conference by taking four of their last five contests, which meant taking both home battles and stealing two on the road. A Turkey Day victory over the Lions would necessitate only three wins to clinch the title. The Packers would end up at 10-4, and the Lions would finish at 9-4-1, if they won the rest of their games. Of course, this was all speculation on Lombardi's part. As always, he was taking them one game at a time, which meant scoring more than LA on the coming Sunday.

The catch to the winning the division crown was doing it with a short roster. Jerry Kramer's season was as good as finished, and Paul Hornung, Ray Nitschke, and Boyd Dowler were all spending their week days in the Army. This left Lombardi with only 32 players for practices. Nitschke was a possible player on Sundays, if he could get a weekend pass and a flight to wherever the Packers were playing. Both Hornung and Dowler had not yet made such an arrangement at their respective posts.

The most needed position to be filled was at placekicker. Men with real experience at that spot were hard to find, but Lombardi came up with one. He signed 42-year-old Ben Agajanian, obtained from the Dallas Texans of the AFL. Agajanian was slated to kick extra points and field goals in place of Paul Hornung who would be unavailable at least for the time being. The new kicker replaced injured Jerry Kramer on the roster.

Good news for the Packers! Boyd Dowler and Ray Nitschke were both in uniform for Sunday's game with the Rams. Starting in Hornung's spot was Tom Moore.

Besides the sellout crowd, around a hundred Packer alumni attended the final home game of the regular season in Green Bay. The former Packer players sat on benches on either side of the team's allotted sideline area.

The Rams took a 7-0 lead in the first two minutes of the game.

That score held until the second quarter. Los Angeles upped the margin to 10-0 before the Packers finally got going offensively. Jim Taylor rumbled 11 yards for Green Bay's first score at the 11:17 mark of the second period. Just 3:22 later, Bart Starr connected with Max McGee for another touchdown, this one from 20 yards out, giving the Bays a 14-10 lead. Starr and McGee hooked up again with 5:00 left in the half, this this time from 10 yards away, to build the lead to 21-10. With just 0:07 remaining in the period, Starr found Boyd Dowler for a 17-yard score to boost the margin to 28-10. After a scoreless third stanza, the Rams tried to make a comeback, scoring a touchdown just 3:37 into the final quarter to cut Green Bay's lead to 28-17. Not to worry, the Packers marched right back down the field and regained their 18-point margin on a one-yard plunge by Taylor, bringing the final tally to 35-17 with the Pack on top.

Looking at the box score, the average fan would have thought the Rams had won the game. They made 19 first downs to 17 for the Packers; 110 yards rushing to 76 for Green Bay; 235 yards passing to just 173 by the Bays. Both teams committed a single turnover. The big difference that favored the home team came in penalties, punts, and punt returns. Green Bay committed only four penalties for 33 yards, while Los Angeles was flagged six times for 89 yards. The Packers booted the ball four times for an average distance of 39 yards, and the Rams punted three times for an average of 24 yards. Green Bay kick returners brought back two punts for a total of 55 yards, while LA failed to return a single kick.

All those numbers add up to the Packers winning the game with efficiency and field position. This was Lombardi football. As time had already revealed in 34 regular season games, the Lombardi method was the key to victory.

The win over the Rams (3-7) eliminated Los Angeles from the division race and kept the Packers (8-2) a game and a half in the lead. Detroit (6-3-1) kept pace with the Pack with a 37-10 thrashing of the Vikings (2-8) who were also out of the running now. San Francisco (5-4-1) climbed over the Bears (5-5), giving Chicago a 41-31 beating. Baltimore (5-5) stayed alive by downing St. Louis (4-6) by the score of 16-0.

In the East, the Giants (8-2) gained sole possession of first place with a 42-21 trimming of Pittsburgh (4-6). Cleveland (7-3) gained a share of second place with a 45-24 whipping of Philadelphia (7-3).

Dallas (4-5-1) held on to a mathematical chance of winning the East by tying Washington (0-9-1).

San Diego (11-0) continued its winning ways in the AFL by pinning a 24-14 loss on Dallas (3-7). Houston (6-3-1) maintained its half-game lead in East with a 49-13 thrashing of New York (5-5) that put the Titans a game and a half behind the Oilers. Boston (6-4-1) held on to second place in the East with a narrow 20-17 win over Oakland (2-8). Buffalo (5-6) remained two and half games out of first by giving Denver (3-8) a 23-10 loss.

With four weeks left in the regular NFL season, the Packers appeared to be on the brink of winning the Western Conference title for the second straight year. They held a game and a half lead over the Detroit Lions, their Thanksgiving Day opponent in the Motor City. A win over the Kings of the Jungle would put the Pack ahead of Detroit by two and a half games with just three games to play. One triumph in any one of that trio would give the Bays the right to play in the NFL title game. But that was looking too far ahead, according to Lombardi. One game at a time was his philosophy.

Bad news and good news for the Packers two days before the turkey day fight. Neither Tom Moore nor Hank Gremminger, both of them injured in the game against the Rams, would be healed enough to face the Lions. On the positive side, Hornung, Nitschke, and Dowler would be suiting up in green and gold. Why the green and gold? Of all things, the Lions' laundry shrunk their Hawaiian blue jerseys, making it necessary for the home team to wear their white road uniforms.

On a rainy day in Detroit when the dew drops turned the field at Tiger Stadium into a quagmire of mud, the Packers intercepted four passes—one each by four different men; Hank Gremminger who made a great catch in the end zone to prevent a possible field goal just before the half, Herb Adderly who took over for Gremminger to set up the second Packer TD, Willie Wood to kill a definite Detroit scoring threat in the fourth period and set up a field goal by Paul Hornung, and Jess Whittenton who grabbed an Earl Morrall throw on the last play of the game.

Detroit's main target was Bart Starr, the league's leading passer, but the Pack's offensive line kept the Lions' active defensive linemen at bay long enough for Starr to complete 13 out of 22 passes, including two key throws to Max McGee and Hornung that set up both Green Bay touchdowns.

John Symank returned the opening kickoff 31 yards only to fumble the ball. Fortunately, Nelson Toburen recovered it on the Green Bay 47. From there, Starr worked the offense down the field to the Detroit 14. On the next play, he had Dowler open in the end zone, but the Bays' receiver slipped on the soggy turf before the ball could arrive for him to catch it. Instead, Dick LeBeau snared the throw for Detroit and put an end to the scoring threat.

After an exchange of punts, the Lions worked the ball down to the Packers six where the drive stalled, and Detroit came away with a field goal. A fumble by Starr in the second period set up another three for the Lions, giving them a 6-0 lead. The Lions had another field goal opportunity just minutes later, but their kicker missed from 27 yards out. From there, Starr worked his magic and directed the offense to its first touchdown, a one-yard plunge by Jim Taylor with 1:20 to go in the second stanza. giving Green Bay the halftime lead, 7-6.

Detroit took the second half kickoff and rolled up five first downs before the Pack defense put a halt to their progress. This set up another Lions field goal, this one from 16 yards, giving the Lions the lead again, 9-7. Detroit's trey was the only scoring in the third quarter, but not the only offense. The Lions were on the move again until Adderly's interception at the Lions' 40. Starr put the Bays into motion again, moving them down to Detroit's four where Hornung took two tries to get the ball to the one. On the next play, the first in the final period, Jim Taylor crashed into the end zone to put the Packers back into the lead for good, 14-9. With 28 seconds left in the game, Hornung kicked an insurance three from nine yards away, making the final score 17-9.

Taylor led all rushers with 94 yards on 19 carries, while McGee topped the Packers in receiving with six receptions for 92 yards. All the individual stats aside, the victory put the Packers a solid two and a half games ahead of Detroit with three games to go in the race for the West title.

With Green Bay (9-2) firmly in control of their own fate in the Western Conference by way of their win over Detroit (6-4-1), the 49ers (6-4-1) edged in a tie for second with a 38-28 beating of the cellar dwelling Vikings (2-9). Chicago (6-5) and Baltimore (6-5) kept their mathematical hopes alive with respective wins over the (3-8) Rams, 28-24, and the hapless (0-10-1) Redskins, 27-6. The Giants (9-2) kept up their winning ways by handing Cleveland (7-4) a solid loss, 37-21.

Reigning NFL champion Philadelphia (8-3) remained right behind New York with a 35-13 bulldogging of the Cowboys (4-6-1). Now out of the running, Pittsburgh (5-6) came away with a narrow win, 30-27, over St. Louis (4-7).

In the AFL, Houston (7-3-1) picked up a half game on Boston (6-4-1) with a 45-14 bashing of Denver (3-9). New York (6-5) kept pace in the East with a 21-14 win over Buffalo (5-7), this eliminating the Bills from contention. Dallas (4-7) remained a distant second to idle San Diego (11-0) handing Oakland (2-9) a sound 43-11 thrashing.

Week 12 started off on the wrong foot for Lombardi. Taking a roll call of healthy players for the upcoming game with the mighty New York Giants at Milwaukee County Stadium, he quickly discovered he didn't have enough men to field an offense. The key man in his line, Jim Ringo, was in the hospital again with an attack of boils, this time to his face and neck. Max McGee and Jim Taylor were both in bed fighting off cases of the flu. Paul Hornung and Boyd Dowler were back in their Army fatigues, neither assured of being available for the game on Sunday. Tom Moore, Hank Gremminger, and Ron Kramer were suffering injuries from the Lions game. Jerry Kramer was still hobbling on crutches. To make matters worse, several players had come down with colds from playing in the rain and near freezing temperatures of Tiger Stadium.

Taking them one case at a time, Ringo's misery with the same infection that resulted in boils a month earlier was so severe this time that he couldn't move his jaw without feeling excruciating pain; even talking hurt. Moore's game pain was getting better by the day, so, he was a possible for the Giants. Gremminger said he could "go" if one of the starters should get banged up in the game. Same with Ron Kramer. Both McGee and Taylor felt they would recover enough to play on Sunday. All the others with colds said they would man up and be ready to go by kickoff. Jerry Kramer was still a definite out of the lineup. As for the men in service, all three were possible for action.

On Tuesday morning in New York, the NFL front office conducted a coin flip session to determine who would play whom and where they would play in case of a tie or ties in both divisions.

In the event of a three-way tie in the East, Cleveland won the bye and New York and Philadelphia would play each other in Philly December 24. The winner would then visit Cleveland a week later.

In two-way ties in the Eastern Conference Cleveland would

host the playoff game if the Browns were one of the participants. If the game was between New York and Philadelphia, the Giants would play host.

The Western Conference would settle one three-way tie with Green Bay getting the bye and Detroit hosting San Francisco. Green Bay would then host the winner. In a second scenario, Green Bay would get the bye and Chicago would be host to Baltimore with Green Bay hosting that winner.

In the first two-way tie possibility, Detroit would be host to Green Bay or to San Francisco if the Packers should lose their last three games and the Lions and 49ers win out. San Francisco would host Green Bay if they tied. If the playoff came down to the Packers against the Bears, Green Bay would host. If Baltimore tied either Chicago or Green Bay, the Colts would be the host.

Of course, the Packers could settle matters in the West simply by winning one more game. The Giants didn't have that luxury. They had to win out to assure themselves of a shot at the NFL title game.

By the time the Packers arrived in Milwaukee, the only player still on the injured list was Jerry Kramer. All the flu and cold victims had recovered from their viruses, and Jim Ringo's boils had cleared up enough for him to play on Sunday.

To make matters even better for Lombardi's team, two of the three soldier boys were on their way to Wisconsin. Only Nitschke would miss the game. Dowler and Hornung were eager for the battle with the Giants. A joyful Lombardi declared his boys were ready to go.

With the temperatures in the upper 40s and no precipitation falling from the sky, the Packers received the opening kickoff and Bart Starr guided them down the field to New York's 16-yardline before stalling. Paul Hornung then booted the ball through the uprights to give Green Bay an early 3-0 lead.

The Giants wasted little time coming right back on their first possession. After returning the kickoff to their own 29, the New York eleven rolled the distance to paydirt, scoring the game's first TD on a 1-yard sneak by Y.A. Tittle. Pat Summerall converted the PAT to give the Giants a 7-3 lead.

Green Bay's next possession sputtered to a halt on the New York 18, necessitating another field goal attempt from Hornung. He did his job, splitting the uprights from 25 yards out and bringing the Packers closer but still trailing, 7-6.

The Gothamites appeared to be on their way to upping their points on the scoreboard until Willie Davis recovered a fumble near mid-field. Starr started the offense moving again, and this time Jim Taylor found the end zone on a 14-yard rumble. Hornung converted the extra point to give Green Bay the lead, 13-7.

Unperturbed, the Giants came right back, marching 70 yards to the end zone. Bob Gaiters gained the final two yards to score the touchdown that tied the score at 13. Summerall's PAT attempt gave New York the lead again, 14-13.

At this point, the game looked like a slugfest with 27 points on the board in just 16:44. This was the point where the defenses took command of play. The only scoring until the fourth quarter was a Summerall field goal just before the end of the half. The Packers were their own worst enemy, losing the ball at the New York one and three on interceptions and at the one again on a Taylor fumble.

Finally, the Packers mounted a last period charge that ended with a three-yard blast by Taylor and a Hornung PAT, to give Green Bay a 20-17 edge with 10:20 to go in the game. The Giants appeared headed for a winning touchdown late in the game. New York had the ball on the Pack's 22 when Coach Allie Sherman called for a reverse. Tom Bettis sniffed out the play and forced Gaiters to fumble after taking the handoff from Alex Webster. Once again, Willie Davis was the man of the hour as he pounced on the loose ball. The Packers then ran out the final two-plus minutes on the clock and came away with the 20-17 victory *and* the Western Conference title for 1961.

The Packers (10-2) clinched the West, while the Giants (9-3) fell into a tie with the Eagles (9-3), winners, 35-24, over Pittsburgh (5-7). This set up a "make-it-or-break-it" game the following Sunday in the City of Brotherly Love between New York and Philadelphia. The winner of that contest might be the Pack's opponent at City Stadium on December 31.

As for the rest of the NFL, Cleveland (8-4) remained masters of their own fate with a 38-17 spanking of the Cowboys (4-7-1). St. Louis (5-7) showed promise for 1962 with a 38-24 win over the very hapless Redskins (0-11-1). Had the Packers lost, Detroit (7-4-1) and Baltimore (7-5) would have remained in contention for the division crown with their elimination wins of 16-15 over Chicago (6-6) and 21-17 over (San Francisco (6-5-1), respectively. In their battle for the cellar, Minnesota (3-9) gave a 42-21 shearing to the Rams (3-9).

The AFL presented their fans with a possible scenario of who might meet in their championship game as the undefeated Chargers traveled to Texas to square off with the Oilers. A league record crowd of 37,845 turned out to cheer Houston's Roughnecks (8-3-1) to a 33-13 victory over San Diego (11-1). Still very much in the running for Eastern Division honors, Boston (7-4-1) took down Denver (3-10) in a close one, 28-24. New York (7-5) handled Dallas (4-8) by a 28-7 score. In the cellar-dweller game, Buffalo (6-7) slipped by Oakland (2-10) in a close encounter, 24-21.

Although the Packers had wrapped up the division crown, they still had two games to play against the West Coast teams. The first was against the 49ers in San Francisco's Kezar Stadium.

The Packers ran into a blazing hot John Brodie who dented the Green Bay pass defense for 329 yards on 19 of 29 passing. Brodie put up a pair of touchdowns; one each to Bernie Casey and R.C. Owens to give the 49ers a 14-0 lead in the second quarter. Green Bay retaliated with a touchdown on a pass from Tom Moore to McGee for 23 yards with 3:11 to go in the half. Bart Starr was tackled in the end zone in the third period to give the 49ers a 16-7 lead. Later in that stanza Bart Starr found McGee for a 13-yard score to bring the Pack within two points, 16-14. Kicker Tommy Davis booted a field goal with 6:53 left in the game to up the 49er lead to 19-14. Starr led the charge down the field to set up Jim Taylor for a four-yard burst into the end zone with 2:12 left on the clock.

Trailing 21-19, the 49ers charged right back. Abe Woodson took the kickoff and raced 50 yards to the Green Bay 45. Brodie completed two passes for 32 yards to the Pack's 13. Three running plays took the ball to the seven, but more importantly, they killed much of the time left in the game. Davis put up another three with just 0:11 left on the clock. The Packers were unable to pull off a miracle, and San Francisco came away with a 22-21 victory.

The loss made no difference to Green Bay (10-3) in the West's standings, but for the 49ers (7-5-1) the victory kept them in the race for the consolation game to be played by the two second-place clubs in each division. Still ahead of San Francisco stood the Lions (8-4-1) who held the Vikings (3-10) at bay, 13-7. The Rams (4-9) broke the Colts, 34-17, spoiling Baltimore's (7-6) chances of a post-season game. The Bears (7-6) eliminated Cleveland (8-5) from the Eastern Conference race with a narrow 17-14 victory. Pittsburgh (6-7) gave the Redskins

(0-12-1) a beating, 30-14. St. Louis (6-7) did likewise to Dallas (4-8-1), handing them a 31-13 loss. In the game of the day, the Giants (10-3) bounced back from their loss to the Packers the week before by edging the Eagles (9-4) in a 28-24 affair riddled with questionable calls by the officials.

The AFL still had a race for first place in the Eastern Division. Boston (8-4-1), winners, 35-21, over Oakland (2-11), continued to trail Houston (9-3-1), victors, 48-21, over New York, (7-6) by one game. San Diego (12-1) won again, 28-10, beating Buffalo (6-8). Meanwhile, Dallas (5-8) nailed down second place in the West with a 49-21 win over Denver (3-11).

Lombardi knew the final game of the regular season against Los Angeles was meaningless to the team, so he didn't hesitate to rest some players who had taken a beating in recent games. He started by announcing that Max McGee would be sitting out the game in LA and Lew Carpenter would play in his place. McGee had suffered cracked ribs and a bruised kidney in the game with San Francisco. Figuring Hornung needed a rest as well, the coach said Tom Moore would be his replacement in the starting lineup. As it turned out, Hornung could not get a pass for that weekend. Ben Agajanian would be in the lineup to do the placekicking for Hornung.

Jim Murray, one of the greatest sportswriters of all time, wrote a piece in the *Los Angeles Times* about the upcoming game between the Packers and Rams.

"Today ... in the Coliseum, the Los Angeles Rams will play the final game of the 1961 season. The opposition will be the U.S. Army.

"... not all the Green Bay Packers are soldiers on leave from the cold war... Just the good ones. They've got so many GIs in the lineup it looks like a stag line at the USO.

"In order to spring them from week to week, the games are officially designated by the NATO high command as bivouacs. And they don't make first downs; they take prisoners.

"...'Red Dogs' are referred to for the day as 'Crimson K-9's' and anyone who drops a pass gets immediately busted to private.

"They won't use a whistle for the day. A bugle. Reveille for kickoff, retreat for the defensive unit, and taps for whoever bumps into Roy Hord on an end sweep. Broken jaws get the purple heart...

"They won't have pep talks between the halves, but mail call. 'Dear John' letters will be saved till after the game.

"The game ball will be awarded to Sgt. York or Audie Murphy. If somebody bumps into Roy Hord and Art Hunter simultaneously, however, the game ball will be awarded to him. Posthumously.

"Press box credentials have been requested for its scouts by Russia. Gromyko will man the field phones. Player rebellions ... will not be tolerated—unless staged by the Rams. Any Packer rebelling will be turned over to the MPs or shot by the half-time gun.

"The Green Bay Packers may be the first team ever to win the cold war and the National Football League Championship the same year, and if so, they will get a unit citation from the White House and a check from Pete Rozelle at the same time. If they get run over by Lamar Lundy or scalded to death by Hamp Pool, they will get a full 21-gun burial in Arlington National Cemetery.

"There will be a camp show between halves, starring Bob Hope, Jayne Mansfield, and the Andrews Sisters. If Bratkowski is on target, the Packers have permission to run up barrage balloons. The card stunts will spell out 'Uncle Sam Needs You.'

"The Packers will probably be the first team in history to win the title by a furlough. Actually, the Rams will also be out on a weekend pass—from the play pen.

"The name of the game is the Old Army Game. Don't buy tickets. Buy bonds. And remember, somewhere out in the wilds of Ft. Riley, Kan., is a boy doing double duty for the absent-with-leave Hornung. That is, he's taking two girls out on one week's pay. Let's have a moment of silence in honor of THAT unknown soldier.

"The point spread, and casualty lists are military secrets. If you see anyone going around talking about them with an accent like a male Zsa Gabor, contact your nearest poolroom and ask for General Intelligence. They'll take your bet there."

By game time in Los Angeles, the Packers were already aware of their opponent-to-be on December 31 for the NFL crown. And it wasn't the Philadelphia Eagles. They didn't think about that game because now they had to face the Rams.

The Packers scored first and last in the game. Tom Moore took a short run to paydirt to give Green Bay a 7-0 lead. The Rams put up a three to keep them in the game. Moore caught a Bart Starr pass for eight yards and another TD before the half to make it 14-3 Green Bay after two periods. The Rams drew closer in the third quarter, 14-10, and then took the lead, 17-14, 35 seconds into the final stanza. Without a blink, Starr maneuvered his team into field goal range. Ben Agajanian connected from 28 yards out to tie the game at 17-all. The Rams made a threat to retake the lead, but Willie Wood ended the drive by snaring a Zeke Bratkowski pass. Starr showed his mastery at moving his team down the field. Starting on the Pack's 34, he completed a 14-yarder to Boyd Dowler on the Green Bay 48. Lew Carpenter picked up five yards on a reverse. Moore picked up six yards and first down on two carries to the LA 41. On the next play, Starr found Dowler again down the middle, this time for a gain 24 yards to the Rams' 17. Elijah Pitts took a handoff from Starr, veered outside the left tackle, and turned on the speed to score standing up with 2:53 remaining in the game. The Packers defense then held the Rams on their final two possessions to give themselves a 24-17 victory.

The win gave the Packers (11-3) the best record in the league, leaving the Rams (4-10) in 6th Place in the Western Conference. New York's Giants (10-3-1) tied, 7-7, with the Browns (8-5-1) who finished in 3rd Place in the Eastern Conference. Philadelphia (10-4) finished in the East by defeating Detroit (8-5-1) narrowly, 27-24. Ironically, the Lions and Eagles would be paired in the Runner-Up Bowl. Chicago (8-6) and Baltimore (8-6) tied for 3rd Place in the West with wins over Minnesota (3-11) and San Francisco (7-6-1). St. Louis (7-7) came in 4th in the East by defeating Pittsburgh (6-8). Washington (1-12-1) broke a long winless streak by beating Dallas (4-9-1).

In the AFL, the Boston Patriots (9-4-1) were all fired up when they faced the San Diego Chargers (12-2) and crushed them, 41-0. The same could be said of the Houston Oilers (10-3-1) who bashed the Oakland Raiders (2-12) by a hefty 47-16 margin. Dallas (6-8) played out the string with a 35-24 win over New York (7-7).

Now it was time for the post-season in both leagues.

§§§

16

The NFL Championship Game: New York at Green Bay

No sooner than the Packers clinched the Western Conference title with their narrow victory over the New York Giants than a major issue hit the fan. The fan in this case was "Joe Fan" who supported the team by buying tickets; season tickets, that is.

For decades the Packers had relied on support from avid fans all across Wisconsin and the Upper Peninsula of Michigan. To accommodate as many of them as they could, they chose to play a portion of their regular season schedule in Milwaukee. The officers and directors of the corporation never dreamed this would someday create a monster of a problem.

Customarily, most sports teams, professional and collegiate, allow their season ticketholders first chance at buying seats for any post-season games. Example: If a fan had four regular season tickets, then he or she could purchase those same four seats for the playoffs or the championship game, should that be the only game to be played after the regular season ended. For every other team everywhere, this was not a problem because they all played their post-season games at a neutral site, such as a college bowl game or a tournament. This two home fields situation that the Packers had with each having its own set of season ticketholders was just one more factor that made them unique in all of professional sports. (Yes, the NBA teams in that era played a few regular season games at neutral sites, but when it came to the post-season, they played at their regular home courts.)

So, what were Dominic Olejniczak and the Packers executive committee to do? No matter what they did, some fans were bound to be upset about it. However, not one of them would swear off his or her allegiance or devotion to the team.

On Friday, December 8, the *Press-Gazette* ran a story headlined:

Joe Fan To Be Taken Care Of: Ole; Title Tickets $10

Of course, this was another subterfuge by the Packers with the assistance of the press. To quote President Abraham Lincoln: "You can fool some of the people all the time, and all of the people some of the time, but you cannot fool all the people all of the time." Not every Joe Fan of the Green Bay Packers was sucked into the plan that Ole and the committee placed before them.

"Joe Fan will be taken care of when it comes to tickets for the championship game on Dec. 31"

Really? How do you "take care of" over 30,000 Green Bay season ticketholders and over 15,000 Milwaukee season ticketholders—a total of over 45,000 season ticketholders—when there would only be 41,000 seats available for the game?

Olejniczak revealed in an address to the North Side-Preble Kiwanis Club that applications will be sent to season ticketholders Monday, December 11 with a letter explaining how the Packers would be handling the ticket situation.

In the meantime, NFL Commissioner Pete Rozelle announced that all tickets would be priced at $10 each and there would be no standing room because 2,500 temporary seats would be erected for the game increasing the seating capacity to 41,100 from 38,669. The game would not be telecast in Green Bay or within a 75-mile radius of City Stadium. Milwaukee, Madison, Wausau, La Crosse, and Michigan's Upper Peninsula would receive the telecast. This game would become the first million-dollar playoff in NFL history. Should the Eastern Conference end in a three-way tie, the championship game would be moved to January 7.

On December 12, the Packers announced the formula for distribution of tickets to season ticket holders for the Championship game. If Joe Fan had one season ticket, he could buy only one ticket to the title game. If he held two season tickets, he could get two seats at the Championship. If three, then he could buy three ducats to the big game. If he owned four, five, six, seven, eight or nine season tickets, he could only purchase four title game tickets. Holding 10 or 11 regular season tickets would allow him to buy five title tickets. He could get six Championship ducats if he held 12 or 13 season tickets; 14-15 got him seven; 16-17 eight; 18-19 nine; and 20 or more would get him 10.

Season ticket holders would be allotted title game tickets on the basis of where they held the greater number of seats, whether they were in Milwaukee or Green Bay. This did not mean they would get the same seats they had during the regular season. Applications for playoff tickets had to be made by midnight December 15. Any tickets remaining after that would be reallocated to season ticket purchasers. There would be no children's tickets. The only other persons getting tickets would be the opposing team, the NFL office, and news media. There would be no public sale at all.

By the time the Packers returned home after their final regular season game against Los Angeles, all the tickets were sold, and most fans were more than satisfied with the result. They were so happy that a crowd of approximately 500 enthusiastic fans met the team at the airport Monday night. The number of well-wishers would have been greater, but the scheduled time of the team's arrival kept changing as the evening wore on. Initially, the plane was supposed to set down around 6:35 pm. This changed to 6:45, then 7:30, 7:25, 7:15, 7:56, 7:50, and finally 7:59. These delays caused some fans with school age children to leave early.

Lombardi wasted no time announcing that Tuesday would be a day for the players to rest and recuperate from their West Coast swing. He had a quartet of banged up starters who really needed the time away from the practice field. The regular routine for preparing for the next game would resume on Wednesday.

Team trainer Bud Jorgensen had at least four severe cases on his hands Tuesday morning. Max McGee with injured ribs suffered in the San Francisco game. Jim Taylor had his back hurt in the Los Angeles game. Norm Masters was still suffering with an ankle injury from the Rams game. John Symank bruised chest suffered in the LA game. Taylor and Symank went to the hospital upon arrival the night before.

The oddsmakers wasted no time installing the favorite to win the NFL title. They made the Packers a three-point pick to defeat the New York Giants at City Stadium. The gamblers cited the home field advantage and the weather as their reasons for making the Packers their choice to win the game.

The *Associated Press* sportswriters named Allie Sherman of the New York Giants as their coach-of-the-year. Lombardi and Norm Van

Brocklin tied for second.

When the Maras couldn't pry Vince Lombardi away from the Packers after the 1960 season, they turned to the man who replaced Lombardi as the Giants' offensive coach: Allie Sherman.

Alexander "Allie" Sherman was born February 10, 1923 in Brownsville, a neighborhood in the borough of Brooklyn, New York City. His parents were Phillip and Dorothy Sherman, Russian Jews who immigrated to the United States in 1920. Having a quick mind with an aptitude for learning, he skipped three grades of school and entered high school at the age of 12. A year later he tried out for the football team at Boys High School of Brooklyn. He failed to make the team because he weighed a slight 125 pounds. The coach said he was too small for such a rugged sport and suggested he try handball instead. Sherman became captain of the handball team and won division titles over the next three years. He graduated at age 16 and entered Brooklyn College.

Sherman gave football another try at Brooklyn College, and this time his coach Lou Oshins gave him a try at quarterback. When Sherman's mother saw how violent football could be, she made him quit the team. Oshins and Allie eventually convinced Mrs. Sherman to allow him to play. During the summer after his freshman year, Allie waited tables at a resort in the Catskill Mountains. Oshins mailed weekly sections of Clark Shaughnessy's book about the T-formation, leading Sherman to refer to himself as "a correspondence school quarterback." Oshins made Sherman the starting quarterback for the next three years at Brooklyn College.

After graduating in 1943 from Brooklyn College, Sherman signed a free-agent contract with Earl "Greasy" Neale, future Hall of Fame coach of the Philadelphia Eagles, for the purpose of teaching his team the T-formation. Much to his chagrin, the Eagles only had 16 players under contract. At the same time, the Pittsburgh Steelers had only six players under contract. Thus, the two teams combined to be the Phil-Pitt Combine, more popularly known as the Steagles. Pitt's head coach was Walt Kiesling, who played in the NFL for 12 years, including two seasons with the Green Bay Packers (1935 and 1936) and he served as Curly Lambeau's line coach in Green Bay for two seasons (1945 and 1946). When the owners of the Eagles and Steelers decided to merge their teams for the 1943 campaign, they could decide which of their two head coaches should be head coach of the

Combine. So, they left it to Neale and Kiesling to figure it out. The two coaches hated each other, and neither would agree to work under the other man. Kiesling wanted to install his single wing as the offense for the Steagles, while Neale wanted the team to learn the T-formation. Neale got his way because Kiesling was delayed in joining the team for its first week of practice. By the time he arrived, Allie Sherman had the Steagles running the "T" as well as he had his college eleven running it. Phil-Pitt finished the season in 3rd Place behind the Redskins and Giants. The Steelers merged with the Cardinals in 1944 as Card-Pitt, while Philadelphia got their Eagles back.

Playing both quarterback and defensive back, Sherman spent five seasons with the Eagles. They finished in 2nd Place in the East three years running (1944-46). In his final year as a player, he helped lead the Eagles to a 1st Place tie with Pittsburgh both teams 8-4. The Eagles defeated the Steelers for the right to face the Chicago Cardinals for the NFL crown. Chicago won the title, 28-27.

Before the next season, Neale advised Sherman to give up playing and take up coaching because he was such a brilliant leader and strategist. Sherman saw the wisdom of his mentor's advice and accepted the head coaching job with the Paterson Panthers, a minor league team in New Jersey. He coached and played quarterback, and the Panthers won their league's championship. Not done advising his protégé, Neale recommended Sherman to the New York Giants to be their backfield coach under Steve Owen. Sherman remained with the Giants for the next four years before resigning after the 1953 season because he was passed over for the head coaching job.

From New York, Sherman went west—and north—to serve as head coach of the Winnipeg Blue Bombers in the Canadian Football League. The Blue Bombers made the playoffs three years running, but they couldn't win the Grey Cup. Homesickness struck Sherman in 1957, so he returned to New York to scout for the Giants. Two years later the man who replaced him on the coaching staff was hired away by the Green Bay Packers, so the Maras promoted Sherman to Jim Lee Howell's staff as offensive coordinator. When Howell retired after the 1960 season, the Maras tried to wrangle their first choice away from the team they thought had promised them they could have him back when Howell hung up his whistle. The Packers said no dice, so the brothers turned to their second choice: Alexander "Allie" Sherman.

The irony of all these coaching maneuvers was Vince

Lombardi replaced Allie Sherman on the Giants staff in 1954, then Allie Sherman replaced Vince Lombardi on the Giants staff in 1959, and now the two first-time head coaches were about to square off in the 1961 National Football League Championship Game. None of this was lost on anybody covering professional football at the time.

John P. Carmichael of the *Chicago Daily News* had this view of Goliath versus David in his piece about the matchup.

"Nobody picked anybody to beat the Packers in the Western Division. After all, they were defending champions. They had a veteran lineup with fullback Jim Taylor wedging his way through opposing tacklers and Paul Hornung, the only quadruple threat in the game (run, pass, kick, and receive passes) as Taylor's vis-à-vis. So when Green Bay finished 11-3 this fall, it occasioned no surprise.

"However, the Giants, caught up in a cycle of rebuilding under a new coach, didn't rate too high. Veterans were fraying, including 14-season-old Charlie Conerly. Third place was about where the Giants figured to be behind the Eagles and Browns. But they won.

"So, there's the American scene: Green Bay's 100,000 versus New York's 8,000,000 and at Green Bay, too, where less than 47,000 seats could be sold for $100 each if they weren't already gone.

"Last year the Packers lost the finale to the Eagles. This is the time and place for the superhuman effort because next year could evolve two other teams in the annual windup.

"On a statistical basis, the Packers and the Giants emphasize their rights to challenging roles for the Eagles' crown. Green Bay rolled up the most NFL points 391, to next-best 368 by New York. The Giants led the league in first downs with 275, while the Packers paced the loop in first downs by rushing with 142.

"This, of course, is a tribute to the prowess of Taylor and Hornung along the ground, which makes quarterback Bart Starr's passing chores a bit easier.

"From a defensive standpoint, these title finalists also finished one-two; the Giants permitting only 220 points in 14 games, while the Packers yielded 223. In this same department, the Giants intercepted 33 passes, most in the league.

"This factor may cause Lombardi to continue directing his major offensive along rushing lines to minimize the chances of losing the ball.

The beauty of this game? Somebody must win between the

cities of David and Goliath.

A week before the title game Lombardi announced that Ray Nitschke and Boyd Dowler had their holiday leaves from the Army and were practicing with the team. That was the good news. The bad news came from Paul Hornung. He reported that he wouldn't be starting his holiday leave for another week, giving him only two or three days to practice with the team. Lombardi indicated not having Hornung for the full week of practice could present a serious issue for his offense.

Two days before Christmas—"Surprise! Surprise!" as Gomer Pyle would have said—Lombardi and the Packers received an early gift courtesy of the U.S. Army. Paul Hornung arrived in Green Bay more eager than ever to get on the practice field and bump heads with his teammates. Lombardi was ecstatic. The gloom and doom that had been shadowing him disappeared into that famous Lombardi grin. There would be a real game in Green Bay on the last day of the year.

While the NFL title game was scheduled for December 31, the AFL championship was set for December 24 at Balboa Stadium in San Diego No worries about the weather in sunny Southern California. The final score was Houston 10, San Diego 3, a low scoring affair due to sloppy play and a baker's dozen turnovers, seven by Houston and six by the Chargers. This was not a game to attract new fans to the nascent league.

Art Daley summed up the coming championship game a very succinct fashion. "Title Imponderables: Giants' Age, Fans, Weather." The Giants average age was much higher than the Packers', for certain. Nearly every New York regular was older than his Packer counterpart. This factor was not figured into the regular season meeting between the two teams, but now that the regular season was concluded age did matter because the recent campaign was 14 games long instead of the 12 in years past. The physical toll on older players was considered to be greater than on younger players. Advantage: Packers. More than 90% of the fans attending the game would be cheering for the hometown team. Advantage: Packers. Lombardi had his boys practicing outside in temperatures as low as five degrees BELOW zero, while Allie Sherman gave his guys a five day-vacation. Advantage: Packers. The oddsmakers made the Packers three-point favorites. Advantage: Giants.

Daley didn't want to jinx the Packers by predicting Green Bay would win the title. He simply wanted his readers to have confidence in their team—like he did.

The big day came, and the fans were ecstatic. Weather? A mild 20-plus degrees. Optimism? Astronomical!

Big Ben Agajanian kicked off for the Packers to get the game started. The Giants failed to make a first down and punted. Three and out for the Packers and they punted the ball back to the Giants. The New Yorkers put together some offense and made two first downs to the Green Bay 46. On third and 10, Kyle Rote dropped Y.A. Tittle's pass on the Pack's 35 to bring up fourth down again. Don Chandler's punt went into the end zone, giving the Packers the ball on their own 20. From this moment forward, the Boys from Green Bay were in complete charge of the contest.

Bart Starr directed the Green Bay offense 80 yards in 12 plays to pay dirt, culminating with a two-yard end run by Paul Hornung. The key play of the drive was a third-and-10 pass from Starr to Hornung for a first down at midfield. Hornung and Jim Taylor carried three times each to gain the next 30 yards. Then NY defender Erich Barnes was called for pass interference at the Gotham seven, setting up the score by Hornung. Green Bay led, 7-0, and never looked back.

The Green Bay defense had been stiff for New York's first two possession, but now they took command of the game. On the next attempt to generate some offense by the Giants, Hank Jordan deflected a pass by Tittle and Ray Nitschke snared the tipped ball and set up the Green Bay offense on New York's 34. In six plays, the Pack lead was doubled to 14-0. Starr completed a pass to Ron Kramer for 16 yards, and then he connected with Dowler for the touchdown.

On the third play of the Giants' next possession, Hank Gremminger picked off another Tittle pass on New York's 49 and returned it 13 yards to the visitor's 36. On seven running plays, Taylor and Hornung ground down the Giants to the New York 14. From there, Starr connected with Kramer again for a six. Hornung's third PAT gave the Pack a 21-0 lead.

Agajanian's kick was returned to the Gotham 39, where New York QB Charley Conerly set up shop. The old man of the Giants drove his offense down to the Pack's six where the visitors had third down and a yard to go. Wells failed to make the first down as Quinlan stuffed him at the line of scrimmage. Instead of going for a field goal, Allie Sherman opted to have his boys go for the TD. A halfback pass to Rote failed to connect, turning the ball over to the Packers once more.

In four plays, Starr maneuvered his team down to the New York 15. The Packers set up for a field goal, but the Giants were called for being offside. With no time on the clock, Hornung booted a field goal, and the jubilant Packers raced into the locker room in complete control, 24-0.

The Giants took the field in the second half determined to get back into the game. A short kickoff was hauled in by Nitschke at the Green Bay 18 and returned 18 yards to the Pack's 36. Failing to make a first down, Dowler punted. His kick was partially blocked, fielded on the New York 38, and returned to their 41. The Giants came up a yard short of making a first down and chose to punt again, this time the kick going out of bounds on the Pack's 15.

After gaining only six yards in three plays, Dowler punted again. Joe Morrison fumbled the kick and Forrest Gregg recovered the ball on New York's 22.

Tom Moore gained six yards on first down. Hornung picked up a yard on second down. Starr's pass to Hornung was knocked down by Barnes. Hornung came through with another field goal from 22 yards out to give Green Bay a commanding 27-0 lead.

New York's following possession ended with a punt to Willie Wood at the Green Bay 42. The Giants were penalized 15 yards when Wells interfered with Wood's fair catch attempt, setting up the Packers at the Giants' 43.

Starr wasted no time. He connected with Dowler for 11 yards to the New York 32. Hornung gained six yards to the 26. Starr hit Dowler for 13 to the 13. Hornung's pass to McGee fell incomplete. Then Starr connected with Kramer for a touchdown with 2:48 left in the quarter. Hornung's fourth PAT put the Packers ahead, 34-0, a lead that was certainly insurmountable at this point.

From this moment on, anything the Giants attempted proved to be superfluous. For the Packers, Hornung's third field goal of the day meant only one thing. It gave him 19 points for the game, breaking the championship game record set by Cleveland's Otto Graham who put up 18 points against the Detroit Lions in 1954. The final score of 37-0 was the widest shutout margin since the Chicago Bears totally annihilated the Washington Redskins, 73-0, in 1940.

That was history. For the present, the Green Bay Packers were Champions of the National Football League for the seventh time, tying them with the Bears. The fans in Green Bay didn't care about the tie with the Bears.

As far as Packer fans were concerned, Green Bay, Wisconsin, the smallest city in major professional sports, was Titletown, U.S.A.

§§§

17

The Off-Season War Resumes

Rumors! Rumors! And more rumors! This time the rumor mill concerned the American Football League holding another early draft.

The *Associated Press* story out of Dallas was responsible for the latest buzz around professional and college football.

"Indications were mighty strong today that the American Football League has pulled a similar stunt to 1960—jumped the gun on the draft. Only this time it violates an agreement with American Football Coaches Association.

"There could be a lot of trouble, especially from the NCAA, but obviously nothing can be done about it except talk."

Apparently, everybody of importance in the AFL knew about the telephone draft with the exception of Commissioner Joe Foss and his AFL office staff. When he heard the rumor of a draft, Foss called a few owners who verified the rumor as a fact.

Three newspapers reported that the secret draft had been held and such college stars as Ernie Davis of Syracuse, Bob Ferguson of Ohio State, Lance Alworth of Arkansas, Roman Gabriel of North Carolina State, and Jim Sexton of Texas were early round selectees. An anonymous official with the San Diego Chargers told Jerry Magee of the *San Diego Union* that "the commissioner knew nothing about this. It was run by the owners."

The club owners were supposed to have held six rounds of the draft by telephone several weeks before Foss set the official date of the draft for December 2, the day of final regular season college games. In announcing the draft, Foss said he was complying with an NCAA request not to hold the player selection until the close of the college season.

The *Dallas News* was the first newspaper to reveal the story of the secret draft. Then came the *San Diego Union*. Finally, the *Houston Post* confirmed the news. The *Union* said Oakland, presently with the worst record in the AFL, made the first pick, taking Roman Gabriel. The *Dallas News* reported hearing of the draft from a Southwest Conference coach, who said he figured there had been a draft because the pros keep calling him about certain players.

Jim Kensil, public relations director for the National Football League, said the NFL had information that the AFL had held a sneak draft. "The immediate concern, however, is not ours. The National League will go ahead with its scheduled draft meeting in Chicago December 4 as announced. The problem is one for the colleges to whom a written commitment was made last August by the other league."

Big Ten Conference commissioner Bill Reed said he would ask Foss to retract the draft, if one had been held, and to halt any and all authorized negotiations between the AFL and the college players that had been drafted.

The brouhaha over the AFL holding a secret draft before the proposed date was wrapped up in Reed's final remark. The secret draft gave the AFL a jump on the NFL in offering those collegians drafted a contract and up-front money. Should any player sign a deal before his school played its last game of the regular season or a bowl game, then that player would be ineligible to play for his school after signing. If he did play after signing, that would cause his school to forfeit any games the collegian had played in. The NCAA's concern was trying to find the truth behind each player who might have signed a deal with the AFL.

So was the dark cloud that appeared over the realm of pro football before the 1961 season ended and the 1962 season began. All the legal beagles grinned and started counting the fees they were to earn while handling this potential mess.

However, cooler heads did prevail with Foss nullifying the AFL's early six-round draft and declaring that all new player contracts dated prior to December 2, 1961 would be declared null and void. The owners merely smiled and went along with it, knowing all too well that their poll, as they called it, would stand when the real draft came along in December.

The actual AFL draft did take place on December 2 as Joe Foss promised. Proof that telephone draft had been nullified by Foss came when the Buffalo Bills made Heisman Trophy winner Ernie Davis their first choice and the New York Titans raised a ruckus over the pick because they had chosen Davis in the previous draft. New York owner Harry Wismer said he would pay Davis $100,000 over three years with a bonus of $25,000 to sign the deal. Buffalo said no soap to the offer, and Foss supported Buffalo's pick.

The NFL draft took place exactly when Commissioner Pete Rozelle said it would; Monday and Tuesday, December 4-5 in Chicago. Washington chose Ernie Davis with the 1st Pick as expected. This set a precedent for the Redskins. (See Chapter 18 for details.) Los Angeles followed up by choosing Roman Gabriel, quarterback from North Carolina State, then traded for Minnesota's 1st Round Pick, Number 3 overall. The Rams chose Merlin Olsen, tackle for Utah State. Dallas had the 4th Pick, which they traded to Cleveland. The Browns selected Gary Collins, end from Maryland. Pittsburgh was next. The Steelers chose Bob Ferguson, fullback from Ohio State. St. Louis then chose Fate Echols, tackle from Northwestern. Chicago picked Ronnie Bull, halfback from Baylor. San Francisco selected Lance Alworth, wide receiver from Arkansas. Baltimore picked Wendell Harris, back from LSU. Detroit took John Hadl, quarterback from Kansas. Cleveland had the next pick, taking Leroy Jackson, a back from Western Illinois. St. Louis had the second pick by way of a trade with Philadelphia and chose Irv Goode, center from Kentucky. New York chose 13th and selected Jerry Hillebrand, end from Colorado.

The Packers had the last pick in the 1st Round. Their brain trust chose Earl Gros, fullback from LSU. In subsequent rounds, Green Bay selected Ed Blaine, guard, Missouri; Gary Barnes, end, Clemson; Ron Gassert, tackle, Virginia; Chuck Morris, back, Ole Miss; Jon Schopf, guard, Michigan; John Sutro, tackle, San Jose State; Oscar Donahue, end, San Jose State; Gary Gutsinger, tackle, Oklahoma State; Jim Tullas, back, Florida A&M; Peter Schenck, back, Washington State; Gale Weidner, quarterback, Colorado; Jim Thrush, tackle, Xavier (Ohio); Joe Thorne, back, South Dakota State; Tom Pennington, back, Georgia; Tom Kepner, tackle, Villanova; Ernie Green, halfback, Louisville; Roger Holdinsky, back, West Virginia; Jimmy Field, back, LSU; Buck Buchanan, tackle, Grambling; Bob Joiner, quarterback, Presbyterian; Jerry Scattini, back, California; and Mike Snodgrass, center, Western Michigan.

Once the two drafts were concluded, it was time for the men who signed the checks to make their offers to the college players they had just drafted with the exceptions of the future draftees, such as Hall of Famer Buck Buchanan.

A day after the draft was concluded Green Bay City Council Alderman Robert N. Johnson presented a 13-paragrph proposal to the Council that suggested the Packers cease playing any regular season games in Milwaukee. Johnson noted how Green Bay's economy and reputation were wrapped up in the Packers. Any city can support a winner, but Green Bay has demonstrated financial support for a losing team over the years.

"Our people cannot rejoice at the many games that have been lost before so many coldly indifferent Milwaukee audiences. When we needed their help—win, lose, or draw—they were not there," said the alderman. Johnson further stated the Council as the "chosen representatives of the people" should inform the Packers of the desires of the people of Green Bay.

Johnson's thesis was sent to the Packers but without the Council's official endorsement.

The first shot was fired in the signing war between the leagues when Ray Jacobs, the big tackle from Howard Payne, was signed by both the Houston Oilers and Dallas Cowboys. Jacobs said he signed with the Oilers before the official draft held on December 2. Dallas representatives said they signed Jacobs on Monday night, December 4, after taking him in the 17th round of the NFL draft.

A few days later Joe Foss started another uproar with the NFL when he approved two contracts of draftees who had also signed with the NFL. The first was with Irv Goode, center from Kentucky. Foss ruled that it was a conditional contract, the condition being that Goode must be selected in the AFL draft to make it stand up. This was done, according to Foss. A similar ruling was made with Howard Payne tackle Ray Jacobs. After Houston signed Jacobs, Tex Schramm, GM for the Dallas Cowboys, hinted he would take legal action.

Then Pete Rozelle asked for a clarification of Foss's rulings in view of the fact that Foss had told him by telephone that the AFL would not approve any contract signed prior to the AFL draft. Foss replied that he did not consider the Jacobs and Goode contracts as final but as promises to sign when drafted. He also explained that this did not violate the constitution and by-laws of the AFL, which forbid signings of players before their college eligibility had ended. Foss made the contention that both Jacobs and Goode had finished their playing seasons.

Foss investigated still another case of double signing. Charley Hinton, back from North Carolina College (North Carolina Central), affixed his signature on deals with both the Dallas Texans and the Cleveland Browns. Foss allowed this was a case of who signed Hinton first and did not violate any of the rules. He declared this matter was between the two teams and for them to work it out.

The Packers announced their first signings for the next season when the team was in San Francisco to play the 49ers. They were No. 3 pick Gary Barnes, end from Clemson; No. 4 pick Ron Gassert, tackle from Virginia; No. 18 pick Bob Joiner, quarterback from Presbyterian; and No. 19 pick Jerry Scattini, defensive back from California. The next day Lombardi announced the signing of their No. 2 pick Ed Blaine, tackle from Missouri.

Bud Adams, owner of the Houston Oilers, fired a salvo at the NFL for "early" signings. He said he had grave concerns over a report that showed the older league had signed "no less than 10 players who still have bowl games to play." Of course, he also stated his club had made no attempts to sign any of the eight players by the Oilers who still had college eligibility left "in accordance with our promise to college coaches."

Adams was responding to a previous story where Clyde Brock, a giant tackle out of Utah State, had been offered a $1,000 in cash to sign with Houston on the eve of Utah State's appearance in New York's Gotham Bowl. Brock was held out of the game because it was rumored that he accepted the offer. Brock acknowledged the proposal was made to him but denied taking the cash. He then signed with the NFL team that drafted him, the Chicago Bears.

In their final practice of the regular season, Detroit's players hung their club's general manager in effigy. Edwin J. Anderson, the GM, refused to comment on the protest by the team. He did say that it was the fault of the AFL signing Detroit's draft choices before the NFL held its draft. The latest of these raids on his choices was allegedly John Hadl, quarterback from Kansas. Hadl denied signing with any team yet because the Jayhawks still had a bowl game to play. Anderson said an investigation by the Lions had revealed Hadl had signed with the San Diego Chargers. He also claimed the Dallas Texans had signed Eddie Wilson, quarterback from Arizona and a Detroit pick. One more Detroit draftee was Bobby Thompson, halfback from Arizona, who had allegedly signed with Montreal of the Canadian Football

League. Anderson failed to offer any proof.

The *Detroit Free Press* quoted the players as criticizing Anderson for "losing our future." One Lion player was quoted as saying, "I don't care what the excuses are. Other teams are signing their players. Why can't we?" Another player claimed that Anderson was not a salesman.

Anderson failed to sign Johnny Robinson from LSU, their Number One choice in 1959, and John Anderson, linebacker from Notre Dame, their Number Two in 1960.

As soon as the regular season concluded for both leagues, AFL Commissioner Joe Foss issued the same challenge to the NFL's boss Pete Rozelle.

"We'll give them the longest afternoon they ever had—any place and any time they want to put a team on the field," said Foss. "They'll have a million excuses to avoid us. They act like they don't want to admit the AFL exists. But they've got plenty of reason to know we're here, we're solid, and we're growing."

Rozelle responded, "The answer has not changed in the past 18 months. You don't consider playing games with people who are suing you for ten million dollars."

Speaking of lawsuits, the Packers had one of their own to defend. Former Packers defensive end Lenny Ford filed a suit in Wayne County (Michigan) Circuit Court seeking $10,000 in damages from the Packers. Ford contended that he signed a contract with the Packers in June 1958, in which he was to be paid $11,000 for that season at $916.66 per game. He said the contract also contained a clause that stipulated he could not be fired without first getting a written notice of his termination.

Ford also stated that despite this he was fired December 13, 1958 without notice and was not paid for the season's last game. His suit contended the dismissal injured his reputation as a player.

Teams in the AFL weren't the only abusers of the agreement with the college coaches' association. The Cleveland Browns signed Villanova end Ron Meyers two weeks before he was supposed to play in a bowl game. Villanova coach Alex Bell had a fit because he was losing his top pass catcher and his punter. He tried to hide his true feelings by saying he had plenty of backups for Meyers.

Meyers admitted to Commissioner Rozelle that he had insisted on signing the contract before the bowl game, and Meyers' father told Rozelle that his son wasn't planning on playing in the bowl game anyway. The Cleveland scout told Rozelle that Meyers insisted on signing then because he wanted the bonus money for Christmas. The commissioner said the contract was approved by his office because it was understood Meyers wasn't planning to play in the bowl game. So, the bottom line here was the NFL could sign players early, but not so the AFL. The fact was Rozelle had a bigger manure spreader than Joe Foss had.

Bill Sullivan, president of the Boston Patriots, remarked in an interview that the NFL had been whipped in its hope that the AFL would fold. "The NFL thought we would never get off that ground, but they've been whipped. They're in the corner now," he said, using a boxing analogy. "In two years, we've signed more than our share of their top draft choices. I've still got the greatest respect for the NFL. They sold professional football on television and created the interest we needed."

The NFL received a huge Christmas gift when Heisman Trophy winner Ernie Davis agreed to terms with the Cleveland Browns. Davis chose to accept the $80,000 deal from the Browns over the $135,000 offered by the Buffalo Bills. Davis was the seventh of 14 1st Round picks sign by the NFL.

Meanwhile, the AFL reported their estimated financial status for the 1961 season. Overall the league owners said their aggregate loss would come in just short of $2,000,000. Boston, Buffalo, and Houston stated they would break even for the year and might even end up in the black when the final tallies came in. Houston led the league in paid attendance with 197,120 customers buying tickets. San Diego came in a close second with 195,014 fans in their seats. The two division winners accounted for nearly 40% of the AFL's 988,608 total tickets sold. These numbers were encouraging for most of the owners, but the losses sustained by Dallas, Denver, and New York—the three teams in the AFL in direct competition with NFL franchises—still cast a dark cloud over the league's future. Commissioner Joe Foss felt encouraged by the numbers and cautious about the year ahead. He didn't say it, but the consensus around the league was Dallas, Denver, and Oakland had to do much better in 1962 or find other homes for their wobbly teams.

The first signing of the New Year for the Packers was Earl Gros, the 220-pound fullback out of LSU. Lombardi described him as a good fit with Jim Taylor, Paul Hornung, and Tom Moore.

Not quite two years into the job, NFL commissioner Pete

Rozelle was given a new contract for five years by the league's owners. He had one year remaining on his original contract. His salary would be $50,000 per year.

Good news on the business front for the NFL. Attendance for 98 regular season games reached a new high of 40,675 per game, an increase of 569 above the record set in 1960. For the year, the total came to 3,986,159 butts in the seats. Cleveland led the NFL in attendance with 436,886. New York was second with 423,919, and Philadelphia third with 412,318. Pete Rozelle credited the increases in average attendance for the last two seasons to the new stadium in Washington. The rules committee passed one landmark change. No longer would it be legal for a defender to tackle a ball carrier by grabbing his facemask.

At the AFL winter meeting, Joe Foss was given a new contract for five years that would keep him in the commissioner's office through the 1967 season. The AFL rules committee joined the NFL in making it illegal to tackle a ball carrier by his facemask. Roster limits were raised from 33 players to 36.

The biggest news of the winter was the NFL signing a contract with Columbia Broadcasting System (CBS) that would give the network exclusive rights to telecast all of the NFL's games in 1962. In return, each team would receive a payout of $320,000. By signing this one network deal, the Baltimore Colts would make less money from television than they had made the year before when they had their own deal with a different network.

At the winter meetings in Miami Beach, Jack Hand, a writer for *United Press International*, wrote a very interesting piece about a survey he took. He made the rounds of each NFL team and asked the general managers or head coaches one simple question. "What do you need most?" Translation: What did each team need to get to the top of their division or stay at the top in 1962? When Wellington Mara gave his answer, he added, "I can't wait to see what Vinnie Lombardi needs."

Well, Lombardi went along with the request from the *UPI* writer. He said he would like another defensive back and a defensive lineman. Trading for one or both seemed out of the question because he felt he would find both defenders in his present class of draftees. Of course, Lombardi failed to speculate about which draft choices might fill those roles.

At those same meetings, rumors abounded about possible

coaching changes in the NFL and the AFL. The one that mattered to the Packers was the story floating around that Bill Austin, Green Bay's offensive line coach, was being interviewed for the head coaching job for the Buffalo Bills. That story appeared one day, and the next day a completely opposite article made the headlines.

Austin admitted "receiving some offers" but he was looking forward to the 1962 season with the NFL champions. "I'm associated with a great man, and I want to continue that association." Of course, he was referring to Vince Lombardi, his boss. "It would be darn tough leaving a championship club."

In an *Associated Press* story late in January, Joe Foss claimed the AFL was ready for a title match with the NFL after the coming 1962 season, He based his claim on the facts that in the 1961 draft the AFL signed 35 of their top 100 and 43 of 100 in the 1962 draft. His argument claimed that the talent his league was signing was fairly equal to that of the NFL. Besides all the signees, Foss said the circuit's contract with ABC for the coming year was practically a done deal, assuring the AFL of even more revenue than the previous season. The biggest barrier to any possible title game between the two leagues was the $10,000,000 lawsuit the AFL was still pursuing against the NFL. Pete Rozelle said bluntly that his loop would not agree to anything with the AFL as long as the litigation stood in the way.

The AFL announced in late February that the league had held a draft of "red shirt" players who still had a year of eligibility remaining. A spokesperson said this was no different than the NFL drafting future players each year. The AFL said their draft was just as legal as the NFL's. Instead of drafting futures during their regular draft, the AFL held a separate draft.

At last on February 26, 1962, the AFL's $10,000,000 anti-trust lawsuit against the NFL went to federal court in Baltimore. The first witness was Lamar Hunt, owner of the Dallas Texans, who testified for four hours, reviewing the exact losses of each team in the AFL in 1960. Hunt also gave a step-by-step account of how he tried to obtain a new franchise in the NFL and how we he was turned down, which led him to form the American Football League. He further stated that George Halas, owner of the Chicago Bears, and NFL Commissioner Bert Bell informed him that the NFL was years away from expanding. Hunt then organized the AFL on August 22, 1959. A week later Halas and the NFL expansion committee announced their league would expand into Dallas and Houston in the 1961 season. Attorneys for the NFL said the NFL had planned to expand into the two Texas cities as well as Minneapolis long "before the American Football League was even a dream."

On the second day of testimony, Lamar Hunt, founder of the AFL, said Clint Murchison, owner of the Dallas Cowboys, offered him a substantial amount of stock in the NFL's initial expansion team, if Hunt would drop his plans to form the AFL. Murchison tried to convince Hunt that the AFL would be a losing proposition and that having two teams in Dallas would be bad business for both clubs.

Hunt also named off a list of NFL owners that he contacted by telephone who told him the AFL would never succeed. He said that he made overtures to the NFL owners that included a single draft by the two leagues and a joint television deal that would blackout games when an AFL club and an NFL club were playing in the same city on the same day. Finally, he remarked on how he was hindered by Murchison and other NFL owners from placing an AFL team in Dallas.

On the fourth day of the trial, the NFL's attorney Gerhard A. Gesell asked the court to explain exactly which cities the AFL was referring to in its suit against his client. The AFL's attorney Warren E. Baker answered that the AFL intended to prove local damages as well as national damages, specifically in the cases of Minneapolis-St. Paul and Dallas, cities where the NFL granted franchises as the AFL was attempting to establish itself. Baker added that he would prove that the AFL franchise in Houston was damaged by the placement of an NFL franchise in Dallas by television coverage of the Cowboys' road games in the Houston area when the Oilers were playing at home.

Judge Roszel C. Thomsen closed the testimony of witnesses at this point until the coming Monday. However, he did agree to allow the AFL's attorney to enter into the record portions of depositions of representatives of 11 NFL clubs who spoke to Lamar Hunt. The three clubs not part of the depositions were the Green Bay Packers, Los Angeles Rams, and San Francisco 49ers.

When the trial resumed the following Monday, Commissioner Joe Foss took the stand to testify for the AFL. He revealed how he wrote a letter to each of the NFL owners just a few days after he was named to his position with the AFL. In that letter, he asked those men running the NFL at that time not to do anything to destroy the new league but to co-operate with the fledgling circuit.

While under oath, Foss acknowledged the fact that the AFL had signed some of the top draft choices of the NFL, although it was testified earlier that the AFL was suffering because of competition with the NFL for players.

After Joe Foss finished his testimony, Jay Michaels, a representative of the Music Corporation of America (MCA), took the stand. He explained to the court that his company negotiated the sale of the AFL's television rights, stating the AFL's market was reduced to one network when NBC contracted to televise the 1960 games of the Baltimore Colts and Pittsburgh Steelers, both NFL teams. CBS, another major network, had earlier signed a contract to televise a majority of the remaining NFL games for 1960. This left the AFL with only one option: ABC. Michaels said the value of the AFL games was approximately $1,795,000, but the league had to settle for $1,200,000 less than this amount.

The next day Ralph C. Wilson, president and owner of the AFL's Buffalo Bills, testified how he was told by Edwin Anderson, the president of the Detroit Lions, that the NFL was interested in expanding only to cities with warmer weather. Anderson followed up by telling Wilson, if he would drop his Buffalo franchise, then he, Anderson, would help Wilson get a substantial interest in an NFL franchise in Miami when the NFL expanded there. Wilson clarified that offer by saying he had tried to get a franchise in Miami for the AFL before he opted for Buffalo.

Wilson said he was surprised and shocked when he learned the NFL was going to grant a franchise to Minneapolis-St. Paul when an AFL franchise had already been awarded there. His shock was due to the fact that the ownership group that had been awarded an AFL team in Minnesota was planning to bale on the AFL and go with the NFL instead. Wilson added that Max Winter, one of the Minnesota group, told him that he "couldn't afford to buck the NFL."

In further testimony, Wilson said his team was injured by the awarding of an NFL franchise in Minneapolis-St. Paul because this left the AFL with no choice except to award a franchise to Oakland in direction competition with the San Francisco 49ers. Oakland, he said, couldn't provide as much attendance as Minneapolis-St. Paul could, thus, reducing the visiting team's share of the gate.

Summing up, Wilson said nearly the exact same thing about the NFL placing an expansion team in Dallas.

In cross examination, the NFL's attorney asked Wilson if the AFL decided to go to Oakland because the prospective owners of the new franchise said it would help the AFL with its antitrust case. The Buffalo owner said he didn't know about that because he was not a part of any such discussion. He added that he had voted against admitting Oakland because he felt it was a poor city for professional football.

The next day Houston owner Bud Adams took his turn on the witness stand. He stated Edwin Pauley, a part owner of the Los Angeles Rams, offered him a franchise in the NFL if he would drop out of the fledgling AFL about a month after the new league was announced publicly. Adams said Pauley told him he should consider the cost of operating a pro football team before going into the sport. Pauley said he had known Adams' father and wanted to do his son a favor. Adams added that Pauley said he would see to it that he got a franchise in the NFL in Houston for the 1961 season. The Texas oilman objected to waiting that long to start up his team. Adams said he had tried for two and a half years to get a franchise in the NFL for Houston before opting to join Lamar Hunt in setting up the AFL. He and Hunt went to Chicago to meet with George Halas, chairman of the NFL's expansion committee. Halas told them the NFL would take in Dallas and Minneapolis into the NFL in the first year of expansion and Houston and another city in the second year. Adams said he and Hunt thought the NFL should add six teams instead of four by putting new franchises in New York and Los Angeles. Halas said this would never happen. Adams concluded the conference when he realized that Halas was operating "a stalling action against the new league." Before ending the meeting, Adams informed Halas he and Hunt were going ahead with the AFL.

Adams was followed to the stand by Barron Hilton, son of hotel magnate Conrad Hilton and owner of the San Diego Chargers. Hilton said Pauley told him in August 1959, that NFL franchises could be made available to Adams and Lamar Hunt, president of the AFL.

Judge Thomsen then recessed the trial until the following Monday.

Nothing of importance came to light at the next session of the trial, but on Tuesday testimony by the NFL proved to be very revealing.

Baltimore Colts president Carroll Rosenbloom took the stand and said plans to expand the NFL took form at the funeral of Bert Bell in October 1959. He also testified that expansion had been a constant topic of discussion among NFL owners since George Halas was made chairman of the expansion committee in January 1958. This was an outright lie. Expansion was discussed at the league meeting that year, but it failed to pass, meaning no committee was set up at that time. As for the remainder of Rosenbloom's testimony, it can only be described as hearsay and therefore inadmissible as evidence.

Then Cleveland head coach Paul Brown took the stand. The only purpose of his testimony was to deny he had ever made a certain statement. "Nobody likes competition. We have a monopoly, and we want to keep it that way." The "we" he mentioned was the NFL.

On Wednesday, Dallas Cowboys owner Clint Murchison, Jr, told the court that the NFL moved up expansion into Dallas by a year in order "to get off on (an) even footing" with the rival AFL. Lawyers for the AFL made the contention the older league expanded into Dallas just as the AFL was preparing to launch a team there as part of a plan to squeeze the AFL out of the professional football business. Murchison further added George Halas told him in February 1959 that the NFL would expand from 12 to 14 teams in 1961. "He (Halas) was definite about expanding into Dallas and Houston." The Cowboys owner said he met Halas again on August 29, 1959 in Houston and asked the committee chairman to make a definite statement about his city's entry into the NFL so he "could negotiate for the Cotton Bowl and so we could dissuade Lamar (Hunt) from starting a new league, which I felt he was doing because he thought there wouldn't be an NFL franchise in Dallas." Halas agreed, and an announcement was made that day. Murchison finished up his testimony by saying he tried to persuade Lamar Hunt and his brothers Bunker and Stewart to join him in owning the Cowboys. When they declined the offer of a partnership with him, Murchison said he offered to withdraw from the Dallas franchise and let them have it. The Hunts declined that offer as well.

The problem with Murchison's testimony was simple. He lied about the timing of his first meeting with Halas in 1959. This was fabricated by the NFL lawyers. Nobody in the NFL was planning on expanding the league until after Hunt and Adams announced they were forming the AFL.

On the following Monday, court resumed, and the first witness for the NFL was their heaviest hitter George Halas. Papa Bear started off by saying he was named chairman of a league expansion committee in 1958. The initial plan to expand was to "go south and west. Houston and Dallas were the leading cities in the southwest and we were heading in that direction." He later corroborated Murchison when he said Halas told him in February 1959 that the NFL was planning to expand into Dallas. This was pure fabrication by both men. (For proof, go back to Chapter 8 and read the statements made by Halas during Week 5 of the 1959 season.)

The next day George Preston Marshall, Washington Redskins owner, gave his testimony. He started by denying he ever made any statement to the effect that NFL expansion was designed to wreck the new league. Marshall did admit to saying that he thought expansion by the NFL was impractical and was opposed to it in order to protect existing franchises. He said the NFL would be better off to leave the rest of the country to another league and that college football would be hurt by expansion, which would eventually affect pro football because the number of quality players coming from the collegiate ranks would be reduced.

Max Winter, president of the Minnesota Vikings, followed Marshall to the stand. He testified that he had been trying to get an NFL franchise for Minneapolis-St. Paul since 1958 and had even spoken to the late Bert Bell about it as early as 1955. Winter added that in July 1959 he was referred to Lamar Hunt and his associates who were just then starting up the AFL. Winter and his group committed to the AFL and were in the midst of organizing a team, even drafting college players, when the NFL announced it wanted to place a franchise in the Twin Cities. Of course, Winter failed to tell this to the court because if he had, then some sort of wrongdoing might have been suspected by the judge.

In his summation of the NFL's case, attorney Gerhard Gesell argued that Bert Bell had stated before Congress in 1957 that he favored the league to expand by the year 1960. Not true again. Bell did testify in front of Congress that year, but the hearing concerned the establishment of a players' union to negotiate with the NFL. Bell did, however, say for the public record that he favored expansion by the year 1961 into the cities of Buffalo and Louisville because both of them had stadiums that were ready for NFL teams. Gesell also held up three newspaper releases from George Halas in 1959 that mentioned the addition of two teams in 1961. The third in August said he would recommend Dallas and Houston. Minneapolis was also mentioned in that release. The problem with this move by Gesell was he was holding up *news releases,* not newspaper articles. Anybody can write a news release and put a date on it, but if the story is never published, then it is NOT news. Gesell's final argument held that the move into Dallas a year of ahead of schedule was necessary to *compete* with the AFL because the new league had announced it was putting a team there in 1960. That's like saying a national fast food chain has to put a store in a small town to *compete* with a mom and pop drive-in restaurant.

The next day, April 26, Judge Thomsen announced, "The issue in the case is whether National Football League actions were to nip the AFL in the bud or to compete more effectively." He said he would study the testimony and arguments of both sides and make his decision in May or June.

Except for a few signings of late round draft choices, the Packers had done little business that winter and spring. This lack of action was partially due to their general manager taking his wife on a month-long vacation to Europe, which included Italy, of course, and an audience with Holy Father, Pope John (St. John) XXIII. After evaluating his team, meeting his obligations as guest of honor at several speaking engagements, and receiving awards and well-earned platitudes from fans throughout the state of Wisconsin, Lombardi finally made a trade on April 26. In a three-way deal, he sent a future undisclosed draft choice to the New York Giants who then traded defensive back Dick Nolan to the Dallas Cowboys who sent their placekicker Allen Green to Green Bay. Nolan was signed as a player-coach, taking over the secondary for head coach Tom Landry.

The Packers already had two placekickers under their control: Paul Hornung and Ben Agajanian. However, their status for the coming season was in flux. Hornung was still under obligation to the Army, while Agajanian was another year older at 43. Lombardi picked up Green as an insurance policy against both Hornung and Agajanian being unavailable in 1962.

Wednesday, May 2, the Packers held their annual stockholders. meeting at the WBAY auditorium in Green Bay. General Manager Vince Lombardi announced several good items from the financial results for the 1961 season. Net profit: $175,075.46, an increase of $59,847.21 over the year before. Surplus in the bank: $573,141.60. Operating income: $1,475,456.56. Gate receipts were higher for home games in Green Bay and Milwaukee than they were for road receipts for the first time in the history of the team: $707,612.90 at home and $626,308.64 on the road.

Lombardi also noted that "an ever-increasing payroll and the competition from the American Football League." He reiterated that no rookie will receive more money on his basic salary than any of the veterans.

Two new directors were elected that night. Frank M. Cowles was voted to fill the remainder of the late J.H. "Tubby" Bero, and Police Chief Elmer Madson was voted to fill the vacancy created by the death of Dr. R.L Cowles. All 15 of the current directors who were up for re-election were given another three years on the board. All other officers and members of executive committee were also re-elected.

Lombardi increased his coaching staff in May by hiring Tom Fears, again as the receivers' coach; only this time his employment was full-time.

Finally, on May 21, Judge Thomsen announced his decision on the AFL's lawsuit against the NFL. He dismissed the monopoly claim, saying the NFL "did not have the power to prevent or unreasonably to restrict competition." He based his finding on a statement in the AFL's official publication where the league boasted that never before in the history of sports had an organization gone so far so fast.

Yes, the AFL had done well in just two years of play, but the point of the suit was the AFL could have gone farther if the NFL had not interfered with its attempt to put teams in Minneapolis-St. Paul and Dallas *after the AFL had announced its intention of going into to those two markets.* The truth was the AFL lawyers had failed to prove that it cost its organization money and prestige because the NFL had done this.

NFL Commissioner Pete Rozelle said Thomsen's ruling was a "complete vindication" of the older league. Of course, this was just an exercise in gamesmanship. He went on to say, "Representatives of the new league have publicly vilified the National Football League for 2½ years...it is now time for the AFL to face up to free and open competition and direct its attention to football."

Makes one wonder how many times Rozelle had to say that in front of a mirror before he could say it without laughing. The so-called representatives of the AFL had every right and every good reason to "vilify" the NFL for its actions. Halas clearly admitted that the NFL had no intention of expanding until 1961, but once it became known that the AFL intended to place teams in Minnesota and Dallas, the NFL hustled to get one team in Dallas in 1960 and convinced the investors of an AFL franchise to withdraw their commitment to the new league and join the NFL in 1961. Who could blame the AFL for being more than a little upset and for suing the NFL?

Judge Thomsen's integrity comes into question by his reason for finding in favor of the NFL. A single quote from the AFL's official publication? What did that have to do with the NFL trying to head off the AFL from entering Dallas and Minneapolis? It all appeared like Thomsen was looking for any straw to break the AFL's case. More than two decades would pass before another judge would rule the NFL had a monopoly over professional football.

The next day Lombardi announced the Packers had sold out all four games to be played in City Stadium for the coming season. This was only for the 38,000 permanent seats that were available for season ticket buyers. The other 669 seats were reserved for visiting teams. He also said the Pack could have sold another 2,000 season tickets if they had the seating for them. As far as the three games set for Milwaukee, Lombardi estimated 25,000 season tickets would be sold eventually. So far, 18,000 had rung up the cash registers.

In early June, Harry Wismer, owner of the New York Titans and present chairman of the AFL's expansion committee, made a very premature announcement that the junior league would expand from eight teams to 12 in 1963. The new teams would be located in three cities without professional football and one that currently had a team in the NFL. Those potential expansion franchises would go to Atlanta, Cincinnati, New Orleans, and Washington., the latter being the home of the Redskins owned by the very vocal George Preston Marshall.

"I can't keep them out of Washington," said Marshall, "but I can keep them out of that stadium."

The Redskins had a 30-year lease on District of Columbia Stadium, which contained a clause that no other professional football team could play there during this period. What he wasn't saying was his lease was only good if he integrated his team with players of color. (See Chapter 18 for more details.)

By the first of June, interests in Atlanta and New Orleans had sent checks for $25,000 each as good faith deposits to the AFL office in Dallas. Investment groups in both cities expressed their desire to join the AFL in 1963.

On June 22, Warren Lockwood, a financier from Maryland, announced his desire to apply for a franchise in the AFL to be located in Kansas City. He said he would put up the earnest money for the club when the AFL held its summer meeting the following Monday in Boston.

The big news coming out of the AFL's summer meeting in Boston was the announcement that the league owners voted unanimously to appeal the decision handed down in May by Judge Thomsen in the AFL's suit against the NFL. Warren Baker, attorney for the AFL, said, "We think the judge erred both in his factual finding and in his legal conclusion." Baker failed to mention that he and his fellow lawyers for the AFL failed to prove their case against the NFL. Instead of pursuing their claim of a monopoly by the NFL, they should have accused the NFL of conspiracy to deny the AFL its legal right to do business in Dallas and Minneapolis-St. Paul. There was absolutely no doubt that Halas and other owners and officials in the NFL worked together to deny the AFL a franchise in Minnesota and in Texas.

Baker said the appeal would probably be heard sometime in the fall and that it would take five to eight months before a decision could be reached. The appeal was planned to be made in a federal court in Richmond.

The next and last day of the AFL meeting the owners voted to table expansion until the fall meeting. More important for the coming 1962 season, the owners voted for a plan to strengthen the two weakest teams in the league in 1961, which were Denver and Oakland. On August 14, a month after training camps started, each team would be required to place 35 players on an "untouchable" list. Then the Broncos and Raiders would be allowed to select three players each from those players left off the reserve list. After that bit of business, the entire league would draft from the same group of players left off the reserve list. Finally, rosters would be limited to 33 players for the season.

Good news for the Packers came in early July. Boyd Dowler and Ray Nitschke were given their discharges from active duty in the Army and would be at training camp when it opened for veterans on July 18. This left only Paul Hornung hoofing it for Uncle Sam.

After more than six months of R&R (rest and relaxation), the veterans from Green Bay's 1961 title team began drifting into town, all of them eager to put on the pads and start their hunt for a repeat of the previous campaign. Lee Remmel, filling in for vacationing Art Daley, wrote several pieces where he interviewed the old pros as they arrived in the city. All of them pretty much said the same thing. The opposition for a crown in 1962 would be tougher than the year before, but they were all ready to meet it head-on with the best each of them had to give.

This was the exact kind of talk Vince Lombardi and his staff wanted to hear. Confidence but not with swelled heads.

§§§

18
Integrating Pro Football

The first man of color to play professional football was Charles W. Follis, known as "The Black Cyclone." He played for the Shelby Blues of the unofficial "Ohio League" from 1902 through 1906. On September 16, 1904, he signed a contract with Shelby. One of his teammates during his first two seasons with the Blues was a fellow named Branch Rickey; the same Branch Rickey who integrated Major League Baseball with the signing of Jackie Robinson. Is that an incredible coincidence? Or was Rickey influenced to make history with Robinson because he had known Charles Follis? More than likely the latter.

Joe Horrigan, historian for the Pro Football Hall of Fame in Canton, Ohio, wrote an excellent article about early professionals in pro football who were men of color. Those pre-NFL players of color who played as professionals were Charles "Doc" Baker (Akron [Ohio] Indians 1906-08, 1911); Henry McDonald (Rochester [New York] Jeffersons 1911-1917); Gideon "Charlie" Smith (Canton [Ohio] Bulldogs 1915; Robert "Rube" Marshall (Rock Island [Illinois] Independents 1919-1921, Duluth [Minnesota] Eskimos 1925; and Fritz Pollard (Akron Pros 1919-1921 and 1925-26, Milwaukee 1922, Hammond [Indiana] 1923-25, Providence [Rhode Island] Steamroller 1925. Both Fritz Pollard and Marshall are considered to be tied as the first men of color to play in the NFL. However, it could be debated that Marshall was actually first because he played in his first NFL game a week before Pollard played in his.

Horrigan also named the men of color who played in the NFL from 1920 through 1933. After Marshall and Pollard, came Paul Robeson, Jay "Inky" Williams, John Shelbourne, Duke Slater, James Turner, Sol Butler, Dick Hudson, Harold Bradley, David Myers, Joe

Lillard, and Ray Kemp. These men fought not just the other team in a football game; they also fought racism of opposing players and fans in the bleachers. Along with Marshall and Pollard, they have to be hailed as heroes with a possible nickname of "The Brave 13" because they led the way for people of color in professional sports.

In 1934, millions of men were out of work as the tragedy of *The Great Depression* lingered across America. For this solitary reason, the NFL owners decided not to hire any men of color to play for them. At the head of this racist move was George Preston Marshall, one of the original owners of the Boston Braves whom he renamed the Boston Redskins in 1933 and moved to Washington. in 1937. He goaded the other owners into denying men of color into the NFL by saying such things as, "It's wrong to have (deleted) playing for our teams and paying them for a job that can be filled by a white man."

Marshall was born in West Virginia in 1896, then moved with his family to Washington, D.C., before World War I, where his father opened up a chain of laundries. Apparently, he was a victim of time, place, and history. His place of birth and that of his parents was West Virginia, and their ancestors could be traced back to Virginia in colonial times. No doubt Marshall grew up in an atmosphere of race bigotry and was ingrained with it from the cradle.

Men of color were once again given the opportunity to play in the NFL and in the All-America Football Conference in 1946. One man he couldn't bamboozle into keeping the NFL all white was Dan Reeves, owner of the Los Angeles Rams. Being a complete opposite of Marshall, Reeves refused to be bullied by the often-cantankerous Washington owner. He decided that the time for change was now, partially because of the signing of Jackie Robinson to a Major League contract on October 23, 1945 by Branch Rickey of the Brooklyn Dodgers and partially because he wanted to have his team play in the Los Angeles Memorial Coliseum. Thus, pressure from the media and fans to integrate his team forced Reeves to stand up to Marshall.

And Reeves did just that when he signed the popular Kenneth "Kenny" Washington, a halfback who had played his college ball at UCLA and who had been playing for the San Francisco Clippers of the Pacific Coast Professional Football League (PCPFL). His deal with the Rams was sealed on March 21, 1946, giving him the honor of being the first man of color to play in the NFL since 1933.

Right behind Washington came Woodrow Wilson Woolwine

"Woody" Strode, who played in the same backfield at UCLA with Washington and Jackie Robinson. Strode signed his deal with the Rams on May 7, 1946.

Later that year, Paul Brown, head coach and general manager of the Cleveland Browns, then of the fledgling AAFC, signed the first two men of color to play in the new league. William Karnet "Bill" Willis, a defensive guard, had played at Ohio State under Brown. He inked his pact with the new Browns on August 6, 1946. Three days later Brown signed Marion Motley, a husky fullback who had played on the Great Lakes Navy Bluejackets coached by Brown.

After the Rams and Browns signed men of color in 1946, other teams followed. In the AAFC, the Brooklyn Dodgers, Chicago Rockets, Los Angeles Dons, and New York Yankees integrated their rosters in 1947. The San Francisco 49ers signed two men of color in 1948 to make the AAFC completely integrated.

The NFL was slow to follow the example of the AAFC. None of their teams drafted a player of color until the Chicago Bears selected George Taliaferro, a halfback from Indiana, in the 13th Round of the 1949 draft. Taliaferro opted to sign with the Los Angeles Dons of the AAFC instead. The first NFL draftee of color to play in the league was Wally Triplett, a halfback from Penn State, picked by the Detroit Lions in the 19th Round of the 1949 draft.

After the Rams, the next team to integrate was the Detroit Lions in 1948. Then came the New York Giants in 1950. The Green Bay Packers picked up end Bob Mann in a trade with the Lions in 1951 for their first ever player of color. Following small-town Packers were the Chicago Bears, Chicago Cardinals, Philadelphia Eagles, and Pittsburgh Steelers in 1952. The Baltimore Colts climbed aboard the integration band wagon in 1953, leaving the Washington Redskins as the only segregated team in all of pro football.

The AFL wasted no time on segregation. Each of their 1960 draft lists and rosters included players of color. Denver's included a particularly unique and versatile man named Gene Mingo.

As a kid growing up in Akron, Ohio in the 1940s and 1950s, Gene Mingo played youth football at the behest of a cousin. He later dropped out of football but went back for a short time before giving up everything to care for his terminally ill mother. He returned to high school and figured out he was pretty good at football. Being older than his classmates, he then quit school to join the Navy in 1956 where he played for a base team and was a star. After his discharge 1959, he went to work at the Goodyear rubber plant where he read in a newspaper that a former opponent who had played for an Army team who was signed by the Denver Broncos. Gene wrote a letter to the Broncos and received a contract. He made the team without ever having even gone to college.

With Denver in the inaugural season of the AFL, Mingo had the first-ever punt return for a touchdown for the Broncos and in the first game ever in the league. He then booted the first field goal, scoring the first points ever for the Broncos in a home game. The next year he threw a 50-yard TD pass to Lionel Taylor from his halfback position in Denver's opener against the Bills in Buffalo. He led the AFL in scoring in 1960 with 123 points and again in 1962 with 137 points. To date, he still holds the Denver record for longest TD run from scrimmage racing 82 yards against Oakland in 1962.

This brings us back to George Preston Marshall who refused to employ men of color on his team despite the changing attitudes of his peers and the dawn of the new era in race relations in America.

For decades after the War Between the States, also known as the Civil War, the United States remained divided in how they dealt with the rights of people of color. All of the former slave states of the Confederacy and the four slave states that remained in the Union, as the war raged between the two factions, continued to practice overt segregation between people of color and whites. A legal case here and another there brought some very minor changes in the North and West, but segregation remained in place there as well, being practiced covertly, especially in big cities.

In professional baseball, racial segregation was often called "a gentlemen's agreement," meaning a tacit understanding because there was no written policy at the highest level of the game. Because their teams depended heavily on playing exhibition games against teams of the National League and the American Association, the International League, a high minor league, voted to discontinue contracting players of color beginning in the 1888 season. This attitude remained as the unwritten rule for all of Organized Baseball until Branch Rickey signed Jackie Robinson and placed him with the Montreal Royals, a team that quite ironically was in the same International League.

The integration of Organized Baseball led to the integration of professional football and jump-started the desegregation of schools at all levels across the country, beginning with the 1954 Supreme Court decision in the *Brown v. Board of Education* case. The NAACP legal team representing the 13 parents suing the Topeka, Kansas Board of Education was led by future Supreme Court Justice Thurgood Marshall. In the initial hearing, the plaintiffs lost. They lost again when they appealed to the three-judge District Court panel. Their next step was the U.S. Supreme Court.

Brown v. Board of Education was combined with four other similar cases filed in South Carolina, Virginia, Delaware, and Washington, D.C.; all to be heard before the Supreme Court as one case. In December 1952, the U.S. Department of Justice filed a friend of the court brief in the case that basically supported Brown and opposed segregation. The following spring Chief Justice Frederick Moore Vinson delayed the hearing of *Brown v. Board of Education* because he knew how his fellow justices would vote on the case; 5-4 in favor of Brown. However, he didn't want the narrowest of decisions; he wanted a unanimous ruling that would once and for all time strike down segregation across the country. Therefore, Vinson, who had already written one opinion of the Supreme Court opposing segregation in the law school of the University of Texas (*Sweatt v. Painter)* delayed the matter until the fall court. Unfortunately, Vinson's true place in the history of civil rights in America was denied him when he died before the Court could convene and rehear *Brown v. Board of Education.*

President Dwight David Eisenhower acted quickly to name a new Chief Justice with his appointment of former governor of California and vice-presidential candidate Earl Warren. Not a lawyer, Warren was, however, an astute politician. He knew how to persuade people to his way of thinking, and his goal in this case was a unanimous decision by the Supreme Court in favor of *Brown*, just the same as his predecessor had wanted. It took him a few months, but Warren finally achieved his desire when he convinced the final holdout on the Court, Justice Stanley Reed, a Kentuckian, to vote with the remainder of their colleagues. Thus, segregation in our nation's schools came to an end.

Some revisionist historians in modern times chastise President Eisenhower for his racist language in private and his failure to offer any verbal support for the Court's decision and for equal rights. What they don't acknowledge about Ike was he was a man of outright action, not a politician mouthing a litany of words to make himself look good in the eyes of voters. Eisenhower supported the Court's decision in favor of *Brown*, showing it in 1957 when he sent federal troops into Little Rock, Arkansas to face down the resistance of Governor Orval Faubus to integration of Little Rock High School. Ike worked to integrate the armed forces and took strong steps to desegregate Washington, D.C. He then lent his support to the effort to pass the Civil Rights Act of 1957.

On a note of interest to the people of Wisconsin, President Eisenhower changed a law prohibiting Native Americans from being patrons of establishments that served alcoholic beverages. Before he became President, Ike took a fishing trip to northern Wisconsin. He hired a local guide by the name of Louis St. Germain, a Chippewa who was respectfully known as Louie No. 1. After a good day's fishing, Ike and his fishing buddies retired to a local watering hole. When they reached the steps to the place, Louie stopped. Ike asked him why. The famous guide said Indians weren't allowed inside such establishments. Incensed, Ike promised Louie he would change that law if he ever got elected President. Eisenhower kept his word.

In his attempts to enforce the Fair Housing Act of 1937 and its subsequent laws, Eisenhower ordered the destruction of so-called ghettos in major cities and the construction of low rent, subsidized housing to replace the slums occupied mainly by people of color. In his plan, apartment buildings consisting of eight family units would be built throughout these cities, scattering them wherever possible. In cities where the municipal government was controlled by Democrat mayors and city councils, these Eisenhower apartment buildings were never built. Instead, these mayors and their city councils took the funds that provided for this urban renewal and built high-rises where the slums once stood. Thus, such cities as Chicago, Detroit, Cleveland, and many others remained segregated.

This author recalls a trip through Chicago in January 1965 when hitchhiking to California where the driver pointed out the tall apartment buildings on the city's south side. "A lot of us were worried those (people of color) would be living in our neighborhoods, but our mayor fixed that." He laughed. "They're called projects. Hell, they're nothing more than new ghettos for the (people of color)."

Racism in housing wasn't just a big city issue; it was also very prevalent in small towns, even in Green Bay, Wisconsin. When Bob Mann, the first player of color to play for the Packers, came to town, he was faced with bigotry at every turn except on the field of play. Still, he stuck it out. Mann and other players of color who came after him were forced to live in small cabins, the YMCA, and hotels. Herb Adderly had to live in a little shack down by the tracks. In 1961, Adderly, Willie Davis and Elijah Pitts shared a one-bedroom place on Velp Avenue. When Emlen Tunnell came to Green Bay in a trade engineered by Vince Lombardi at the start of his tenure with the Packers, the coach pulled some strings with other Packer officials and arranged for His player to stay at the Northland Hotel. Rumor had it that Lombardi even paid for Tunnell's room and board.

Although President Eisenhower did what he could to integrate America, it wasn't enough, and the one man in the National Football League who took full advantage of this lived in our nation's capital. His name was George Preston Marshall, bigoted owner of the Washington Redskins.

Marshall wasn't the only person in pro football who was basing his decisions on racial bigotry. The AFL had its problems as well.

In their first year of play, the Houston Oilers and Dallas Texans obeyed the segregation rules of the state of Texas for seating people of color in areas away from whites. With the start of the 1961 campaign, these laws were challenged from the start of the season.

The National Association for the Advancement of Colored People (NAACP) asked the players of color for the visiting Oakland Raiders to refuse to cross the anti-segregation picket lines the NAACP had set up for Oakland's game at Houston against the Oilers. This demonstration by the NAACP was a protest against segregated seating in the stadium. Mrs. Hosea Evans, executive secretary of the Houston chapter of the NAACP, said she sent telegrams to each of the four players of color on the Oakland roster, asking them each to use their influence as professional athletes to the NAACP in getting integrated seating at their games. The Oilers played their home games at a public high school in Houston. A spokesperson for the school board said it was their policy for seating to be segregated in public school stadiums.

The AFL wasn't the only league dealing with racial issues. A month later two opposing groups demonstrated for their causes at the game between the New York Giants and the Washington Redskins at the new District of Columbia Stadium in Washington. A band of men wearing khaki uniforms with swastika armbands emblematic of the American Nazi Party paraded on a grass plot opposite the entrance to the stadium. They carried picket signs that read: "Mr. Marshall, keep

Redskins white." The other group, composed of members of the Congress of Racial Equality (CORE), picketed along the stadium wall next to the entrance. Their signs read: "We carry the rifle. Why can't we carry the ball?"

October 18, 1961, George Preston Marshall offered to trade a second-round draft choice to Cleveland for speedy halfback Bobby Mitchell, who would be going into the Army on November 2. This would make Mitchell the first ever man of color to play for the Washington Redskins. Paul Brown, Cleveland coach and general manager, gruffly rejected Marshall's tongue-in-cheek offer.

"I have a feeling Mr. Marshall is trying to project me into his racial problem," Brown said through a spokesman. "This is unfair to a player who still has some games to play for us."

Marshall was under pressure from Secretary of the Interior Stewart Udall, whose department operates the stadium where the Redskins played their home games. Udall threatened to break the contract with Marshall's club if the Redskins continued to operate without the services of a player of color.

On the same day of Marshall's attempt to embarrass Paul Brown, an incident in Lexington, Kentucky added fuel to the inferno that was growing across the nation opposing segregation. Two players for the Boston Celtics were refused service at the coffee shop in the hotel where their team was staying before playing an exhibition game in Lexington.

Boston owner Walter Brown was furious over the incident. "The Celtics will never play another exhibition game in the South or any other place where they might be embarrassed," said Brown. He also cited another incident that had happened at Charlotte, North Carolina. "I'm not so hungry for money that I'd arrange games where my players might be embarrassed. Never again."

Teammate Frank Ramsay, who played at the University of Kentucky—in Lexington—spoke out against the hotel employee who refused to serve Sam Jones and Tom Sanders. "No thinking person in Kentucky is a segregationist," he said. I can't tell you how sorry I am as a human being, as a friend of the players involved, and as a resident of Kentucky for the embarrassment of this incident."

This was the second such racial incident in a week. Boston players were also refused service at a Marion, Indiana restaurant after an exhibition game there. That encounter had a much better outcome.

Local police intervened on behalf of the players involved, and they were then given service.

Finally, the national press was bringing more attention to the public with its coverage of these peaceful racial confrontations. Every day there seemed to be some mention of race relations, either in the newspapers or electronic media. A majority of the country seemed to be speaking out against segregation.

George Preston Marshall, the last holdout against integration for the National Football League, finally succumbed to overwhelming social and political pressure to integrate his Redskins. The final straw came from Attorney General Robert Kennedy and President John F. Kennedy. Both leaders made it clear to Marshall that his team would be homeless in 1962 if he didn't act immediately to add men of color to his team. Marshall realized that he was the loser in this battle, but he still did nothing to integrate the Redskins for the remainder of the 1961 season. Instead, he used the Number One Pick in the college draft to accede to the demands of the President and his brother. He picked Heisman Trophy winner Ernie Davis of Syracuse to be Washington's racial groundbreaker.

Unfortunately for Marshall, Davis had other ideas. "I wish they would quit bringing up this race stuff," said Davis. "I don't want to be another Jackie Robinson. I just want to play football, and I'll go where I can get the best offer." He added, "I don't worry about the racial issues. (George Marshall) is a good business man. If he makes me the best offer, I'll take it."

Three days later the Redskins *signed* their very first player whose ancestors had their origins in Africa. His name was Ron Hatcher. He played his college ball at Michigan State as the Spartans' fullback for three seasons. George Marshall made a big deal about this signing. He spoke with Hatcher before the signing, but the actual event was done by head coach Bill McPeak and other team officials. Marshall refused to pose with Hatcher for the photographers who were present.

Marshall said, "This boy was signed as a player. His name was put on our draft list by Bill McPeak last August as one of the top football players available. He was signed on his football ability and not for racial exploitation. I don't want him to be handicapped on (the) Redskins because of his race."

What Marshall *wanted* and what really happened with Hatcher were two different outcomes. Hatcher made it through training camp and was inserted into three games in 1962. He never touched the ball once. Then he was released. Marshall allowed the signing of Hatcher because he needed to get the Secretary of the Interior off his back. Nothing more, nothing less.

On December 15, the announcement of a blockbuster trade in the NFL hit the sports pages throughout the country. The Cleveland Browns had obtained the rights to Ernie Davis, the Heisman Trophy winner from Syracuse University and the Number 1 overall draft pick of the Washington Redskins. Cleveland gave up star halfback Bobby Mitchell and the rights to Leroy Jackson, a speedy halfback from Western Illinois, who was picked in the 1st Round of the 1962 NFL Draft. The actual trade had been made on the day of the draft, but both parties had kept it secret until Washington signed Ron Hatcher.

For as much as he didn't like his team being integrated on paper, George Preston Marshall saw this trade as a victory for him. He would keep his team playing in D.C. Stadium, and that was the whole purpose in signing Hatcher and obtaining the services of Mitchell and Jackson.

At last, after a long struggle, professional football joined the ranks of the other major sports leagues as a racially integrated entity. No longer would discrimination be allowed. This pleased one man in particular.

Almost from childhood, Vincent Thomas Lombardi had felt the emotional sting of discrimination. Why? Because his ancestors had come from southern Italy and were darker-skinned than Italians from central and certainly from northern Italy where many were actually blond and blue-eyed. More than once young Vince had been called a "n----- Dago" by non-Italians. He often fought physically with such bigoted cretins. From a modern perspective, it's easy to believe that some people stalled his career in coaching because they considered him to be a person of a minority. Why else would a man of his obvious talent and integrity have been denied the opportunity to be a head coach in the game he loved so much?

Yes, Vince Lombardi was happy that professional football had finally been completely integrated, but he was still unsatisfied with his part in it. He had much more to prove, and nothing would get in his way.

§§§

19
To Repeat or Not to Repeat

Coach Lombardi opened the campaign to win a second straight NFL title when the majority of his rookies and free agents reported to camp on July 15 and hit the practice field the next day. A total of 20 rookies checked in at St. Norbert College in nearby De Pere. Lombardi said he would give all of them a good look and hoped he could find some help for the two lines and defensive backfield.

All the veterans from the previous season were expected to return with the single exception of Emlen Tunnell who decided to retire after 14 seasons in the NFL, 11 with the Giants and the last three with the Packers. A total of 19 vets checked into camp a day early. Vets not expected into camp yet were Paul Hornung, Herb Adderly, and Elijah Pitts, who were still on active duty with the Army. Rookie Preston Wright was also working for Uncle Sam at this time. Three other rookies—Earl Gros, Ed Blaine, and Ron Gassert—were practicing with the College All-Stars for the upcoming game against the Packers at Soldier Field in Chicago.

Among non-players, Carl "Bud" Jorgensen returned for his 39th year as Packer trainer. Domenic Gentile, West De Pere High School basketball coach, returned as assistant trainer for his second year with the Packers. Dad Braisher came back as equipment manager. Dr. James W. Nellen presided over the physical examinations of the players.

The first big news out of camp was the trade of Tom Bettis to the Pittsburgh Steelers for an undisclosed draft choice. This move by Lombardi elevated Nelson Toburen up a notch on the depth chart. As for Bettis, he left the team with indecision about whether he would report to the Steelers or spend more time at his off-season job.

Jack Salamon, rookie end from American International, was the first player cut from the roster.

While the Packers and other pro teams were opening their training camps across the country, AFL Commissioner Joe Foss was in Seattle for a speaking engagement at the convention of the Western Association of Game and Fish Commissioners. The uncredited writer of the newspaper story about his speech tried to make Foss look like an idiot by stating the AFL boss said it wouldn't be long before the two pro pigskin leagues would have their own "World Series" featuring the champions of the AFL and NFL. Any fairly knowledgeable sports fan knows a "series" means two teams playing three or more games to determine a champion. Foss meant a title game between the champions of the two circuits.

"That championship game," said Foss, "will fill any stadium in the country and be the biggest television package ever. That's what both leagues are in business for. We love football, but we want to make a buck."

This was some prediction. It would have been an even greater prognostication if Foss had prophesized the year this game would come to reality.

The second rookie to hear from "the Turk" was the end from West Virginia Bob Timmerman. He made it through four days of camp before being waivered by Lombardi.

After the team's first scrimmage, Lombardi reduced the roster by three on Monday morning. Handed their pink slips were Andrew Griffin, fullback from American International; Rudy Simko, tackle from Cincinnati; and George Versprille, halfback from Howard.

On July 24, Paul Hornung and Herb Adderly were given their discharges from active duty with the Army. Hornung reported the next day, but Adderly took a little longer. In the meantime, the date for Elijah Pitts to be discharged remained a military secret.

The Monday before the Packers were slated to play the College All-Stars in Chicago Lombardi trimmed the roster by releasing five players on waivers and trading one. Failing to make the team were Don Ellersick, a halfback who was on the Pack's taxi squad the year before after having earlier shots with the Rams and Vikings; Jerry Scattini and Roger Holdinsky, both halfbacks; George Haney, center; and Tom Kepner, tackle. Gone to the Dallas Cowboys in exchange for a future draft choice was John Sutro, tackle from San Jose State. This left 47 players on the roster; 12 rookies and 35 veterans.

The Packers went into the College All-Star game as 20-point

favorites and came away as 22-point winners. Seeing the final score, 42-20, might have given a reader the idea that the Pack had an easy time of it. Not so. The All-Stars gave Green Bay a real game—for much of three quarters. They held leads of 7-0, 10-7, and 17-14. The "Pros from Dover" then took over.

Bart Starr completed his third touchdown pass of the game, his second to Boyd Dowler to put Green Bay up for good. Starr then connected with Max McGee for Starr's fourth scoring toss. The pair hooked up again when Starr hit McGee with the quarterback's fifth passing TD of the game.

Green Bay's final score came on a three-yard run by Elijah Pitts who had only joined the squad two days earlier.

After the College All-Star game, Lombardi waived two more rookies from the roster. Released were Jack Novak, guard from Miami (Florida) and Peter Schenck, halfback from Washington State. Novak spent the 1961 season on the taxi squad.

The Packers played their first pre-season game in the Cotton Bowl in Dallas against the Cowboys. Not much of a game. The crowd of 54,500 sweated through 90-degree temperatures to watch the Bay Boys hammer their Wranglers, 31-7. Although the victory was basically meaningless, it did extend Green Bay's pre-season win string to 15.

After the Dallas game, Lombardi announced yet another trade. This one involved rookie halfback Ernie Green from Louisville. He was sent to the Cleveland Browns for an undisclosed draft choice. Paul Brown had hopes that Green could replace Heisman Trophy winner Ernie Davis in Cleveland's backfield. Davis was already declared out for the season due to contracting leukemia.

Green Bay squared off against the St. Louis Cardinals in the Gator Bowl in Jacksonville, Florida for the Packers' next pre-season contest. Again, the Boys from the

Bay overwhelmed the competition, this time, 41-14. This game wasn't all offense for the Packers. Two of their six touchdowns came on pass interceptions.

Lombardi's first move after the Cardinals game was to trade big Ben Davidson, defensive end, to the Washington Redskins for a future draft choice. Apparently, the coach didn't think Davidson was on his way to becoming a candidate for the Hall of Fame, although he did become a three-time All-Star in the AFL.

The 13th Annual Midwest Shrine Game in Milwaukee was next on the Packers' pre-season schedule. Facing them were the Monsters of the Midway, the Chicago Bears. No big deal there. It was a meaningless game for all but the charity because for the first time ever the game was sold out. All 44,235 seats were reserved two days before the game. For the fans from Chicago, the game was fine through three quarters, but in the fourth the Packers broke a 21-21 tie and came away with yet another pre-season victory, 35-21. This raised Green Bay's winning streak in exhibition games to 17.

Beware of the Giants! Or so the newspaper stories warned. Fans in Green Bay giggled at the reports that the New Yorkers were coming to town seeking revenge for the shellacking they had taken the previous winter when their Packers slam-dunked the Gothamites over the crossbars of City Stadium. The 2nd Annual Bishop's Charities Game had no real meaning for them other than a chance to see their boys in action because the coming season's home games in Green Bay were sold out. New York gave as good as they got in all departments but one: kick returning. Green Bay's punt returners and kickoff men dominated the visitors return defenses, setting up scoring chances for the home team in a 20-17 win. Oddly, all four of the games between the Giants and Packers had scores totaling 37 points.

With one pre-season tilt to go, Lombardi decided the time had come for a major cut to his roster. He started by trading Paul Dudley, halfback from Arkansas, to the Giants for an undisclosed draft choice. Then the Turk put veteran player-coach Ben Agajanian on waivers with Dick Davis, free agent defensive end from Kansas, and Bob Joiner, the longshot quarterback from Presbyterian. Howard Williams, defensive back from Howard University, was placed on the injured waiver list (Injured Reserve). The next day the general manager sent Lee Folkins, tight end from Washington, to the Dallas Cowboys for an undisclosed draft choice. This gave the Packers six extra picks in the 1963 NFL Draft at this time.

Without too much trouble, the Packers ended their pre-season slate in Columbus, Georgia with a 20-14 victory over the revitalized Washington Redskins. This was pre-season win number 19 in a row for the men who represented the smallest city in all of professional sports in the United States. Now all they had ahead of them was a rugged 14-game regular season and hopefully another shot at the NFL title.

The AFL kicked off its season with a Friday night game in Denver with the Broncos beating San Diego, 30-21. On Saturday night in Dallas, the Texans downed Boston, 42-28. In the Sunday games, New York started well with a 28-17 victory over Oakland; and Houston continued its winning streak by holding off a mad second-half rush from Buffalo to defeat the Bills, 28-22.

On cut-down day, Lombardi released rookie Oscar Donahue, offensive end from San Jose State, in order to get the Packers down to the roster limit of 36 for the season. This left the Packers with 32 vets from the previous season and four rookies from this year's draft. The men returning were quarterbacks Bart Starr and John Roach; running backs Jim Taylor, Paul Hornung, Tom Moore, and Elijah Pitts; ends Max McGee, Ron Kramer, Boyd Dowler, Gary Knafelc, and utility man Lew Carpenter; offensive linemen Forrest Gregg, Bob Skoronski, Norm Masters, Fuzzy Thurston, Jerry Kramer, Jim Ringo, and Kenny Iman; defensive linemen Bill Quinlan, Willie Davis, Dave Hanner, Ron Kostelnik, and Henry Jordan; linebackers Bill Forester, Dan Currie, Ray Nitschke, and Nelson Toburen; and defensive backs Willie Wood, Herb Adderly, Hank Gremminger, John Symank, and Jess Whittenton. Rookies who made the team were running back Earl Gros, guard Ed Blaine, offensive end Gary Barnes, and defensive end Ron Gassert.

First on the schedule for the Packers were the Minnesota Vikings of Coach Norm Van Brocklin. Only seven original Vikes made the team for 1962. One other faced a two-year hitch in the U.S. Army. This was all that remained of the 36 players selected from the expansion pool from the year before. Besides the seven originals, the Minnesota roster was made up 13 players picked up in trades, 11 from the 1961 and 1962 drafts, and six free agents. Even with all the new faces in camp Van Brocklin had put together a very competitive team for the coming campaign.

The oddsmakers for the season placed the Packers and Giants at the tops of their respective divisions and would meet in the title game in New York at the end of December. For the season opener in Green Bay against Minnesota, the Packers were favored by 17 points, a hefty margin to say the least. Lombardi worried that his boys might be a little too confident because of the spread and the Vikings might be extra fired up for the game.

A sellout crowd waited anxiously for the opening kickoff, all the Packer Backers wishing and hoping for a stunning victory over the visiting Vikings. They got their wish granted.

The Packers jumped out to a 14-0 lead in the first quarter on two touchdowns by Paul Hornung from six and seven yards out. He added a field goal in the second period to give Green Bay a 17-0 lead at the half. Ron Kramer caught an 18-yard scoring toss from Bart Starr in the third stanza and Hornung kicked his second field goal to build the lead to 27-0 through three. Hornung scampered 37 yards in the fourth quarter to give the Packers a 34-0 lead and 28 points for himself in the contest.

Minnesota avoided a shutout by scoring a touchdown with a mere minute and 45 seconds left in the game to make the final score Packers 34, Vikings 7.

Offensively, the Pack was fairly dominant, totaling 334 yards against Minnesota's 229. The major difference in the outcome was created by five Fran Tarkenton passes being intercepted by the ball hawks in Green Bay's secondary. Willie Wood hauled in the first of them off a tipped ball by Bill Forester. Wood intercepted another in the second quarter. Herb Adderly pulled down a pass tipped by Jess Whittenton just before the half to halt a potential Viking scoring drive. Hank Gremminger snagged a Tarkenton pass on the Minnesota 44 and carried it all the way back for a touchdown that was called back because of a penalty on Willie Davis for an illegal block. Adderly intercepted for the second time in the fourth quarter, returning it 18 yards to the Vikings' 44, setting up Hornung's final TD of the day.

Jim Taylor picked up 75 yards on 17 carries. Hornung gained 67 on 10 attempts. Starr completed seven of 14 passes for 108 yards. Hornung threw for 41 yards. Boyd Dowler caught three passes for 95 yards; Max McGee two for 34 yards; Hornung two for two; and Kramer one for 18 yards.

Lombardi commented after the game that he was pleased that the ground game was back after seemingly being missing in the last two pre-season games. The win gave the Packers a 3-0 record over the Vikings all-time.

Around the rest of the NFL, Cleveland topped New York, 17-7; St. Louis upset Philadelphia, 27-21; Chicago gave a pounding to San Francisco, 30-14; Baltimore slipped by Los Angeles, 30-27; Detroit hammered Pittsburgh, 45-7; and Dallas tied Washington, 35-all.

In the AFL's second week, the Denver Broncos (2-0) slipped by the Buffalo Bills (0-2) by a field goal on Saturday night., 23-20. On Sunday afternoon, Boston (1-1) clipped Houston (1-1) behind former Packers quarterback Babe Parilli, 34-21; and San Diego (1-1) crushed

New York (1-1) behind the passing combination of Jack Kemp to Lance Alworth, 40-14. Dallas and Oakland had the weekend off.

Good news for the AFL. After the first two weeks of play, attendance was up for the league by more than 50%. In 1961, the average attendance per game was 17,800. For the current year, it was 26,939, which was 9,139 more fans in the stands than the previous season for the same time. This was good for the AFL, but odious for the NFL. If this trend were to continue, the NFL owners knew it would only be a matter of time before the AFL would go to war with them for services of players, whether veterans or college draft picks.

Three Packers were guests at the Downtown Lions Club lunch on the Monday after the Viking game. Boyd Dowler, Henry Jordan, and Bob Skoronski all agreed during a question and answer period that success of the new league (AFL), now in its third season, would not hurt the caliber of professional football. Dowler said he expects the salary fights between the leagues to level off as the AFL becomes stabilized. None of the three could predict if or when the two leagues would come together for a mutual player draft.

The one big question the trio couldn't answer in agreement was, "How do (the coaches) select the positions the (players) play?"

"It's easy," Jordan quipped. "They try them all out on defense, and if (they don't) pass the physical, (the coaches) make ... offensive player(s) of (them)."

Next on the Green Bay schedule was St. Louis at Milwaukee. The Cardinals were figured to finish at or near the top of the Eastern Conference for one reason. John David Crow was back in their lineup and as healthy as ever. Cards' coach Wally Lemm was more to the point. "What Jimmy Brown is to Cleveland, what Paul Hornung is to Green Bay, John is to us." In the opener for St. Louis, Crow gained 70 yards on 22 carries and scored three touchdowns.

Come Sunday, rugged Jim Taylor cracked the tough St. Louis defense for 122 yards, but Paul Hornung and Max McGee busted the visitor's goal line once each to carry the Packers to a 17-0 win over the Cardinals. Green Bay's defense once again rose up and shut down the opposing offense, holding the St. Louis running game to a mere 16 yards and the desperation passing attack to 172 yards. Boyd Dowler snared five passes for 82 yards, Taylor four passes for 40 yards, Ron Kramer four for 26 yards, and Max McGee two for 33 yards and Bart Starr's lone touchdown toss.

The win got the Packers (2-0) off to a solid start in the Western Conference. Keeping pace were the Lions (2-0), big 45-24 winners over San Francisco (0-2); the Colts (2-0), who stomped the Vikings (0-2) by the same score as Green Bay had the week before, 34-7; and the Bears (2-0), who were narrowly victorious over the Rams (0-2) in Los Angeles, 27-23.

In the Eastern Conference, Washington (1-0-1) pulled off a big upset over Cleveland (1-1) by the score of 17-16, putting the Redskins in first place. The Giants (1-1) downed the Eagles (0-2) in Philly, 27-13. Down in the heart of Texas, the Steelers (1-1) nipped the Cowboys (0-1-1) by a safety, 30-28.

The AFL was showing promise of real excitement in its third week of action. Once again former Packer Babe Parilli led the Boston Patriots (2-1) crushing the Denver Broncos (2-1) in Boston, 41-16. Saturday night in Buffalo, New York (2-1) took down the Bills (0-3) by a score of 17-6 before irate fans who littered the track around the field with beer cans and other debris at the end of the game. The Sunday games saw Houston (2-1) put a 42-17 hurt on San Diego (1-2) behind the running of Billy Cannon and Charlie Tolar, the stout fullback who worked as an oil well fire-fighter in the off season; and Dallas (2-0) remained the only unbeaten in the league with a 26-16 victory over Oakland (0-2).

The opponent for the Packers' third straight home game was none other than the Chicago Bears. Papa Bear George Halas whined that his team was riddled with injuries and might not be up to par for the game in Green Bay. Wounded but not critical were Mike Ditka, Fred Williams, Willie Galimore, Charley Bivins, Rick Casares, and Bill George. Bivins and George failed to heal enough to play in the 87th clash between the Bears and the Packers.

Packer Backers went to sleep Saturday night "just wishing and hoping and thinking and praying" for a big victory over the Bears the next afternoon. When all was said and done Sunday evening, all their desires were fulfilled.

After a scoreless opening quarter, the Packers threw their game into high gear and put 14 points on the board, while keeping the Bears off the scoreboard for another 15 minutes. Jim Taylor barreled in from a yard out with 9:26 left in the half, and Bart Starr connected with Ron Kramer for 54-yards and the second six with 1:16 before the gun.

Taylor broke away for a 26-yard gain to the Chicago two, then cracked through the Bear defense for the score to up the Pack's lead to 21-0. After Bill Quinlan tipped a Rudy Bukich pass to Ray Nitschke at the Chicago 21, Elijah Pitts raced around right end to the end zone to up the ante to 28-0. Bukich's next pass was picked off by Hank Gremminger on the Chicago 24. A 15-yard holding penalty on the Packers pushed the ball back to the 41. Pitts broke loose for a 31-yard gain, then Taylor banged his way to pay dirt from the 10 to put Green Bay ahead, 35-0.

The fourth quarter saw the Packers mount a 72-yard scoring drive in nine plays. Starr connected with Dowler for 23 yards and Pitts for another 29. A 10-yard toss to Dowler put the ball on the Bears' three. Chicago stopped two runs for a yard loss by each, then Starr ran five yards around left end for the score, making the unsurmountable lead 42-0. Willie Wood made his second interception of the game on the Bears' next possession. Herb Adderly snared a Bill Wade pass at the midfield stripe and raced 50 yards for the last six of the afternoon.

Packer fans everywhere couldn't have been happier that their boys in green and gold had blasted their archrival by the largest margin in the history of the series between the two teams, 49-0. Not since 1934 when they shutout the Cincinnati Reds and Chicago Cardinals on consecutive Sundays had the Packers held two regular season foes scoreless in back-to-back games.

Taylor led the ground game with 26 yards on 17 carries. Pitts, filling in for Hornung who was hurt early in the contest, racked up 64 yards on nine attempts. Starr finished with nine completions out of 12 throws for 154 yards and a TD. Dowler hauled in five passes for 57 yards, and Pitts snared two for 40 yards. Taylor also scored three TDs.

Going into Sunday's NFL action, the Western Conference standings had a four-way tie for first place with four unbeaten teams. The Packers (3-0) dropped one of those, Chicago (2-1) from the perfect ranks, while Detroit (3-0) nailed down the fourth, Baltimore (2-1) by the score of 29-20. San Francisco (1-2) picked up its first win of the year by beating winless Minnesota (0-3) in a struggle, 21-7. Los Angeles (0-3) suffered another defeat, 27-17, at the hands of the Dallas Cowboys (1-1-1). Surprising Washington (2-0-1) stayed on top of the Eastern Conference with 24-14 victory over St. Louis (1-2). New York (2-1) kept pace with the Redskins, slipping by Pittsburgh (1-2) by the narrow margin of 31-27. Philadelphia (1-2) got into the win column with a 35-7 thrashing of Cleveland (1-2).

In Week 4, the races were beginning to shape up in the AFL as Dallas (3-0) remained the only undefeated team with a 41-21 win over the Buffalo Bills (0-4). Denver (3-1) stayed in the hunt with a 32-10 beat down of the New York Titans (2-2). San Diego (2-2) made their presence known in the Western Division, hanging a 42-33 on winless Oakland (0-3). Idle were Boston (2-1) and Houston (2-1).

For the fourth week in a row, the Packers would be facing a team that had not lost a game during the regular season of 1962. Who should be rolling into Green Bay on Sunday afternoon October 7 than the Detroit Lions. For their three wins, the Lions had beaten Pittsburgh, 45-7; San Francisco, 45-24; and Baltimore, 29-20. Detroit's three victims had an aggregate record of 4-5. For the Packers, their trio of opponents were 3-6 so far. Detroit's offense had posted 119 points in their three games and had surrendered 51. Green Bay had scored an even 100 points and had allowed a mere 7. Detroit was a plus-68, while the Pack had an edge of plus-93. Throwing all those numbers into their computers, the oddsmakers favored the Packers to win in a tight one.

Over the years, the Packers and Lions had met 58 times. Green Bay had won 33 of those games, lost 24, and tied one. Records aside, their games were almost always close and certainly hard-fought on both sides. Only during the years between Lambeau and Lombardi did the Lions dominate the Pack. Before and after, the Packers reigned supreme.

The gamblers seldom make bad predictions on sports. This game proved no different.

Rain started falling long before the kickoff, and it never really let up throughout the game. The foul weather hurt both teams when they had the ball and aided both teams when they were on defense.

Paul Hornung scored all of Green Bay's points. The Golden Boy kicked a 15-yard field goal to put the Pack up 3-0 in the first quarter. Detroit took the lead, 7-3, on a Danny Lewis run of six yards following a fumble by Bart Starr. Hornung booted another 15-yarder to close the gap to one, 7-6, in the third period. Neither team could do any scoring until the final two minutes of the contest.

Detroit made two first downs before the clock was stopped for the two-minute warning. The Lions had the ball on their own 47, first and 10. Nick Pietrosante and Lewis managed to gain just three yards on one carry apiece, and the Packers called time out after each run. This left 1:25 on the clock. Then came the pivotal play of the game.

Milt Plum had been successful on two consecutive third down tries before the two-minute warning, so Detroit Coach George Wilson called for the same passing play, only this time to a different receiver. Plum fired in the direction of Terry Barr, his top pass catcher. Barr slipped slightly in making his cut, which allowed just enough room for Green Bay's sneaky pass thief Herb Adderly to slide in front of Barr and snare Plum's throw on the Packer 42. From there, the cagey back from Michigan State rambled 40 yards to the Detroit 18.

With a minute left to play, the crowd erupted with eager and livid anticipation of what could happen next. Green Bay's offensive 11 charged onto the field, each man knowing this might be their last opportunity to "make-it-or-break- it." With one precious timeout left, Hornung and Jim Taylor each gained two yards and moved the ball to the center of the field. Starr used that last stoppage of play to give the field goal team the chance to get on the field and gain their composure for the kick that would decide the outcome. Dan Currie ran out with a towel to wipe off the square toe of Hornung's kicking shoe, just in case any mud had caked there from the quagmire of the rain-drenched turf of City Stadium. Starr knelt down, patted the ground to give it some kind of firmness, held out his hands in preparation of catching Jim Ringo's snap, and gave the signal. Ringo rifled the ball perfectly to Starr's waiting hands. He put it down on the spot he had just made for the tip of the ball. Hornung stepped forward, whipped his kicking leg at the ball, and sent the ball into the air. A mighty struggle between the two lines erupted in front of Starr and Hornung. Defenders reached high to slap at the ball, but to no avail as the kid from Notre Dame boomed his third and final three of the game through the uprights to give the Pack a 9-7 lead that would hold up for the final 33 seconds of the game.

The crowd held its collective breath until the referees under the goal posts threw up their arms to signal the field goal was good. Then every loyal Packer Backer erupted into a euphoric cheer heard all across Packerland. Final score: Green Bay 9, Detroit 7.

In spite of the poor weather conditions, the Packers managed to gain 319 yards as a team. Taylor led the way with 95 yards in 20 carries. Starr completed 18 of 26 passes. Max McGee had a good day with five catches for 69 yards. And Hornung added nine points to his league-leading total, now at 56 points.

By defeating Detroit (3-1), the Packers (4-0) were now the only team remaining unbeaten and untied in the NFL. Washington (3-0-1), with its 20-14 win over Los Angeles (0-4) could also claim unbeaten status but not untied. Chicago (3-1) posted a shutout, 13-0, over the Vikings (0-4), to join the Lions in second place in the West. The 49ers (2-2) climbed a notch in the standings with a 21-13 victory over the Colts (2-2). Back East, New York (3-1) stayed in stride with the Redskins with a 31-14 win over St. Louis (1-3). Cleveland (2-2) won one for "The Elmira Express" Ernie Davis, who was sidelined for good with a terminal case of leukemia. The Browns downed Dallas (1-2-1) in Cleveland, 19-10. In a rare Saturday game this early in the season, the Steelers (2-2) handed the struggling Eagles (1-3) a tough loss, 13-7.

In the AFL, Denver (4-1) crushed Oakland (0-4) in a Friday night game, 44-7. Babe Parilli once again led the Boston Patriots (3-1) to a lopsided win, 43-14, over the New York Titans (2-2) Saturday night. In the Sunday matches, San Diego rookie John Hadl took the reins from Jack Kemp who had a broken finger on his throwing hand and was shuffled off to Buffalo. The Chargers (3-2) rode over the Texans (3-1), bringing an end to their hope of an unbeaten year, 32-28. Houston (3-1) shaded the Buffalo Bills (0-5) by a field goal, 17-14. Denver sat atop the Western Division with Dallas a half-game behind and San Diego a full game back. In the East, Boston and Houston were tied for the top spot with New York a game behind. Buffalo and Oakland occupied the cellar of their respective divisions a sad three and a half games out of first.

Like a lot of football coaches, Lombardi worried that his team might see their next match-up as a trap game because the Packers would be playing the Vikings in Minnesota at a time when Green Bay had just duked it out with the team that might have been their toughest opponent of the season. After winning a big one like that, many teams would suffer a deep letdown in morale, which often cost them a game they should win. Of course, Packer fans didn't believe that could happen to their boys in green and gold, especially since they would be facing the winless Vikes, a team they had already handled quite easily in the season opener. Lombardi took every precaution against his team getting fat-headed about Minnesota.

The late NFL Commissioner Bert Bell coined the phrase: "Any team can beat any other team on a given Sunday." Well, this wasn't to be one of those Sundays.

Just like the first time the two teams met, the game wasn't much of a contest. The Packers put up 27-first half points to seven for the Vikings. Green Bay coasted home in the second 30 minutes by scoring 21 points to Minnesota's 14. No drama in this game except for the six injured players the Packers sustained.

Bill Quinlan took to the bench with rib and leg hurts. John Symank twisted an ankle. Jess Whittenton got a leg banged up. Ron Kostelnik took one to the shoulder. Bob Skoronski suffered a leg injury. But the biggest injury of all happened to Paul Hornung. He scored the Pack's first touchdown and was five yards from scoring the second when Cliff Livingston hit him low and flipped the Golden Boy into the air. Hornung came down hard on his knee and had to leave the game.

On a positive note, Jim Taylor had another huge day, gaining 164 yards on 17 runs. Bart Starr completed his first 10 passes of the day, 20 of 28 overall, for 297 yards and three touchdowns. Max McGee caught 10 passes for 159 yards and two touchdowns. Boyd Dowler pulled in seven passes for 124 yards and a touchdown. Green Bay's defense intercepted three more passes to give them 16 on the year, and they sacked Fran Tarkenton for 28 yards on the day.

Starting the season, no other team in the NFL doubted that the Packers (5-0) were the team to beat in 1962. Now after five weeks the Boys in green and gold were proving it. Detroit (4-1) continued to hang in with Green Bay, narrowly winning, 13-10, over the "Sad Sack" Rams (0-5). Baltimore, San Francisco, and Chicago—all tied for third (3-2)—still had hopes of overtaking the Packers. The Colts showed signs of getting their offense back on track with a 34-14 whopping of Cleveland (2-3). San Francisco took down the Bears, 34-27. In the Eastern Conference, Washington (3-0-2) picked up a half-game on the Giants by holding St. Louis (1-3-1) to a 17-all tie. Pittsburgh (3-2) moved into a tie with New York (3-2) for second, beating the aging Gothamites, 20-17, in Yankee Stadium. Dallas Cowboys (2-2-1) pulled the biggest surprise of the day by handing a 41-19 stinger on the Eagles (1-4), now in last place.

The AFL started Week 6 of their season on Friday night with Dallas visiting Boston in a rematch of their first meeting in Texas to start the season. Dallas won the opener, 42-28, but the Patriots, with Babe Parilli at the helm now, felt their chances for victory were better at home. It wasn't to be for the Pats. The Texans (4-1), behind the running of Abner Haynes and the passing of Len Dawson, posted a 27-7 victory over the New Englanders (3-2). Saturday night's game featured the Bills hosting the Chargers. Winless Buffalo (1-5) pulled off a major upset, 35-10, over San Diego (3-3) behind the running of fullback Cookie Gilchrist. Sunday's games saw the Oilers (4-1) coming together offensively as they put a 56-17 hurt on the Titans (2-4). The ageless George Blanda threw a record seven touchdown passes in the lopsided affair. Denver (5-1) continued to hold down first place in the West by handing Oakland (0-5) yet another loss, 23-6.

Lombardi's only worry for the next game—against the 49ers in Milwaukee—was the health of the six players who left the romp over the Vikings. John Symank's ankle appeared to be okay on Monday. Ron Kostelnik had a dislocated shoulder that made him questionable for the next game. Jess Whittenton had pulled a muscle in one leg. Bill Quinlan had sore ribs, but he was expected to be full recovered by game day. Bob Skoronski still had a sore knee on Monday, but he was considered to be good enough to go against the 49ers.

This left Paul Hornung. X-rays of his knee showed no bone damage, and an examination for torn cartilage or worse proved to be negative. Lombardi termed Hornung's injury to be a bruised knee and only time would tell if it might actually be worse. The other five men on the wounded list had a man ready to step in if any of them couldn't go on Sunday. Hornung was a different matter. The versatile back from Notre Dame would need three men to replace him in the lineup. Jerry Kramer to do the placekicking. Tom Moore to run at halfback. Willie Wood to do kickoffs.

Lombardi could only say he'd have to see how everybody felt on Sunday morning before making any decisions about who would and who wouldn't play that day. He did caution that the two with the least likely chance to play were Kostelnik and Hornung. On Thursday, the coach declared Hornung would not play against San Francisco, but the other walking wounded would be on the field at County Stadium and in uniform ready to go.

Two days before the game San Francisco Coach Red Hickey announced, "We're 100 per cent healthy for the first time this season. So, we have no complaints there. There's no doubt about it, our club has come on in the past three weeks. It's more aggressive and more determined."

Leading the 49ers on offense were quarterback John Brodie,

fullback J.D. Smith, and halfback Bill Kilmer. Hickey had deserted the mostly passing shotgun formation of recent years for a T-formation running game resembling those of the Packers, Bears, and Giants. Like the Cleveland Browns who relied heavily on fullback Jim Brown to carry the load for them, the 49ers put their fortunes in the hands of Smith. He had carried the ball 31 times in each of San Francisco's last two games, both of which the 49ers had won. Of course, he wasn't running against the number one defense in the NFL—which belonged to the Packers—in either of those games.

Red Hickey figured the only way to beat the Packers was to control the ball. For the first 20 minutes of the game, his plan worked. The 49ers held the ball for 37 plays to eight for the Packers. In that time, San Francisco kicked two field goals to take a 6-0 lead, and the 49ers had the ball again. John Brodie threw a pass that Willie Wood intercepted, ran out of bounds, and promptly found himself being trampled by 49er feet. This set a fire under the Packers.

Still trailing 6-0, Tom Moore scored on a 14-yard run to put Green Bay ahead, 7-6. Just before the half ended, Jerry Kramer put his toe into a 27-yard field goal attempt and made it for a 10-6 lead at the intermission.

Undeterred, the 49ers regained the lead on a punt return of 85 yards by Abe Woodson. This put San Francisco on top again, 13-10. That was the end of their scoring.

Jim Taylor then went on a rampage. In less than three minutes, he bolted for touchdowns from 17 yards and 25 yards to put Green Bay ahead for good, 24-13. Ron Kramer's shoestring catch of a nine-yard Bart Starr in the fourth quarter finished the scoring on the day, giving the Packers a 31-13 victory over San Francisco.

Taylor gained 160 yards on 16 carries, while Moore chipped in 84 yards on 14 runs. Starr connected on 10 of 12 passes for 107 yards. Ron Kramer puled in four passes for 67 yards.

Green Bay (6-0) added a game to their lead in the West with their win over San Francisco (3-3). Detroit (4-2) slipped a notch, losing to the Giants (4-2) in a close one, 17-14. The Bears (4-2) rejoined the Lions in second place by hammering Baltimore (3-3) by 20 points, 35-15. In a battle to escape the cellar, Minnesota (1-5) punished Los Angeles (0-6) with an offensive barrage, 38-14. In the Eastern Conference, Washington (4-0-2) continued its winning ways with a 27-21 win over Philadelphia (1-5). Dallas (3-2-1) took it to Pittsburgh

(3-3) by a score of 42-27, gaining third place in the process. Cleveland (3-3) moved into a tie with the Steelers for fourth by giving a 34-7 crushing of St. Louis (1-4-1).

Friday night's AFL game had the Chargers in Boston to face the second place Patriots. San Diego pulled out to a 20-3 halftime lead that had the Boston crowd booing their team for 30 minutes. The second half was completely different as former Packer Babe Parilli rallied his guys with two TD passes and some clutch ball-carrying, while the Boston (4-2) defense held San Diego (3-4) scoreless to win, 24-20. On Saturday night in Buffalo, the Bills (2-5) won their second straight game, 14-6, beating Oakland (0-6) before a rain-soaked crowd of 21,037 exuberant fans. Cookie Gilchrist led the way for the Bills with 144 yards on 19 carries. Sunday's game saw Denver (6-1) keep its hold on first in the West with a 20-10 win over Houston (4-2). Dallas (5-1) kept pace by defeating New York (2-5) by a field goal, 20-17.

A newspaper writer came up with the wildest rumor of the season. He wrote the AFL wanted the Chargers to leave San Diego for New York; the Raiders to bolt Oakland for Kansas City; and the Titans to fly south to New Orleans. He offered a fistful of malarkey to back up his tale. According to him, the Titans couldn't compete for fans in New York because the Giants were so entrenched there. The Chargers, a better team than the Titans, would fare better in Gotham. As for the Raiders, his argument was they could do better no matter where they went as long as there was no other team within 100 miles of them. Of course, the league office denied all of this and added that the Chargers were doing just fine in San Diego. Harry Wismer, the primary owner of the Titans, had no comment; however, it was widely known that he was looking for someone to buy him out and take over the franchise.

One sore on Lombardi's record as head coach of the Packers was his boys had yet to beat the Colts in Baltimore. Actually, the Pack had lost four-straight in the Maryland city, going back to the 56-0 licking under Scooter McLean. The Colts were led by Johnny Unitas at quarterback, Lenny Moore at slot back, and Tom Matte at halfback. When all three were cruising on all cylinders, the Colts were nearly impossible to beat. Lombardi had other ideas, of course.

The Packers showed their championship class by holding back a mighty effort by the charged-up Colts. Neither team offered any quarter as they drew a combined 163 yards in penalties before a crazed crowd of 57,966 fans in Memorial Stadium. Green Bay won, 17-6, to keep their record for the year untarnished.

Lombardi's bunch worked two perfect touchdown plays to get the victory. Bart Starr connected with Ron Kramer for a 25-yard score, and Jim Taylor reeled off a 37-yard scoring run. The other three points came via Jerry Kramer's toe. Baltimore piled up more yards, 309, than Green Bay, 252; but yardage doesn't show on the scoreboard, the only place where the numbers count.

Taylor managed only 64 yards for the game, but those markers moved him into second place all-time in Packer history for rushing yards. He now had 3,917 career yards to Clark Hinkle's 3,877. Taylor trailed only Tony Canadeo who had 4,197 yards for his Hall of Fame career.

The big highlight of the day came during the playing of the National Anthem. As all stood for playing of the tune by a huge band, Baltimore's mascot, a real live pony, made his prediction for the outcome of the game. When the band marched away once *The Star-Spangled Banner* was completed, a steaming pile of barnyard waste was discovered on the playing field. This had to be removed before the opening kickoff, but it was too late. The pony had made his point.

Halfway through the season now the Packers (7-0) remained the solid leader in the West with their win over Baltimore (3-4). The Lions (5-2) kept pace with a weird win, 11-3, over the Bears (4-3). Los Angeles (1-6) finally made the win column, 28-14, over San Francisco (3-4). Minnesota posted its second win of the year, 31-21, over the faltering Eagles (1-6). Y.A. Tittle tied an NFL record by completing seven touchdown passes in New York's 49-34 victory over the Redskins (4-1-2). St. Louis (2-4-1) upset Dallas (3-3-1) in a close game, 28-24. Cleveland (4-3) climbed back into the Eastern race with a 41-14 bashing of the Steelers (3-4).

Boston (5-2) began the AFL weekend Friday night by defeating Oakland (0-7) in Beantown, 26-16. Gino Cappelletti scored 20 of the Patriots' points. In the Sunday games, Len Dawson drove the Texans (6-1) into first place in the Western Division with a 31-7 smacking of the Oilers (4-3) in Houston. Buffalo (3-5) extended its winning streak to three with a 45-38 comeback win over Denver (6-2). The Titans (3-5) kept their Eastern Division title hopes alive with a 23-3 victory over the sliding San Diego Chargers (3-5), now three and a half games behind Dallas in the Western Conference.

On paper, Green Bay's first half didn't look all that impressive to most NFL aficionados. They would argue that the Pack had played five of their seven at home, giving them a solid advantage. Then they would add that the Packers second half wouldn't be so easy. They had Chicago, Philadelphia, Detroit, San Francisco, and Los Angeles on the road and Baltimore in City Stadium and Los Angeles in Milwaukee County Stadium. Not an easy path for Lombardi's men seeking an undefeated season.

Lombardi knew better than to look ahead of the next game, especially when that next game was in Wrigley Field against the Big Bad Bears. Hunters say that a wounded bear is much more dangerous than a bear without any pain. Lombardi made this perfectly clear to his team as they prepared to face the Monsters of the Midway in Week 8. The Bears weren't just hurt; they were infuriated over the 49-0 beating they had taken from Green Bay the first time around. They were crazy for revenge, and Lombardi knew it.

Wally Cruice, the Packers' head scout, pointed out one important fact. "And don't forget the Bears aren't hurt like they were the last time." He was so right. Chicago played without Bill George, Fred Williams, Willie Galimore, and Mike Ditka. Furthermore, several other Bears were playing in subpar condition that day.

The ivy on the outfield walls of Wrigley Field had already lost its leaves by the Sunday the Packers met the Bears. Not a big deal for the 48,953 fans who showed up. But the biting cold wind whipping the rain was. The standing-room only crowd didn't hang around for the end of the game. Well, at least not the Chicago fans. They went home wondering why they had bothered to show up at all.

Green Bay took the early lead on a 70-yard drive that ended with Jim Taylor slanting in from two yards out. The Bears came roaring right back with a 79-yard drive culminated by a four-yard pass from Bill Wade to end John Adams. Jerry Kramer kicked a 17-yard field goal to make the score 10-7 at the half.

Taylor's second TD was on a one-yard plunge in the third frame, putting the Pack up, 17-7. Two more touchdowns by Taylor and one by Earl Gros in the final stanza and no scoring by Chicago gave Green Bay its eighth win of the year, 38-7. Taylor amassed 124 yards on 25 carries.

The Bears did more to lose the game than the Packers did to win it. Chicago committed seven turnovers to none for Green Bay. Bart Starr had a good day in spite of the weather conditions, with 14 completions in 26 passes.

Green Bay (8-0) continued its hold onto first place in the West, while the Bears (4-4) fell back into a tie for third with Baltimore (4-4), winners, 22-3, over the rapidly fading 49ers (3-5). Detroit (6-2) kept pace with the Pack with another close win, 12-3, this time over the Rams (1-7). Minnesota (2-6), on the verge of elimination already, lost, 39-31, to Pittsburgh (4-4). Washington (4-2-2) fell into second place in the East, losing big, 38-10, to Dallas (4-3-1). Cleveland (4-3-1) now matched the Cowboys for third place because Philadelphia (1-6-1) held the Browns to a 14-14 tie. The big win of the week went to the Giants (6-2) who moved into first in the East with a close win, 31-28, over St. Louis (2-5-1).

In the AFL, the Patriots traveled to Buffalo for a Saturday night game with the resurgent Bills. Fullback Cookie Gilchrist carried 20 times for 102 yards and a pair of touchdowns to get the Bills (3-5-1) out in front, but Babe Parilli rallied the Pats (5-2-1) in the second half to tie the game at 28-all. Buffalo fans were dismayed when a touchdown interception was canceled by an official who had blown the play dead before the pass was thrown. With six weeks left in the season, the Titans (4-5) got back into the race in the Eastern Division, handing a 31-21 loss on Oakland (0-8) in front of 11,000 fans at the Polo Grounds in New York. The Oilers (5-3) avenged their defeat at the hands of the Texans (6-2) the previous week by a 14-6 score in front of 29,017 fans in the Cotton Bowl in Dallas. The last game of Week 9 saw the Broncos (7-2) take back first place in the West by a field goal, 23-20, over the Chargers (3-6) before 20,827 patrons in Balboa Stadium in San Diego.

Bigger news in the AFL that weekend was the announcement by New York Titans owner Harry Wismer that he was putting his 90% ownership of the club for sale. "I've spent one and three-quarter million dollars, and I have gone about as far as I can go," said the former radio sports announcer. "I will take in some partners or I'll sell out completely." His asking price was $2,500,000, which included the 30-year lease he had signed for the use of a new stadium now under construction in the Flushing Meadows area of Queens. Finances were so bad for the Titans that the league had to loan Wismer money to pay his players for the coming week.

The last meeting that meant something between the Packers and the Eagles was the title game in 1960. Since then, Green Bay had continued to rise in the NFL, while Philadelphia had fallen on hard times. Not that the Eagles didn't have some star players—they did in QB Sonny Jurgensen, receivers Tommy McDonald and former Packer Timmy Brown, and halfback Clarence Peaks—but they were missing the kind of coaching they'd had in 1960 that brought them the title. Philly also led the NFL in passing, but the running game and the defense that led them to a title was missing as well. Did this give the Pack the edge for the upcoming meeting of the two in the Quaker City? The bettors thought so, making Green Bay the favorite to cop their ninth win of the year. (Also known as the City of Brotherly Love, this was hardly the case at sporting events held in Philadelphia.)

When Sunday came and went, the Packers might as well had stayed in Green Bay and played a pickup game with the Knights of local St. Norbert College. Philadelphia was just about that tough. More than 60,000 fans turned out to see a record-setting performance by the Pack. Green Bay's defense held the Eagles to three—that's right, three—first downs, one by penalty. Philly totaled all of 54 yards. Those weren't the records set by the Packers; these were:

PACKER RECORDS
37 first downs to beat the old mark of 35 by Pittsburgh 1958
623 total yards to beat the old Packer mark of 539 set in 1942 against the Chicago Cardinals
7 PATs by Jerry Kramer, tying Don Hutson in 1945 and Paul Hornung in 1961 and 1962
4 touchdowns by Jim Taylor tying Don Hutson in 1945, Paul Hornung and Taylor who did it twice before
6 touchdowns rushing set in 1941 against the Detroit Lions and tied in 1961 against the Cleveland Browns

The Packers mounted scoring drives of 86, 89, 85, 76, 71, 66, and 65 yards, and they didn't score in the final period.

TD #1: 86 yards in 11 plays ending with Tom Moore scoring from the three.

TD #2: 89 yards 7 plays ending in Taylor scoring from the five.

TD #3: 85 yards in 3 plays ending in Moore scoring from the seven.

TD #4: 76 yards in 9 plays ending on a 25-yard pass from Moore to

Boyd Dowler.

TD #5: 71 yards in 9 plays ending in Taylor scoring on an end run to the left for the final five.

TD #6: 66 yards in 10 plays ending in Taylor scoring from the one.

TD #7: 65 yards in 9 plays ending in Taylor around right end for the final four at 1:30 to go in the third quarter.

Imagine how badly the Packers would have beaten the Eagles if Lombardi hadn't showed some good sportsmanship and pulled most of his starters on offense in the fourth frame.

By Green Bay (9-0) winning, 49-0, three teams in the West felt the sting of being eliminated with five weeks to play in the 1962 season. Los Angeles (1-8) lost, 14-2, to Baltimore (5-4). Minnesota (2-7) lost, 31-30, to Chicago (5-4). San Francisco (3-6) lost, 38-24, to Detroit (7-2). Besides the humiliation they had suffered on their own field to the Packers, the Eagles (1-7-1) were also forced from the field in the Eastern Conference. First place New York (7-2) pasted a 41-10 beating on Dallas (4-4-1). Washington (5-2-2) put a 17-9 hurt on Cleveland (4-4-1). Pittsburgh (5-4) handed a 26-17 loss on St. Louis (2-6-1).

All eight teams played on Sunday in the AFL's Week 10. Dallas (7-2) moved back into first place in the West by giving the Titans (4-6) a 52-31 thumping before 13,275 fans at the Polo Grounds in New York. Boston (6-2-1) stayed on top in the East by a 33-29 score over the Broncos (7-3) in front of 28,187 fans in Denver. Houston (6-3) kept pace with the Patriots with a 28-20 come-from-behind victory over the hapless Raiders (0-9) before an estimated crowd of 11,500 loyal fans in Kezar Stadium in San Francisco. Buffalo (4-5-1) stayed alive in the East with a 40-20 shellacking of the Chargers (3-7) whose divisional title hopes were nearly extinguished in the West with their loss at home with 22,204 spectators in attendance.

After clobbering the Bears and Eagles, the Packers squared off again with one of the two opponents who had given them trouble the first time around. Detroit practically gave them their game back in early October, but the Colts had been just about as tough as the Lions when Green Bay met them in Baltimore. Now for the rematch at home in friendly City Stadium.

The Packers won the game with clutch defense and minimal offense. Baltimore rolled up an impressive 380 yards, but the Colts could only score a single TD and a pair of field goals. Green Bay was limited to 116 yards by the bucking Colts, but the Packers stood tall at the goal line on more than one occasion.

In the first quarter, Ray Nitschke recovered a fumble by R.C. Owens at the Green Bay two. In the second stanza, the Colts reached Green Bay's one for a first down and trailing the Pack, 10-3. The Green and Gold line stiffened on three straight plunges before Bill Forester chased down Johnny Unitas for a 13-yard sack on fourth down. In the final frame, the Colts banged their way to the Green Bay seven with four minutes to play and the Packers ahead, 17-13. Herb Adderly once again proved to be the hero of day as he batted down a Unitas pass aimed at Jimmy Orr in the end zone. Baltimore had one more shot, but Bill Quinlan and Willie Davis sacked Unitas on fourth down to end the threat.

Baltimore scored first with a field goal, but the Packers struck back immediately as Adderly took the ensuing kickoff three yards deep in the Pack's end zone and bolted straight up the middle through the Colt defenders before breaking into the clear and racing to pay dirt to give Green Bay the lead. Jerry Kramer kicked a field goal to extend the lead to 10-3. Baltimore tied the score before the half, then took the lead once more in the third period. Tom Moore zipped outside right tackle with 46 seconds gone in the last stanza to score the final TD of the game from 23 yards out. After that, it was all defense.

Jim Taylor only gained 46 yards on the day, but they were enough for him to break Tony Canadeo's career record for yards gained rushing. The previous mark was 4,197, and now Taylor had 4,228.

Green Bay (10-0) now had eliminated Baltimore (5-5) from the race in the Western Conference. This left only Detroit (8-2), winners, 17-6, over Minnesota (2-8); and Chicago (6-4) who won, 34-33, with a late field over Dallas (4-5-1), with any chance of catching the Packers. San Francisco (4-6) continued to play for pride, beating Los Angeles (1-9) by a touchdown, 24-17. New York (8-2) put a firmer hold on first place in the East with a 19-14 win over Philadelphia (1-8-1), while the Redskins (5-3-2) continued to see their season slip away, losing, 23-21, to Pittsburgh (6-4). Cleveland (5-4-1) stayed alive in the race, winning, 38-14, over St. Louis (2-7-1).

The AFL East race saw Houston (7-3) snatch first place from Boston (6-3-1) with a 21-17 win over the Patriots in front of a home crowd of 35,250 Texans. Bad news for Boston was the injury to Babe Parilli who had been leading his team since the second week of the year. Buffalo (5-5-1) nipped Oakland (0-10) by a 10-6 score in front of another sparse crowd of 11,700 in Kezar Stadium. The Texans (8-2) added to their lead in the West with a 24-3 win over the second-place Broncos (7-4) as 23,523 fans looked on in Denver.

For 11 consecutive years, the Packers spent Thanksgiving Day in Detroit as guests of the Lions. During that decade-plus-one, the Lions came away winners eight times. In Lombardi's tenure so far, the Packers were 2-1 over Detroit. Although his boys were doing well on Turkey Day, Lombardi was quite anxious about this visit because the Lions of 1962 were the best the league had seen in a while. Of course, the Packers fit the same description, so fans for both teams were really expecting a bang-up battle between the top two teams in the Western Division, and maybe the whole league.

The bad news for the Packers going into the short week was Nelson Toburen was pronounced done for the rest of the season with a dislocated vertebra from tackling Johnny Unitas. This left his only backup to this point, Ken Iman, in a precarious situation. Iman was a center who had only played middle linebacker at little Southeastern Missouri where his job was to stop the run. But in the Packers scheme, his job would be to stop the short passes on his side of the field. He was put on a crash course to learn the position along with *his* new backup Earl Gros who did play some outside linebacker while leading the offense at LSU.

Leading the Lions offense was quarterback Milt Plum and his backup Earl Morrall. Their top runner was former Notre Dame fullback Nick Pietrosante who many said was as tough a load to stop as Green Bay's Jim Taylor. Pass catchers were Pat Studstill, Jim Gibbons, Gail Cogdill, Terry Barr, and Dan Lewis. They made a fair attack, but Detroit's real measure as a team was on defense. Lead by Yale Lary who also did the team's punting, the defending list was filled with stars. Dick LeBeau. Joe Schmidt, Alex Karras, Roger Brown, Darris McCord, Sam Williams, and Dick "Night Train" Lane—every man an all-star—matched up better with the Packers than any other team in the league.

Art Daley started his game report in the *Press-Gazette* with: "The inevitable has happened. The Packers lost." He followed that by stating, "This was no disgrace." He followed that by making excuses for the Pack. Of course, that was his job, and he did it well, as always.

The truth was simple. Lombardi's men were tired, and the Lions were more rested for the game. Green Bay had just played the very tough Baltimore Colts, and Detroit had squared off with the Vikes in Minnesota. The Packers had taken a beating, while the Lions had an opponent that was still new to the league. Lombardi and company had to travel the day before the game, while George Wilson's crew slept in their own beds the night before Thanksgiving. And all that showed in the first half of the game when the Lions roared out to a 23-0 lead. They added another three points in the third period, and for all practical purposes, the game was over before the start of the final frame. Green Bay did score two token touchdowns on the way out the door to make the final score, 26-14.

Statistically, nobody had a good day for Green Bay. Ron Kramer and Boyd Dowler came the closest with four catches each and 62 and 41 yards, respectively. Then it was back to Wisconsin for some much-needed rest and the beginning of preparations for the final three games of the season against Los Angeles in Milwaukee, followed by the annual West Coast swing into San Francisco and then Los Angeles.

The loss to Detroit (9-2) did spoil the hopes of a perfect season for the Packers (10-1) and their fans, but Lombardi was quick to point out it wasn't the end of the world for them. Two games against LA (1-9-1), who managed a 24-all tie with Minnesota (2-8-1), should be the clinchers for Green Bay. The Bears (7-4) still had a shot at second place thanks to their 57-0 creaming of the Colts (5-6). Although the 49ers (5-6) won over St. Louis (2-8-1) by a TD, 24-17, San Francisco still appeared to be easy pickings for the Packers. In the East, New York (9-2) put the kibosh on Washington (5-4-2) by a 42-24 margin, practically ending their hopes for a first-place tie. Cleveland (6-4-1) did much the same to Pittsburgh (6-5) with a 35-14 win over the Steelers. Philadelphia (2-8-1) took down Dallas (4-6-1) by doubling up on the Cowboys, 28-14, as both teams continued to play out the string.

The AFL initiated their own Thanksgiving Day game in order to get a big share of the holiday television audience. They scheduled the game between the Titans and Broncos in Denver because it would start after the Packers-Lions game had finished. An what a whale of a battle they gave viewers across the country and the meager 15,776 who showed up to watch in person.

New York jumped out to a 17-0 lead early in the second stanza before Denver's offense came to life. Denver QB Frank Tripucka, a 1949 graduate of Notre Dame and drafted by the Philadelphia Eagles and immediately traded to the Detroit Lions, started what looked like a game-winning rally. Tripucka completed a TD pass to Bob Scarpitto, also from Notre Dame and a 1961 draft choice of the San Diego Chargers. Two field goals by Gene Mingo, the first player of color to be a placekicker in professional American football, brought the halftime score to 24-13 in favor of New York. Denver came out smoking in the second half with a 69-yard TD return of a NY fumble by Bud McFadin, from Texas, and another Scarpitto TD on a four-yard pass from George Shaw, from Oregon, to take the lead, 27-24. New York got a safety and a touchdown pass from Johnny Green, from Chattanooga (now Tennessee Chattanooga), to Don Maynard, from Texas Western (now UTEP), to go back on top, 32-27. Lionel Taylor, from New Mexico Highlands, caught a three-yard pass from Shaw for another six to start the final frame and regain the lead, 35-32. Jim McMillin, from Colorado State, continued the fun for Denver with a 48-yard run to boost Denver's lead to 42-32. Mingo added another field goal, and it looked like the Broncos had the game sewn up at 45-32. That is, until NY recovered a Denver fumble with less than four minutes left on the clock. Johnny Green wasted no time connecting with Dick Christy, from North Carolina State, on a six-yard score to bring the Titans within a touchdown at 45-39. Denver gave up the ball on downs on their next possession, and Green marched the New Yorkers 62 yards to the Denver three where he connected with Art Powell, from San Jose State, for the tying score. Placekicker Bill Shockley, from West Chester, calmly booted the PAT, giving the Titans a 46-45 victory.

This game was to the American Football League what the title game of 1958 between the Baltimore Colts and New York Giants was to the National Football League. Each game put their league on the map of professional football. Millions of American viewers caught the excitement of watching games in both circuits. For the AFL owners, the Denver-New York contest was the gem that gave their league the status they had been seeking for three years. For the NFL owners, it was the death knell for their monopoly of pro football in America.

In the remainder of the AFL schedule, Houston (8-3) took down San Diego (3-8) by six, 33-27, to gain a hold on first place in the East, while Dallas (9-2) clinched a tie for first in the West with a 35-7 throttling of Oakland (0-11).

All the Packers needed to do to eliminate the Bears from the race for first was beat the Rams in Milwaukee or have a Chicago loss.

To beat out the Lions, they had to win all three remaining games or have combination of wins and losses for the two teams that added up to three, such as two Green Bay wins and one Detroit loss or one Green Bay win and two Detroit losses. First things first, though. The Rams in Milwaukee.

The Rams had once been the most talent laden team in the West, but bad management, bad drafting, and bad coaching had ended that legend. They were as bad as their record indicated. But, like Coach Vince always said, don't be fooled by a weak opponent; this was the NFL and on any given Sunday…

Los Angeles played more like lambs than Rams. LA put up a three in the first quarter and a seven in the final stanza. The Packers scored in all four quarters.

Paul Hornung returned to the lineup and paid a dividend right away, catching a 30-yard touchdown pass from Bart Starr to give the Packers the lead they would never relinquish. Jerry Kramer capped off the scoring in the first period with a field goal to give Green Bay a 10-7 lead. Jim Taylor scored the first of his two TDs from one yard out in the second quarter to up the ante to 17-3. With 40 seconds left in the half, Ron Kramer snared a Starr pass from four yards away to boost the halftime margin to 24-3. Jerry Kramer booted another field goal in the third stanza for the only scoring in that frame. Taylor burst over from the two for his second TD. Earl Gros scored from 15 yards away to put the final score on the board for Green Bay, giving the Pack a 41-10 victory to maintain their one-game hold on first place in the West.

The win by the Packers (11-1) ousted the Bears (7-5) from any contention for first place as they lost to New York (10-2) by a narrow margin of 26-24. Detroit (10-2) did keep pace with Green Bay by slipping past Baltimore (5-7) by a touchdown, 21-14. San Francisco (6-6) moved into fourth place with a 35-12 win over Minnesota (2-9-1) still in sixth ahead of the cellar-dwelling Rams (1-10-1). With the Giants having clinched first in the East, the only goal left was second place, which Pittsburgh (7-5) took over with a 19-7 win over St. Louis (2-9-1). Cleveland (6-5-1) still had a shot at the runner-up spot in spite of losing, 45-21, to Dallas (5-6-1), also still in the running. Washington (5-5-2) continued to fade in the standings after losing, 37-14, to the once mighty Eagles (3-8-1).

The AFL Western Division title was settled when the Texans backed into ownership of the crown. Dallas (9-3) lost, 23-14, to the

Bills (6-6-1), but so did the Broncos (7-6) lose, 34-17, to Houston (9-3). The Oilers continued to hold a half-game lead over Boston (8-3-1), winners, 24-17, over the Titans (5-7). San Diego (4-8) rounded off the weekend by defeating Oakland (0-12) comfortably, 31-21.

Lombardi sent the team out to sunny California on Monday to give them a chance to rest and get accustomed to the time zone change. When he arrived the next afternoon, the coach called for a meeting of the boys to go over the plan for their week in Palo Alto.

Looking ahead to the 49ers again, the game would mark the 119th consecutive game for center Jim Ringo. On the other side of the ball, San Francisco's Leo "The Lion" Nomellini would be taking the field for the 159th straight game of his career, breaking the record of 158 set by Emlen Tunnell. A ceremony before the game was set to honor Leo with a plaque for his achievement.

San Francisco coach Red Hickey said before the game that his boys weren't going to make it easy for Green Bay. He was only right.

J.D. Smith, from North Carolina A&T, put the 49ers up, 7-0, before Jerry Kramer kicked a field goal to close the quarter at 7-3. John Brodie, from Stanford, connected with Monty Stickles, from Notre Dame, from three yards out to boost the Frisco lead to 14-3. Tom Moore smashed through the 49er line for a five-yard TD run, closing the gap to 14-10. Then before the half could end, Brodie found Clyde Conner, from University of the Pacific, for a five-yard touchdown to end the half at 21-10 San Francisco.

The second half was all Green Bay. Moore exploded on a quick-opener to close the deficit to 21-17 in the third period. Jim Taylor busted into the end zone early in the fourth frame to give the Pack the lead, 24-21. Bart Starr tossed an eight-yard pass to Ron Kramer with 1:11 to go in the game to seal the deal at 31-21.

No Packer had a particularly big day on offense, but Taylor's touchdown tied the NFL record for TDs in a season. One more against the Rams and the record would be his.

Their victory over the 49ers (6-7) guaranteed the Packers (12-1) at least a tie for first place in the Western Conference. Detroit (11-2) continued to hang in the race with their 37-23 win over the hapless Vikings (2-10-1). The Bears (8-5) dumped the Rams (1-11-1) by a decent 30-14 score. In a Saturday game between the Colts and Redskins, Baltimore (6-7) downed Washington (5-6-2) by a 34-21 margin. New York (11-2) polished off the Browns (6-6-1) with a 17-13 win. St. Louis (3-9-1) pulled off a huge 52-20 upset of the Cowboys (5-7-1). Pittsburgh (8-5) continued to show new life with a 26-17 win over the Eagles (3-9-1).

In the AFL's Saturday contest, Cookie Gilchrist busted his way through the New York (5-8) defense to lead the Bills (7-6-1) to a 20-3 victory. Dallas (10-3) beat Denver (7-7) by a 17-10 margin. Boston (9-3-1) stayed in the hunt in the East with a 20-14 win over San Diego (4-9). The Oilers (10-3) pasted Oakland (0-13) in Houston, 32-17, to hold on to the top spot in the Eastern Division.

Lombardi moved the team to Long Beach to prepare for the final regular season game against the Rams at the Coliseum. Except for some minor bumps and bruises inflicted on them by the 49ers, the team was in good shape. Paul Hornung came down with a touch of the flu in mid-week, but he recovered sufficiently enough to play in the game.

The big news of the week was the announcement by the league office that Jim Taylor had been voted Player of the Year. After that, the NFL revealed the names of the All-Pro team for the year. The Packers landed 10 men on that list. Taylor, Jerry Kramer, Forrest Gregg, Ron Kramer, Jim Ringo, Willie Davis, Henry Jordan, Dan Currie, Bill Forester, and Herb Adderly. Four more made the second team. Fuzzy Thurston, Bart Starr, Ray Nitschke, and Willie Wood. Nearly a third of the two teams were Packers; 14 out of 44 players. Were these guys great or what?

Lombardi wanted a third straight conference title, but he didn't want to back into it. He didn't get his way. Early in the second quarter of the LA game and the Packers leading, 7-0, on a 45-yard pass play from Tom Moore to Ron Kramer on Green Bay's first possession, the public address announcer revealed the outcome of the game back in Chicago: Bears 3, Lions 0. The Packers didn't make any handsprings and jump-arounds for joy. They merely exchanged firm handshakes to congratulate each other on winning the West for a third consecutive year. Then it was back to business because their coach would have it no other way.

The Rams followed Kramer's touchdown with a field goal to close the gap to 7-3. Jim Taylor broke the NFL touchdown record for one season on a run of 28 yards to boost the margin to 13-3. LA caught a break when Max McGee bobbled the snap on punt attempt and threw his first NFL pass, which Merlin Olsen, rookie defensive tackle from Utah State and future television actor, intercepted and lumbered 20 yards to the end zone to cut the spread to 13-10 at the half. Neither team scored in the third stanza, but both put up seven in the final frame, the Packers nailing theirs on a picture-perfect pass play from Bart Starr to Paul Hornung for 83 yards to go up 20-10. LA came right back with their own last score of the game to bring the final to 20-17.

Workhorse Taylor had a big day, gaining 158 yards on 23 carries and setting the team record for yards in a season with 1,476.

Green Bay (13-1) became the first team in the NFL to win 13 games in a regular season. LA (1-12-1) wasn't the first to lose 12, but that was no consolation prize. The Lions (11-3) became the first team to win 11 games and finish in second place in their conference. Chicago's Monsters of the Midway (9-5) would have been a happier lot if they had changed their defensive coach a few weeks earlier and won a few more games. Next year, Bears. The up-and-down Colts (7-7) wished they had played more games like they did the last week, beating the Vikings (2-11-1) with four touchdowns in the final period, 42-17. The Giants (12-2) won their eighth in a row, beating the steadily improving Cowboys (5-8-1) by 41-31 score. Pittsburgh (9-5) looked like a team on the rise with a 27-24 win over Washington (5-7-2). St. Louis (4-9-1) beat out the Eagles (3-10-1) for sixth place, 45-35. The Browns (7-6-1) appeared to be in decline, even though they did beat the 49ers (6-8) in a Saturday game, 13-10.

In the AFL, the Houston Oilers (11-3) finished their regular season schedule by handing a 44-10 rout to the New York Titans (5-9) in the Big Apple. This gave the boys from Texas the Eastern Division title for the third straight year. Dallas (11-3) closed out their regular season with a 26-17 win over Denver (7-7). The Broncos had two totally opposite halves, going 6-1 in the first half and 1-6 in the second. In the last game of the regular season for the AFL, the Raiders (1-13) took advantage of the heart-broken Patriots (9-4-1) who had no reason to play hard on Sunday because the Oilers had won their division on Saturday. Oakland broke its 18-game losing streak, 20-0, and hoped this would be the beginning of a new life for their franchise and team.

The 1962 regular season campaigns for both leagues were now complete. This left only the two championship games for them. Dallas against Houston in a Texas shootout, and Green Bay at New York in a rematch of the 1961 game. Both promised to do their parts in stirring the ardor of professional football fans across the nation.

§§§

20
Title Game 1962

Packers vs. Giants. David vs. Goliath. Same song, different dance hall.

Unlike previous title games in New York, this one would be a massive sellout. Not just a sellout, but the-hottest-ticket-in-town kind of attendance. Fans from all over the metropolitan area surrounding the Five Boroughs, including New Jersey, Connecticut, and especially Upstate New York, wanted tickets to the game at almost any cost. Why? They were certain that this year their Giants would do a number on those rubes from Wisconsin.

The Giants changed home fields in 1956, moving from the Polo Grounds in Upper Manhattan to Yankee Stadium in The Bronx. They moved because "the house that Ruth built" had better seating for football than the old stadium below Coogan's Bluff. Fans were closer to the action, and they were willing to pay a bit more to watch a game there.

Football capacity at Yankee Stadium was 62,800. Once the Giants clinched their conference title the box office began taking orders for tickets. The first 45,000 seats were already reserved for the season ticket holders. Another 10,000 were sold in a public sale to fans wherever. The last 7,800 were apportioned among other league teams. Within hours of the end of the regular season, no more tickets were available except through scalpers or fans who had other plans for the holidays and wouldn't be using them. In other words, if you wanted to go to the game and needed a ticket, then you might need to take out a second mortgage on your home or pay a visit to your local loan shark; this was New York, after all.

While the Packers and Giants were still practicing for their title tilt, the Dallas Texans and the Houston Oilers played for the AFL crown on December 23 in Houston. And what a game it was! Max B. Skelton of the *Associated Press* told the story of the contest with all the enthusiasm of a true professional football fan.

"A slight drizzle trickled off Tommy Brooker's helmet. The clock showed 2 minutes, 54 seconds of the second sudden death overtime period had elapsed. The opposing lines tensed as the ball was snapped back. Len Dawson put the ball down on the 25-yard line stripe.

"Brooker kicked and the Dallas Texans were the champions of the American Football League with a 20-17 decision over Houston's two-time titlists in the longest game in professional football history that came replete with a Fred Merkle boner."

Skelton's article rippled with excitement as he detailed more than the action on the field in the battle that lasted 77 minutes and 54 seconds.

"The game turned out to be three-part production. Dallas won the first half, 17-0. Houston took the second half by the same score. Then they went to the finale before *an overflow crowd of 37,981 and a national television audience.*"

Yes, a national TV audience! That Sunday pro football fans had only one game to watch on their boob-tubes. (Remember! It was 1962. Television sets were already being chastised for drawing America away from outdoor activities.) And because it was Sunday no college bowl games were being played. The AFL had the sports world all to itself, and the upstart league delivered the goods with good play and drama that surpassed that of the NFL and its greatest moment four years earlier.

"Dallas won the toss at the start of the overtime, and it was Abner Haynes' decision to make on whether to receive, kick off, or take the option of selecting the favorable end of the field. Inexplicably Haynes gave the Oilers the first advantage without a second ticking off when he elected to kick off."

Haynes committed a version of "Merkle's boner."

The date: September 23, 1908. The place: Polo Grounds in New York City. The circumstance: the Chicago Cubs and New York Giants were tied for first place in the National League and playing each other that day. The bonehead: Fred Merkle, a 19-year-old rookie first baseman for the Giants.

The game was tied in the bottom of the 9th inning. Two outs, a Giant on third and Merkle on first. A hit to the outfield by the Giants' shortstop. Giant fans rushed the field in their exuberance over their team winning the game. Merkle cut short his trip from first to second base. Cubs' second baseman Johnny Evers saw Merkle leave the field. He called for Cubs' outfielder Solly Hofman to throw him the ball. The outfielder did just that. Evers touched second base, and the umpire called Merkle out; thus, the winning run was canceled.

All sorts of controversy followed over the next several days. The final ruling by National League president Harry Pulliam was Merkle was out and the game ended in a tie. The Cubs and Giants were still tied for first place at the end of the season, so Pulliam ordered a replay of the game. The Cubs won, 4-2, and went on to win the World Series, their last until 2016, 108 years later.

So, that was Merkle's boner and how it applied to what Abner Haynes did when he told the referees the wrong thing at the flip of the coin for overtime in the 1962 AFL championship game.

Fortunately for the Texans, Houston failed to capitalize on their advantage. The Oilers had the ball with the wind at their backs and went three and out. They punted and put Dallas in poor field position. The whole quarter went that way.

In the second overtime period, Houston quarterback George Blanda, from Kentucky, threw an interception that was picked off by Bill Hull, from Wake Forest, who returned it 23 yards to the Houston 48. From there, Dawson completed a 10-yard pass to Jack Spikes, from Texas Christian. Spikes then ran for 19 yards to the Houston 19, putting the Texans in field goal range. Brooker made the kick, and the Dallas Texans were 20-17 winners of the 1962 AFL championship.

This game and the one played Thanksgiving Day in Denver between the New York Titans and the Broncos showed America that pro football could be a lot of fun to watch on television. More than that, it convinced thousands of fans throughout the areas where the AFL had teams to dig into their pockets and buy season tickets for the coming season.

While the AFL owners rejoiced, the NFL owners began asking themselves how the Packers and Giants were going to beat what the Oilers and Texans did. Longest game in history? How do you top that? As the NFL moguls fretted, the two coaches spent their energy preparing for their rematch for the title.

Meanwhile, back at the Stadium, Allie Sherman started the boys practicing to beat the Packers. Sherman had been selected the NFL's Coach of the Year again, mostly because he had directed his aging team to grander heights than he had the prior year. He still had ageless Y.A. Tittle at the helm. Gone was the venerable Charley Conerly who retired at the end of the 1961 season. The Giants had a younger backup for Tittle in 1962. He was Ralph Guglielmi, the 1954 All-American from Notre Dame.

Other members were fullback Alex Webster, from North Carolina State; fullback Joe Morrison, from Cincinnati; receiver Del Shofner, from Baylor; halfback Frank Gifford, from USC, who was actually coming back from retirement; end Joe Walton, from Pitt; halfback Paul Dudley, from Arkansas and originally drafted by Green Bay in 1961 and traded to the Giants; safety Allan Webb, from Arnold College; linebacker Bill Winter, from St. Olaf; guard Jack Stroud, from Tennessee; Greg Larson, from Minnesota; halfback Phil King, from Vanderbilt; tackle Roosevelt Brown, from Morgan State; guard Darrell Dess, from North Carolina State; center Ray Wietecha, from Northwestern; placekicker Don Chandler, from Florida; cornerback Dick Pesonen, the former Packer from Minnesota-Duluth; defensive tackle Roosevelt Grier, from Penn State; defensive end Jim Katcavage, from Dayton; safety Jim Patton, from Mississippi; cornerback Dick Lynch, from Notre Dame; defensive tackle Dick Modzelewski, from Maryland; defensive end Andy Robustelli, from Arnold College; linebacker Sam Huff, from West Virginia; linebacker Tom Scott, from Virginia; and cornerback Erich Barnes, from Purdue.

Both head coaches remarked that the Giants were a better team in 1962 than they had been in 1961. Neither of them said a thing about whether the Packers were as good or better or less of a team as they had been in 1961 when they stomped the Gothamites, 37-0, in Green Bay. The oddsmakers had the Packers winning by six and a half points. Many NFL insiders felt the difference in the final score would be closer. Some even said the Giants had improved so much over the previous year when the quarterback position was split between Charley Conerly and Y.A. Tittle that the home team just might pull off an upset over the favored visitors.

Sunday morning. Game Day. Championship Game Day. The weather was miserable. Temperatures 17-20 degrees. Howling winds up to 40 miles per hour. Swirling snow. Typical December weather—for Green Bay, Wisconsin. But this was New York City. Not ordinary conditions for the Big Apple.

Much more accustomed to the climate conditions than the

opposition, the Packers came out determined to silence the chants of the 60,000-plus crowd who wailed "Beat Green Bay" throughout much of the game. Offense played little part in the contest as neither team could mount any real consistency. Thank you, Old Man Winter. Jerry Kramer booted a 26-yard field goal in the first quarter. Jim Taylor scored on a seven-yard burst into end zone in the second stanza. After New York scored their only touchdown in the third period, Kramer kicked his second field goal from 29 yards out. Then Kramer put the icing on the cake in the final frame with a 30-yarder with just 1:50 on the clock to bring the final score to 16-7 Green Bay.

For the millions of viewers sitting in the cozy comfort of their living rooms across the country, the 1962 NFL title tiff was hardly an exciting game. Too much defense, not enough offense, too little scoring. Of those people who watched the AFL championship game the week before, this was a real yawner. Pro football fans were beginning to think that NFL stood for the "No Fun League" and that AFL stood for the "All Fun League."

But to Packer Backers across the nation and around the world, beating New York for the second straight year was a really sweet treat. To them, this game was proof that their boys from little old Green Bay were the true World Champions of professional football.

As for the man who engineered the victory, Lombardi summed up his feelings in one terse paragraph when he was asked about the advantage New York had statistically.

"I'm not interested in statistics. All I'm interested in is the final score, and I don't know what that was. All I know is we won and that's enough for me."

That was Vincent Thomas Lombardi talking. What a man! What a coach! But he wasn't done fulfilling his destiny. Not yet. Not for five more years.

§§§

Summary

By now the reason for breaking *Lombardi's Destiny* into two volumes has become apparent to you, dear reader. There is simply too much history to tell about Lombardi, about the Packers during his time with them, and about the history between the NFL and the AFL and how Lombardi had his place within that context. Therefore, these stories must be divided into two books to do them justice for the serious fan and history buff.

The Packers were back. Lombardi had brought them there. No one could dispute that. Not then, not now.

But three division titles and two league crowns simply were not enough for the man from Brooklyn. He wanted more, and so did his players and all those millions of Packer Backers across the nation and around the world.

Lombardi took the pieces handed to him in 1959, added some more by way of trades and the draft, and molded them into one of the greatest teams in National Football League history—to that time. As he said so many times in 1960, winning a division sets you up for a much more difficult season the following year. Winning a league title puts a big old bull's-eye on your back. Winning two league crowns in a row marks you for extinction by every team on your schedule the next year.

Lombardi was quite aware of all this, but he was up for the challenge. He showed his team that they could be up for the challenge as well.

In four seasons, Lombardi had built the foundation for a real dynasty. The players he inherited from the worst Packer team in their 38-year NFL history were talented, but they were raw because their coaches of 1957 and 1958 had not managed to make winners out of them. Lombardi did that—one season at a time. He pushed them to a winning record—7-5—in his first season with them. Not satisfied, he bullied them to a better finish in 1960—8-4—and a division title. Now that he had their confidence in him, he drove them harder than they had ever been driven before, and they won it all in 1961. Did he let up then? Aw, hell no. Vince Lombardi was not a man to sit back on his laurels and say, "Look what I did." He wanted more. Lots more. He wanted a second NFL championship, and his boys delivered it to him wrapped up in pretty green and gold ribbons.

Although he would never admit it publicly, Lombardi did take great satisfaction in beating his former team twice in the big game. The one in Green Bay was good, but the fight in New York in Yankee Stadium before all those Giant fans was even sweeter. Oh, so much tastier.

Curly Lambeau had won three straight NFL titles from 1929 through 1931. In the NFL's first four decades, he had been the only coach to accomplish that feat.

Lombardi wanted to equal Lambeau's mark and possibly beat it. On New Year's Day 1963, he contemplated doing just that and he went to work the next day with that in mind. Could he do it? Could his boys in green and gold do it? Only time would tell.

For Lombardi, that time was too far away. He wanted that third title in a row right now. Could he get it? We'll see in Part 2 of *Lombardi's Destiny.*

§§§

BIBLIOGRAPHY

Books

The Baseball Encyclopedia, Sixth Edition, Revised, Updated & Expanded, edited byJoseph L. Reichler, Macmillan Publishing Co., Inc., 1985

George Halas and the Chicago Bears, George Vass, Henry Regnery Company, 1971

The Green Bay Packers, Pro Football's Pioneer Team, Chuck Johnson,Thomas Nelson & Sons, 1961.

The Green Bay Packers, The Story of Professional Football, Arch Ward, G.P. Putnam's Sons, 1946.

Halas on Halas, George Halas with Gwen Morgan and Arthur Veysey, McGraw-Hill Book Co., 1979

History of American Football, Allison Danzig, Prentice-Hall, Inc., 1956.

The NFL's Official Encyclopedic History of Professional Football, Macmillan Publishing Co., Inc., 1973

Official 1985 National Football League Record & Fact Book.

The Packer Legend: An Inside Look, John B. Torinus, Sr., Laranmark Press, 1982

This Day In Packer History, Jeff Everson, Angel Press of WI, 1998

The Pro Football Digest, edited by Robert Billings, Digest Books, Inc., 1978

The Scrapbook History of Pro Football, Richard M. Cohen, Jordan A. Deutsch, Roland T. Johnson, and David S. Neft, The Bobbs-Merrill Company, 1977.

VINCE, A Personal Biography of Vince Lombardi, Michael O'Brien, Quill, 1987

Lombardi: His Life and Times, Robert Wells. Wisconsin House, LTD, 1971

Lombardi: Winning Is the Only Thing, Jerry Kramer, World Publishing Co., 1970

NEWSPAPERS

Chicago Sun, The

Chicago Daily News, The

Chicago Herald-Examiner, The

Chicago Tribune, The

Daily Georgian and Sunday American

Green Bay Gazette

Green Bay Press-Gazette, The

Iron Mountain News, The

The Los Angeles Examiner, The

Los Angeles Times, The

Milwaukee Journal, The

Milwaukee Sentinel, The

New York Daily News, The

New York Times, The

Packer Report, The

The South Bend Tribune, The

PERIODICALS

Collier's

Time

Sport Magazine

Sports Illustrated

Touchback, The

Look

Green Bay Packers Media Guide, 1986 Green Bay Packers Media Guide, 1987 Green Bay Packers Media Guide, 1988 Green Bay Packers Media Guide, 1989 Green Bay Packers Media Guide, 1990 Green Bay Packers Media Guide, 1991 Green Bay Packers Media Guide, 1992 Green Bay Packers Media Guide, 1993 Green Bay Packers Media Guide, 1994 Green Bay Packers Yearbook.

§§§

About the Author

"The day I met John Torinus, Sr., was the day I began focusing on the fascinating history of the Green Bay Packers." John's first hand stories about the Packers sparked Names into digging deep into researching the history of the most unique sports franchise in the world. He has made it his mission to separate fact from fiction and tell the real story of the history of the Green Bay Packers.

Larry Names has had 44 titles published to date, 28 novels, and the remainder non-fiction all dealing with sports teams or sports figures. He is a recognized authority on the Green Bay Packers, Chicago Cubs and Chicago White Sox.

He resides in central Wisconsin with his wife Peg on a family farm that has been in his wife's family since 1854. They have a son, Torry and a daughter, Tegan, a klepto-cat - Cleo, an escape-artist palomino named Lucky Moondancer, an Arabian mare named Amerrah, a Tennessee Walker named Windy and an award-winning Arabian stud colt named Micah.

Larry has four children from his first marriage: daughter Sigrid, an author in her own rite; son Paul; daughter Kristin, an award-winning screenwriter; and daughter Sonje. He also has 17 grandchildren and two great-grandchildren.

The author was born in Mishawaka, Indiana and has lived in nine different states during his life and went to eleven schools growing up and three colleges after serving his country in the Navy. He is an avid researcher, genealogist, and traveler.

For more information about Larry Names and his books, go to www.larrynames.com

"Like" Larry Names on his Facebook Fan page at:
https://www.facebook.com/LarryNames/

§§§

INDEX

B

C

D

E

F

G

H

I

J

K

L

M

N

O

P

Q

R

S

T

U

X

Y

Made in the USA
Monee, IL
17 December 2019

18986906R00184